TURKEY
AND THE
WEST

Sevgili Soner,

İzinde gitmeye çalışıyorum!

Umarım beğenirsin.

En iyi dileklerimle,

Kemal

4 Mayıs 2018

GEOPOLITICS IN THE 21ST CENTURY

For a quarter century since the fall of the Berlin Wall, the world has enjoyed an era of deepening global interdependence, characterized by the absence of the threat of great power war, spreading democracy, and declining levels of conflict and poverty. Now, much of that is at risk as the regional order in the Middle East unravels, the security architecture in Europe is again under threat, and great power tensions loom in Asia.

The Geopolitics in the 21st Century series, published under the auspices of the Order from Chaos project at Brookings, will analyze the major dynamics at play and offer ideas and strategies to guide critical countries and key leaders on how they should act to preserve and renovate the established international order to secure peace and prosperity for another generation.

TURKEY

AND THE

WEST

FAULT LINES IN A
TROUBLED ALLIANCE

KEMAL KIRIŞCI

Brookings Institution Press
Washington, D.C.

The Brookings Institution is a private nonprofit organization devoted to research, education, and publication on important issues of domestic and foreign policy. Its principal purpose is to bring the highest quality independent research and analysis to bear on current and emerging policy problems. Interpretations or conclusions in Brookings publications should be understood to be solely those of the authors.

Library of Congress Cataloging-in-Publication data are available.

ISBN 978-0-8157-3000-2 (cloth : alk. paper)
ISBN 978-0-8157-3001-9 (ebook)

9 8 7 6 5 4 3 2

Typeset in Sabon and Scala Sans

Composition by Westchester Publishing Services

*In loving memory of my late parents who were a constant support
and helped me learn to transcend borders*

Contents

CHAPTER ONE

Turkey and the West

A Troubled Alliance

AS THE SECOND DECADE of the twenty-first century moves beyond its midpoint, the transatlantic alliance faces growing instability on multiple fronts. The conflict in Syria has entered a new stage since the Russian-imposed cease-fire in December 2016 and the April 2017 U.S. missile attack on a Syrian air base to punish the regime for its chemical attacks on civilians. Though considerable gains were made against the self-styled Islamic State (IS) in Iraq and Syria during 2016 and 2017, IS continues to threaten not only the future of the Middle East but security in Europe and the United States as well. Iran's gradual reincorporation into the international community has failed to bring an element of order to the region. At the time of completion, the summer of 2017, Yemen and Libya are still in the grip of civil war, while Tunisia, the only success story among the Arab Spring countries, is not yet on solid ground. Russia's actions in the post-Soviet space and its growing military assertiveness in the Middle East and eastern Mediterranean region continue to cloud Moscow's relations with the West. The European Union is trying to put itself back together after the global financial crisis of 2008–09 and is struggling with the consequences of the migration crisis that began in 2015, while nationalism is on the rise in a number of EU member countries. The issue of Brexit remains unresolved more than a year after the referendum and continues to constitute a challenge to the future shape of the EU.

This grim picture is accompanied by growing concerns about the ability of the transatlantic community to confront these challenges together and uphold the international liberal order. A major question clouding predictions is whether the U.S. president Donald Trump will continue to support the U.S.-led post–World War II global liberal order. Considerable uncertainty persists as to the direction of U.S. foreign policy in the immediate future. This contrasts starkly with the United States that emerged as the "liberal Leviathan" after World War II and fashioned "a world of multilateral rules, institutions, open markets, democratic community and regional partnerships."[1]

The bulk of the institutions that would form the basis of the international liberal order emerged between 1944 and 1951 in the form of the Bretton Woods institutions—the International Monetary Fund (IMF) and the World Bank—the United Nations, the Marshall Plan, the General Agreement on Tariffs and Trade (GATT), the Organization for Economic Cooperation and Development (OECD), and the North Atlantic Treaty Organization (NATO). Turkey was quick to join all these organizations. Membership to NATO in 1952 was particularly critical and was seen by the then U.S. ambassador to Turkey, George C. McGhee, as a sign the country was becoming "an integral part of Europe and the West."[2] Regional organizations such as the Council of Europe, founded in 1949, and the European Economic Communities (EEC), the precursor to the EU, all encouraged by the United States, also emerged during this period. Turkey became a founding member of the Council of Europe and applied for associational membership in the European Economic Community (EEC) in 1959. Turkey's membership in these institutions bound Turkey to the West and was in line with the objective of the founders of the Turkish republic, to orient the new country toward Western civilization, and membership became a part of Turkey's post–World War II traditional statecraft.[3]

Initially this liberal order remained constrained to Australia, Canada, Western Europe, Japan, New Zealand, and the United States. This picture changed dramatically when first the Berlin Wall came down and then, after decades fraught with tension, an exhausted Soviet Union in the late 1980s began a quiet collapse from the inside. Eastern bloc countries, released from the sphere of Soviet influence, turned to the West for a new chapter in military security and political affiliation. NATO and the EU expanded into Central and Eastern Europe, instilling in the region an unprecedented sense of security and creating a basis for growing economic prosperity as well as liberal democratic governance.

There was hope in some quarters that these developments heralded a "unipolar moment" as the rest of the world, not just the global north, seemed to be moving toward an international liberal order spearheaded by the United States.[4] John Ikenberry, a prominent scholar of international affairs, argued that this post–World War II U.S.-led order was turning into "a sprawling global system."[5] Emerging economies such as Brazil, India, and South Africa advanced toward greater democracy and a market economy, and China was expected to follow suit, along with Russia.[6] Indeed, the number of democracies around the world increased substantially in the two decades following the end of the Cold War.[7] In addition to the BRICS—Brazil, Russia, India, China, and South Africa—a large number of countries nurtured their economies, narrowing the welfare gap between the developed and the developing world.[8] The exception to this trend was the Middle East, where the Arab countries seemed stuck in authoritarian political systems and autarkic economies, as was strikingly exposed in the United Nations Development Program's *Arab Humanitarian Development Report 2002.*[9] Yet many anticipated that the George W. Bush administration's Greater Middle East Initiative would eventually break through the exceptionalism of the Middle East and bring the region into the fold of the international liberal order.[10] This did not happen, and the state of world affairs today is starkly different from what was envisioned at the end of the Cold War.

Turkey joining Western institutions might have not occurred had it not been for the fear of Soviet expansionism and territorial demands made by Joseph Stalin on Turkey during the closing months of World War II, as well as the growing domestic calls for democratic reforms. Modern Turkey had emerged from the collapse of the Ottoman Empire at the end of the World War I when Atatürk and his colleagues fought back occupying European powers to win the independence of the country in 1923. Atatürk's reforms had led to a steady growth of Westernization that was guided by a vision of secularization. However, ruined by wars and population displacements, the country had adopted a Soviet-like planned economy and a one-party political system. During the course of World War II, İsmet İnönü, Atatürk's successor, followed a policy of neutrality and resisted Allied calls to join the war against Germany until February 1945. This experience would leave an important legacy in Turkey's relations with the West.

During the course of the Cold War, Turkey's democracy evolved hesitantly and was interrupted by military coups on a number of occasions. Domestically, its membership in the transatlantic community and especially NATO was periodically questioned. It would not be until the

1980s that Turkey would start transforming its economy from a primarily state-led import substituting to a liberal market economy. A slow and highly contested process of democratization would then follow this from the late 1980s on. Eventually these two developments would open the way in 2005 for membership talks with the EU, and it increasingly seemed that Turkey was becoming solidly anchored in the international liberal order. By the time the EU and the United States had entered into one of their worst economic recessions in 2008, Turkey was being touted as a model for countries aspiring to join the international liberal order. Its rising soft power, constructive foreign policy, and economic engagement of its neighborhood (the Balkans, countries bordering the Black Sea, the South Caucasus, and the Middle East) were seen as assets for bringing this neighborhood into the international liberal order. Yet this did not last long. The international liberal order began to encounter challenges from within, as both the United States and the EU experienced economic difficulties and challenges from outside powers, especially China and Russia, which sought an alternative order. Furthermore, Turkish democracy began to recede, its economic dynamism started to fade, and its leadership, increasingly driven by an Islamist agenda, became embroiled in the conflicts of the Arab Middle East.

GLOBAL LEADERSHIP AND THREATS TO THE WORLD ORDER

The revolving heart of this picture is the question of global leadership, especially the extent and nature of U.S. involvement. Some have advocated that the world continue to be led by the United States as the power that remains "in a class of its own."[11] Others disagree, adducing in support of their position notions of "the decline of the West" and "the rise of the rest"—China in particular.[12] The greater role of the G-20, whose members account for 80 percent of world trade and two-thirds of the world population, relative to that of the G-7 in steering the global economy through the first stages of the economic crisis of 2008–09 reinforced this broader view of a more dispersed global leadership.[13] Furthermore, the Chinese economic model of state capitalism and the Russian (Putin's) political suasion of sovereign democracy have exhibited staying power as alternatives to their Western counterparts. Thus some have espoused the idea that the twenty-first century will not be America's, China's, or Asia's; it will be no one's.[14]

The question of a continuing leadership role for the United States in the international liberal order has come to be discussed most ardently in relation to developments in the Middle East. Compared to the depth and scope of U.S. involvement in Central and Eastern Europe in the 1990s and in the Middle East during the 2000s, the country remained relatively inactive during the Obama presidency. The mass protests that erupted in Iran following the presidential elections of June 2009 offered an opportunity for the United States to support the prospects of a democratic opening in the country. Yet Obama remained reticent, fearing that any sort of outside intervention would be regarded as imperialist meddling and would weaken the hand of the reformists in government.[15] It was the Arab Spring uprisings, which erupted in Tunisia in December 2010 and spread to other Middle Eastern countries, that suggested an impending democratic breakthrough. Those hopes also proved short-lived: the situation in Libya, Syria, and Yemen quickly worsened, and the West could not be effective in preempting the violence between domestic actors, who were often supported by rival Arab regimes.[16] In Egypt, the government of Mohamed Morsi succumbed to the "temptations of power," drifted into majoritarian rule, and was later violently overthrown by the military in July 2013.[17] Some placed the blame at least partially on Washington's inertness, arguing that the United States had reduced itself to a "dispensable nation."[18] Interestingly, the only success story, though a fragile one, was Tunisia, where the democratization process was led by local actors (political parties, trade unions, and civil society groups) rather than by Western outsiders. The influential politician and moderate Islamist Rachid Ghannouchi's unique leadership in devising a power-sharing arrangement in governance—a sure sign of his commitment to reconciling Islam with democracy—also proved critical to Tunisia's success.[19]

The question of finding the right measure of U.S. involvement in the Middle East has been complicated by the civil war in Syria. The protests against the regime of Bashar al-Assad, which began in March 2011 in the context of the Arab Spring, gradually dissolved into civil war, pulling a growing number of external actors into the fray. The wavering U.S. commitment to hew to its "red lines" in Syria, coupled with the decision to reduce troop levels in Iraq, did not improve the security situation in the region.[20] The rise of IS in 2014 aggravated the chaos in both Iraq and Syria, triggering what the UN High Commissioner for Refugees has described as a protracted displacement crisis.[21] This soon evolved into a security concern for Europe: the IS fighters, in possession of Western passports, became a growing threat, as some masterminded or carried out bomb attacks. In the meantime, Europe became the final destination for some of the millions of Syrian refugees fleeing the chaos in the region.

These developments in turn fueled the rise of xenophobic right-wing groups across Europe and were drawn on to justify calls for stricter border controls. Fearful that extremists might have planted themselves among these flocks of refugees, some EU member states jettisoned the burden-sharing schemes of the European Commission. These developments have raised concerns about the viability of keeping together the very fabric of the EU.[22]

U.S. domestic politics have also been upended by the rise of right-wing populism and anti-immigrant feelings. This exclusionary sentiment has already translated into travel restrictions placed on the nationals of a group of Muslim-majority countries, including drastic limits on the admission of Syrian refugees, by the new administration. The international agreement applicable to refugees, put in place by the United States in the aftermath of World War II, is based on the principle that the protection of refugees is an international responsibility and one that should be shared globally. That these developments occurred despite the disposition on the part of the U.S. public to help Syrian refugees is contributing to the weakening of the very international liberal order the United States once helped to promote.[23]

Finally, Russia has reemerged as a threat to the liberal world order.[24] The first conspicuous manifestation of this threat materialized with the Russian military intervention in Georgia in 2008. The scope of Russia's ambitions and capabilities became clear with the annexation of Crimea and the subsequent support extended to separatists in eastern Ukraine. These actions not only violated the sanctity of the territorial integrity of states in Europe, they also threw obstacles onto Ukraine's path of transforming itself into a stronger democracy.[25] The trade sanctions against Russia put in place by the United States and the EU have been ineffective, attracting instead Russia's own sanctions in a tit for tat, which further disrupted the liberal environment in Europe. Security in Western Europe is also threatened by Russia's infringement on the Baltic airspace and by Russian support for right-wing nationalist movements in European countries.[26] Russian cyber campaigns and allegations of interference in U.S. presidential elections continue to roil U.S. politics, while similar concerns have also been expressed by European countries with respect to their own elections.[27] These policies, reminiscent of the Cold War, seem intended to roll back the achievements of a "Europe whole and free" (called for by then president George H. W. Bush in May 1989) and to introduce fracture lines into the Western association, which had been united behind a single, liberal U.S. leadership.[28] Last but not least, the inaction of the United States and its European allies in the face of the humanitarian crisis that unfolded after Russia's direct involvement in the Syrian conflict in October 2015 has signaled an erosion of Western power. Initial Russian success in brokering a cease-fire agreement also points to that country having the upper hand in shaping outcomes in the Middle East. It is not yet clear whether the U.S. decision to strike an air base in Syria in April 2017 and send a representative to the Russian-led talks in Astana the following month will evolve into a policy of greater engagement. This could move the focus from the narrowly defined objective of capturing Raqqa from IS to the search for a settlement that would be sustainable for all parties involved. The latter outcome would clearly be much more desirable since it would help reinforce the tenets that still bind the international liberal order at a time of increasing challenges to its viability.

THE CURRENT ANGLE OF TURKEY'S GEOPOLITICAL AXIS

Turkey's deteriorating relations with the United States and the EU and its dramatically weakened commitment to liberal democracy and a market economy have been a source of concern to many observers. Turkey has been part of the international liberal order since the end of World War II, and any signs of its moving away from this engagement are cause for alarm. Turkey has also been an important player in the defense of the U.S.-led global order in its neighborhood, and its "crossing the floor" into a realm populated by countries such as China, Iran, and Russia would undoubtedly chip away at the effectiveness of its longtime Western allies. That this is happening at a time of growing challenges from the rise of populism and right-wing politics in Europe further complicates matters. Turkey sits in a geography where various arcs of turbulence—humanitarian, geopolitical, economic—intersect dangerously. Ensuring Turkey's cooperation and support will be critical in addressing such issues as managing the Syrian refugee crisis, fighting IS, finding a sustainable diplomatic solution to the war in Syria, stabilizing the wider Middle East, strengthening NATO, and countering Russia's growing assertiveness.

Turkey's relationship with its Western allies with respect to Syria has been a difficult one. Initially, both sides seemed keen to see the replacement of the Assad regime and a transition to a more democratic form of government. However, as the conflict in Syria persisted, major differences of opinion on what should be given priority in Syria—whether to over-throw Assad first, or defeat IS, or prevent the Syrian Kurds from domi-nating the northern part of Syria—kept the sides from uniting around a concerted effort.[29] The ongoing fight against IS has also locked the part-ners into a conundrum as the Turkish president, Recep Tayyip Erdoğan, reacted sharply to the cooperation that formed between the West—the United States in particular—and the Kurdish opposition groups in Syria, actors the Turkish government considers terrorists. Erdoğan even blamed the United States for turning the region "into a pool of blood" and demanded that the United States choose between a NATO ally and the Kurds—all of which has produced a dire predicament.[30] The reality is that Turkey and the United States need each other to bring the broader conflict in Syria to a successful resolution, yet it is not clear whether they will be able to work out a basis for cooperation.[31] Time will tell whether both sides will be able to rise above their differences and pave the way to a more harmonious partnership in Syria and elsewhere. The bigger un-known is whether the two countries will be able to reengage each other over an agenda supportive of democratization in Turkey. Democratic regression in Turkey accompanied by a lack of interest on the part of the U.S. administration in supporting democracy is not very promising in terms of the future of the international liberal order.

Turkey's relations with the EU have also been strained to the break-ing point. This is partly because of the mutual recriminations over the implementation of the March 2016 deal to address the European migra-tion crisis, whereby Turkey agreed to accept the rapid return of migrants from Greece in exchange for its EU membership bid being "reenergized." It is also partly driven by simmering Turkish resentment at the EU's fail-ure to express solidarity with Turkey after the coup attempt in Ankara in July 2016. These events have occurred against the background of long-standing criticisms by the EU of the shortcomings of Turkish democ-racy, especially with regard to the Kurdish minority. Their cultural rights and economic well-being had improved considerably with reforms made in the early years of the Justice and Development Party (AKP), mainly as part of the effort to start EU accession negotiations. Erdoğan's later out-reach to the Kurdish Workers' Party (PKK) was most welcome as a step that would finally bring an end to the violence, destruction, and displace-ment that had shaken the country since the 1980s.

The hopes have fast been eroding with the start of clashes again be-tween the state forces and the PKK insurgents beginning in the summer of 2015. The antiterror laws introduced by the government and the arrest of several Kurdish politicians, including Selahattin Demirtaş and Figen Yüksekdağ, coleaders of the Kurdish People's Democratic Party (HDP), marked a return to the repressive policies of the 1990s. Another major source of concern for European observers has been the imposition of restrictions on the freedom of expression, which played an important role in the European Parliament's November 2016 call to freeze EU accession negotiations with Turkey. The decision of the Parliamentary Assembly of the Council of Europe (PACE) to reintroduce a monitoring process for Turkey in the aftermath of a contested referendum in April 2017 that granted enhanced powers to Erdoğan has been a significant blow to the relationship. The measure was met with indignation by the AKP, the very same government that had succeeded in getting a similar monitoring process lifted in its early years in power.[32]

Turkey's once highly praised "zero problems with neighbors" policy was considered an "engine of convergence" that could help bring its neighborhood into the fold of the international liberal order.[33] By employing its soft power, observers thought, Turkey could mediate conflicts in the region (for instance, by holding proximity talks between Israel and Syria), and this was a quality that made Turkey invaluable in efforts to achieve greater stability and security in the region. Public opinion surveys conducted in various Middle Eastern countries only a few years ago demonstrated solid support for Turkey's leadership and policies.[34] The exuberant welcome extended to Erdoğan when as prime minister he visited Cairo in September 2011 cannot be easily forgotten.[35] Also noteworthy was his speech, delivered to an enthusiastic audience, emphasizing the virtues of a democratic and secular form of government. His speech was also a gentle nudge to the Egyptians to ensure their embrace of the international liberal order—a feat no Western politician could have undertaken in that part of the world.

Today, Turkey is far from enjoying the same clout in the region. Its policy of zero problems with neighbors is in tatters, drawing sarcastic comments such as "zero neighbors without problems."[36] There is no dearth of animosity in Turkey's relations with many states in its proximity as the leadership has found itself in serious conflict with the governments of Armenia, Cyprus, Egypt, Iraq, Israel, Libya, Russia, and Syria. No diplomatic relations exist with Armenia and Cyprus to this day, and the Turkish government frequently resorts to recalling ambassadors from countries with which it disagrees—a diplomatic practice sparingly employed otherwise.[37] An unexpected U-turn in Turkey's relations with Israel and Russia in July 2016, on the other hand, has raised the prospects of Turkey reviving stronger relations with these two countries.[38] Time will tell whether this reorientation toward a zero-problems policy and greater pragmatism can be sustained. On the whole, however, Turkish foreign policy has lost credibility and the admiration it once enjoyed.[39]

Turkey's diminished influence and reputation became particularly apparent at the United Nations. Turkey's failure to be reelected as a nonpermanent member of the UN Security Council in 2014, when it lost out to Spain by a margin of 60 to 132 votes, was sobering.[40] Six years earlier, in 2008, Turkey had received 151 votes out of 193, garnering decisively the right to hold a seat on the UN Security Council during 2009–10. The subsequent downward trend was interpreted by a senior adviser to Erdoğan as a sign that Turkey now occupied a position of "precious loneliness"—a term intended to imply the administration's preference for upholding noble ethical standards over realist and pragmatic considerations.[41] Yet for many pundits, Turkey's state of loneliness is no more than the dismal result of an orientation in foreign affairs that substituted ideologically driven policies for realistic ones.[42] This has set Turkey in conflict and competition with its traditional allies and shows how dramatically Turkey has lost its positive international standing compared to 2010.[43]

Domestic politics is another area in which the luster of Turkey's record has dimmed. The intricate relationship between domestic affairs and the conduct of foreign policy in Turkey, a phenomenon made all the more striking during AKP rule, calls for a close look at these dynamics together. Signs of growing authoritarianism at home gradually undermined the democratic credentials the AKP had been careful to build during its early years in power, though it is difficult to pinpoint an exact time or event signaling the beginning of the trend. The issue has often been discussed in Turkey around the question of whether Erdoğan and the AKP leadership had any genuine intentions of steering the country toward greater democracy. To use a Turkish expression, they were suspected of performing *takiye* (disguising their true intentions) even as they seemed to act in accordance with the principles of democracy and to adhere to the values of the international liberal order. A frequently cited remark in this context comes from 1996, when Erdoğan compared democracy to a tramcar, to be disembarked once it has served its purpose. He would disown these words four years later, saying they had been misconstrued and he had indeed internalized democracy.[44] The situation today contradicts him unless he had been professing all along a majoritarian form of democracy. Recent developments, such as restrictions on the media, massive purges after the coup attempt of July 2016, and the controversial referendum of April 2017 that granted him vast powers, have led to several commentaries that profess to have uncovered through hindsight some early signs betraying an underlying authoritarian streak within the AKP all along, with the typical lamentation that they should not have been overlooked or ignored.[45]

The resounding victory that the AKP achieved in the 2011 parliamentary election can also be seen as a point when the weakening of democratization became increasingly more visible.[46] The strong electoral performance coincided with the emergence of an increasingly majoritarian understanding of democracy that was much more willing to disregard diversity and minority views. This led one observer of Turkish politics to remark that Erdoğan evidently took his 50 percent vote share in 2011 "as a mandate to refashion the country according to his values."[47] This was also the point at which restrictions on the freedom of expression, increasing state penetration into citizens' private lives, and the reconstruction of a judicial edifice along lines more palatable to his political ambitions began to be unmistakably visible. These developments caused grave concerns in Turkey as well as abroad, validating the similarities that had been drawn between Erdoğan and Vladimir Putin and reinforcing the perception that Turkey was becoming another Russia.[48]

The resentment that was building against the government for this step-by-step centralization of control erupted with the Gezi Park protests of May and June 2013. What started as a peaceful demonstration against a construction project in one of the few remaining green spots in central Istanbul grew in scope and spread across the country before being violently repressed by the AKP government. The crackdown caused loss of life, the participants were harshly prosecuted, and businesses that supported the protesters were harassed by tax inspectors.[49] Censorship was imposed on the internet and social media. In hindsight, the leadership's reaction to the Gezi Park protests can be seen as a harbinger of the AKP's new mode of governance.

Erdoğan's becoming Turkey's first popularly elected president in August 2014 after campaigning for an executive presidency to replace the parliamentary system marked another step toward greater authoritarian control.[50] In April 2017, as president, Erdoğan succeeded in obtaining the approval of the Turkish electorate—with 51.4 percent of the votes—for a series of amendments to the constitution that gave him vast powers with few checks on it. The referendum results remain contested, and the number of commentaries calling him "effectively a dictator" has been increasing by the day.[51] But this state of affairs is unsurprising in light of the damage inflicted on democratic institutions in Turkey, notably the media and the judiciary, over the past decade. Turkey's performance in Freedom House's *Freedom in the World* reports has steadily weakened with respect to civil liberties, and its media have been listed as "not free" since 2014. Ironically, it was under the AKP's reign, between 2004 and 2011, that Turkey achieved its best freedom rating of 3 (1 being most free and 7 least free); the rating has been slipping since then.[52] Reporters Without Borders also placed Turkey in its "bad" section for 2016, citing media censorship and massive purges since the coup attempt; Turkey now ranks 155 among 180 countries, "just four ranks ahead of Brunei, Kazakhstan, Iraq and Rwanda, while lagging behind countries such as Russia, Belarus, Singapore and South Sudan."[53] More disturbing is the growing number of reports on the use of torture against detainees since the coup attempt, a practice that again the AKP governments had eradicated, which earned them great praise.[54]

These domestic developments have called into question Turkey's commitment to the values central to an international liberal order. There exists a widening gap between Turkey's foreign policy pursuits and those of its traditional allies, a gap that to an important extent is a function of the decline in its democratic credentials at home. The rise of authoritarianism in Turkey has conspicuously coincided with its growing involvement in the Middle East in the aftermath of the Arab Spring.[55] Initially, Turkey was expected to constitute a model for several Arab countries in their aspirations to transition to democracy. As Turkey increasingly found itself in the grip of an authoritarian streak and rapidly undermining its own democratic reforms, however, its soft power status in the region began to suffer as well. This also meant a decline in Erdoğan's popularity among Turkey's Arab neighbors and their leadership, a position that had afforded him abundant leverage before.[56] More strikingly, all this was happening at a time when Turkey was carrying most of the burden of looking after an ever-increasing number of Syrian refugees.

Turkey's involvement in the Syrian civil war, the efforts it has made to ensure a regime change, has been most troubling. The very fact that

Turkey supported the radical groups—factions outliers to the moderate opposition—led to doubts about its credentials as a dependable NATO member; its slow response to preventing the flow of foreign fighters and the logistical help that it extended to the extremists came to be challenged heatedly.[57] The words of a former U.S. ambassador to Turkey, Robert Pearson, and his co-author describe the situation well: "Turkish President Recep Tayyip Erdoğan's flirtation with radical Islam in Syria and march from liberal democratic reformer to illiberal populist authoritarian have confused Americans trying to deal with Turkey."[58] This picture became further complicated when Turkey sent its military into northern Syria in August 2016, ostensibly to fight IS but more with the aim of striking the Kurdish groups allied with the United States, which was then followed by close cooperation with Russia for a cease-fire agreement.

These events marked a stunning reorientation from the AKP's earlier days, when Barack Obama lauded Turkey's now erstwhile democratic achievements in his address to the Turkish parliament in April 2009 and expressed confidence in a future U.S.-Turkey partnership.[59] As late as 2012, Erdoğan was among the top five world leaders whom Obama cited as trustworthy.[60] Four years later, however, Obama sounded very bitter when he referred to the same Erdoğan as "a failure and an authoritarian."[61] In turn, Turkish resentment of Obama went so deep that an analyst close to the AKP government accused him of being "white in his ideas, behavior and policies" and suggested Obama had delivered Syria to the Russians on a golden platter.[62]

Yet none of this changes the reality that Turkey remains, at least in the formal sense of the word, a member of the main institutions of the transatlantic alliance and is still a candidate for EU membership. Turkey is deeply integrated into the global, and especially European, economy. It is a long-standing member of NATO, where it plays a critical role in a number of operations and participates in UN peacekeeping efforts. The current challenges in its neighborhood only add to its importance. Turkey may today appear at loggerheads with its Western allies, yet this was not the case until a few years ago. Hence it is important to understand this dramatic change in Turkish politics and foreign policy to determine whether and how the U.S. administration may reengage its erstwhile ally. The EU can also benefit from a similar exercise, especially as recent elections in some key member countries ended with pro-European politicians prevailing over their right-wing opponents. The nature of this reengagement will be instrumental in bringing a degree of order to Turkey's neighborhood. This in turn will also depend on how the U.S. administration crafts its future policy toward Turkey, not to mention the broader transatlantic alliance. The results of the April 2017 referendum in Turkey offer important possibilities. Despite the absence of a level playing field during the run-up to the vote and allegations of fraud at the ballot box, close to half of the Turkish electorate objected to a constitution that undermines Turkish democracy and promises a one-man rule. Hence it will be very important for Turkey's transatlantic allies to adopt policies that continue to support democratic reform in Turkey. The advice of *The Economist* ahead of the referendum, that Turkey should not be abandoned, regardless of the result, is therefore apt.[63] Turkey's geographic location and long-standing relationship with the Western alliance will remain critical in addressing the challenges to the international liberal order. Turkey still holds the potential to evolve, once again, into a robust promoter of the liberal order in its region. The risk of seeing the fault lines with its traditional allies widening even further remains serious, however, and should be addressed carefully. With this in mind, this book explores the following questions:

What factors are driving the deterioration in Turkey's ties with its traditional allies? Why was it not possible to anchor Turkey solidly in the transatlantic alliance, a country that had been part of this partnership ever since the arrival of USS *Missouri* in the Istanbul harbor in 1946 as a gesture of support against Soviet territorial demands on Turkey? How did Turkey's foreign policy of zero problems with neighbors turn into the dismal state of zero neighbors without problems? What kind of "order" are the rulers of contemporary Turkey seeking? How compatible is it with American and broader Western preferences? Can the current rift with the West be overcome? What would be the advantages of reengaging Turkey?

TURKEY: AN IDENTITY CAUGHT BETWEEN EAST AND WEST

Turkey's deviation from its trajectory of a long and slow process of convergence with the international liberal order is deeply connected to the larger and heavily charged issue of identity. It is now commonplace for political scientists to refer to Turkey as a "most obvious and prototypical torn country," but when Samuel Huntington introduced the term in

1993 he was describing a country trapped between rising Islamist sentiments and the secular republican elite, a divide that fed European reluctance to engage Turkey as an eventual member of the EU.[64] The historian Selim Deringil's observation that Turkey is a country in constant search of its identity also dates from a period before the AKP's rise to power.[65] The period of successive AKP governments beginning in 2002 brought its own set of complications to an alliance with the West that has never quite flourished. The AKP's espousal of liberal, economic, and political principles in its early years was a source of inspiration for many, who hoped that stance would finally ensure Turkey's place in the Western community. The term "Muslim democrats," in clear reference to the Christian Democrat parties in Europe that emerged after World War II, was frequently used to define the AKP's leadership. The AKP itself shied away from the term, preferring "conservative democrats," which in the view of the party leaders better conveyed the message that they did not approve of involving religion in politics. Indeed, for most of the first decade of the twenty-first century the AKP was a conglomeration of political views, ranging from political Islam to conservative nationalism and liberalism.[66] The leadership also seemed at ease in its relations with the United States, the EU, and even Israel.

The diversity in the AKP's makeup began to disappear with its third election in 2011, however. A number of founding members of the party, including some of the most prominent advocates of liberal policies, lost their positions both in government and in the party over the years. The party has over time changed into a coalition of Islamic-leaning parliamentarians, mainly the remnants of the Millî Görüş (National Outlook) tradition, and champions of religious nationalism. Loyalty to Erdoğan has been a major cohesive factor binding these groups together.[67] In conjunction with the change in the party, the old elite, the class of Western-oriented politicians adhering to the Western vocation promulgated by the founders of the republic, was displaced by a new elite, a class of more conservative politicians who problematized Turkey's identification with the West. This shift was accompanied by policies and actions, such as controversial court cases brought against high-ranking military officers and government employees, that sought to weaken the role and influence of bureaucrats, thus dealing a blow to the continuity of the state.[68] Pro-government media played an important role in this transition, sometimes going so far as to question the suitability of democracy for Islam.[69]

The AKP's successive victories at the ballot box since 2002 have brought a more majoritarian understanding of democracy, a trend that can be tracked in Erdoğan's pronouncements over the years. The calls for unity that marked his early postelection speeches have become less frequent, just as his promises to engage the electorate in its entirety, irrespective of party affiliation or lifestyle, have disappeared. The tone has become more divisive as Erdoğan has increasingly sought to distinguish "us," meaning his unquestioning followers, from "others"—anyone who disagrees with him, especially Turkey's former elites.[70] Erdoğan's grudge against the latter, in particular the military and the judiciary, has become more pronounced: he has repeatedly targeted them as the enablers of a "tutelage regime" that had long disregarded the AKP's right to exercise *millî irade* (national will), phraseology indicating the party's control of a large electorate, with little respect for pluralism.[71] As resentment against the tutelage regime was broadly shared, the growing disregard for diversity aggravated a polarization between Erdoğan's political base and the secular opposition and liberal circles.

The coup attempt of July 2016 and the government's reaction in its aftermath have further aggravated polarization. The general view in Turkey holds the Gülen movement, a former ally of the AKP leadership, responsible for the uprising, which started in the military on July 15.[72] The Gülen movement became identified in recent years with a series of schemes aimed at eliminating supporters of the secular establishment from key institutions, such as the army, the police, and the judiciary. Named after the cleric Fethullah Gülen, the group was known for a long time as a charitable organization and so received support from successive governments beginning in the 1970s. The Gülen community shared with the members of the AKP a worldview based on Islamic principles, and acquired prominence over the years by building a large network of high-quality schools at all levels, both in Turkey and abroad. The extent of their reach and their human capital are generally recognized as having benefited the AKP during the decade in which the two organizations operated as close allies.[73] The coalition gradually eroded, however, and they eventually found themselves locked in a fierce power struggle. Since the coup attempt the government has introduced draconian measures in an attempt to eliminate Gülenist sympathizers from state institutions and civil society.

The language adopted by the AKP administration has also become increasingly imbued with Islamic motifs. The religious mission that the

AKP claims to have taken on itself has been repeatedly invoked through the use of such terms as *kutlu yolculuk/yürüyüş* (holy march) and *dava* (mission).[74] Gestures such as long-winded salutes to the Islamic world at the beginning of speeches have become common. The absence of the usual EU contingent and the presence of several Arab leaders, mostly from the Muslim Brotherhood, at the 2012 AKP party congress can be interpreted as the party carrying out *dava* and uniting preferentially with the *ummah*, the broader Muslim community—which, especially in the Arab world, is represented by the Muslim Brotherhood.[75] It is hard to believe that the same party was in power in 2007 when both Shimon Peres, the Israeli president, and Mahmoud Abbas, the Palestinian president, addressed the Turkish parliament together.[76] The strong Muslim Brotherhood orientation at the 2012 party congress suggested the AKP was moving away from its embrace of diversity and pragmatism, the bedrock of the regional cooperative approach it had previously upheld. Instead, a politically divisive and religiously sectarian dimension began gaining ground in AKP circles, shaping not only domestic politics but also the conduct of foreign policy.[77]

The emphasis on close relations with the Muslim Brotherhood has been most evident in post–Arab Spring policy orientations. This marked a major shift from the traditional statecraft that had guided Turkey's foreign affairs for more than seven decades.[78] Championing the cause of the Muslim Brotherhood largely aligned with the "strategic depth" doctrine launched by Ahmet Davutoğlu, a former academic who served as minister of foreign affairs and then prime minister from March 2009 to May 2016.[79] Now largely discarded as overly ambitious, even mocked as manifesting "strategic shallowness," Davutoğlu's aspiration was to seek an ideologically and religiously motivated political leadership for Turkey in the post-Ottoman space.[80] The Büyük Restorasyon (Grand Restoration) project that Davutoğlu initiated to reunite the Muslim *ummah* of the Middle East never materialized in the quagmire that the region has turned into with the civil war in Syria.[81] The vision of an Ikhwan (Muslim Brotherhood) belt stretching from Tunisia to Libya, Egypt, and Syria also fell victim to the ousting of Egypt's Mohamed Morsi in 2013, which provoked Turkey's anger toward the United States in particular for failing to defend a democratically elected leader.[82] This was further complicated by the rise of IS and other extremist groups and unclear signals from Turkey as to the role it might expect to play in the fight against them.

The shift in the pendulum toward the Middle East marked a major departure from the AKP's earlier emphasis on the pursuit of EU membership. Erdoğan had seemed committed then to ensuring that Turkey met the Copenhagen political criteria, a list of conditions candidate countries were expected to fulfill before starting accession negotiations. The AKP certainly deserves credit for the reforms it initiated in its early years and for starting accession negotiations in 2005. It was during this period that the then minister of foreign affairs, Abdullah Gül, worked closely and constructively with the Turkish bureaucracy and in particular with those ambassadors and Ministry of Foreign Affairs officials responsible for handling relations with the EU.[83] However, the lukewarm response from the EU curbed the enthusiasm, which was further weakened by the realization that Turkey's admission would face strong resistance from the European public. Not surprisingly, Turkish support for EU membership dropped steadily from its peak of 73 percent in 2004 to its lowest level of 38 percent in 2010.[84] The trend was not only a reaction to the EU's reluctance to accept Turkey; it also derived from the diminished value of membership after the euro crisis. The Turkish economy had grown around 9 percent in 2011–12 while the EU had barely maintained a 2 percent growth rate. Meanwhile, the Turkish per capita income also moved from about 26 percent of the euro area average in 2006 to 30 percent in 2014.[85] The "Eurosarcasm" that emerged as a result was certainly a new phenomenon, a sentiment only aggravated by events since then, adding further doubt as to whether Turkey would maintain its Western orientation.[86]

TURKEY TODAY IS RUDDERLESS. The coup attempt of July 2016 and the much-contested referendum of April 2017 that all but secured a one-man rule for Erdoğan have further widened the gap between Turkey and the West. The political gamble in the Middle East did not bring about the leadership position that Davutoğlu had envisioned for Turkey. The recent rapprochement with Russia and Israel, in light of Prime Minister Binali Yıldırım's poignant remark that Turkey needed "to increase the number of friends and reduce the number of enemies," points to a return of some pragmatism but fails to assure observers that it is the result of a well-thought-out policy.[87] The earlier hopes invested in the BRICS as a potential compass for Turkey did not last long either as an economic downturn undermined the prospects of "the rest" reshaping the international order. The AKP also seems to have missed the point that a correlation exists between the adoption of democratic principles and the political and economic gains that follow thereafter. It is a sad irony that Turkey's regression today occurred under the AKP, the very party that had propelled Turkey closer to the EU and deeper into the transatlantic community.

A deep-seated skepticism where the United States is concerned continues to motivate Turkey in its search for new alignments. The United States had supported Turkey's bid for EU membership through several steps in the process: from the EU-Turkey Customs Union agreement in 1995 to Turkey's appointment as a candidate country in December 1999, and later to open the accession negotiations in October 2005. Backing Turkey's bid was a strategic component of the U.S. policy to anchor Turkey in the transatlantic community. The United States even became the target of criticism from some EU leaders for its aggressive advocacy of the Turkish cause. An illustrative incident was the rancorous spat between French president Jacques Chirac and the U.S. president George W. Bush at the 2004 NATO summit, Bush arguing that as a European power, Turkey belonged in the EU, and an openly frustrated Chirac accusing the American president of wading into territory that was not his.[88]

This U.S. enthusiasm for Turkey's EU membership did not shield the U.S.-Turkish relationship from being adversely affected when the United States invaded Iraq in 2003. The many warnings from the Turkish government and diplomatic corps against such an undertaking, along with the havoc it created in the region, brought the relationship to a state of crisis. Public skepticism toward the United States has been on the rise ever since: as shown by Pew opinion polls, the people of Turkey have grown more anti-American than the populations of other Muslim countries, with the exception of Jordan, primarily since the intervention in Iraq.[89] The resentment has persisted: a Turkish national survey conducted in 2016 found that 52.9 percent of respondents "[had] a problematic outlook on Turkey-USA relations." More strikingly, the U.S. approach to Turkey was characterized as "untrustworthy, colonialist, hostile, opportunistic, and hypocritical" by 67.1 percent of respondents.[90] The United States is regularly seen as perpetrating, if not confecting, conspiracies in Turkey and in the region. For Turkish leaders, launching such charges has traditionally served as propaganda to drum up domestic support, but skepticism has been a part of Turkish attitudes at least since the 1960s. Skepticism was also on display after July 15, 2016, when many officials, including a cabinet minister, openly accused the

United States of being involved in the coup attempt.[91] Subsequently, Turkey's persistent requests that the United States extradite Fethullah Gülen, who has been in self-exile in Pennsylvania since 1999, became another thorny issue.

Turkey's future trajectory depends on how its relationship with the EU and the United States develops. National elections in Austria, France, and the Netherlands in 2017 have suggested pro-European integration centrist leaders prevailing over populist and nationalist leaders. Should a similar result follow Germany's elections in September 2017, it is likely that regardless of policies and actions Erdoğan may pursue, the EU may continue trying to engage Turkey and strengthen EU-Turkish relations. (This is not set in stone, and much depends on how well these leaders also manage the challenges that the EU faces from within.) The greater challenge emanates from a U.S. administration that so far appears in its foreign policy to have put more emphasis on Realpolitik and transactional relations with authoritarian leaders than on shoring up the international liberal order.[92] The lack of consistent messaging from the American White House additionally leaves a question mark over the United States' continuing commitment to anchoring Turkey in this liberal order.[93]

FLUCTUATING RELATIONS: ENGAGEMENTS AND FAULT LINES IN THE TRANSATLANTIC PARTNERSHIP

Going forward, at least three structural factors are likely to deflect the Turkish leadership from its anti-Western ideological trajectory and move its foreign policy more in the direction of pragmatism. First, Turkey is deeply integrated into the politico-military institutional structures of the transatlantic community: it is part of NATO and the Council of Europe, and also participates in economic organizations central to the international liberal order, such as the World Bank, the IMF, and the World Trade Organization. This level of integration is a leading factor distinguishing Turkey from many other emerging economies and the BRICS.[94] These economic, political, and security connections linking Turkey to the transatlantic community are likely to persist. Despite a deep-rooted anti-Westernism, Turkey's current governing elite is ill prepared to bear the cost of severing these bonds. As a close observer of Turkish foreign policy has noted, Turkey "is tied to the Western order by bonds that are thicker than the sometimes adventurous impulses of Turkey's elites."[95]

Second, the loss of important export markets as a result of the turmoil in the Middle East and the sanctions by Russia enhances the value of Turkey's economic relations with the transatlantic community. The EU has remained one of the few major destinations for Turkey's products, somewhat offsetting the drop in Turkey's exports to the Arab Middle East and Russia in 2015–16. More important, Turkey's membership in the EU-Turkey Customs Union, besides offering Turkey preferential access to the EU's internal market, has also led to the adoption of EU standards for Turkish industrial export goods, which has increased their competitive value outside the EU as well. And despite the distance, Turkey's exports to the United States have in the last two years been more than twice the volume destined for Russia, its neighbor across the Black Sea. By and large these exports have included industrial goods, which have greater value added than the agricultural products that Turkey exports to Russia.

Similarly, around 62 percent of foreign direct investment in Turkey originated from the EU in 2016. This influx of investment is critical to the Turkish economy, which is notorious for failing to generate enough savings and technological knowhow of its own. Traditionally, tourism has been an important source of income, amounting to 3 percent of Turkey's GDP at its peak in 2014. More than half the nationals visiting Turkey that year came from European countries other than Russia. The negative impact that the collapse of tourism in 2016 had on the Turkish economy as a result of growing insecurity and instability speaks for itself. The fall in revenue from almost U.S. $28 billion to around $17 billion has adversely affected employment levels and living standards along the Aegean and Mediterranean coastal regions of Turkey.[96] Government efforts to mobilize tourism from the Gulf countries, Iran, and Russia have fallen well short of compensating for the loss of European tourists. Russia's ability to hurt Turkey with economic sanctions, especially in the tourism sector, as it did after Turkey's downing of Russia's jet, is well recognized.[97] Hence all indications are that Turkey will have to turn its attention to the West once again to revive its sluggish economy.

Security considerations are a third factor pushing for a reorientation of Turkey's policies. The mayhem in Syria has gravely affected Turkey's security over the last two years—more than 410 lives have been lost in numerous terrorist attacks since June 2015.[98] Some of the attacks are known to have been led by IS, while others were perpetrated by the PKK. Additionally, a number of separate attacks have been carried out by the

PKK-affiliated splinter group known as the Kurdistan Freedom Falcons. The PKK's close alliance with the Democratic Union Party (PYD) and People's Protection Units (YPG) in Syria is another major issue threatening Turkish national security. Turkey's relations with Russia seem to have taken an upturn since Erdoğan's apology for the downing of the Russian warplane, but Putin's sanctions and aggressive language have caused Turkey to remember the usefulness of NATO membership.[99] This may also be the explanation for Erdoğan's enthusiastic participation in the Warsaw NATO summit in July 2016 and his determination to strengthen Turkey's commitment to NATO.[100] Despite close Russian-Turkish cooperation on Syria, there is nevertheless a recognition on the Turkish side that the relationship has become deeply asymmetric in power terms and that the two countries' longer-term interests in Syria do not necessarily converge.[101] The meaning of the "accidental" killing of three soldiers in Syria in February 2017 by a Russian air strike is well understood as signaling the harm that Russia can inflict on the Turkish military.[102] The annexation of Crimea by Russia and Russia's role in undermining the territorial integrity of Ukraine, Moldova, and Georgia have also been duly noted by Turkish officials, who remain wary of the potential threat from the north. Most Turkish officials, in other words, are conscious of the danger of getting too close to Russia.[103] The prevailing argument seems to be that Turkey's "anger at the United States and its Western allies notwithstanding, it needs the protection the alliance offers. Without it, the Russians would be able to intimidate Ankara at will."[104] This appears to be borne out by the Turkish public that maintained almost 62 percent support for continued NATO membership.[105]

These three structural realities are likely to create the circumstances that prevent Turkey from further slipping away from its transatlantic allies (the West) and encourage closer engagement among the United States, the EU, and Turkey. They are offset, however, by at least three major divisions, or fault lines, that currently hold sway in Turkey's relations with the West.

The first major divide concerns popular opinion with respect to seeking closer ties in the first place. Advocates of a closer partnership with the non-Western world—"the rest"—are likely to continue to push back against proponents of maintaining tighter bonds with the transatlantic community. The "Eurasianists" in Turkey are likely to continue to seek closer relations with Russia and China. Their influence over the government has increased since the coup attempt and may well be reinforced by the outcome of the referendum. The long-standing Eurasian voice in Turkish politics has now merged into Erdoğan's notion of a "new" Turkey, along with its emphasis on authoritarianism and Islamization. Together they are poised to shore up Turkey's perennial status as a "prototypical torn country" whose identity remains caught between East and West. Nevertheless, this new Turkey will continue to enjoy strategic importance in the eyes of the West; its cooperation will be needed in tackling a catalogue of issues. Common interests are expected to provide the foundation for a transactional relationship that could be effective in the areas of regional security architecture, foreign trade, energy, and the provision of humanitarian assistance to Syria and Iraq.

Another fault line with the West lies in Turkey's diminished commitment to democratic values, a deficit that has become particularly conspicuous since the July 2016 coup attempt. The ensuing purges conducted by the government, the attack on the judiciary, and the numerous detentions and arrests that were carried out raised serious questions about the rule of law in the country. The imposition of emergency law has also laid the groundwork for a number of practices, such as the detention of Kurdish members of parliament, the extension of detention periods without trial, and the alleged widespread use of torture, that sharpen this concern. It remains to be seen whether Turkey will return to the days when its democracy was on the rise, when it contributed favorably to the fate of the international liberal order, especially by promoting accountable and transparent government and improving human and minority rights at home and in its neighborhood.

This steady deterioration in Turkey's democratic credentials is reflected in a recent study examining the role of five rising democracies; the study is not particularly hopeful about Turkey.[106] The adoption of the constitutional changes sought by Erdoğan to increase his powers in the tightly contested April 2017 referendum may further distance Turkey from the prospect of returning to the days when great hopes were entertained about the quality of its democracy. Under these circumstances, it is difficult to envisage a relationship of the kind that was assumed in Obama's "model partnership," while the nature of future relations with the U.S. administration cannot be predicted.

The final fault line is the result of the conflicting interests of the EU, the United States, and Turkey on a range of specific issues. The separation is likely to deepen if the sides cannot reconcile their differences even in the transactional sense of the word. The exclusion of Turkey's trading concerns from the Transatlantic Trade and Investment Partnership negotiations was a bitter source of grievance for Turkish leaders. Also, the disagreements with the United States over co-opting the PYD, an entity critical for the United States in the fight against IS but posing a threat to Turkey's national security, will strain bilateral relations if a compromise arrangement cannot be found. Nor is it clear how Erdoğan's policy of courting Russia will play out in the near and more distant term, with respect to both Turkey's bid for EU membership and finding a diplomatic solution to the conflict in Syria.

Turkey's relations with the EU are in no better state. The accession process is at a standstill. The migration deal between the EU and Turkey continues to cause deep consternation on both sides over its implementation. This impasse leaves only trade relations as an area that may enjoy some improvement because of the economic interdependency of the two sides and the ongoing discussions on upgrading the EU-Turkey Customs Union. Improving economic relations between the United States and Turkey could provide room for cooperation if the shadow the U.S. administration has thrown over free trade agreements can be dispelled. This may be possible in Turkey's case because Turkey runs a trade deficit with the United States and is keen to institute a more "fair" trade with the United States.

In sum, the future state of an already troubled alliance between Turkey and its traditional transatlantic partners does not seem promising. Possibly the best outcome might be one that prevents the existing fault lines from widening.

What is quite evident is that Erdoğan's new Turkey will be caught between structural factors that pull it toward the West and the fault lines in the transatlantic relationship that push it away. This dynamic is consonant both with Turkey's liminal identity and with the fluctuations that have historically characterized Turkey's relations with the West: in some periods Turkey's Western vocation has come to the fore, only to be countered by a domestic wave of anti-Westernism that puts into question Turkey's ties to NATO as well as to the EU. The attempt in the 1970s to develop closer relations with nonaligned countries and the Soviet Union illustrates one excursion of the pendulum. The immediate aftermath of the Cold War was also a difficult period when questions emerged about where Turkey belonged, and Turkish leaders sought to unite in what they called a Turkic world, stretching from the Adriatic Sea to the Great Wall of China. Deep distrust crept into Turkey's relations with the West, then, before the tension eased somewhat with the start of a reform process, which was at least partly nudged into being by the United States and the EU.

Turkey's integration into the transatlantic community and the Western-led international liberal order reached its peak in the early years of the AKP and Erdoğan's reign. This outcome owed as much to the AKP's readiness to cooperate with the existing bureaucracy in Turkey as it did to the policies laid out by earlier governments. The Turkish economy during this period also benefited from the reforms that had been put in place before the AKP's rise to power. That this transformation mostly occurred on the watch of an elite with deep roots in political Islam raised hopes that Turkey would indeed be able to marry democracy and Islam. Had the attempt been successful, Turkey would not have had to sail the choppy seas of international relations like a rudderless boat. The country might now be at a point where it could draw strength from the unique position of being a predominantly Muslim democracy. Unfortunately, Turkey could not live up to the expectations that arose in the early years of AKP rule and turned away from the principles of the international liberal order. The new Turkey that Erdoğan is pursuing appears at times to be trying to make a break with the West, as manifested in Erdoğan's threat to hold a Brexit-like referendum on Turkey's EU membership bid and his periodic calls to Putin to help him join the Shanghai Cooperation Organization. All of that might well be posturing, however. Only the passage of time will reveal whether a major rupture with the West does or does not occur. A number of possible scenarios might unfold under Erdoğan's reign as Turkey moves toward its centenary. These are described in the concluding chapter of the book, which also offers some brief recommendations for overcoming or at least mitigating the impact of the fault lines on the troubled alliance.

CHAPTER TWO

Turkey and the Transatlantic Alliance in the Cold War Era, 1947–91

From Blissful Honeymoon to Fragile Alliance

THE EMERGENCE OF AN ASSERTIVE Turkey on the world stage in the mid-2000s and the unmistakable debut of this assertiveness during the Justice and Development Party (AKP) administration precipitated a debate on Turkey's geopolitical axis shifting away from the West, or in other words Turkey surrendering its Western orientation in favor of a pivot to the east. Turkey, some claimed, was being "lost."[1] Others interpreted the shift as a sign of Turkey's newfound economic and political self-confidence and a corresponding interest in engaging the world beyond its traditional partners and commitments.[2]

The process of joining the West was not without stress, however. As an observer of Turkey, reflecting on these years, noted, "The U.S.-Turkey relationship and indeed Turkey's general relations with the West have been more contentious and uneasy than usually assumed."[3] Nevertheless, this alliance was considered vital for the security interests on both sides: Turkey's strategic position next to the Soviet Union and the Middle East meant that Ankara and Washington were prepared to overlook the flaws in their partnership and would pursue realist policies to prevent their "fragile alliance" from fracturing.[4] The Cold War years were also a time when Turkey's relations with Western Europe and first the European Economic Community (EEC) and then the European Communities (EC; the plural name denotes the three constituent communities) expanded and became institutionalized. Turkey's relations with the EEC and the EC were strained by domestic political developments, especially when the Turkish military staged coups in 1960 and 1980 and forced a civilian government out of office in 1971. Issues of democratic governance continued to strain Turkey's relations with the EC throughout the 1980s. However, these matters did not seem to affect U.S.-Turkish relations adversely. Instead, it was the U.S. military presence in Turkey, especially in the 1960s, that triggered anti-Americanism: leftist politics rose to a more prominent position in Turkey, accompanied by calls for a more nonaligned foreign policy. The 1970s saw U.S.-Turkish relations at their worst when the U.S. Congress imposed an arms embargo on Turkey following its intervention in Cyprus. The embargo, coming as it did on top of the anti-Americanism of the previous decade, engendered considerable distrust of the United States. However, the Soviet invasion of Afghanistan, which began in December 1979 and lasted nine years, and the corresponding increase in military and diplomatic tensions between Eastern and Western blocs helped revamp military and strategic cooperation between Turkey and the West. The following decade saw relatively warmer relations with the Soviet Union especially in trade, while Turkey's relations with the West became strained over human rights issues. However, strategic and defense cooperation with the U.S. deepened.

This chapter traces the trajectory of Turkey's integration into the U.S.-led international order. It explores how this uneasy relationship evolved over time and the ways in which the process became incorporated into Turkish statecraft. Having the Soviet Union as a common enemy—and its containment as a common objective—facilitated Turkey's entry into the emerging international order led by the West. Despite their mutual interests, however, a persistent mistrust hampered Turkey's relations with the United States and Europe, and the sources of this mistrust remain active today, steadily feeding skepticism toward the West on the part of the Turkish public and leadership.

EARLY COLD WAR ERA, 1947–60

The Bretton Woods institutions—the World Bank and the IMF—established in the closing years of World War II, were the first pillars of the international liberal order. The descent of the iron curtain across Europe lent urgency to the elaboration of similar institutions and architectures and gave rise to the Marshall Plan, the Truman Doctrine, NATO, and the European integration project, all of which are at the core of this order in Europe.

Turkey's bid for membership in these institutions, or rather its first statement that it wanted to be included in the fold of this emerging world order, came in March 1945. It happened when the Soviet Union made territorial claims to the northeastern provinces of Turkey and demanded privileged shipping access to the Turkish Straits—the Bosphorus, the Sea of Marmara, and the Dardanelles—which was not envisaged in the Montreux Convention Regarding the Regime of the Straits of 1936.[5] Turkey was still a young country, born out of the ashes of the Ottoman Empire, a multiethnic nation with an Islam-based state structure and a centuries-old history of domination over a large region. The Turkish Republic had come into being in 1923, following a long period marked by wars and deprivation. The founding principles of the republic emphasized the sanctity of national borders and the need to shun any move that could be interpreted as expansionist by the rest of the world. Because of Turkey's long history of hostilities with Russia, dating back to Ottoman times, Moscow's territorial threats caused significant concern for the leaders of the young republic. In a way, the Cold War with Moscow began earlier for Turkey than for the United States, with the Turkish Straits crisis. For Turkey, the Soviet threat had already emerged in 1945, at a time when Soviet and American troops were still embracing each other across the Elbe.[6]

It took some effort for Turkey to direct Washington's attention to Moscow's expansionist agenda. After a period of fighting a lonely "war of nerves" against Moscow, as Turkey's then minister of foreign affairs put it,[7] Turkey did receive a symbolic measure of support in April 1946 when the USS *Missouri* was dispatched to Istanbul, a gesture that, though meaningful, would initially prove mostly ineffective in the face of Soviet pressure on Turkey.[8] The Kremlin ceased its territorial demands only after the March 1947 declaration of the Truman Doctrine, which promised U.S. support to Turkey and Greece against the USSR. This was a cause for celebration in Turkey—almost an affirmation that the United States, "a great nation, the most powerful in the world, was interested in [Turkey's] independence and integrity."[9] Fear of the Soviet Union was a powerful motive: it convinced Turkish decisionmakers that an alignment with the West was and would be in the country's best interests. The lesson was in due course woven into traditional Turkish statecraft and the principle remains in place today, though Turkey's statecraft has changed dramatically.

The alignment with the West marked a break from the policy of neutrality that the Republic of Turkey had pursued until then. Its rulers, many of whom had served as Ottoman officers or diplomats, had experienced the benefits of maintaining a policy of active neutrality, which had kept their country out of World War II.[10] The posture of neutrality arose out of Ankara's realization that Turkey could not remain completely aloof from the course of the war. On the one hand, Turkey had to honor the terms of the Cooperation Agreement of 1939, signed with Britain and France; on the other, it had to make sure it did not appear unnecessarily hostile to Germany, whose forces had reached the Turkish border with Greece and Bulgaria. Turkey was under pressure from both sides. With the German armies locked in drawn-out battles inside the Soviet Union and desperately struggling to reach the Caucasus, Germany needed Turkey on its side. The Allies, for their part, also pressed Turkey into joining their ranks to deal a coup de grâce to Germany as the tide of the war began turning against that country.

Nevertheless, Ankara continued to resist a full alignment with a wartime alliance against Germany. This attitude frustrated the British and provided the Soviet Union with an excuse to threaten Turkey. Yet what was deemed essential for President İsmet İnönü, the successor to Atatürk, who had died in 1938, and his top diplomats was ensuring that Turkey stayed out of the war and that the Ministry of Foreign Affairs navigated those dangerous waters without any major compromise. It should be noted that this was a policy led by a group of individuals whose psyche had been deeply shaped by their own experiences of war. The horrors and destruction they had observed in the late Ottoman era, beginning with the Balkan Wars and continuing through World War I, were still fresh in their memory. Many of them had participated in the resistance movement against the Allied occupation following the disintegration of the Ottoman Empire and were well aware of the ruinous state of the land and its people when national independence was regained in 1923. In the end, on February 23, 1945, Turkey declared war against Germany, but this was no more than a symbolic necessity, executed with the aim of securing a seat at the postwar conference that would lay the foundations of the United Nations. Throughout the war Turkey had remained neutral; in its aftermath the country began moving, clearly and consciously, toward the "democratic front"—in other words, the West.[11]

To some extent, this shift was not surprising. According to the historian Bernard Lewis, Turkey would eventually have aligned its foreign policy with that of the Western powers; it was only a matter of strategic timing. For Turkey had undergone profound internal changes during its founding years.[12] Subscribing to an Ottoman tradition that stretched back to the early nineteenth century, Atatürk was deeply committed to Turkey's Westernization. In the late 1920s and early 1930s, he pushed into effect a series of reforms that aimed to transform Turkey into a modern state, fashioned in the image of its European counterparts. This, Atatürk reasoned, would elevate Turkey to "the level of contemporary civilizations," which he and his successors equated with the West.[13] In a sense, Lewis (and his line of historiography) explains Turkey's alliance with the Western powers in terms of the Kemalist desire to associate Turkey with Western civilization.[14] Indeed, this did play a role in maintaining a strong commitment to anchor Turkey in the Western alliance since Turkish leaders wished to be considered European and not Middle Eastern.[15] İnönü himself had remarked that one aim of NATO membership was to enable Turkey to be seen as a "respected member of the civilized world,"[16] which explains parliament's unanimous support in favor of joining NATO.[17] The Kemalist view of Turkey as a strictly European state, then, was instrumental in buttressing efforts to be included in this liberal order, yet İnönü's statements leave doubts as to whether, in the absence of these political and economic realities, Ankara would have pursued NATO membership with the same vigor and enthusiasm.

There also existed a combination of political and economic factors that propelled Turkey's foreign agenda throughout the Cold War and, at times, weighed more heavily in the politicians' calculus. Westernization was a top-down process that unfolded under the one-party political system of the Republican People's Party (CHP).[18] Its chief objective, to forge a homogenous and secular nation-state out of the once cosmopolitan Ottoman Empire, meant that the leadership would show little regard for minority and religious rights. The emphasis on homogeneity and strict secularism stirred up discontent among the Turkish public and even some of the CHP membership.[19] The elite recognized that "[by] 1945, the political alliance which had provided stability since 1923 had broken down and a new political balance needed to be established once the war was over."[20] In his address to the Turkish parliament in November 1945, President İnönü even remarked that Turkey's political structure had to be rethought in light of the "changed circumstances of the world," a reference to the victory of democracies over fascism.[21] Honoring this promise, the CHP allowed the formation of an opposition party, thus leading the way to the first-ever competitive elections in 1946. Four years later, in 1950, the CHP handed power over to Adnan Menderes's center-right Democratic Party (DP) following the latter's decisive victory at the polls. This peaceful transfer of power through the ballot box marked a critical turning point in Turkey's tumultuous journey to membership in the transatlantic community.

A major change introduced while the DP was in power was the softening of etatism, the principle that privileges the state in matters of economic and social development. The regulation of the economy by the state was one of the six guiding principles adopted by the CHP leadership in the early 1930s; its significance was captured symbolically by an arrow in the party emblem, which also featured symbols of five other principles—republicanism, nationalism, populism, secularism, and reformism.[22] In practical terms, etatism was an economic policy dictated by the dire circumstances in which the country found itself in the aftermath of World War I and its subsequent exposure to the effects of the Great Depression of 1929. The absence of a private sector also meant the heavy involvement of the state in economic matters, one manifestation of which was the preparation of five-year economic plans modeled on the Soviet example.[23] Despite these efforts, however, Turkey remained severely underdeveloped on the eve of World War II, its per capita income having improved only slightly from 1929 to 1945.[24] Measures introduced during the war years, such as price and currency controls and an unrealistic exchange rate to the U.S. dollar, had stifled the economy and increased inflation.[25] Domestic pressures for economic openness had been building up, which explains Turkey's keenness to become a member of a cluster of economic institutions—the IMF, World Bank, OECD, and GATT.

Political factors also played a role in drawing Turkey into the Western camp. Soviet actions in Iran, Czechoslovakia, and Berlin (in 1948), in addition to the threat of a few years earlier, were fanning Turkey's concerns for its national security. Many believed that membership in NATO would bolster Turkey's security and democratization efforts.[26] However, the leadership's aspirations to become a founding member of NATO were thwarted,[27] and worse, two subsequent applications for membership were turned down.[28] Turkey was unsuccessful partly on the grounds of geography, as it was not located in the North Atlantic space, and partly on the grounds of identity: some NATO members felt that Turkey was insufficiently "Western" and should rather be part of a Middle Eastern mutual defense arrangement.[29]

NATO membership became possible only after Turkey responded positively to the UN's call for reinforcements in the Korean War and dispatched troops to the region in July 1950. The stunning performance of its military gave the Turkish administration another chance to apply for membership. The Turkish hand meanwhile had been strengthened by the NATO countries' realization that Soviet expansionism could be contained only through a more global approach.[30] The accession of Turkey to NATO membership in 1952 was interpreted as the young nation's crowning achievement, and the fact that it had been the result of efforts by the first democratically elected party did not go unnoticed.

Membership in NATO, however, was not uniformly welcomed by the Turks. Some regarded it as a major departure from established policy of neutrality,[31] a stance that would fuel objections in later decades, thus contributing to an important fault line in Turkey's alignment with the West. Nonetheless, in the words of a longtime observer, joining NATO was indeed "Turkey's most important foreign policy change since the 1920s."[32] The dire circumstances of Atatürk's time—the collapse of the Ottoman Empire, the heavy toll of the struggle to regain independence against Western powers, and the urgency to rebuild the country in the aftermath— had led him to adopt a noninterventionist, nonexpansionist policy in foreign affairs. This was best captured in his famous maxim, "Peace at home, peace abroad,"[33] and guided his successors through World War II.

Had Turkey not been under pressure from Soviet expansionism, would it have continued its policy of active neutrality and nonalignment with either Eastern or Western bloc after the war? An exchange with former president İnönü in the 1970s is illuminating in this respect. Şadi Koçaş, a former Turkish senator, deputy prime minister, and contemporary of İnönü, argued, on the basis of a conversation with İnönü, that he believed İnönü's personal preferences would have been in support of a policy of nonalignment, and quoted İnönü as saying this would have been the case "had Stalin not pushed us into the Western bloc."[34] According to Koçaş, İnönü was sympathetic to the idea of adopting policies similar to those of Tito, Nehru, and Nasser. Clearly, the Soviet threat had radically altered the rules of the game for him. Yet the aspiration for a foreign policy independent of the West persists to this day. The desire to challenge the established Western-oriented statecraft became particularly conspicuous beginning in 2009 under the stewardship of the former minister of foreign affairs and prime minister, Ahmet Davutoğlu, and continues under the current president, Recep Tayyip Erdoğan.

TURKEY'S FIRST DECADE AS a member of the transatlantic community is often described as a "honeymoon" or "golden era."[35] Three developments put their stamp on this period. First, Turkey and the United States strengthened their military alliance, thereby deepening Turkey's integration into

NATO. Second, Turkey took its first tentative steps toward liberalizing its economy and benefiting from developmental assistance, grants, and credits. Third, at the end of the decade a military coup overthrew the elected government.

With U.S. assistance, Turkey was able to modernize its military infrastructure, revamping its organizational capacity and physical facilities to a higher standard, one that would serve the needs of the U.S. operations and military personnel.[36] Even though Nikita Khrushchev was less hostile to Turkey's territorial integrity than his predecessor Stalin had been,[37] Turkey's commitment to the alliance did not waiver, eventually earning it a reputation as an "unsinkable aircraft carrier" and a "bulwark" against the Soviet Union.[38] Prime Minister Adnan Menderes paid particular attention to displaying energetic solidarity with Turkey's transatlantic allies,[39] leading some to call him "more Dullesian than Dulles." He was wary of Arab socialism in the Middle East, which he saw as an instrument that would facilitate the expansion of communism. He spoke against the nationalization of the Suez Canal and supported NATO-like alliances, such as the Baghdad Pact and CENTO, for the defense of the Middle East against Soviet intrusion.[40] To reaffirm and reinvigorate Turkey's agency in the transatlantic space, the Menderes government followed policies similar to those of France with respect to Algeria and voted against Algerian self-determination at the UN in 1954—a policy move that, according to contemporary commentators, should have been an embarrassment to a young republic.[41] Similarly, at the Bandung Conference, the first large-scale conference that brought together the newly independent Afro-Asian states, the Turkish delegation dismissed nonalignment as an option; such policies, the delegation head remarked, only furthered Moscow's agenda.[42]

Turkey's membership in NATO also led to a transformation in the economic domain, the second major development for Turkey in the early Cold War era. The amount of assistance Turkey received from NATO was larger than the amount of aid that had been allocated to Turkey under the Truman Doctrine and the Marshall Plan. The total amount of assistance between 1952 and 1962 reached almost $1.4 billion, a significant sum for a country whose annual revenue from exports did not exceed $320 million during the 1950s.[43] Turkey could not have maintained a robust economic growth, financed major infrastructural projects, modernized its agricultural sector, or invested heavily in its defense architecture without Western assistance. This was also a period that benefited from the DP's liberal policies, which helped increase economic openness and attracted larger amounts of foreign direct investment. As put by the then president Celal Bayar, the main motivation behind all this was the desire to transform Turkey into a "little America." [44]

Impressively, these policies ensured close to $18 billion in foreign direct investment throughout the 1950s. However, the introduction of liberal economic policies and the partial opening up of the economy were accompanied by problems that eventually led to a growing current accounts deficit, increased borrowing, and mounting inflation. [45] As the economic situation deteriorated, political stability became harder to maintain, triggering repressive measures on the part of the government. Members of the opposition became concerned that the United States, to protect its strategic interests, would turn a blind eye to the dictatorial proclivities and practices of the incumbent regime. [46] These factors were marshaled to justify an intervention by the military in May 1960—the first coup in the history of the Turkish Republic and the third development of the period. The civilian government was toppled; President Bayar and Prime Minister Menderes were tried for treason, and Menderes was subsequently executed. The CHP was returned to power. In the aftermath of the coup the military, and subsequently the civilian government, now led by İsmet İnönü, were careful to reiterate their unequivocal commitment to Turkey's alliance with NATO and the West. This attitude did not, however, prevent a deep and growing skepticism toward the United States and the West from taking root in the country during the 1960s. Ironically, this was a consequence of a more liberal political environment that permitted criticism of policies by the establishment.

Turkey's Place in the European Integration Project

Turkey's alliance with the West also took shape in relation to Europe's economic integration project, which aspired to create a common market among member states. The Schuman Declaration of 1950 laid out the framework for the establishment of first the European Coal and Steel Community (ECSC) in 1952 and then the EEC in 1957 to encourage economic integration among West European states and thereby promote peace on the continent. The hope was that such close cooperation would also strengthen the resilience of these nations against the Soviet Union. Turkish leaders, for their part, had long found value in the idea of European integration and had shown keen interest when the French premier and minister of foreign affairs, Aristide Briand, proposed as early as 1930 the formation of an organization of a federal European union.[47] Hence, when a similar notion made a forceful comeback in the aftermath of World War II, Turkey was more than ready to come on board. The Menderes government applied for an association agreement with the EEC two years after that organization's founding in 1957. The EEC member countries were already major trading partners with Turkey, which was an incentive in itself; more important, EEC membership was seen by the Turkish leadership as a chance to reverse the country's economic downturn. A desire not to lag behind Greece, which had already submitted an application for membership, was also instrumental in Turkey's decision—a point that can be better understood by considering the beginning of difficulties between the two countries over the pending independence of Cyprus.

The leadership was ready to seize any opportunity that could bring Turkey closer to Western institutions.[48] After signing the Association Agreement in Ankara in September 1963, İnönü remarked, "The EEC is, in my opinion, the highest achievement of human intelligence to date [the highest achievement in human history] and likely to be the best legacy to future generations. . . . Today, we have signed an agreement that forever ties Turkey to Europe."[49] His European counterparts echoed İnönü's sentiments. The president of the European Commission, Walter Hallstein, for instance, interpreted the agreement as not just a recognition that "Turkey [was] a part of Europe" but as a sign that "one day Turkey will surely become a full member of the community."[50] As the Turks are painfully aware, that day has not yet come. The Ankara Agreement nevertheless merits attention because it set out a framework for establishing a customs union between the two sides, determined the financial provisions to support this transition, and spelled out the guidelines for the agreement's implementation.[51] Thus began the slow, highly contested, and an important project of integrating Turkey into Europe—a critical pillar of the U.S.-led post–World War II international order—and the gradual emergence of economic and structural factors that would ground Turkey in the transatlantic alliance.

THE EMERGENCE OF FAULT LINES, 1960–80

As Duygu Sezer, an analyst of Turkish foreign policy, has observed, Turkey "[had become], for all political and strategic intents and purposes, a member of the West" within a decade of joining NATO.[52] However, as the decade of the 1950s drew to a close, so too did the honeymoon. The next two decades would witness the growth of fault lines in especially the U.S.-Turkish relationship.

The military coup of May 1960 did not sap energy from U.S-Turkish relations, nor would the discord arise because of the sentences of capital punishment handed down to the elected leadership of the DP. In fact, the leaders of the coup, Alparslan Türkeş and Cemal Gürsel, promptly announced that Turkey remained committed to NATO, and, in a move intended to secure American support for the new administration, added that previous agreements with the United States would remain intact and in effect.[53] The flaws in Turkey's democratic edifice were obvious, but they did not seem either pressing or salient enough to prompt rumblings from Washington. The United States was busy dealing with its own domestic challenges to democracy in terms of ending segregation.

What instead caused a rift between the sides was the manner in which the United States withdrew its Jupiter missiles from Turkey in 1962. (Until then, the United States had only short- and medium-range missiles and needed a site from which to launch them against the Soviet Union in case of war.) The United States had informed the Turkish government of the impending removal the previous year, but the fact that the decision was made as part of a secret deal with Khrushchev to resolve the Cuban missile crisis provoked consternation in Ankara. The Turkish leadership resented what it perceived as the United States riding roughshod over Turkish interests to accommodate the Soviets.[54] Many were beginning to realize that Turkey's security interests were at risk of being bargained away by the United States to secure a more advantageous deal with Turkey's main adversary. This instilled in Turkish officials a "lingering suspicion" toward the United States.[55] It would be fair to say that suspicion of U.S. motives and trustworthiness persists to this day.

This crisis in confidence in the United States was aggravated in 1964, when President Lyndon Johnson sent a letter to İnönü. The communication was prompted by Turkey's threats to intervene militarily in Cyprus to rein in the growing violence between the Greek and Turkish communities, a move largely motivated by the fear that intercommunal tensions were poised to escalate into a state of war between the respective countries. The letter warned İnönü—rather crudely, according to the Turkish side—against using weapons supplied by the United States in executing such an interventionist policy and stated that if a step taken by Turkey triggered a military reaction from Moscow, NATO might not feel bound by its defense obligations.[56] This incident would surely have reminded İnönü of a similar threat by Winston Churchill, who toward the end of World War II had hinted at the possibility of Turkey standing alone against an aggressive Soviet Union after the war unless it joined the Allied camp.[57] İnönü's response to Johnson expressed his disappointment in the lack of solidarity; more significant, it also made clear that the American president's response to the affair had raised questions in İnönü's mind as to whether NATO was a reliable alliance for Turkey. The matter was closed when the two leaders met in Washington at the invitation of the American side.[58] But the damage had been done.

The confidence held by İnönü personally, and Ankara more generally, in the benefits of nurturing various forms of partnerships with the United States and other Western countries was shaken. In an interview with *Milliyet* in April 1964, İnönü said, "If our allies don't change their attitude, the Western alliance will break up and then a new kind of world order will be established under new conditions, and in this world Turkey will find itself a place. I had faith in the leadership of America, which carries great responsibility within the Western alliance. I am suffering now as a result of this attitude."[59] These bitter words still resound in the institutional memory of the Turkish Foreign Ministry. At the time, they captured the substance and essence of the skepticism that had been developing in Ankara toward the West and explain why Turkey, only a decade after joining the Western alliance, was embarking on a search for an alternative.

Domestic Turbulence during the 1970s

This search commenced in the 1960s as some in the military in power began to advocate a return to "Atatürk's foreign policy," which they now called a third-worldist approach to international relations.[60] Many young officers and their supporters did not hide their preference for a Nasserite regime.[61] The 1924 Turkish constitution was reformed after the coup—remarkably, along more liberal lines, leading to the emergence of political space for left-wing movements. The 1960s also witnessed the election of Turkey's first openly Marxist political party to the parliament, and it was in this period that left-leaning labor unions began to emerge in large numbers. The circumstances were ripe for the rise of a politicized youth, especially at the university level. A number of radical, violent groups also came into being during these years, most notably the Kurdistan Workers' Party (PKK), founded in 1977. Street protests against NATO, the U.S. military presence in Turkey, and the Vietnam War were common occurrences; in February 1969 the car belonging to the U.S. ambassador Robert Komer was overturned and set on fire at the Middle East Technical University as a sign of protest against Turkey's pro-Western orientation.[62] These left-wing organizations also clashed with the nationalist and Islamist groups that proliferated during this period. Alarmed by these developments, the U.S. embassy decreased the number of its personnel in Turkey, and Peace Corps operations were terminated in 1970.[63] Against the backdrop of this new political environment, the consensus of the honeymoon years began to fall apart. And with the unstable domestic environment, many observers started to question Turkey's fitness to be a NATO member.

Yet both the subsequent administration under Süleyman Demirel—the leader of the Justice Party, which was established in place of the DP when the latter was shut down by the military—and the liberal business elite continued to be staunch supporters of amiable relations with the West.[64] The Demirel government made efforts to expand Turkey's web of partners, reaching out to a community of nations beyond the strict confines of the Western world, including not only the developing economies but the Soviet Union as well.[65] Apart from growing doubts as to the U.S. commitment to Turkey's defense and security, the outbreak of the Cyprus conflict in 1974 also provided an impetus to expand the country's network of relations. Ankara began to realize, based on President Johnson's earlier reactions, that it would be alone in pursuing its interests in Cyprus.

The Turkish leadership did not receive a more encouraging response from the camp of the nonaligned, whose support was lukewarm. The Soviet invasion of Czechoslovakia in 1968, on the other hand, provided a striking reminder that a threat still loomed across the Black Sea. The domestic opposition to NATO subsided as a result[66]—the events in Czechoslovakia even led some leftist leaders to denounce Moscow's actions as a revival of Stalinism.[67] Government circles were now joined by the ranks of the opposition in a newfound appreciation of the value of NATO membership. A pattern seemed to be emerging: while frustration over what the Turkish side identified as the West's half-hearted interest in Turkey's integration sent its leadership on a search for alternative alignments, the Soviet threat had Ankara walk its steps back into the transatlantic fold.

As the 1970s wore on, the U.S.-Turkey relationship was once again marked by conflict. Turkey's intervention in Cyprus in the summer of

1974 triggered an arms embargo by the U.S. Congress that remained in effect from 1975 to 1978. Bülent Ecevit, the leader of the CHP administration, who had returned to power as prime minister in 1977, was critical of the capitalist order; he saw Turkey as evolving into an "economic colony."[68] Ecevit hailed from the left of center of the political spectrum and was an advocate of policies steeped in a tradition that had its roots in the leftist movements of the 1960s and the notion of "left Kemalism."[69] His motto, *Haysiyetli dış politika* (Foreign policy with dignity), guided him in his frequent questioning of Turkey's close relations with the United States. He even remarked that Turkey's NATO membership was an impediment to Turkey's own economic development.[70]

Ecevit, however, never aimed to pull Turkey out of NATO. Instead, he called for an equitable distribution of responsibility that would also serve Turkish national interests; in his words, "our contribution to NATO in the future would be and should be commensurate with NATO's contribution to Turkey's security."[71] He also pursued a foreign policy that targeted stronger relations with countries in the neighborhood, as attested by his choice of Yugoslavia for his first official visit in 1977 and Moscow for a visit the following year. Ecevit crafted a new defense policy in light of the understanding that the real threat to Turkey would come not from the Soviet Union but from Greece.[72] Indeed, Greek-Turkish relations were particularly tense under his leadership in the latter part of the 1970s.

Turkey's Relations with the EEC during the 1970s

Turkey also experienced some turbulence in its relationship with the EEC during the decade of the 1970s. The adoption of the Additional Protocol in 1973, a supplement to the 1963 Association Agreement with the EEC for the purpose of streamlining the process of lowering customs tariffs, meant a new phase for both sides. In addition, Turkey was expected to adapt to a series of measures introduced with the objective of preparing the country for a customs union by 1985.[73] The Turkish government, however, failed to follow the guidelines and resisted opening its economy to competition. All this injected more friction into an already fraught dynamic, deepening the crisis of confidence that fuels today's fault lines.

It was not only Turkey's failure to follow through that hampered relations: Europe's actions also made it difficult for the parties to see eye to eye. For instance, the EEC member states were reluctant to grant easier access to the common market for Turkish textiles, Turkey's only industrial product at the time that would have had a competitive advantage in the European market. They also found the prospect of unrestricted circulation of Turkish labor unpalatable. Germany in particular proved intractable in amending its position especially on labor, speculating that the number of Turks in its cities might increase to 10 million by 1990.[74] These limitations on the movement of goods and labor frustrated Ankara at a time when Turkey's economy had to grapple with a cluster of other difficulties resulting from an increase in oil prices and a shortage of foreign exchange reserves. The view from Ankara was that Europe was deliberately impeding Turkey's economic development, a conviction that easily converged with Ecevit's fears of Turkey becoming an "economic colony," and as such constituted one of the fault lines that divided the country from the Western alliance. This mental proclivity would mark EEC/EU-Turkish relations well into the 1990s.

On the side of the EEC, the approach to Turkey was mostly defined by the structural challenges the West European countries had to face during an economic recession. A downturn had hit the continent in the mid-1970s as the EEC was reeling from the first round of enlargement, which had severely strained its resources. Furthermore, the EEC was also striving to expand concessional relations with a string of Mediterranean countries. It is not hard to understand that under the circumstances, rethinking Turkey's ties to the European market in a way that would benefit Turkey's economy would not take precedence on the EEC's agenda. As a close observer of Turkey's relations with the EEC wrote in 1976, Turkey "no longer had a special status, and had to be considered like any other third country."[75]

The rise of Necmettin Erbakan on the political scene in the 1970s also complicated relations with Europe. Erbakan emerged at the political forefront as the head of an Islamist opposition party that objected to Turkey's becoming a member of the European community on ideological grounds derived from the National Outlook movement (Millî Görüş). Instead, he found value in the idea of forming an Islamic common market.[76] Motivated by the more etatist constitution of 1961, the opponents of Turkey's integration with Europe organized interest groups that propped up resistance to putting into effect the Additional Protocol. Having doubts of his own about Turkey's relations with the EEC, Prime Minister Ecevit suspended implementation of the protocol. The idea of a common market as pursued by the Europeans, he reasoned, would turn Turkey into a "market for them" without much benefit for Turks, who would become no more than "gardeners" for Europeans.[77]

Improving Relations with the United States during the Late 1970s

Unlike the situation with Europe, Turkey's relations with the United States dramatically improved toward the end of the 1970s. The period of détente during the mid-1970s in Soviet-U.S. relations, which had already been under duress as a result of the growing arms race between the two countries, ended in 1979 with the Soviet invasion of Afghanistan. This reminded the Turkish leadership that the small states bordering the Soviet Union remained vulnerable to Moscow's territorial machinations. Now that the need to safeguard itself against a potential Soviet invasion had intensified, Turkey started to dial down some of the tension in its bilateral relations with the United States.[78] A new Defense and Economic Cooperation agreement was signed in March 1980 to undo the damage inflicted on Turkey by the sanctions regime of 1975–78. Economic and military aid from the United States increased by a significant margin. Most important, the agreement made possible a higher level of cooperation in transferring technology and thereby developing Turkey's defense industry. The opening of a production line for F-16s in Turkey was a case in point, a step that also strengthened Turkey's structural bonds with the West.[79] From Ankara's vantage point, though its relations with the United States and Europe were disappointing at times, the presence of the Soviet threat was sufficient motivation for Ankara to overlook these concerns and once again seek safety within the transatlantic fold.

THE CLOSING YEARS OF THE COLD WAR, 1980–91: HEIGHTENED UNCERTAINTY

Another watershed moment in Turkish history, the military takeover of the civilian administration in September 1980, came amid the political turmoil and profound economic crisis resulting from the collapse of Turkey's import substitution policies after the oil shock of the mid-1970s.[80] The coup triggered a new round of uncertainty in Turkey's transatlantic relations. Once at the helm, the military authorities suspended the constitution and dissolved parliament. The country would be handed back to civilian authorities in 1983, but only after a new and restrictive constitution had been formulated the year before. This backsliding in democratic standards did not hamper Turkey's relations with the United States, nor would Turkey's numerous human rights violations impinge on bilateral relations. Both sides at this time remained more focused on managing the geopolitical challenges posed by the Soviet Union. In contrast, the European Parliament's condemnation of the coup in Turkey was unequivocal; it also suspended the implementation of financial aid packages until the European Commission had affirmed that effective steps had been taken to restore democracy.[81] Simultaneously, Turkey was put on a watch list at the Council of Europe, which monitored its civil and human rights track records.[82] Eventually, elections were held in 1983, and the rise of the Motherland Party (ANAP) to power ushered in a new phase in Turkey's relations with the EC. The new government, under Turgut Özal's leadership, was indeed keen to mend ties, and Turkey's formal application for membership was submitted on its watch in 1987. The EC's response two years later was not positive; the EU turned the application down on the grounds of democratic and economic deficiencies and unresolved conflicts with Greece and Cyprus.[83] Nevertheless, the Commission did reassure Ankara that Turkey was still eligible in principle, leaving the door open for Turkey to join this pillar of the international liberal order in the undetermined future.[84]

U.S.-Turkish cooperation against the Soviet Union continued, but a number of disagreements flared up during this period that would resonate well beyond the 1980s. When the U.S. Congress considered recognizing the Armenian genocide in 1987, it precipitated a major diplomatic crisis between the two countries, including Turkey's withdrawal of its ambassador from Washington and cancellation of the Turkish president's visit to the United States.[85] Similarly, human rights groups called the international community's attention to the actions of the Turkish security forces toward the Kurdish minority in the southeast, and started applying pressure on Ankara to recognize the Kurdish identity. As the Cold War began to ease and particularly when the Berlin Wall came down in 1989, it became increasingly difficult to keep human rights and civil liberties off the agenda of U.S.-Turkish discussions. The economy, however, was an area of convergence. Özal had worked closely with the military in implementing an earlier decision to liberalize the Turkish economy; in collaboration with the IMF and the World Bank, he pushed through critical structural reforms that would transform Turkey's economy from an import substitution economy to a dynamic export-oriented one.[86] By abandoning import substitution policies in favor of those based on the Washington Consensus, the Turkish economy acquired a head start in its integration into the post–Cold War international liberal order. The liberalization of Turkish democracy would take much longer.

CONCLUSION

In the aftermath of World War II, a critical factor that brought the United States and Turkey together was the common goal of containing Soviet expansionism. Turkey's founding fathers' commitment to Turkey's modernization, which they equated with Westernization, was another engine of propulsion. Britain and France represented the ultimate model for their ambitious project—an irony in itself, since it was mainly against these two countries that they had led a war of resistance not long before, between 1919 and 1922. To Ankara, Britain and France, together with the United States, were the "great powers" that had withstood and combated the machinations of an expansionist Germany during World War II and the Soviet Union thereafter. Germany and the USSR, by contrast, were seen by the Turkish leadership as having very little regard for the independence and sovereignty of smaller states. Safeguarding Turkey's territorial integrity was Ankara's chief objective, which meant taking the necessary precautions that would allow the country to defend itself against any threats emanating from Moscow. This line of reasoning brought Turkey into the fold of the emerging transatlantic alliance. In return, Turkey's geostrategic location and its determination to challenge Soviet expansionism became invaluable assets for the United States and the broader West.

It is more difficult to determine whether a genuine interest in strengthening democracy played a role in Turkey's incorporation into the transatlantic alliance. The Truman Doctrine was critical, for it effectively named Turkey (along with Greece) as a country of the "free world." But "being free" had a specific meaning then that is not recapitulated in today's world. Invoked in a geopolitical context, a desire for freedom during the Cold War equated with a desire to be protected against Soviet domination. The decade of the 1950s was an early phase in Western Europe's economic and political reconstruction; liberal democracy as understood today had not yet taken root. Likewise, the United States was far from representing liberal democratic values. The decade was marked by McCarthyism and racial segregation; the civil rights movement had not yet been set in motion. In the case of Turkey, the issue of democracy, or the question of how democratic the country was, does not appear to have been a major topic of discussion, let alone a point of contention, during the membership negotiations with NATO.[87] (Portugal was a dictatorship when it became a founding member of NATO in 1949.) Yet as one Turkish academic has pointed out, beyond Turkey's value to the West in terms of security there was also a second motive of wanting to make Turkey "a showcase of fast economic growth within the framework of capitalism and democracy."[88] It was meant to counter the Soviet economic model for the third world. Nevertheless, this motive did not lead the United States to condemn the two military coups, in 1960 and 1980, that ousted elected civilian administrations in Turkey.[89] Neither were democracy and respect for human rights brought up as a major issue by the EC or the Council of Europe until after the second coup. On the Turkish side, it is difficult to determine whether Turkey's democratic transition from a one-party to a multiparty political system was driven solely, as some have argued, by a calculation that such a move would ensure Turkey's acceptance into the Western alliance.[90] What is clear, however, is the role of the constant Soviet menace in facilitating Turkey's integration into a string of transatlantic institutions, ranging from the Bretton Woods system to GATT to regional West European organizations. These institutional ties would play an important role in integrating Turkey into the emerging international liberal order.

Another question that is difficult to answer is whether Turkish democracy would have matured had Turkey not become a member of this international liberal order, or again, whether Turkey would have adopted a liberal market economy. Would the military have handed back the reins of power to a civilian administration after both coups had Turkey not been a part of the international institutional web? It is unlikely. Moreover, these institutional and geopolitical forces of circumstance effectively helped balance the influence of the anti-Western circles in the country, whose deep skepticism of the United States in particular often led to a search for alternative alignments.

The benefits of being part of the transatlantic alliance were many for Turkey. With the Soviets kept at bay, Turkey emerged from the Cold War on the winning side. Its military earned esteem for its role in holding down twenty-four Soviet divisions, thus helping to relieve the pressure on the central and northern fronts in Europe.[91] The alliance also made possible a significant modernization of Turkey's military, a process that eventually led to the production and even exportation of warplanes such as the F-16s. Its economy opened up, industrial production expanded, and exports of consumer goods increased. Ironically, Turkey even reached a point where it could offer export credits to the Soviet Union. This was quite a departure from the previous state of affairs, when Turkey relied on the Soviets for the long-term loans it desperately needed for its industrialization in the early days of the republic and as late as the 1960s and 1970s.[92] Turkey during the Cold War became the recipient of the most economic aid outside the Warsaw Pact countries.[93] But the influx of aid did not spare Turkey from the negative effects of the structural problems in its economy; cyclical crises during these years led to frequent interventions by the IMF.

The end of the Cold War would bring new challenges to Turkey's relationship with the West. As discussed in the next chapter, some of these were of a nature that would heighten Turkey's strategic importance, while others risked peeling away its value. Meanwhile, both the United States and Europe constantly reminded Turkey of the need to address its democratic shortcomings. The leadership in the 1990s and early 2000s, including the incumbent Justice and Development Party (AKP) in its first two terms in government, did indeed set Turkey on a pro-EU agenda centered on democratization. In this regard, Turkey seemed to be moving onto a promising trajectory and started to meet the criteria outlined in the EU acquis—the body of laws, covenants, and regulations binding on all EU member states—for eventual membership in the EU. The train of economic reforms set in motion in the early years of the AKP administration transformed the country into what became known as an economic success story.

All this increased Turkey's prestige in the region and bestowed on the country unprecedented levels of soft power.[94] In return, Ankara found itself in a position to facilitate the region's integration into the liberal international order. It came to be viewed as "doing the European Neighborhood Policy for the EU," or, put differently, as creating a "ring of friends" around the EU.[95] For the Middle East, Turkey had evolved into a source of inspiration: it showcased the perks of economic liberalization and demonstrated to the international community that Islam was indeed, or could be, compatible with democracy.[96] This was a country, a partner, and an ally that upheld the interests of both the EU and the United States. And it was the Turkey with which the Obama administration envisaged developing a "model partnership"—a clear indication that the days of a fragile alliance were in the past.[97]

This partnership, however, never blossomed into the model the U.S. president had in mind. Instead, Turkey's relations with its allies turned increasingly bitter and its EU membership prospects became contested. This turnabout was driven as much by internal developments as by external factors. Deep-seated skepticism in Turkey toward the West and the EU's feigned commitment to Turkey's accession derailed the prospects of anchoring Turkey in this liberal world order held together by common interests and shared values. There was also the weakening of the consensus over traditional statecraft with its Western orientation and a general tendency to keep foreign policy insulated from domestic politics. The post–Cold War era saw growing discussion of alternative worldviews and approaches to Turkish foreign policy, a trend that became pronounced during Ahmet Davutoğlu's term as minister of foreign affairs from 2009 to 2014. Furthermore, domestic politics and foreign policy became increasingly intermeshed, particularly in the aftermath of the Arab Spring. The next chapter takes up the evolution of Turkey's relationship with its transatlantic allies in the post–Cold War era and explores how the relationship saw periods that brought the two sides together and others that pushed them apart. Yet at the same time, this would also be the era that saw Turkey's increasing structural integration with the economic, political, and security institutions and architecture of the transatlantic community.

CHAPTER THREE

The Post–Cold War Years, 1991–2017

THE END OF THE COLD WAR brought sweeping changes to the global north. The collapse of the Soviet Union rearranged geopolitical alignments among hardened adversaries and eased military tensions, especially for countries within the ambit of Soviet influence. Countries on Russia's friends and enemies lists traded places overnight as the young federation's democratically minded foreign minister, Andrei Kozyrev, fought for Russia to have a place among the global institutions of the economically developed West. Russia's new policy of respect for the sovereignty of independent states, respect for the sanctity of international borders, and a focus on treaties of friendship and economic cooperation allowed countries in a large swath across Europe and Asia to emerge from the shadow of the Soviet Union and begin to build peacetime relationships of their own.

Turkey had benefited from the policies of glasnost and perestroika pursued by the eighth and last president of the Soviet Union, Mikhail Gorbachev, in the late 1980s, especially in the realm of trade. Nonetheless, the dissolution of the Soviet Union still came as a major relief to Turkish decisionmakers, who were also gratified by the number of newly independent states emerging in the post-Soviet space.[1] Ankara was quick to recognize them since their existence ensured that Turkey, for the first time since the late seventeenth century, when Russia captured the Azov fortress north of the Crimean peninsula, and with the exception of a brief period between 1918 and 1921, when the republics of the southern Caucasus were independent, would no longer share a border with Russia.

With the Soviet Union removed as an obstacle to an eastward orientation, many in Turkey also dreamed of the rise of a Turkic world that would extend from the Adriatic Sea to the Great Wall of China and as such could offer an alternative vocation to the West. In the vision laid out by Prime Minister Süleyman Demirel in 1992, Turkey deserved to be at the helm of this enormous Turkic world.[2] Optimism over the region's future had its limits, however, since a series of conflicts, including Iraq's invasion of Kuwait, the Israeli-Palestinian conflict, and clashes in the former Yugoslavia and the South Caucasus, served as constant reminders to the Turkish leadership that Turkey was still situated in a volatile neighborhood. This recognition highlighted the continued need for pragmatism in foreign dealings that had historically shaped Turkey's statecraft. It also dictated caution over any "daring" policies that might put Turkey's membership in the transatlantic community at risk.[3]

Some of the strategic challenges that arose at the end of the Cold War were met by the transatlantic community in close cooperation with Turkey. Convergent policies emerged in areas of common interests, such as in the Balkans and the Caucasus, and together with Turkey's assistance elsewhere—as a modest mediator in Middle Eastern conflicts and a contributor to various peacekeeping efforts in Afghanistan, the Balkans, and Africa—these policies played an important role in strengthening ties with the West. This was accompanied by U.S. and EU initiatives to encourage democratic reforms in Turkey, where internal demands for a greater recognition of freedoms and diversity had already begun to emerge, especially in the context of allowing greater cultural rights for the Kurdish minority in the country. The latter was a particularly sensitive issue because after the military coup in 1980, the public use of the Kurdish language was banned and repression increased. The situation was further aggravated when in 1984 the Kurdistan Workers' Party (PKK) took up armed struggle against the Turkish state with the declared intention of setting up a Marxist-Leninist independent Kurdistan in areas populated by Kurds. Nevertheless, calls for reform continued to gain momentum as Turkey sought to integrate more closely with the EU, which brought the need to consider seriously whether the two sides could converge on values and not just on common interests.

The chapter dedicates a large section to Turkey's EU membership saga owing to its centrality to long-standing fundamental issues such as Turkey's identity and its place vis-à-vis the Western world in general. The democratization process enters the discussion mainly as an area where

Turkey's internal dynamics often intersected with the conduct of foreign policy. For all Turkey's cooperation efforts with the West since the end of the Cold War, however, and despite its status as a candidate for EU membership, Turkey's position in the international liberal order remains precarious. On several occasions Turkey and its Western allies, particularly the United States, found themselves at loggerheads in the Middle East. Differences in the way in which each side has approached the Kurdish minority in the region have proved to be a persistent source of friction, one that continues to separate them. Recently, the AKP's weakening commitment to democratization has widened the gap that always existed between Turkey and its Western allies.

AREAS OF CONVERGENCE WITH THE WESTERN ALLIANCE

At the end of the Cold War, Turkey was propelled from serving as a "flank" state—an outpost propped up by the U.S. and NATO to help contain the Soviet Union in a highly unstable region—to acting as a "front-line" state, tasked with managing this instability. The country sat in the middle of thirteen of the sixteen conflict zones of immediate concern and interest to NATO[4] and was entrusted by the Western consensus with a stabilizing role.[5] Successive U.S. administrations during the post–Cold War period would envisage Turkey as a model to help expand democratic and secular governance as well as liberal market practices throughout its region.[6] On the Turkish side, fears that the end of the Cold War would reduce Turkey's strategic value for the Western alliance were thus allayed.

The Iraqi invasion of Kuwait in 1990 propelled Turkey into the limelight.[7] Initially, President Turgut Özal seemed eager to collaborate closely with the United States, noting that Turkey could in this fashion "kill three birds with one stone" (*bir koyup, üç almak*), a reference to the significant benefits—economic, political, and strategic—he expected in return for a more proactive role in the new world order. Özal's move was challenged, with the strongest reaction coming from Turkey's chief of staff, who resigned in protest of any plan that would require the deployment of Turkish troops to dislodge Iraq from Kuwait.[8]

Turkey ended up following a "middle of the road" policy. It did not directly participate in military operations; instead, it implemented the UN sanctions on Iraq by cutting the flow of oil through the Kirkuk-Ceyhan pipeline and showed its support for the West by allowing the

United States access to its military facilities for logistical needs. Cooperation with the United States also extended into the aftermath of the operation that pushed the Iraqi military out of Kuwait, when a huge displacement crisis resulted from punitive actions mounted by the Iraqi government, with large number of refugees, mostly Kurds, streaming into Turkey. Turkey spearheaded the diplomatic efforts that culminated in the adoption of UN Security Council Resolution 688, which created a "safe haven" in northern Iraq and set in motion Operation Provide Comfort, with the objective of safely repatriating refugees to their homes.[9]

Operation Provide Comfort had coincided with growing violence between the PKK and the Turkish military. The Kurdish groups that had remained committed to peaceful means, on the other hand, were becoming increasingly assertive in their demands, which covered a large spectrum, from cultural rights to self-rule. All this led to a serious concern in Turkey at both state and public levels as to the stability and territorial integrity of the country. Western sympathies for Kurdish aspirations were particularly poorly received, fueling the long-existing skepticism that Turkey faced a conspiracy aimed at challenging its very existence as a unitary state. Operation Provide Comfort, therefore, was an instance in which cooperation in one area, to ease the plight of Kurds fleeing Saddam Hussein, led to divisions in another—how to address the long-term aspirations of Kurdish groups in the region. (The Kurds, who had enjoyed considerable autonomy under the Ottoman Empire, became separated into Iraq, Syria, and Turkey after the end of World War I. They also constitute an important minority in Iran. Since then many Kurds have aspired to create a pan-Kurdish state, a goal precluded by divisions among themselves, resistance from the states in which they live, and also the realities of international relations that complicate the emergence of a new state.[10]) Turkey's attachment to the notion of a unitary and homogenous state has complicated the introduction of reforms recognizing the separate cultural rights of Kurds and other ethnic and religious groups on its territory. This resistance to allowing for greater diversity and pluralism in the country has been one important reason for its marginal (contested) place in the international liberal order.

Turkey's response to the Iraqi invasion of Kuwait did establish a template for cooperating with the West in general, and the United States in particular, for the next decade. For instance, in the aftermath of the Kuwait crisis Turkey championed U.S. efforts to promote peace between Israel and its Arab neighbors, and participated in the multilateral track talks that emerged from the Madrid Conference in 1991.[11] The Oslo Accords in 1993 and the subsequent breakthrough in the Israeli-Palestinian peace process two years later opened the way for Turkey to upgrade and expand its economic and especially military ties with Israel.[12] Prior to that bilateral relations had remained at a low point; the 1970s and 1980s were marked by a foreign policy increasingly aligned with the pro-Palestinian sentiments of the Turkish public despite Turkey's position as the first country in the Muslim world to recognize Israel, which it did in 1949.[13] After the Oslo Accords, Turkey also engaged the Palestinian Authority by extending economic assistance, as well as by supporting peace-building projects.

In the early 2000s, after a long period of tension, Turkey succeeded in improving relations with Syria, and later in the decade it even managed to install itself in the role of mediator in the conflict with Israel. This coincided with a time when Turkey's support was deemed critical for George W. Bush's Broader Middle East and North Africa (BMENA) initiative, which was promoted by his administration with the aim of democratizing the region.[14] Though reluctant, Turkey made an indirect contribution to the effort by engaging the Middle East through economic channels. The result was an increase in the volume of trade with the region, as well as growing Turkish foreign direct investment in countries such as Egypt, Iraq, Libya, and Tunisia.[15] At the same time, Turkey introduced a liberal visa regime to encourage a greater movement of people, thereby granting persons from the Middle East the benefits of unrestricted travel, which had been denied them by the EU and its "fortress Europe" policies.[16] Considerable prestige ensued for Turkey from these developments, with growing soft power to influence the political trajectory in the Middle East.

These policies were readily associated with the motto "zero problems with neighbors," much publicized by the AKP and its foreign policy architect, Ahmet Davutoğlu.[17] Yet this regional orientation had in fact had its start under previous governments. Despite all the disagreements of the preceding decade between Turkey and its Western partners, Turkish policymakers had demonstrated a keen interest in addressing long-standing bilateral disputes and in supporting greater economic and social integration with the international community. The origins of this trend can be traced back to the aftermath of the military coup of 1980, when relative isolationism, which had determined Turkey's statecraft until then, began to be abandoned with the return to democracy after three years of military rule.

In this respect, Turgut Özal, who rose to power as prime minister and leader of the Motherland Party after the 1983 elections, is recognized as a more daring politician than his predecessors. He was willing "to depart from established policies, to take calculated risks, and to search for new alternatives and options."[18] In domestic politics he was the first leader to openly acknowledge the existence of a separate Kurdish identity, going so far as to publicly reveal his Kurdish roots, and advocated for cultural rights. His economic policies helped Turkey adopt a more liberal, export-oriented economic model, which necessitated greater access to and integration with the world. Restrictions on Turkish nationals' ability to travel abroad were lifted, and at the same time, visa requirements for nationals of the Soviet Union—and later for Russians and most residents of the Soviet successor states—were liberalized. He led the establishment of the Organization of the Black Sea Economic Cooperation, a novel arrangement at the time.

Özal also pursued efforts to resolve Turkey's long-standing bilateral disputes, especially with Armenia with respect to the recognition of the Armenian genocide and the opening of the land border between the two countries, and, with Greece, territorial issues in the Aegean Sea and minority rights of their respective coethnics, though without much success. He was deeply conscious of the need for peace building in the Middle East. Much as Gül and Erdoğan would emphasize twenty years later, he advocated the view that the Muslim world should adopt secularism and liberal democracy, along with a vision for "a pro-Western outlook" to predominate in the region.[19] Most important, though, he sought to engage the EU in support of greater integration. His book *Turkey in Europe and Europe in Turkey* revealed his disposition to see Turkey's European vocation as consistent with the nation's cultural orientation and the long Ottoman history that lay behind. For Özal, closer ties with Europe were expected to enhance both Turkey's regional power and its strategic value in the eyes of the West.

A similar emphasis on reconciliation and integration marked the tenure of Hikmet Çetin, foreign affairs minister between November 1991 and July 1994, and that of İsmail Cem, who served in the same position from June 1997 to July 2002. Çetin was successful in improving relations with Israel even as he expanded ties with the Palestinians. Like Özal, he made a point of revealing his Kurdish origins during his May 1992 address to the European Parliament, a bold move in light of the heavy lid kept on Kurdish identity until then. Improvements in the area of cultural rights for the Kurds would also be on Cem's agenda later when he advocated for greater minority rights, in which effort he was joined by Mesut Yılmaz, then serving as deputy prime minister. Cem's legacy is better known today for the rapprochement with Greece: he worked with his Greek counterpart, George Papandreou, to break the cycle of conflict between the two countries and pave the way for a new level of cooperation. Relations with the Middle East were another area in which Turkey made progress during Cem's tenure. Together with Papandreou he visited Israel in April 2002; the visit included a meeting with Yasser Arafat, then under house arrest in Ramallah, in an effort to spur a reconciliation similar to the one between Greece and Turkey. As part of a vision to secure greater cooperation among the countries neighboring Iraq, Cem also focused on improving relations with Syria. In this regard, he is credited with initiating the Neighborhood Forum to manage the difficult regional situation resulting from the conflict between Iraq and the international community and from the UN sanctions. These constituted the initial seeds of the AKP's zero-problems policy to come. His initiatives for regional engagement can also be regarded as a precursor to Davutoğlu's more ambitious regional integration projects.

Cem's criticism of traditional Turkish statecraft preceded Davutoğlu's similar comments on the topic. As revealed in *Turkey in the New Century*, Cem complained that the country's foreign policy "lacked 'depth' with respect to time, and 'breadth' with respect to space."[20] He envisioned an "assertive" Turkey, on its path to becoming a "world state," capable of exploiting its geographic advantage and willing to bring together "a unique blend of civilizational assets, historical experience and strategic attributes." Furthermore, Cem was uncomfortable with the view that Turkey was standing between East and West. In his view, Turkey was "already European," but recognizing that orientation did not mean disavowing Turkey's "Asian identity." As he put it, Sultan Mehmed, the conqueror of Istanbul, had "styled himself both as the 'Sultan of Islam' and as 'Caesar and Emperor of Rome.'"[21] In his commitment to Turkey's European vocation, Cem seemed to agree with Özal, and he was part of the cabinet that saw Turkey receiving candidate status for EU membership in December 1999. Lastly, he pushed forward Atatürk's legacy, which to him constituted a "role model for nations with parallel cultural backgrounds" where Davutoğlu sought to restore the Ottoman legacy.[22]

These policies can be seen as the precursor of a foreign policy orientation that would later be adopted by the AKP. The seeds of the much-touted zero-problems policy promoted by Davutoğlu were indeed sown in the 1990s.[23] When the AKP rose to power in 2002, it found a Ministry of Foreign Affairs willing and capable of working with the new political leadership, especially during the tenures of Yaşar Yakış, Abdullah Gül, and Ali Babacan as ministers of foreign affairs during the course of the 2000s.[24] With the chaos that followed the Arab Spring there would also come a gradual drift away from the letter and spirit of zero problems with neighbors, altering these dynamics dramatically and walking back the many economic, political, and social benefits that had been gained earlier.

TURKISH COOPERATION FROM THE BALKANS TO AFGHANISTAN

In dealing with the conflicts that erupted in the Balkans and in the post-Soviet space in the early 1990s, Turkey and the United States shared much common ground. In both sets of conflicts the Turkish government was under domestic pressure to take action because of kinship links with the Bosnian Muslims, who were at war with the Serbs in the former Yugoslavia, and with the Azeris, who clashed with Armenia over Nagorno-Karabakh. (The ethnic Armenian enclave of Nagorno-Karabakh is recognized de jure as part of Azerbaijan, but has declared itself an independent republic and seeks to unite with Armenia.)[25] In each situation Turkish decisionmakers sought to pursue a course that contributed to peacemaking efforts while keeping Turkey out of direct involvement. The plight of the Bosnians in particular dominated Turkey's foreign policy agenda and engendered considerable skepticism toward the EU, whose response to Serbian attacks on the Bosnian population had fallen short of expectations.[26] Turkey, however, would not undertake unilateral action, partly for geographic reasons, partly because of the impracticality of hewing to a different course from its Western allies. Instead it mounted an energetic effort to mobilize international support for a UN-authorized intervention to stop Serbian aggression.[27]

Turkey played the discreet partner in the U.S.-led effort to establish a Bosnian-Croat federation. It also lent its full support to the formation of the UN Protection Force (UNPROFOR) in the former Yugoslavia and eventually contributed a military unit. Following the December 1995 signing of the Dayton Accords, which set out a framework peace agreement for the warring factions and states in Yugoslavia, Turkey's role was mostly visible in providing humanitarian assistance and military training to the newly established Bosnia-Herzegovina. A similar approach was taken with respect to the Kosovo conflict in 1999, in which the Turkish government supported NATO operations against Serbia even though the UN did not authorize them. Subsequently a large contingent of Turkish troops was dispatched to join the NATO-led Stabilization Force in Kosovo (KFOR). All this did not prevent Turkey from seeking improved relations with Serbia, by then a reformed country. The process was handled with such skill that even the recognition of Kosovo's independence in 2008 did not damage bilateral ties. Turkish decisionmakers also supported EU and NATO enlargement in the region, which strategically contributed to the weakening of Russia's hand in this space.[28] They felt that besides strengthening their links with NATO, they had played a positive role by helping to stabilize and pacify the region after the initial tragic period of conflict.[29] Turkey had never before been in a position to make such visible and concrete contributions to NATO.[30]

The situation in the South Caucasus was somewhat more complicated. When the Soviet Union dissolved, Turkey quickly recognized the independence of Armenia, Azerbaijan, and Georgia. Bilateral efforts were pursued with Armenia in the hope of resolving the long-standing issue of the Armenian genocide and to establish diplomatic relations. These overtures came to a halt with the eruption of hostilities between Armenia and Azerbaijan over Nagorno-Karabakh.[31] This was another context in which the Turkish government had to navigate its foreign policy under acute domestic pressure because of Turks' kinship ties with the Azeris. Geographic proximity to the war zone, coupled with some belligerent language used by President Özal, was another factor that might have tilted the decisionmaking process in favor of direct involvement. But the government steered away from such a course.[32] Action came in the form of a blockade imposed on Armenia, more as a show of solidarity with Azerbaijan than to project a serious threat. Turkey also froze ongoing efforts to establish diplomatic relations after the Armenian occupation of territories in Azerbaijan beyond the disputed Nagorno-Karabakh region. The move was accompanied by the expression of support for resolving the conflict by diplomatic means, including the Organization for Security and Cooperation in Europe (OSCE) initiative through the Minsk Group, set up in 1992 in an effort to find a peaceful solution to the Nagorno-Karabakh conflict.

The Minsk Group has yet to succeed in its mission. In the meantime, however, Turkey expanded its political relations with both Azerbaijan and Georgia. It also advocated for closer relations between Georgia and NATO and provided considerable military training support to Georgia.[33] Russia's invasion of Georgia in 2008 came as a shock, but it also created an opportunity for Turkey to improve relations with Armenia. Intense diplomatic activity, which also involved Switzerland and the United States, resulted in bilateral protocols between the two countries that, if implemented, would have opened the border between them and ensured the establishment of diplomatic relations.[34] However, the political shadow of the Armenian genocide and the Armenian occupation of Azeri territories prevented the terms of the protocols from being realized, to the disappointment of many.

Turkey contributed to Azerbaijan's and Georgia's economic development, helping those post-Soviet independent states better connect with the world and reduce their dependence on Russia. Turkey signed a free trade agreement with Georgia and subsequently became its largest trading partner; Turkey also granted Georgian nationals access to the labor market in Turkey. In a similar but informal manner, Turkey allowed Armenian nationals to travel relatively freely and enabled some trade with Armenia to take place through Georgia.[35] In 2015, Turkey was Armenia's fifth-largest partner for imported goods, after Russia, the EU, China, and Iran.[36] Most significant, working closely with the U.S. Turkey helped launch the Baku-Tbilisi-Ceyhan (BTC) oil pipeline, subsequently supplemented by TANAP, to create an East-West energy corridor.[37] Together with Azerbaijan and Georgia it pushed forward efforts to realize the Baku-Tbilisi-Kars (BTK) railway as a critical section on the Transport Corridor Europe-Caucasus-Asia (TRACECA), the "Iron Silk Road of the 21st Century," linking China to European markets.[38]

The motivating force behind this wide array of cooperative efforts was the conviction that economic cooperation and interdependence were key to resolving conflicts. This was a view put forward at the end of the Cold War by Prime Minister Özal in particular. A testament to this policy orientation can be found in the then minister of foreign affairs Hikmet Çetin's remark that "the surest way for nations to advance as peace-loving, politically stable partners is sustained economic development and increasing welfare."[39] The establishment of the Black Sea Economic Cooperation Organization in 1992 was an early step in this direction; it involved countries bordering the Black Sea, along with Armenia, Azerbaijan, and Greece.[40] A similar effort was made with the launching of the Economic Cooperation Organization (ECO), which sought to deepen the economic integration among its membership, comprising the former Soviet states of Azerbaijan, Kazakhstan, Kyrgyzstan, Tajikistan, Turkmenistan, and Uzbekistan, and, beyond the post-Soviet space, Afghanistan, Iran, Pakistan, and Turkey. These steps prepared the ground for the AKP's later initiatives to promote Turkey's role in its neighborhood. They did serve as the basis for some of the foreign policy achievements of the AKP rule, garnering much credit for the party leadership but little for its predecessors.

Peacekeeping and Humanitarian Operations during the 1990s and Beyond

The decade of the 1990s saw Turkey's increased participation in peacekeeping operations led by the UN, NATO, and the EU. This was in sharp contrast to the Cold War years and geographically extended well beyond the Balkans, where Turkey had earlier made similar contributions. Turkey supported international peacekeeping efforts in Africa, the Middle East, and Asia.[41] In Afghanistan it played an important role in the NATO-led International Security Assistance Force right from its start in December 2001 until it was replaced by Resolute Support Mission in 2014, which was commanded by Turkish officers on two occasions. Çetin himself served as the senior civilian representative for Afghanistan between 2003 and 2006, a position filled by another Turkish official in 2014. Turkey received praise for its development strategy in Afghanistan and was cited as "a valuable example that the West can use to develop its own ideas."[42] The schools for girls that Turkey established in Afghanistan were especially recognized by an official, who viewed it as a project that only Turkey could have undertaken and a contribution with greater potential impact for the country's development than a combat division.[43]

Turkey's activism in developmental and humanitarian assistance is relatively new and has its origins in the closing days of the Cold War. Turkey launched a modest humanitarian assistance program at that time for a wide range of countries from Armenia to Cuba, including many African countries.[44] The initiative expanded dramatically over time, leading to the founding of two key agencies, the Turkish Cooperation and Development Agency (TIKA) and the Disaster and Emergency Management Authority (AFAD). In the span of a few years Turkey came to be recognized as among the top donors in the world.[45] TIKA today supports development projects in more than 140 countries. In 2015 it commanded a budget of $3.91 billion, increased from $85 million in 2002. Similarly, AFAD provides emergency and humanitarian assistance to more than forty countries, spending more than $6.4 billion in 2014 alone.[46] As stated by the Turkish Ministry of Foreign Affairs, the objective of this program is to "contribute to the creation of a more peaceful and stable environment in the neighboring regions."[47] Davutoğlu as the minister of foreign affairs in 2013 argued that these efforts were part of Turkey's efforts to keep up with an accelerating "flow of history" and become a "compassionate and powerful state."[48]

Somalia presents a relevant example in this respect. After September 11, 2001, the fear of global terrorism called attention to the failed states' need for state building.[49] Somalia's dire situation gained some traction, and Turkey's efforts not only to extend humanitarian assistance but also to launch developmental and state-building projects became especially important. In less than a decade, Turkey invested large resources to stabilize Somalia through broad developmental assistance. That Erdoğan visited the country twice—in 2011, as the first nonregional leader to pay an official visit, and again in 2015—highlights the extent of Turkey's commitment to this project. The second visit came on the heels of a violent attack by al Shabaab on a compound that was hosting the Turkish officials preparing for the visit.[50] The Turkish government's resolve to continue its support and maintain a presence remained constant through a series of attacks aimed at Turkish nationals in Somalia. In the words of a group of Western analysts, this resolve clearly demonstrated that Turkey was "contributing to addressing shared international challenges."[51]

The Turkish government has also taken an interest in the broader developing world. For example, it committed itself to help meet the UN's Millennium Development Goals (MDGs) and gradually increased its international assistance budget as a means to do so.[52] It also hosted the Fourth UN Conference on Least Developed Countries (LDCs) in Istanbul in May 2011, where the Istanbul Programme of Action was adopted, containing specific steps to be undertaken to achieve sustained and equitable growth for LDCs. Turkey offered to monitor the progress of the program and promised $200 million annually to LDCs.[53] As part of this commitment, in May 2016, Turkey undertook the first comprehensive midterm review of the implementation of the Istanbul Programme.[54] At the G-20 summit in Antalya in November 2015 the Turkish government emphasized the importance of making sure that LDCs benefited from the "inclusiveness" focus of the summit.[55] Finally, in May 2016 Istanbul hosted the first World Humanitarian Summit, organized under the auspices of the UN Office for the Coordination of Humanitarian Affairs—a symbolic recognition of Turkey's engagement in humanitarian and development assistance.

SINCE THE END OF the Cold War, Turkey has acquired a place in world politics that goes well beyond being a bulwark against the Soviet Union. Turkey's post–Cold War activities show considerable convergence of interests with Turkey's transatlantic allies. At the strategic level, Turkey followed policies to help newly independent countries reduce their dependence on Russia, and supported NATO's enlargement as a means to strengthen the West's strategic interests in Europe. Turkey's broader policies in support of economic interdependence, peace-keeping, conflict resolution, and state building have also strengthened the institutions and norms of the Western-led liberal international order.

BEYOND COMMON INTERESTS, THE ISSUE OF SHARED VALUES

The end of the Cold War abruptly ushered into existence a world that was much more complicated for the West to deal with. The Western model of democratic governance and liberal economy had prevailed over the Soviet communist system, but the world still faced a multitude of security challenges. Operating in a region that had become particularly volatile, Turkey navigated a course that was in line with the interests and policies of its transatlantic allies.

The post–Cold War era also brought growing Western criticism of Turkey in the areas of human rights and democratic freedoms. Three main reasons may account for this reaction. First, the West no longer faced an immediate threat from a colossal adversary, making it much more difficult to keep human rights issues on the sidelines. There was now opportunity for them to take precedence in the foreign policy agendas of the United States and the EU. A second reason was the growing conviction that security in a broad sense of the word was tied to better governance, a concept closely associated with accountability, transparency, and the promotion of liberal democracy. Third, Turkey's strategic value arose from the expectation that it could serve to ensure stability and advance democratic values in its neighborhood. Turkey therefore came under increasing pressure to improve its democracy, which aggravated its differences with the Western world. All the while, efforts continued to anchor Turkey more strongly in the international liberal order, which led to the formation of a customs union with the EU and offered considerable hope for Turkey's eventual membership in the EU.

Turkey's historical relationship with the EU has unfolded not only along political pathways, through economic interactions, or in the arduous process of adopting the EU acquis—the laws, regulations, and covenants of the EU. It is also heavily linked with Turkey's identity. Europe represented an ultimate model to emulate for the modernizers of the late Ottoman era; they admired European civilization, despite the threat it posed to the viability of the Ottoman state. The Turkish Republic was founded by leaders who saw the adoption of the European model as the only path toward progress. Contemporary civilization was largely equated with Europe, especially Western Europe. The young republic of Turkey was erected on a penal code adopted from Italy, an understanding of secularism (*laïcité*) borrowed from France, a civil code imported from Switzerland, and a commercial code that came from Germany.

That history, however, has not prevented constant debate over whether Turkey belongs in Europe, and the debate is conducted both within Turkey and Europe. For all their craving for European ways, Turks have always been unsure whether they felt at home in Europe. Religion and culture have constituted an important schism between Europe and Turkey, one that the common aspiration of secularism has not succeeded in bridging. While a large segment of the Turkish population has traditionally hoped to integrate with Europe, other Turks, both secular and religious, have imagined a better future as part of the Islamic *ummah* or in Eurasia. The EU saga has also been heavily tied to the question of democracy in Turkey. It has cut deeply across such vital issues as the rights of minorities and tolerance for pluralism. Turks have been divided over these issues, with some groups supporting greater levels of democracy and pluralism and others exhibiting tendencies more in line with nationalism, if not xenophobia. Hence it is not surprising that Turkey was called a "torn country" in the past, or that it has been described as a country in constant search for its own identity.[56]

The question of whether Turkey belongs to Europe or its periphery, or nowhere at all, also resonates across the EU. Europe has been of two minds on the issue, depending on what sort of identity it envisions for itself. Those who urge cultural diversity see a place for Turkey in Europe as long as Turkey demonstrates a commitment to secular, pluralistic, liberal, and democratic principles, whereas those who consider the EU a cultural project a priori based on Judeo-Christianity do not see any possibility of Turkey joining the EU under any circumstances. Hence the liminal status attributed to Turkey, neither of Europe nor outside it, feeds back into Turkey's own struggle with its identity.[57]

This neither-here-nor-there status of Turkey is of relevance to the United States as well because of the general U.S. policy of supporting Turkey's integration with the EU, mainly as a means of anchoring Turkey in the transatlantic alliance. The end of the Cold War dramatically altered Turkey's relations with the EU. The eastward expansion undertaken by the EU first included the neutral countries of Austria, Finland, and Sweden in 1995, followed by Central and East European countries, then Cyprus and Malta in the next decade. This was also a period during which member states began to share an increasingly larger part of their national competences with the supranational bodies of the EU.[58] Turkey, meanwhile, lodged a membership application in 1987 and was subsequently turned down in 1989. In an effort to soften the blow and also in recognition of Turkey's new strategic importance, a decision was made by the member states in June 1992 to expand relations with Turkey.[59]

This would have both sides moving into the final stage of creating a customs union as envisaged in the Ankara Association Agreement of 1963. The benefits would be to remove all tariffs on industrial and processed food products traded between Turkey and the EU. Furthermore, Turkey would be required to adopt current and future EU standards concerning these products and implement the EU's Common Customs Tariff. The willingness of the Turkish side to take on these obligations was testament to the success of Özal's export-oriented policies; it was also a sign that the economy was open enough to face external competition. The hand of business firms, especially members of the Turkish Industry and Business Association (TUSIAD) and the Union of Chambers and Commodity Exchanges of Turkey (TOBB), and other constituencies that supported the customs union, was thus strengthened.[60] The agreement also received the backing of all political parties except the one led by the Islamist Necmettin Erbakan.[61] These factors facilitated the successful completion of negotiations and the signing of the EU-Turkey Customs Union agreement in 1995.

Once approved by the European parliament, the customs union took effect in 1996.[62] Initially, some circles in the country were skeptical as to Turkey's ability to fulfill the requirements set out in the agreement and questioned whether Turkish industries could stand up to the competition from the EU. This concern was mitigated swiftly. The EU-Turkey Customs Union dramatically improved the competitiveness of Turkey's industries as the country introduced a series of reforms in an effort to adjust to the EU's trade and competition rules.[63] This is an ongoing process, since the EU is continuously adopting new measures. A meaningful indicator of Turkey's participation as a trading partner is that more than 55 percent of European economic legislation had corresponding provisions in Turkish law in 2013, which effectively meant that Turkey had become a part of the EU economy.[64] Closer economic ties with the EU have also made Turkish exports more attractive to many countries outside the region. This situation at least partly explains why Turkish exports to the EU increased from 48 percent of Turkey's overall exports in 1996 to 52 percent in 2000 before falling to 38 percent in 2012, the lowest level in the post–Cold War period, as the country's exports to its neighborhood and beyond increased. Conversely, Turkey in the meantime became the EU's sixth-largest foreign trade partner.[65]

However, the customs union was also related to a problem area that involved Turkey's prospects for full EU membership. At the time of negotiations, the Turkish side considered the customs union a temporary arrangement, preceding the ultimate goal of accession. This was reflected in a remark made by Tansu Çiller, then prime minister of Turkey, to Felipe Gonzáles, her Spanish counterpart, and Jacques Chirac, the French president: "The Customs Union is not enough for us; our chief goal is full membership in the European Union."[66] These words also aimed to allay fears in Turkey that the customs union would be the last stop in any form of bonding with the EU and that it would mainly serve to force Turkey to accept "economic rules it never would be able to influence."[67] This concern was well founded: Turkey's relations with Greece were problematic, and Greece made sure that the customs union could go through only if the EU pledged to include Cyprus among the list of countries slated for enlargement.[68] Furthermore, there was also concern that, owing to identity issues, the EU would not be interested in further engaging Turkey beyond objective economic and political criteria. Many in Ankara believed that this "explained" the EU's decision in December 1997 not to list Turkey among the group of prospective members.[69]

A breakthrough came at the European Council summit in Helsinki in December 1999, when Turkey was finally recognized as a candidate country. A number of factors played a role in the decision. One was the transition of power in Germany from the Christian Democrats—traditionally opposed to Turkey's membership on cultural grounds—to a coalition of Social Democrats and Greens, who were open to the idea of accepting Turkey as an EU member as long as the country met the Copenhagen criteria.[70] On the Turkish side, a new coalition government that had formed in 1999 under the leadership of Bülent Ecevit was favorably disposed toward political reforms. Most critically, it was determined to follow through with a ruling of the European Court of Human Rights that sought a stay on the sentence of capital punishment passed against the PKK leader Öcalan, who had been captured earlier in the year.[71] One last factor was the process of reconciliation with Greece, which received a further boost with the exchange of assistance following the earthquakes that hit both countries. Relations were now at a point that Greece could support Turkey's membership aspirations.[72]

The decision at Helsinki required Turkey to meet the Copenhagen political criteria "sufficiently" to be able to start accession negotiations.[73] This meant Turkey was expected to adopt a series of reforms under the watchful eye of the EU, which had been clamoring over the shortcomings of Turkish democracy since the 1980 military coup. (Turkey's poor human rights record and repression of its Kurdish minority had been an important reason behind an earlier rejection for membership application.) By the 1990s a diverse range of interests within the country, including the business community, had begun to push for democratization; these forces, combined with some demands imposed by the EU in the context of the ratification of the customs union agreements, eventually led to some initial reforms.[74] The pace of reform after the Helsinki agreement, however, did not pick up noticeably before the rise of the AKP on a ticket that promised commitment to EU membership.[75] The reform process that went into effect thereafter included a host of packages covering the following issues: expanding freedom of association and expression, revising the penal code, abolishing capital punishment, terminating emergency rule, improving the rule of law, and strengthening the rights of all minorities, notably the Kurds.[76]

Beyond meeting the Copenhagen political criteria, Turkey had to resolve its bilateral disputes with Greece and the issue of the division of Cyprus. In 1974, further to a coup in Cyprus the president Archbishop Makarios was overthrown, with the intention of uniting Cyprus with Greece. The Turkish military intervened to protect the Turkish Cypriot minority and occupied a large portion of Cyprus. In 1983 the Turkish Republic of Northern Cyprus was unilaterally declared and recognized solely by Turkey. Numerous rounds of diplomatic talks to reunite the island failed until a highly contested domestic decisionmaking process eventually led to Turkey supporting a reunification plan for the island that had been prepared by UN Secretary-General Kofi Annan.[77] After a number of revisions, the plan was finally submitted to a referendum vote in April 2004 on the island.[78] In contrast to the Turkish Cypriot side, which voted in favor of the plan, the Greek Cypriots overwhelmingly rejected the plan, and hence the UN plan could not be put into effect. The island remained divided, but this did not stop the Greek Cypriot part of the island from becoming a member of the EU. This development, together with an ongoing thaw in Greek-Turkish relations, culminated in a Greek decision not to seek resolution of its bilateral disputes at the International Court of Justice, as had been envisaged by the Helsinki decision, but to continue to pursue a diplomatic track.[79] Subsequently the European Commission, in its assessment of Turkey's progress, recommended to the EU member states that accession negotiations be started. Accordingly, in December 2004 the European Council decided to set the process in motion in October 2005.

Since then the accession process, which involves negotiations between a candidate country and the EU for the incorporation of the body of rules and regulations by the acceding country aspiring to become a member, has not gone smoothly. The acquis is incorporated into thirty-five chapters that need to be opened to negotiations by the EU, then negotiated by the two sides. Once the candidate country is deemed to have completed the adoption of the acquis, the chapters are closed. It is only then that the path for membership is complete. In the case of Turkey, as of June 2017 only sixteen such chapters have been opened, and just one has been closed. Eight chapters have been blocked by the EU as a result of a decision made in 2006 in response to Turkey's unwillingness to expand the customs union to cover Cyprus. (Croatia, by contrast, which started its accession process at the same time as Turkey, completed its negotiation of these thirty-five chapters in 2011 and became a member of the EU in 2013.) Some of the reasons why Turkey's accession process stalled can be attributed to Turkish domestic politics; others are related to the dynamics within the EU itself. Despite the setbacks, however, the decision to open membership negotiations with Turkey was still historic and constituted a turning point in terms of anchoring Turkey in the transatlantic community.

Relations between Turkey and the EU: The U.S. Perspective

Turkey's willingness to negotiate requirements with the EU and cool its heated relationship with Greece, as well as its support for the unification of Cyprus, upheld U.S. strategic interests. The United States had consistently supported strong links between Turkey and the EU, even if the level of this support varied from one administration to the next.[80] U.S. support became particularly visible during the Clinton administration, especially during the run-up to the conclusion of the customs union and the adoption of the Helsinki decision.[81] The George W. Bush administration reiterated its interest in having the EU and Turkey set a date for the opening of accession negotiations. However, Turkey-U.S. relations during the early 2000s were clouded by the protracted negotiations over opening a northern front in Turkey to facilitate the U.S.-led invasion of Iraq and the Bush administration's disappointment over the Turkish parliament's no vote. Furthermore, while the Clinton administration considered Turkey's being anchored in the EU as a liberal democracy a strategic gain, the Bush administration seemed more focused on the potential benefits devolving to the United States from Turkey's geographic location on the border of Iraq.[82] Despite some differences in approach, the commitment to anchor Turkey in the West remained firm as both administrations lobbied energetically on Turkey's behalf in Europe while remaining cognizant of the need for the country to improve its democratic record.

The U.S. efforts played out not only in European capitals but also targeted the institutions of the EU, the European Parliament in particular. And they were not always welcome. The European commissioner for enlargement, Gunter Verheugen, "warned the U.S. to keep out of Turkey's EU talks," claiming that U.S. involvement would adversely affect Turkey's chances.[83] Similarly, the French president Jacques Chirac scolded Bush for championing Turkey's membership, noting that "he [Bush] has nothing to say on this subject. It is as if I were to tell United States how it should conduct its relations with Mexico."[84] Yet considerable U.S. lobbying effort went into urging the EU to grant Turkey candidate status in 1999 and to agree to start accession negotiations in 2004.[85]

Many other groups were involved in lobbying for democratization in Turkey. Especially during the Clinton administration, Turkey's poor record on human rights, marred by reports of torture, limitations on freedom of expression, and restrictions on the rights of minorities, particularly the Kurds, raised concerns. The need for democratic reform was raised prominently in a speech by Bill Clinton to the Turkish parliament in 1999, when the U.S. president was participating in the OSCE summit being held in Turkey. The U.S. had played a critical role in the apprehension of Abdullah Öcalan, the leader of the PKK, in Kenya, as a terrorist, and his return to Turkey earlier that year, lending Clinton considerable leverage and popularity in the country.[86] The Bush administration continued to push Turkey to sufficiently meet the Copenhagen criteria; in policy circles, it was believed that a democratic Turkey could be a partner in the U.S. drive to support democratization in the Middle East. Thus not only the geostrategic importance of Turkey to the United States but also what were regarded as shared values lay at the root of encouraging Turkey to enact democratic reforms.[87]

Turkey's supporters among the EU member states acted for similar reasons. They were aware of Turkey's significance for Western countries' security. Turkey's geographic location could help secure energy corridors, and the country could also prove crucial in democratizing and developing the neighborhood around the EU member states. These factors were highlighted in a 2014 report prepared by the Independent Commission on Turkey in support of Turkey's eventual EU membership. In line with the debates that revolved around reconciling Islam with Western values, the report stressed the Turkish case as an opportunity to show such a reconciliation was possible.[88] This thinking echoed the ideas articulated by Bill Clinton in his 1999 address to the Turkish parliament when he said that Europe was as much an idea as a space where diverse opinions, cultures, and faiths were committed to democratic values.[89]

The United States also saw Turkey as coming into its own as an important economic player with an expanding economy and a growing foreign trade. As Turkey's economic prowess gained more traction, it was identified as an emerging economy and thereby acquired more clout in the region as a member of the G-20—all helpful in its bid for EU membership. The "volume of trade, the multiplicity of EU-Turkey business relationships and the potential for growth make a compelling case for further integration," noted the second report of the Independent Commission on Turkey, disseminated in September 2009.[90] The United States had recognized Turkey's economic potential already in the 1990s. The Clinton administration listed Turkey among the top ten emerging economies of the world and, through the Joint Committee on Economic Cooperation, advocated closer business relations; the development of a liberal economy was seen as a stepping-stone to further consolidating Turkey's democracy.[91]

All parties—Turkey, the United States, the EU member states—seemed about to converge around common interests and, for Turkey, on a path to EU membership. However, the progression to membership was not automatic: Turkey had to prove it shared the values that form the basis for the Copenhagen political criteria, which range from ensuring the rule of law and protecting the rights of minorities to establishing a transparent and accountable government. Some unanticipated developments blocked Turkey's progress toward meeting these criteria and widened the gap between Turkey and the EU.

THE ASSERTIVE FACE OF TURKEY'S RELATIONS WITH THE WEST

Against the more constructive aspects of Turkish foreign policy in the post–Cold War era must be set a streak of assertiveness, even aggression, in its conduct, especially with respect to regional relations.[92] According to some, Turkey became a "coercive regional power."[93] A number of bilateral conflicts attest to this dynamic. Turkey reached the brink of war with Greece in 1996 over a territorial dispute in the Aegean Sea, with Syria in 1997 for harboring Öcalan, and with Cyprus over the latter's attempts to acquire S-300 missiles in 1997. Furthermore, Turkey mounted a major military operation into northern Iraq to dislodge the PKK in March 1995. According to a retired Turkish diplomat, the country was surrounded by a "veritable ring of evil," which necessitated a readiness to fight "two and a half wars" simultaneously—against Greece, Syria, and the PKK.[94] The tensions with Greece and Syria softened by the end of the 1990s as Turkey's foreign policy gradually eased the country into a more constructive and conciliatory relationship with its neighbors. But in the Middle East, ever a fertile ground for protracted, violent conflicts with wide-ranging repercussions, there was no shortage of issues that would persistently test Turkey's relations with the West and its place in the transatlantic alliance.

Former U.S. ambassador to Turkey Morton Abramowitz was correct in observing that "the acid test of the U.S.-Turkish relationship is likely to come in Iraq when Saddam departs the scene."[95] Turkey's decision-makers had been wary of Washington's policies in Iraq since the early 1990s. Initially they disagreed over sanctions; later, they clashed over the gradual emergence of a Kurdish entity in the northern parts of the country. The UN sanctions on Baghdad significantly undermined Turkey's previously buoyant trade with Iraq, a nation at the top of Turkey's list of foreign trade partners. A decade later, Turkey was estimated to have lost approximately $100 billion in trade; in addition, the economic livelihood of the communities in the border regions was direly affected.[96] The clashes between the Turkish security forces and the PKK had also given rise to negative consequences for the region. The safe zone created in northern Iraq came to be used by the PKK as a sanctuary and a military base from which to attack targets inside Turkey. This engendered a deep resentment on the part of Ankara toward the United States, leading to allegations that Washington intended to weaken Turkey by supporting the PKK and using Operation Provide Comfort to create a Kurdish state. All this fueled further anti-Americanism, though some of the policy and public relations efforts of the Clinton administration helped mend the rift by the late 1990s.[97]

The relative calm in U.S.-Turkey relations would last only until the Bush administration's decision to invade Iraq and the pressure it subsequently applied to Turkey to allow the U.S. military to travel through the country and use Turkey's military and logistical facilities. This was the first foreign policy challenge for the AKP. The Turkish parliament's no vote reflected domestic opinion in Turkey, which was strongly against the U.S. policies in Iraq.[98] Ironically, the earlier U.S. support for democratization efforts in Turkey and for giving greater say to the people now, apparently, had culminated in a denial of a U.S. request of the Turkish government.

Turkey actively sought to dissuade the United States from intervening in Iraq after the events of September 11, 2001. A host of officials in Ankara voiced concerns about the consequences of such an action for the stability of the region and strongly urged that the crisis be resolved through dialogue and diplomacy. Abdullah Gül, the interim prime minister and then minister of foreign affairs, refused to endorse Washington's plan to intervene,[99] instead moving forward with a last-minute "active diplomacy for peace," trying to persuade Hussein to cooperate and thereby avoid a military disaster.[100] He failed. When the invasion was finally carried out, beginning in March 2003, it was profoundly resented in Turkey. Not surprisingly, public opinion in the country toward the United States, which had improved during the Clinton years, now turned even more anti-American.[101] The ensuing chaos and the daunting task of stabilizing Iraq confirmed Turkey's worst fears, leaving it to face many challenges, ranging from the violence of the PKK and other extremist groups to the influx of refugees from the region, all of which were made worse by the loss of lucrative export markets in Iraq and beyond, in the Gulf countries.

Iraq's territorial integrity presented a problem to Turkey, particularly in relation to the Kurdish issue. The question was whether an independent Kurdish state would emerge in the event Iraq disintegrated.[102] Intensifying the concern was a de facto Kurdish-administered entity that had been formed in the regions dominated by the Kurdistan Democratic Party (KDP) and the Patriotic Union of Kurdistan (PUK). The fact that the PKK was based in northern Iraq and that it had terminated the ceasefire with the Turkish state in 2004 alarmed Turkey's national security advisers. Ankara had entered negotiations with the United States in the first place to be able to have a say in managing the situation in northern Iraq and determining the future of Iraq.[103] The advocates of this approach had hoped that a deal with the United States would enable Turkey to avert such a turn of events and make it possible for Turkish forces to confront the PKK in northern Iraq rather than on home ground.

Its opposition to the emergence of an independent Kurdistan did not hold Turkey back from developing close economic and political relations with the Kurdistan Regional Government (KRG).[104] This was a direct result of a 2007 decision by President Bush and Prime Minister Erdoğan to enhance cooperation against the PKK.[105] Ironically, the United States would again need to step in, this time to issue a warning, as the KRG's oil exports to Turkey without the consent of the central administration in Baghdad began to raise concerns. From the U.S. perspective, "closer energy ties might push Baghdad's Shiite government closer toward Tehran and threaten Iraqi unity."[106] The issue of defeating the PKK remains a major fault line between Turkey and the United States today. This has become especially aggravated since the collapse of Turkey's peace process with its own Kurds. The U.S. reliance on the Kurdish Democratic Union Party (PYD) and its armed wing, the People's Protection Units (YPG), as a partner in the fight against the Islamic State (IS) is highly problematic because Turkey considers the same group an extension of the PKK. The main concern for the Turkish government is the possibility that an empowered Kurdish group on its border could pave the way for the creation of a separate Kurdish state or autonomous area. The appearance of photographs in the media featuring U.S. Special Operations Forces wearing PYD insignia drew an irritated response from Turkish officials, who interpreted the phenomenon as a far-reaching consequence of the initial U.S. intervention in Iraq in 2003.[107] Matters became even more tense after the Trump administration approved substantially arming Syrian Kurds, a decision made just as a Turkish delegation, including the Turkish chief of staff, was holding meetings in Washington, D.C., ahead of Erdoğan's visit in May 2017.[108]

The association of Turkey with the concept of "moderate Islam," promoted as a panacea to Islamic extremism, has been another thorny issue.
The idea gained currency in the context of George W. Bush's "war on
terror" and the launch of the BMENA initiative. In 2004 Bush argued in
Istanbul that "Turkey as a strong, secular democracy, a majority Muslim
society . . . stands as a model to others."[109] More striking was a remark
by the then secretary of state Colin Powell in discussing the future of Iraq
earlier in the year: "There will be an Islamic Republic of Iraq just like
other Islamic republics, such as Turkey and Pakistan."[110] These words
caused concern for secular Turks, who became even more entrenched in
their conviction that the West was seeking to weaken secularism in Turkey through its support of moderate Islam and the AKP leadership.[111]
Islamists have not felt comfortable with such statements either. On numerous occasions, Erdoğan has spoken against the notion that there can
be different formats for the expression of Islam, such as "moderate" or
"extreme." During his speech to the Turkish parliament in April 2009,
Obama strategically avoided any utterance that might have triggered
similar unease. Yet the damage caused by the earlier debate persists.

The ongoing chaos in Syria has pushed Turkey and the United States
further apart. The two countries seemed to be on the same page in the
early stages of the crisis, calling in unison for Assad's departure. Both
predicted his imminent fall and acted in the expectation that a democratically minded administration, led by the opposition, would eventually come to power. As subsequent events have shown, the Syria matter
has turned out to be much more complicated. The public protest that
began as part of the Arab Spring in 2011 has turned into a quagmire,
drawing in multiple adversaries—both the main opponents and numerous proxies—along with allies pursuing conflicting interests.

The war in Syria proved to be a key turning point in Turkey's relations
with the West. The first signs of differences over the approach to the
Syrian war became apparent when Erdoğan reacted sharply to Obama's
failure to act on his "red lines" against the use of chemical weapons by
the Assad government. On one occasion in September 2012, Erdoğan
did not shy away from stating that the U.S. stand in Syria was "lack-
ing . . . initiative."[112] In its obsession with the overthrow of the Assad
regime, the Turkish government bolstered its support for radical Islamist
groups that were fighting against Damascus. That move, however,
prompted serious accusations that Turkey as a country was falling short
of meeting its responsibilities in preventing the flow of foreign fighters

into the ranks of the IS—Turkey was even harshly criticized for extending logistical support to the group.[113] In contrast to the United States, the Turkish government saw the Kurdish groups in Syria, and especially the PYD, as a greater threat to Turkey than IS until the bombing of the Istanbul airport in June 2016, perpetrated by the IS.[114]

Managing the flow of refugees into Turkey has become another point of contention. In the absence of robust international support for the protection and upkeep of refugees, the Turkish government called for the establishment of safe zones in Syria, across from the Turkish border. Since the cabinet reshuffle in May 2016 that saw the replacement of Davutoğlu, the author of Turkey's Syria policy, there has been a softening of Turkey's categorical insistence on Assad's departure, and a rapprochement with Russia has been obvious.[115] The latter opened the way in August 2016 for a Turkish military intervention, called Euphrates Shield, in parts of northern Syria to prevent the PYD from making further territorial gains and to fight the IS while creating a de facto safe zone for displaced persons. However, the legacy of the U.S. policy in Syria will be seen as one that adversely affected Turkish national security and stability, much like the U.S. legacy in Iraq.

The fault lines between Turkey and the West are visible not only in the Middle East. Turkey's refusal to recognize the Ottoman massacre of Armenians as genocide has long plagued its relations with the West. Every time the leadership of a Western state has tried to adopt a resolution in favor of recognizing the events as genocide, it has triggered public protests as well as intense Turkish diplomatic activity to prevent the adoption of such legislation. In 2007 and 2010, for instance, when subcommittees in the U.S. Congress passed resolutions with similar content, Ankara withdrew its ambassador from Washington; eventually, these bills died before moving forward to the plenary.[116] Turkey's opposition also explains why Barack Obama, despite having promised on the campaign trail that he would recognize the Armenian genocide, subsequently used the Armenian term "Meds Yeghern" (commonly translated as "Great Catastrophe").[117] Similar diplomatic reactions were received by France in 2011, when it passed legislation that criminalized the denial of the Armenian genocide, and by Germany in 2016, when the Bundestag recognized the genocide.[118] On the other hand, as it stands today, twenty-four countries and many parliaments, including the European Parliament, have so far adopted resolutions recognizing the Armenian genocide.[119]

Another source of resentment was the accession of Cyprus to the EU despite the Greek Cypriots' refusal to support the unification of the island under the Annan Plan. It took considerable courage and effort for the newly elected AKP government to overcome the rancor and steer the Turkish military and security establishment toward lending their support to the plan. Prime Minister Abdullah Gül had well understood that support for the Annan Plan and resolving the conflict was critical to forwarding Turkey's EU ambitions.[120] However, the outcome of the referendum left the government in a very awkward situation. After it became a member of the EU, Cyprus embarked on a path of obstructionism. Initially it blocked well-meaning EU efforts "to put an end to the isolation of the Turkish Cypriot community and to facilitate the reunification of Cyprus by encouraging [its] economic development."[121] This weakened the hand of the government against those who were reluctant to cooperate in the first place and led to Turkey's decision not to extend the terms of the EU-Turkey Customs Union to Cyprus. This decision in turn triggered the EU's suspension of the opening of eight chapters in Turkey's accession negotiations in 2006; Cyprus then blocked the opening of an additional five chapters in 2009.[122] These developments undermined the EU's credibility in the minds of Turkey's leadership and raised questions about its promise of membership—all of which fueled Euroskepticism in Turkey and slowed Turkey's reform process.[123] The Cyprus conflict remains unresolved to this day, and the EU's handling of the issue is seen as symbolizing manifestation of the EU's "double standard" with respect to Turkey, which generates further mistrust.

Finally, Turkey's strategic relationship with the United States and its relations with NATO have at times constituted sources of disagreement that deepened the divide. One such disagreement arose over Iran's nuclear program: the United States and Europe were concerned that Iran was pursuing a nuclear weapons program, especially during President Mahmoud Ahmadinejad's years in government, whereas the Turkish government saw Iran's nuclear program more as a peaceful one and seemed much less concerned about it, leading some in the United States to conceive that Turkey was turning its back on the West.[124] Turkey also opposed both the use of force against Iran and sanctions, advocating instead diplomacy and engagement with Iran.[125] Hence Turkey together with Brazil negotiated with Iran a deal to relocate enriched uranium out of Iran. This was followed by Turkey's decision as a nonpermanent member of the UN Security Council to vote against a U.S.-sponsored resolution imposing sanctions on Iran. This provoked considerable criticism of Turkey, and Obama felt that the no vote undermined his efforts to achieve a "model partnership" with Turkey. He is reported to have said that Turkey had "failed to act as an ally."[126]

Iran reemerged as an issue in U.S.-Turkish relations when the Turkish government expressed its reluctance to participate in a NATO missile defense system that would openly target Iran. However, once agreement was reached on wording that did not name a third country, Turkey announced in September 2011 its decision to host the missile tracking parts of the system.[127] The decision was received with considerable jubilation in the West and was dubbed the "biggest strategic decision between the United States and Turkey in the past 15 or 20 years."[128] However, the issue of ballistic defense missiles remained a source of disagreement between Turkey and its NATO allies once the government elected in 2013 to purchase a Chinese system. The decision once more provoked doubts about Turkey's commitment to NATO, even though it was partly driven by cost considerations but also, and perhaps more important, by an interest in technology transfer and failure on the part of its allies to take Turkish national security concerns seriously.[129] These concerns did include the recognition that in earlier regional security crises, such as the one in 1991 and the one in 2003, some NATO allies had vetoed the deployment of ballistic defense missiles as requested by Turkey.[130] In November 2015, stiff resistance from NATO and the United States led Turkey to drop plans to purchase the Chinese system and decide to pursue a national project to develop ballistic missiles of its own. However, the issue made a quick comeback in 2017, when this time Turkey began to pursue an effort to procure the Russian-made S-400 surface-to-air missile system. These episodes have entered the annals of deep divergence and mounting sources of mistrust between Turkey and its NATO allies.

CONCLUSION

The end of the Cold War came as a surprise to Turkey, as it did to the West. On the eve of the fall of the Berlin Wall, Turkey was close to finalizing an agreement with East Germany that would have opened consulates in Leipzig and Istanbul and was on the brink of war with Bulgaria over an influx of Turkish and Muslim minority refugees fleeing that country's repressive policies. But it also heralded a new era. In the twenty-five years since the end of the Cold War, the foreign policies of Turkey and the West converged with respect to a host of issues, such as trade, energy routes, democratic governance, ranging from the Balkans and the South Caucasus to the Middle East. This was also a period when Turkey became an important economic player, facilitating the economic development of a number of countries in its neighborhood and their integration into the global economy. At the same time, its role as an emerging contributor to development and humanitarian assistance around the globe was widely acknowledged. The Turkish government introduced measures to encourage greater regional integration and made efforts to improve relations with neighboring countries, particularly Greece and Syria. This trend was continued and expanded on during Abdullah Gül's stewardship of Turkish foreign policy, which was conducted in close cooperation with Turkey's diplomatic establishment. Some of the more prominent examples of this cooperation include the support given to Kofi Annan's plan for the reunification of Cyprus, the EU decision to start the accession process, the negotiations leading to the ill-fated protocols with Armenia, and continued improvements in relations with Greece and Syria. These achievements, later labeled the "zero problems with neighbors" policy by Davutoğlu while he was serving as chief foreign policy adviser to Erdoğan, gradually drifted into "zero neighbors without problems" during his tenure as minister of foreign affairs from 2009 to 2014.

Turkey and its transatlantic allies also disagreed over a cluster of issues, such as the U.S. intervention in Iraq, what to do about the Assad regime in Syria, the failure to ensure the reunification of Cyprus, and the arming of Kurdish militias in Syria. However, the most significant divergence by far has been over Turkey's EU accession bid. Turkey in fact never came closer to acquiring EU membership than in the 2000s; even then, membership did not appear within its grasp.[131] The United States saw Turkey's integration with the EU as a way to improve democracy in the country and more firmly anchor Turkey's position in the international liberal order. EU membership for Turkey was expected to contribute to regional as well as transatlantic security and prosperity. Indeed, considerable progress was achieved in this regard: the more Turkey became integrated with the EU, the more it came to be seen as a model to be emulated by countries aspiring to transition to democracy and liberal markets. Yet a slowdown followed by a reversal in the EU's engagement coincided with Turkey's own struggle to maintain the gains it had achieved in the areas of democracy and liberal economy. The result was growing doubt as to whether Turkey could sustain its commitment to the transatlantic community and continue a relationship with the West based on shared values, not only on immediate interests.

The decade of the 1990s was on average characterized more by convergence and cooperation than by divergence and conflict, in particular with respect to Turkish ties with the United States.[132] A similar statement can be made with respect to EU-Turkish relations as the reform process in Turkey slowly but surely paved the way for Turkey to become a candidate for EU membership. The pace would gather speed following the AKP's rise to power, eventually bringing the country to the point of starting accession talks. At that moment the fault lines between Turkey and its transatlantic allies seemed to be narrowing, but it would not last long. The U.S. intervention in Iraq in 2003 became a source of major conflict and instability that has since adversely affected Turkey's interest. Growing chaos in the aftermath of the Arab Spring was one reason. Another was the domestic situation in Turkey, where the democratization effort showed signs of regression. However, the most important factor undermining the prospect of embedding Turkey in the international liberal order may well have been the EU's failure to see Turkey and the Turks as part of its "self." Europe's sense of its own identity may well have constituted the most significant fault line that destined the relationship to become the troubled alliance it has. This is in stark contrast to perceptions during the Cold War, when Turkey in Western Europe "was no longer represented as the 'Other' of Europe, a representation dating back to Ottoman times, but as part of the European 'Self': an important security provider against the Soviet Union."[133]

CHAPTER FOUR

The Rise of the AKP and Turkey's Exposure to Liberal Democracy

ONE PERSISTENT AREA OF contention in Turkey's relations with the West has been the problematic state of Turkey's democracy and economy. The country's shortcomings in both domains have been especially visible in the post–Cold War era. Turkey early on became a test case for Francis Fukuyama's "end of history" thesis, which held that Western-style democracies and liberal markets would prevail over the Soviet model and eventually dominate the world.[1] Turkey's gradual transformation toward greater democracy and a market economy came on the heels of the September 1980 military coup d'état. Turgut Özal, prime minister since 1983, even felt confident enough to apply for EU membership in 1987. However, the collapse of the Soviet Union in 1991 left Turkey in a deeply troubled neighborhood. The raging ethnically based conflicts, political instability, and economic dereliction that marked the post-Soviet space and a good part of the Balkans posed serious security challenges for Turkey. The Iraqi invasion of Kuwait in 1990 and the subsequent economic sanctions against Iraq also had a direct impact on Turkish politics and economics through loss of business and trade with Iraq and the Gulf region.

Even as Turkey sought to deal with security issues affecting its immediate neighborhood, Turkey faced a set of internal challenges in the decade 1991–2001.[2] Leading the list, the rise of political Islam came to be defined by the political elites and the state establishment, especially the military, as a threat to the secular nature of the Turkish Republic. As a result, the coalition government led by Prime Minister Necmettin Erbakan, the leader of the Islamist Welfare Party, was forced to resign in

1997 by the military—an episode that would infamously become referred to as the "postmodern" coup. The second major challenge was Kurdish nationalism and the fear that it might undermine the unitary structure of the Turkish Republic. The militarized confrontation that ensued between Turkish security forces and the Kurdistan Workers' Party (PKK), led by Abdullah Öcalan, left its imprint on the whole decade of the 1990s. During this time the Turkish political scene was also characterized by a series of short-lived and unstable coalition governments (eleven coalitions were formed, with thirteen foreign affairs ministers serving during the 1990s) that very much remained within the shadow of the influential Turkish military.[3] As the military entertained little affection for liberal democracy and civil society, the circumstances were far from being favorable to address the diverse attitudes emerging in society. Turkey had begun to display growing signs of a *Kulturkampf* between religiously conservative groups and the segments of society that had traditionally professed loyalty to Atatürk's ideals of Westernization and secularization. But the country was not ready for a healthy dialogue.[4] In a way, the Turkey of the 1990s would have fitted well Fareed Zakaria's definition of an "illiberal democracy," even though he himself was hesitant to cite Turkey as an example.[5]

The Turkish economy did not fare any better. Özal's policies had given Turkey a head start in terms of liberalizing the economy and transforming it from a classic import substitution economy, with all its drawbacks, to a more dynamic, export-oriented model. However, a series of structural problems continued to plague the Turkish economy in the 1990s: corruption scandals, rising inflation (67 percent for the period 1991–2001),[6] reduced investment as a result of high interest rates, large current account deficits, and growing public debt, which eventually culminated in the financial crises of 1994 and 1998. The subsequent bailouts by the International Monetary Fund (IMF) required, in addition to a series of currency devaluations, some major structural reforms, but in the absence of political will, these reforms were often set aside and not undertaken. The result was a massive collapse in confidence in Turkish finances in February 2001. It would be the most severe economic crisis in the republic's history: an estimated 20 percent of the Turkish GDP evaporated overnight.[7] By the end of the year the GDP had contracted by a staggering 6 percent.

The roller-coaster ride at the end of the 1990s was in line with the trend toward violent fluctuations that had characterized the Turkish economy over the whole decade. The decade had started with a 9.2 percent growth rate (in 1990) that contracted to 4.7 percent in 1994, later rising to 7.9 percent in 1995.[8] The crisis in 2001 left Turkey's finances in such a dire state that the government had to secure a source of external funding equaling a quarter of the total amount of its foreign borrowing since its foundation.[9] In return for large IMF loans, the government put in place a radical economic policy. This was primarily designed and led by Kemal Derviş, who was at the time serving with the World Bank. Derviş, a special appointee to the cabinet granted extensive powers, got the economy back on track. The introduction of a floating exchange rate mechanism for the Turkish lira and the privatization of state-owned enterprises were among the measures taken; more significant, a series of structural reforms, such as the establishment of regulatory bodies, ensured stability in the longer term. The Justice and Development Party (AKP), which rose to power soon afterward, would be the primary beneficiary of the positive results so achieved, skillfully using them to increase its political capital.

Although the 1990s are retrospectively labeled the "lost decade" for the time it lost in introducing fundamental economic and political reforms, some timid steps were taken toward liberalization.[10] A number of reforms were introduced to protect human rights and support freedom of association, primarily to ensure the ratification of the customs union agreement by the European Parliament. The government also came under increasing pressure from civil society to establish a more liberal form of democracy. The Union of Chambers and Commodity Exchanges of Turkey (TOBB) and the Turkish Economic and Social Studies Foundation (TESEV) in 1995 commissioned a report on the situation of the Kurdish minority in Turkey that discussed its causes and made policy recommendations.[11] The ban on the public use of the Kurdish language had recently been lifted in 1991, but using Kurdish publicly was still quite a courageous step to take in the mid-1990s.[12] The issue was so sensitive that the title of the report could not even have the word "Kurd" in it. The initiative caused a considerable uproar, but Pandora's box had been opened, and the public debate that ensued would eventually pave the way for reform.[13] Another study published in 1997 by the Turkish Industry and Business Association (TÜSİAD) called for drastic democratic reforms, including the granting of cultural rights to the Kurds.[14] The Turkish general staff's response was bitter and even precipitated internal recriminations within TÜSİAD, a situation that did not heal until 2014.[15]

The end of the decade was marked by two massive earthquakes in 1999 that shook the industrialized northwestern corner of Turkey, costing 18,000 lives and inflicting extensive damage. The political consequences were no less significant. The experience revealed the incompetence of the state in dealing with such emergencies, while at the same time it provided a platform for civil society to demonstrate its effectiveness. Mounting criticism targeted the government, along with calls for governmental reform.[16] It was also in 1999 that the leader of the PKK, Abdullah Öcalan, was apprehended with U.S. help and brought to justice. His trial would not conclude before a military judge in the court was removed under pressure from the Council of Europe. The coalition government, which included a right-wing Turkish nationalist party, decided to stay the execution of Öcalan's death sentence in deference to the European Court of Human Rights until the court could rule, on Öcalan's application, whether he had faced unfair court proceedings. A divisive debate within the country had preceded this development; nevertheless, a series of reforms focusing on cultural rights was introduced and duly noted by the EU, regardless of how half-hearted the whole process had in fact been.[17] By the end of the year, Turkey had been granted candidate status for EU membership. This in turn ushered in an initially slow and contested reform process that would quicken its pace once the AKP came to power in November 2002, paving the way to the opening of accession talks with the EU in 2005.[18]

Against such a background, it did seem as if developments in Turkey would substantiate Fukuyama's hypothesis concerning the eventual world dominance of Western-style democracies, though in Turkey's case with a delay of almost a decade. During the early years of AKP governance, Turkey showed signs of quickly moving toward absorbing the standards and values of the international liberal order in the spheres of democratic government, economics, and foreign policy. The "spirit of democracy," to use Larry Diamond's term, seemed to engulf Turkish politics and society, and its booming economy began to be cited among the emerging economic powers.[19] This period witnessed some notable improvements, ranging from the adoption of minority rights—hitherto unprecedented— to the emergence of a liberal climate that permitted an open discussion of the darker chapters of Turkish history, particularly the fate of the Armenian community in the last days of the Ottoman Empire, which, according to Armenians and many historians, was subjected to a genocide. This remarkable performance, many thought, demonstrated that

Islam could indeed be compatible with not only democracy but that AKP was actually transforming the country towards "a tolerant liberal Turkey."[20] Furthermore, Turkey was emerging as a model for the Muslim world; one expert went so far as to use the accolade "the twenty-first century's first Muslim power."[21]

The developments during this period were nothing short of a miracle. Prior to the AKP's initiatives in its first years in power, no serious effort had been made to reach out to understand the concerns of those on the other side of the negotiating table, whether it was the Kurdish or the Armenian issue. No period in Turkish history had brought more prosperity to the people than the first decade of successive AKP governments. And the emerging hope that Islam and democracy could actually be reconciled meant a great deal not only to conservative Turks but to the Muslim world at large.

This situation did not last very long. The positive atmosphere could not survive the rising tide of authoritarianism, and Islamism beginning to engulf Turkey. Nonetheless, the political and economic reform process undertaken by the AKP during its "golden years" introduced the Turkish people to a semblance of liberal democracy, however short-lived it would later prove to be. The following sections trace the peculiar circumstances that led to the emergence of the AKP, its break from the established Islamist agenda by adopting a pro-reform and pro-EU political stance, and its rise to power on an electoral tsunami.[22]

THE EMERGENCE AND RISE OF THE AKP

Religion has long been entwined in Turkish politics. Islamic principles were deeply ingrained in the Ottoman state structure; they also underlay social rules. A gradual move toward secularization was first initiated with the modernization effort that marked the late Ottoman era.

The founding of the Turkish Republic in 1923 went some distance toward curbing the influence of religion on governance and education. At the popular level, religion continued to dominate daily life for the masses, or the periphery, which mostly inhabited the Anatolian backwater. The center, on the other hand, was represented by the urban bureaucracy and the intelligentsia that surrounded the Republican People's Party (CHP) and embraced its nationalist, secularist policies.[23]

The first multiparty elections in Turkey were held in 1946. The major opposition to the CHP came from a splinter faction of disenchanted deputies, who formed the new Democratic Party (DP). The party drew attention with its promise of welfare for the periphery; it was also able to appeal to the religious sensitivities of certain segments in society, especially the conservative masses that mainly populated the areas outside Istanbul, Ankara, and İzmir. The founders of the DP were well aware of the resentment toward the CHP's militant secularism, and they were equally willing to give conservative circles a voice without challenging the basic premises of the republican regime. Installed in office in 1950, four years after its founding, the DP became the first political party in Turkey to take up the reins of government as a result of competitive elections. Its message of respect for Islamic traditions and its claim to act as the voice of the periphery had been effective.[24]

Instrumentalizing religious sentiments for political gains would become a common practice for center-right politicians, such as Süleyman Demirel, Turgut Özal, Tansu Çiller, and Mesut Yılmaz. In the following decades, they would all pursue this path while also maintaining their commitment to secularism and Westernization.[25] The ultimate manifestation of this phenomenon came in form of the "Turkish-Islamic synthesis," an initiative promoted, ironically, by the Turkish military, otherwise known as the guardians of secularism and the state.[26] This happened soon after the coup d'état in September 1980, when the military instituted the introduction of a nationalized adaptation of Islam into school curricula against the influence of radical leftist ideology, which they believed had adversely influenced the minds of the young during the pre-coup period.[27]

This was preceded by the emergence a decade earlier, in 1970, of the National Order Party (Millî Nizam Partisi) as the first party with an explicit Islamic political agenda. It was shut down by the Constitutional Court the following year on grounds of antisecular activities. This would evolve into a trend that would affect later parties with a similar focus. The National Salvation Party (Millî Selamet Partisi), the Welfare Party (Refah Partisi), and the Virtue Party (Fazilet Partisi) all met the same fate subsequently, while the Felicity Party (Saadet Partisi) still remains active. Mostly established and guided by one leader, Necmettin Erbakan, these parties espoused a religio-political ideology known as the National Outlook (Millî Görüş)—the very perspective that had problematized Turkey's Westernization process. The teachings of Necip Fazıl Kısakürek and Sezai Karakoç proved to be powerful sources that fed this line of thinking. In their view, a direct link existed between the fall of the Ottoman Empire and the Western orientation that had marked its later phase: a glorious Islamic state had come tumbling down because of policies that were a mere imitation of the West's.[28] In a more general sense, the approach rested on a fundamental conflict between Western civilization, defined as Judeo-Christian, and Islamic civilization.[29] To Erbakan and many from the Welfare Party, secularism was "the crux of all problems."[30] They were particularly critical of the secular elite in Turkey, especially the CHP, for having followed what they consider to be policies hostile to Islam and the Islamic way of life.

Erbakan was in favor of a state run by devout Muslims. In his electoral campaigns, for example, he called for the appointment of a "political staff" at different levels of the Turkish state that "prays five times a day, fasts, reads the Qur'an."[31] He was also known for his criticism of capitalism, and often advocated for a state-led economic development and protectionism. He viewed Western democracies as deficient and majoritarian,[32] while apparently failing to recognize that his own conception of democracy was vulnerable to similar criticisms. In line with the National Outlook perspective, he deeply believed in political authority and a legitimacy derived from the idea of an "authentic Muslim identity," which raised his expectation that "true" Muslims could and would vote only for him and his party. Erbakan elaborated this argument so far as to suggest that, since the overwhelmingly Muslim electorate in Turkey would eventually be drawn to his party, elections would no longer be necessary.[33] He clearly had little concern for or any conception of pluralism and liberal democracy.[34]

Eventually, Erbakan became the first prime minister of Turkey with an openly Islamist political agenda in a coalition government formed after the 1995 elections, when the Welfare Party emerged as the leading party, with 21.4 percent of the votes. In the local elections the previous year, the Welfare Party had won similar percentages and gained control of municipal governments in a string of major cities, most notably Istanbul, where Recep Tayyip Erdoğan first rose to national prominence as the new mayor. Welfare Party rule, especially at the local level, did earn praise for its service-oriented approach to municipal governance, while its socially conservative policies often raised eyebrows. Corruption diminished during this time, but only to give way to various types of patronage practices discriminating against non–Welfare Party supporters.[35] Eventually the inflammatory rhetoric adopted by the party leaders, along with idiosyncratic, Islamic-themed policy ventures, provoked, in February 1997, what became known as a postmodern coup by the Turkish military.[36] The latter had particularly been disturbed by a "Jerusalem Night" organized in a Welfare Party–governed township near Ankara earlier that year, during which a crowd chanted radical slogans and a local party official promised to "inject Shari'a [into] the secularists by force."[37] The coup eventually precipitated the collapse of the coalition government; it also led to the revision of Turkey's National Military and Strategic Concept in a way that elevated the threat of "reactionary Islam" (*irtica*) to top priority, ahead of Kurdish separatism.[38] In January 1998, the Constitutional Court ruled for the closing down of the Welfare Party and banned Erbakan from engaging in political activity for five years.

This episode intensified the ongoing debate within the National Outlook movement that had pitted the "traditionalists" (*gelenekçiler*) against the "innovationists" (*yenilikçiler*), with Erdoğan leading the latter.[39] His rise marked a break from the idea of political Islam that he professed in the early 1990s, when his views on secularism, democracy, and the West strongly echoed Erbakan's line of thought. His remark in 1996 that "democracy is no different than a tramcar, and when the car arrives at the right station, one would get off and walk in the direction one deemed correct," had become particularly contentious, agitating secularists' worst fears of religious rule in Turkey.[40] Another incident, in which he recited a verse from a popular poem comparing minarets to bayonets, domes to helmets, mosques to barracks, and believers to soldiers, led to his prosecution for inciting violence and advocating the establishment of an Islamic state.[41]

The banning of the Welfare Party precipitated a debate among Islamist intellectuals, who questioned the established views of the traditionalists and loyalists of Erbakan. This was a period when Erdoğan had publicly abandoned the practice of politicizing religious symbols.[42] He and his innovationist colleagues engaged in a leadership struggle within the newly set up Virtue Party in May 2000. Their defeat by a small margin opened the way subsequently for Erdoğan and his colleagues to establish, in 2001, the AKP. As reflected in the *Development and Democracy Program*, the first such document published by the new party, their policies in many areas promised to diverge from the traditional ones espoused by the National Outlook movement.[43]

The AKP's Program of Liberalization

A striking aspect of the AKP's first program was its emphasis on human rights, civil liberties, and the role of civil society. As two leading experts of Turkish politics have observed, the AKP's notion of democracy was "more pluralistic than majoritarian in contrast to that of the RP."[44] The innovationists had also distanced themselves from Erbakan's accusatory rhetoric toward seculars, or the "puppets of Western imperialists," as he called them. Instead, the new movement revealed an effort to find a middle ground between an "Erbakan-style Islamism," on the one hand, and "Kemalist state laicism" on the other.[45] The emphasis was more on the freedom of religion—starkly different from Erdoğan's predecessors' guiding principle of "assertive secularism," which was predicated on the control or repression of religion in the public space.[46] The approach was accompanied by an understanding of secularism as applying only to states and forms of governance, not necessarily to the individual.

Another sphere in which the new movement differed from the classic National Outlook movement was the economy. In contradistinction to Erbakan's etatist, protectionist stand, the AKP's position was unequivocally in favor of liberal market policies. It also embraced the structural reforms put in place by the preceding government after the financial meltdown of 2001.[47] This was not surprising. By then a number of industrial and commercial urban centers, fittingly called "Anatolian Tigers" for their dynamism and future potential, had emerged as a result of the export-oriented liberal policies of the 1980s. These represented, to a large extent, a politically conservative economic sector led by "Islamic Calvinists," which also acted as a natural constituency for the AKP.[48] The party program openly advocated a commitment to a free market economy, with all its rules and institutions. Possibly the sharpest break from previous practice was in the area of relations with the EU. The AKP did not shy away from declaring in its program that it would diligently continue efforts toward joining the EU. This would have been absolutely unacceptable to Erbakan, who once announced that a step in this direction would be tantamount to "treason against our history, concept of civilization, culture and most important of all, our independence,"[49] and had even promised to abrogate the customs union between the EU and Turkey.[50]

These stark differences led many at the time to conclude that the AKP had little in common with its Islamist predecessors, and that it seemed "hardly distinguishable from a conservative or liberal party of the Western type."[51] Some observers saw the AKP as a "Muslim democrat" party, even though its leadership preferred the term "conservative democrat."[52] The innovationists succeeded, with their ideas and policy suggestions, in bringing together a broad coalition of interests that went beyond religious conservatives. They did indeed manage to include Western-oriented liberals as well as the center right in their fold. The traditional center right, once represented by the Motherland Party under the leadership of Mesut Yılmaz, and the True Path Party, led by Tansu Çiller,

Figure 4-1. Voting Patterns in National and Local Elections, 2002–15

Percentage of votes

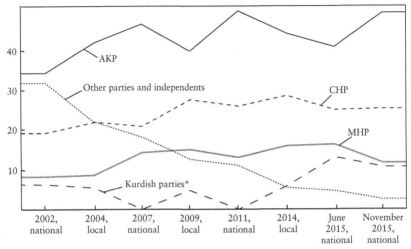

| 2002, national | 2004, local | 2007, national | 2009, local | 2011, national | 2014, local | June 2015, national | November 2015, national |

Source: Archives of the Supreme Election Council of Turkey (*Yüksek Seçim Kurulu*), Parliamentary elections archives (www.ysk.gov.tr).

AKP: Justice and Development Party (*Adalet ve Kalkınma Partisi*), CHP: Republican People's Party (*Cumhuriyet Halk Partisi*), MHP: Nationalist Action Party (*Milliyetçi Hareket Partisi*).

*In 2007 and 2011, Kurdish candidates entered the elections as independents.

had become discredited as a result of corruption scandals and incompetence. All this greatly helped the AKP broaden its base; hence its success in garnering more than 34 percent of the votes in the national elections of November 2002 (see figure 4-1). This gave the party two-thirds (363) of the seats in parliament—a comfortable majority to form a government in a way that had not been possible in Turkey since the late 1980s.

TOWARD LIBERAL DEMOCRACY: REFORMS AND MIRACLES

Possibly the one factor that had the greatest agency in sweeping the AKP to power was its leadership's commitment to EU membership. The notion of "credible conditionality," that is, improved prospects for membership if a country met the standards for EU accession, was an important incentive for the AKP, which duly set out to pursue this goal. Aided by an ability to mobilize an effective and supportive coalition, it quickly began to adopt a series of reform packages.[53] This brought about meaningful improvements in Turkey's notoriously poor human rights record, along with a ban on capital punishment. Civil liberties, such as freedom of association and expression, were expanded, and the Turkish parliament introduced a series of cultural rights for minorities, most notably the Kurds.[54] Some of the measures in the reform packages were aimed at reducing the influence of the military in politics and placing Turkey's National Security Council under civilian control. The dominance of the Turkish military over elected civilian governments since the first coup by the military in 1960 is a well-known phenomenon in Turkey's modern history.[55] Pressure to redefine civilian-military relations had been building for some time. These developments would eventually lead the European Commission to conclude in 2004 that Turkey had sufficiently met the Copenhagen political criteria and recommend that accession negotiations be started.

The adoption of these reforms and Turkey's transformation as a result was no small feat. Resistance to the reforms came from numerous circles, ranging from the military and parts of the state establishment to the nationalist camp. Several of the reforms concerned issues that directly and vitally affected Turkish national security; therefore they had to be "desecuritized" first and imported into "normal politics."[56] The significant structural and political barriers to reform that had to be overcome led the then European commissioner for enlargement, Günter Verheugen, to call Turkey's democratic transformation the "second revolution after the establishment of the republic."[57]

It is against this background that Turkey began to show signs of a relatively liberal democracy, despite some problems that persisted in the area of freedom of expression. The term "liberal democracy" here should be understood in the sense of a polity being able to pursue "normal politics" in an environment that allows much freer debate on sensitive or taboo topics. Additionally, it suggests an orientation toward recognizing Turkey's cultural and political diversity.[58] In such an environment the rule of law reigns, transparency improves, and government is rendered more accountable, especially with respect to the economy and the delivery of public services. The course taken by the government soon after the 2002 elections seemed to promise all that, if not immediately, then surely in the near future. A long-missed climate of optimism began to return to public life.

Miracles after Reforms

The steps taken on the path to a liberal democracy were so consequential that they can perhaps best be understood by calling them miracles.

Because historical and political circumstances had always meant the viability of the state was the uppermost concern in the minds of Turkey's leaders when they sought to negotiate such fraught issues as minority rights and civil and individual freedoms, the initial years of AKP rule stand out as a unique moment.

The miracles in question manifested in three main areas, the first of which was relations with the Kurdish minority. The Turkish state had long denied the existence of a separate Kurdish identity, even considered its public recognition a threat to the national security and territorial unity of the country.[59] Repressive measures against the Kurds had played an important role in the formation of a separatist Kurdish national movement, led by the PKK, in the 1980s. The long years of confrontation between the PKK and Turkish security forces[60] had led to the loss of more than 40,000 lives[61] and the displacement of large numbers of Kurds from their rural communities into urban areas,[62] and had cost the country billions of dollars.[63] The state of confrontation was also marked by severe restrictions on freedom of expression, especially with respect to Turks advocating the cause of the Kurds—an act prosecutable under Turkey's sweeping anti-terror laws. As a result, many academics, journalists, and intellectuals faced prosecution, and some were sentenced to serve prison terms. Any criticism of the government's policy with respect to the Kurds was considered unacceptable, if not criminal. In one striking case, a parliamentarian was publicly accused of being drunk by a colleague who was reacting to him expressing similar criticism.[64] Some Kurdish parliamentarians, among them Leyla Zana, were stripped of their parliamentary immunity and subsequently sent to prison in 1994 for speaking Kurdish in the parliament and for their alleged affiliation with the PKK.

The late 1990s witnessed a change, however slow, in the Turkish political climate to accommodate a more open debate on the Kurdish issue. What shifted the internal dynamics was the capture in 1999 of the leader of the PKK, Abdullah Öcalan, and Turkey's evolution into a candidate country for EU membership. The major breakthroughs, however, did not occur until the AKP's rise to power. The lifting of the state of emergency rule in Kurdish-populated provinces, the extension of cultural rights to Kurds and other ethnic minorities, and the release of Leyla Zana and her colleagues from prison were all important reforms that were finally pushed into effect in the early years of the AKP's governance. There was also a willingness to take the issue beyond the strict confines of the EU accession process; calls were made to find a genuine political solution to the Kurdish problem.[65] The climate was such that a prominent ambassador, though retired then, felt confident enough to note publicly that the time had come to discuss the option of secession for the Kurds and submit it to a referendum.[66] As highlighted by a commentator, the mere mention of such a divorce indicated great change; it meant that the topic was no longer taboo, which in itself spoke to the progress being made with respect to freedom of expression and democracy in Turkey.[67] Another taboo collapsed when the then Turkish president Abdullah Gül, on his way to a meeting with Kurds in northern Iraq, did not shy away from referring to the region as Kurdistan; when challenged by a journalist, he noted that the appellation was quite normal.[68] Gül also lent his open support for the "Kurdish opening," an initiative launched by the government in 2009 to reach a broader political settlement of the Kurdish problem in Turkey.[69] Gül's position was that providing guarantees "for the freedom and rights of those who think differently from the majority" was important. Accordingly, the "existing diversity" should indeed be considered a source of richness for the development of "modern democracy in Turkey."[70] A member of the leadership approaching the issue from such a perspective would have been inconceivable in the previous decade. It was surely the consciousness of moving toward a liberal democracy that had prepared the ground for such outreach.

Another topic, one that had long been taboo in Turkey before being placed on the agenda for open debate, was the Armenian genocide. Armenians, as well as most historians around the world, claim that 1.5 million of their ancestors were deliberately and systematically deported and killed during World War I. Turkey has not only challenged this figure but, more important, has refuted Armenia's designation of the circumstances surrounding the deportations and deaths as genocide. The Turkish government contended that the Armenian losses had to be understood in the turbulent context of World War I, that they were not the result of a systematically orchestrated plan but had occurred amid other massacres that were actually committed against large Ottoman Muslim communities.[71] This view was rarely challenged in Turkey; diversion from this line was liable to prosecution under Article 301 of the Turkish Penal Code, which criminalized any acts or statements amounting to the "denigration of Turkishness." Though the narrative of the Turkish state has remained mostly unchanged to this day, the "wall of silence" over the fate of Ottoman Armenians "began to crumble," especially since the mid-2000s, which saw the emergence of a lively dialogue on the topic.[72]

The Armenian issue was brought into the open and debated in the public space as well. A watershed moment was the holding of an academic conference at Bilgi University in September 2005 under the title "Ottoman Armenians during the Decline of the Empire."[73] The event provided the first public venue for a frank discussion of the topic despite protests, some even in the form of physical attacks on the participants, coming from many circles. Its significance was enhanced by the fact that an effort to hold the conference earlier in the year had been blocked by the then justice minister, Cemil Çiçek, who had rejected the idea in fierce language. Such an attempt, he had stated, would be tantamount to treason, no less than a "stab in the back of the Turkish nation."[74] In contrast, Erdoğan, serving as prime minister at the time, demonstrated a completely different attitude with respect to a court ruling that sought to ban the second attempt to hold the conference. He remarked that "although you may not approve of a point of view, that does not mean you should prevent others from expressing it."[75] Some of the print media sought to dismiss the Doomsday effect attributed to the whole affair; one newspaper noted, for example, that "the conference was held and all hell did not break loose."[76] A lively debate ensued, allowing even some of the most unlikely figures, such as a retired career ambassador who had long served the Turkish state, to recommend an official apology as the best course of action for Turkey, which could then be followed by an offer of citizenship to the descendants of Armenians killed in 1915.[77]

The emergence of attitudes that allowed the discussion of a highly contentious topic, prohibited for so long, can be considered a miracle in itself. In 2007 the assassination of Hrant Dink, the Turkish Armenian journalist who had long lobbied for open debate and for this had run afoul of state authorities and nationalist circles, moved the issue to another dimension.[78] Tens of thousands of people poured into the streets of Istanbul for his funeral, carrying banners and chanting "We are all Hrant Dink, we are all Armenians."[79] This expression of solidarity—not just with the Dink family but with Armenians at large—was particularly noteworthy insofar as the faintest sign of association with Armenian identity had long been frowned upon in Turkey. Erdoğan himself had taken particular offense at insinuations that he might be of Armenian descent, which he saw before anything else as undermining his populist claim to be a purely ethnic Muslim Turk.[80] The massive turnout at Hrant Dink's funeral also led to a campaign under the rubric "I apologize," an online initiative led by a group of Turkish intellectuals that rejected the official denial of the massacres and supported an apology.[81] As expected, the petition provoked strong outcries from Erdoğan and Turkish nationalists and failed to receive a sizable number of signatures; nonetheless, it is difficult to see how such a small gesture would have been possible without at least a semblance of liberal democracy.[82] The significance of these developments was captured by Thomas de Waal, an expert on Armenian Turkish relations and author of the *Great Catastrophe*, who rightly called it the "Turkish thaw."[83]

Another miracle in the making was the possibility that the AKP might succeed in bridging Islam, secularism, and democracy. Erdoğan's remarks at Harvard University in January 2003—"I do not subscribe to the view that Islamic culture and democracy cannot be reconciled"[84]—in particular set the scene for accepting such an outcome. Subsequent democratic reforms were further complemented by a discourse of inclusiveness. As late as early 2011, Erdoğan was still reinforcing the AKP's conservative democrat identity, emphasizing its intention to respect freedom of expression as well as individuals' lifestyles regardless of "the way they may dress, eat and drink, or pray."[85] In contrast to its predecessors, the AKP, and especially Erdoğan, argued unambiguously that "political practice through and by means of religious propaganda is detrimental to democracy."[86] Erdoğan also considered secularism important, though he advocated a more "passive" version that entailed softening the earlier practices of "assertive secularism," deemed too strict toward the religious sensitivities of certain groups, rather than attempting to Islamize society through state power. AKP policies came to be seen as instrumental in finessing the more rigid aspects of Kemalism while avoiding Erbakan-style Islamism.[87] Lifting the ban on headscarves (known as *türban* in the Turkish context) on university campuses is one commonly cited example. The ban had prevented Abdullah Gül's wife from enrolling in a university, and an elected female deputy had not been allowed to take her seat in the Turkish parliament after the 1999 national elections because she wore a headscarf.[88]

There did, though, remain skeptics who feared that the AKP's reforms and liberal discourse were no more than an attempt to cover a hidden agenda, a kind of double-talk known in the Turkish context as *takiye*. This was a group that deeply doubted that the AKP had genuinely become a staunch supporter of secularism and asserted that its temporary subscription to democratic values would end the day it secured a form of autocratic government.[89] Their voice was suppressed by those who advocated otherwise. According to one observer, any suggestion that the

AKP was exploiting the reform process for the purpose of establishing an authoritarian state was outright preposterous.[90] The view that was gaining traction, especially in academic circles, was that the policies pursued by the AKP did play an important role in bridging the divide between conservatives and secularists, thus helping to consolidate Turkish democracy."[91] The fact that this was happening shortly after the events of September 11, 2001, and at a time when Islam was becoming associated with extremism and terror accentuated the significance of the AKP experience. Actually, this experience did lead many in the West, including U.S. presidents George W. Bush and Barack Obama and many EU leaders, to view Turkey as a country that could set an example for aspiring democracies in the Middle East. Their hopes were especially elevated when Abdullah Gül, as minister of foreign affairs, criticized the state of democracy in the Muslim world at a meeting of the Organization of Islamic Cooperation in May 2003, and urged his fellow Muslim leaders to improve the situation.[92] Erdoğan took an even bolder step by calling on the newly elected Mohamed Morsi in Cairo in September 2011 and recommending a secular constitution for Egypt. He stated, "[Egypt should not fear] secularism because it does not mean being an enemy of religion. I hope the new regime in Egypt will be secular."[93] The significance of Erdoğan's position was captured by Ali Al-Bayanouni, a former leader of the Syrian Muslim Brotherhood, when he praised the AKP's neutrality on religion and noted that the AKP "neither imposes religion upon Turkish citizens, nor does it seek to fight it." He then went on to say that "for this reason we find it [the AKP] to be an excellent model."[94]

One last miracle occurred in the realm of economics. This development must be evaluated in the context of liberal democracy that pervaded the Turkish political scene at this time. The AKP's stated commitment to the rule of law, transparency, and accountability was crucially important in preparing the ground for economic growth, and a series of structural reforms put into effect after the massive financial crisis of 2001 further helped the outcome. These reforms not only earned Turkey praise from the EU for being a "functioning market economy," they also generated comments that they were leading to "something akin to the economic miracle of the 1950s in Western Europe."[95] Indeed, Turkey's economic growth was impressive: during the first decade of the AKP's governance, Turkey's total GDP grew almost five times faster than the EU's.[96] In 2013 Turkey's GDP per capita reached its highest level ever at $12,542, bringing it closer to that of the high-income group of countries listed by the World Bank.[97] Turkish exports were valued at $152 billion that same year—a significant increase from $36 billion in 2002. As Turkey became integrated into the global economy, the share of its foreign trade in GDP reached almost 50 percent, a remarkable growth from 37 percent in 2002.

Inflation was also brought down significantly in this period, and in October 2004, six zeros were removed from the Turkish national currency. The fall in interest rates spurred a better investment climate. Private enterprise expanded beyond the traditional industrial centers of western Turkey, such as Istanbul and its environs together with İzmir, boosting business and employment opportunities across the country. Turkey also saw its middle class expand dramatically, hand in hand with government efforts to reduce poverty. Improvements in public services were conspicuous, mainly in education and health. The transportation sector also saw a massive expansion in air routes, super highways, and metro lines, along with major railroad upgrades. Such improved socio-economic performance boosted Turkey's soft power, which in turn attracted higher FDI and an ever-growing number of foreign visitors. It was in this atmosphere that Erdoğan claimed in November 2012 that Turkey had met the Maastricht economic criteria for EU membership.[98] He was also especially proud that Turkey would be able to pay off all its debts to the IMF as of May 2013. It is this "economic miracle" that played a critical role in sustaining ever larger majorities for the AKP in the 2007 and 2011 national elections (see figure 4-1), boosting Erdoğan's popularity at home and abroad.

CONCLUSION

The miracles—the positive economic, social, and political changes—resulting from the AKP's early policies did not unfold without a good measure of resistance and suspicion, especially in certain secular circles. One prominent opinion widely shared in these milieus was that the AKP was performing *takiye*, or hiding its real intentions behind a mask of a seemingly democracy-loving, liberal-oriented party. The increasingly visible turn away from democratic principles especially since the early 2010s and the sharp increase in acrimonious relations with the West make it easier to agree with this view. Whether the AKP was ever genuine in its early intentions may never be known with certainty. To delve further into the question is perhaps moot.[99] One certainty, however, is that the AKP's earlier policies helped the party gain the support of groups beyond its electoral base. The party's espousal of an EU affiliation was welcomed by the business world at large, including groups traditionally associated with the secular establishment, such as TÜSİAD and TOBB, and the mostly conservative Anatolian Tigers, represented by the Independent Industrialists' and Businessmen's Association (MÜSİAD). The AKP's stand against an overpowering military also ensured support from liberal circles, including well-known intellectuals.[100]

The AKP came to power in 2002, only months after it was founded. The votes it was able to garner from religious conservatives and the center right gave the party a comfortable majority in parliament, two-thirds of the seats. The liberal policies advocated by the AKP set it apart from the National Outlook movement, out of which it sprang in the first place. Erdoğan differed from his mentor Erbakan, who had problematized Turkey's Western vocation. The AKP's emphasis on EU membership and its keenness for a free market economy meant a clear break from the ideology and rhetoric of the Islamist tradition.

Despite its origins in a nationalist, Islamist movement, the AKP succeeded in striking a middle ground between Erbakan's Islamism and the "assertive secularism" of the Kemalists. It presented itself as a change agent that would set the country on a path toward democratization, with a greater emphasis on human rights, civil liberties, and a freer exploration of religious identity. Releasing the military's grip on Turkey's politics and banning capital punishment were also identified as reforms that would shape Turkey into a state in line with Western standards and consistent with the EU acquis. After decades of estrangement, there was a greater recognition of Kurdish cultural rights. In addition to the package of reforms introduced by Erdoğan, the announcement of the peace dialogue between the leadership and Öcalan confirmed the executive branch's interest in finding a political solution to the Kurdish problem. The nation also witnessed an unprecedented dialogue on the Armenian genocide. As the AKP pressed ahead with the economic policies that had been adopted under the previous government, it set in motion a train of reforms that transformed Turkey into a success story, to use a description often heard at the time. In the eyes of many, the Turks had never had it so good. Today that statement sounds sadly ironic.

The positive developments in the early years of AKP rule solidified Turkey's ties to the international liberal order. Progress toward EU membership helped strengthen the structural factors that bound Turkey to the Western bloc. This was a time that saw the traditional fault lines with the West narrowing, raising hopes that the country was on its way to sharing a set of values with the West, not just strategic interests. By the mid-2010s, however, the erosion of these economic, political, and social gains could not be denied. Though it is difficult to pinpoint a particular date for the start of the downturn, the Gezi Park protests of 2013 and the manner in which they were crushed were an unmistakable sign of growing authoritarianism. Since then, Turkey both economically and politically has entered a period somewhat reminiscent of the 1990s. The government's relationship with the Kurds has turned violent once more, which has led to many Kurdish deputies seeing their immunities lifted and their party leaders detained. Radical Islamic terrorism perpetrated by the self-styled Islamic State has hit Turkey a number of times, with strong adverse impacts on the economy and especially tourism. The coup attempt in mid-July 2016, perpetrated by a renegade group of officers and their civilian allies, led to the introduction of a state of emergency, with the executive branch assigning itself special powers. This situation in turn has exacerbated repression and fueled concerns about the freedom of the media and expression, the rule of law, and the separation of powers. Though in relative terms the Turkish economy continues to perform reasonably well, it is considered to have been caught in a middle-income trap, and per capita income has fallen steadily from its peak in 2014. The collapse of tourism and the disruption caused to the economy by the coup attempt are likely to aggravate this downward trend. Chapter 6 takes up the politics behind this retreat from a liberal democracy and a dynamic economy that Turks enjoyed under the AKP leadership. The pendulum has swung in the opposite direction, toward deeper divisions; the reasons for this trend are also explored in chapter 6. The next chapter evaluates what Turkey won and lost through its alignment with the West and the factors contributing to either side of the ledger.

CHAPTER FIVE

Skepticism and Identity

Gains and Losses from Turkey's Integration into the Transatlantic Community

TURKEY REALIZED MANY GAINS from its association with the transatlantic community. Some of the gains proved difficult to sustain, for various reasons. The journey toward full integration into the transatlantic community was shadowed by serious disagreements of the kind that go beyond policy matters. Despite periods when Turkey converged with the EU and the United States (or the West) on strategic matters, Turkey's incomplete and less than wholehearted adoption of the values of the international liberal order—democracy, respect for diversity and minority rights, the rule of law, transparency, and accountability—has proven a persistent source of resistance. Turkey's failure to anchor itself more completely within the transatlantic community is also rooted in a deep skepticism of the West and its intentions toward Turkey. This anti-Western sentiment, which derives from multiple sources, strongly influences public attitudes and Turkish foreign policymaking. And at least for now, it seems these will continue to fuel the fault lines in its relationship with the West.

Some part of Turkey's reticence with respect to the West owes to Turkey's narrative of exclusion and marginalization. There is a widely shared conviction that the West wants to finish the incomplete job, left over from World War I, of dividing Turkey into smaller states and pushing Turks out of Europe. From the Islamist perspective, the West wants to keep Turkey as a Muslim country down and deny it the possibility of leading the Muslim world. The political elite in the country often finds it convenient to exploit the narrative of marginalization for

its own purposes, which complicates efforts to build a constructive dialogue with the West and underwrites some part of the anti-Western
sentiment.

Europe for its part entertains a broad uncertainty regarding Turkey's
place in the West, which in turn reinforces Turkey's narrative of exclusion and marginalization. Turks have always been the other in Europe,
except for a brief period during the Cold War when Turkey formed part
of Europe's self as both faced a common adversary, the Soviet Union.[1]
The end of the Cold War ushered into existence a very different geopolitical environment: the EU countries' embrace of Central and East
European countries expanded the fold of Europe's self without including Turkey. And ironically, the closer Turkey came to meeting the criteria for EU membership, the more Europe's resistance to considering Turkey part of the European self increased. Turkey was "too big, too poor,"
and—most important—"too different." No matter how far it progressed
politically and economically, Turkey felt, the doors of the EU would remain closed. The actions and statements of EU officials and politicians,
who advocated a "privileged partnership" rather than membership for
Turkey, reinforced this conviction.

Nonetheless, Turkey gained recognizable economic and political benefits from being part of the transatlantic community, some of them devolving from its efforts to access EU membership and some from being a
member of the Western security alliance, NATO. Owing to the preva-
lent skepticism in Turkey with regard to the West's intentions, however,
these gains were underappreciated in the popular opinion, which
wrapped the West's intentions in malevolent conspiracy theories. The
EU's engagement of Turkey, which initially helped bring Turkey to the
edge of becoming an accomplished liberal democracy, succumbed to
the EU's own indecision and lack of commitment, frustrating those in
Ankara who wanted to see Turkey's full incorporation into the international liberal order and reinforcing the credibility of those who espoused
a more critical view of the West. This particular complex dynamic has
brought Turkey's relations with the West to where they are today, in a
state of crisis, deep conflict, and mutual distrust. It is ironic that the very
people who worked with the West intimately and brought Turkey the
closest it came to a liberal democracy, Recep Tayyip Erdoğan and his
team, are now imposing on the country an increasingly authoritarian
and autocratic form of governance with little regard for the rule of law,
accountability, transparency, or diversity.

WHAT TURKEY GAINED FROM BEING PART
OF THE TRANSATLANTIC COMMUNITY

Turkey has no real peer country for comparison in its post–World War II journey. Yugoslavia under Josip Broz Tito and Egypt under Gamal Abdel Nasser both pursued policies of neutrality, somewhat similar to what Turkey did until 1945, and those who in the 1960s and 1970s advocated an anti-Western orientation for Turkey sometimes pointed to these countries as examples Turkey should emulate.[2] Yet Yugoslavia ceased to exist as a political entity after a series of ethnically based civil wars and insurgencies, and its constituent republics, after declaring their independence, have either joined or are in the process of joining the EU and NATO. Egypt did not follow a steady path to economic and political development either. By contrast, Turkey is still territorially intact and relatively stable, despite the raging instability in its region. And the country was able to realize important political and economic gains through its association with the transatlantic community and its efforts to meet EU accession criteria, which required meaningful internal reforms.

Political Gains: Strategic and Regional Influence and Stability

Turkey's relative stability in a region embroiled in tumultuous conflicts should not be taken lightly. Two of its neighbors to the south, Iraq and Syria, which once were leading members of the nonaligned movement, are now in a state of disarray or collapse. To the north, Moldova, Ukraine, and Georgia have seen part of their territories occupied by Russia or its proxy forces. Armenia and Azerbaijan to the northeast are locked in a conflict that leaves their domestic politics and economic development vulnerable to Russia's manipulation. The only neighbors of Turkey that stand out as relatively better off are Bulgaria, Greece, and Romania—all relatively solid members of the international liberal order. It is not a coincidence that Georgia and Moldova have sought to deepen their relations with the EU and NATO, motivated both by political convictions and by the hope that this alignment might help them push back against external challenges to their territorial integrity.

One main factor that has helped ensure Turkey's security since the Cold War has been its NATO membership. During the Cold War, membership in NATO served to deter the Soviet threat. Thereafter it continued to provide a security umbrella at a time when ballistic missiles proliferated and a number of Turkey's neighbors, including Iran, Iraq, and Syria, obtained weapons of mass destruction.[3] Under the auspices of NATO, Turkey also developed an impressive training capability that it put to use for peacekeeping operations during the Bosnian conflict. Furthermore, its membership in NATO provided Turkey with considerable leverage and prestige that came from being on the winning side of the Cold War. More significantly, Turkey, which had never fared well in wars against Russia, would no longer be sharing borders with a post-Soviet Russia and instead be neighbors with the newly independent states of the former Soviet Union. The importance of this development was highlighted by a journalist close to Ahmet Davutoğlu, minister of foreign affairs and prime minister from 2009 to 2016, and underlined as the elimination of a centuries-old threat.[4]

Turkey might not have been able to carve out a sphere of influence that stretched from the Adriatic Sea to the Great Chinese Wall, an aspiration of Turgut Özal and Süleyman Demirel in the 1990s.[5] Yet, owing to its close strategic relationship with the United States, Turkey enjoyed considerable influence in certain parts of this geography. In the South Caucasus, for instance, Turkey managed to transform itself into a key transit country for energy supplies flowing from the Caspian basin to the West, which thereby bypassed Russia and Iran on the way to world markets. Turkey also enjoyed influence in the Balkans, especially the western Balkans, and in Afghanistan, where it contributed to Western-led peacekeeping and state-building efforts.

Strategically, Turkey's most important gain came at the start of its EU membership negotiations in 2005. The zero-problems policy, combined with deepening integration with the EU, boosted its influence and prestige in its immediate region. Building on earlier policies that laid the groundwork for a constructive approach, successive governments of the Justice and Development Party (AKP) forged ahead, not only actively trying to resolve Turkey's disputes with its neighbors but also taking on a role as mediator on issues that divided other countries, including the Arab-Israeli conflict. (In 2005 Abdullah Gül, then serving as minister of foreign affairs, visited both the West Bank and Israel, and in 2007 he hosted Mahmoud Abbas and Simon Peres together in Ankara.) In recognition of its new role in the Middle East, Turkey was invited to participate in the Annapolis Peace Conference in November 2007, and even urged Washington to include Syria among the nearly fifty states represented, as was subsequently done.[6]

Figure 5-1. Comparative Turkish per Capita Growth, 1960–2014

GDP per capita (constant 2005 US$)

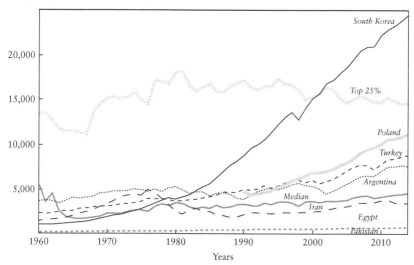

Source: Data made available by the World Bank (http://data.worldbank.org/).

Turkey's international influence reached its peak in 2006–08, when Turkish diplomats facilitated indirect talks between Israel and Syria.[7] Though Turkey could not have brokered a deal without direct U.S. involvement, it took a notable leadership role in attempting to soften old antagonisms and realign regional interests by working with all parties.[8] Turkey thus came to be seen by the West as a country that could make a valuable contribution to the EU's role in its neighborhood and perhaps in global affairs.[9] Many officials, including the Turkish leadership, recognized the correlation between Turkey's growing use of soft power and its deepening relationship with the EU. The strong belief that both sides would benefit from greater integration persisted until about 2013 and the Gezi Park protests, which, from the West's perspective, showed Turkey in an entirely different light.

Economic Gains

Turkey's economic gains from its association with the West are easier to substantiate than the political and strategic gains. Figure 5-1 plots Turkey's per capita GDP growth (measured in 2005 U.S. dollars) from 1960 to 2014, compared with that of six other World Trade Organization

(WTO) member countries of similar demographic and economic size, as well as the median and third quartile members of the WTO (it is assumed that the WTO represents the rules and values of the international liberal order). Of the top 25 percent of WTO member countries in terms of per capita income, most are also members of the Organization for Economic Cooperation and Development (OECD), an association of developed and largely liberal-democratic countries. Turkey's economic performance shows a trend steadily converging toward the top 25 percent during this period. The accelerating rate of this convergence is striking: the slope of the curve for Turkey increases moderately in the 1980s and 1990s, then rises substantially in the 2000s. Turkey had transitioned to a liberal economy and signed the customs union agreement with the EU in the 1980s and 1990s. In the following decade, Turkey pushed through a series of political and economic reforms to meet the EU's Copenhagen criteria and thereby start accession negotiations, while also earning recognition as a "functioning market economy," as noted in the European Commission's 2005 progress report.[10]

When Turkey's economy is compared with the economies of Argentina, Egypt, Iran, and Pakistan, on the one hand, and those of South Korea and Poland on the other, the benefits derived from Turkey's integration into the Western alliance become clearer. Argentina outperformed Turkey until the late 1980s, when it began to pursue economic and financial policies that conflicted with the standards set by the international financial institutions, including the International Monetary Fund (IMF). Iran's economy started to underperform after the 1970s, following a period of good performance that depended significantly on oil exports; the later years' underperformance can be attributed not only to fluctuating oil prices but also to Iran's conflicts with the West and the Western sanctions imposed on the country. Egypt and Pakistan have rarely followed policies in line with the international liberal order, either economically or politically. Since the mid-1990s Turkey has been performing better economically than these four countries. Although other factors may have contributed to Turkey's relative economic success, most analysts agree that its inclusion in the transatlantic alliance—and its adoption of economic and political policies aimed at meeting the standards of this community—has played a major role. Kemal Derviş, a former minister of economic affairs, has highlighted the growth of the Turkish economy between 2003 and 2013 as being "almost 5 times as fast as the EU in terms of total GDP and 3.5 times as fast in per capita terms."[11]

The World Bank supports similar conclusions. In its study on the transition of Turkey's economy, the World Bank emphasizes the impact of a pro-market consensus, improved regulatory institutional environment, structural reforms, greater social inclusion, and integration with the world economy as factors that helped increase income levels in Turkey.[12] The report also draws attention to the role of the EU-Turkey Customs Union in improving Turkey's productivity and export capacity, thereby fueling economic growth.[13] This analysis comes, on the other hand, with the warning that Turkey might well be stuck in a "middle income trap"[14]—a note of caution that was voiced at a time when Turkey's democracy was deteriorating and its economic regulatory and institutional infrastructure was weakening.[15] The situation corroborates the hypothesis that democratic governments exhibit greater openness with respect to modernizing economic institutions and adopting reforms that maintain growth.[16] In return, these measures facilitate further integration into the international liberal order. It is therefore not surprising that Poland, since embarking on EU accession negotiations in the late 1990s, and especially following its full membership in 2004, did considerably better than Turkey. Figure 5-1 also shows how South Korea's phenomenal ascent became possible through economic growth and democratic consolidation. The World Bank warns that for Turkey's income to grow, "[Turkey] would have to improve . . . the quality of its economic institutions . . . significantly to match the levels of [income of] countries that have successfully transitioned to high income in the past decade, such as the Republic of South Korea or Poland."[17]

Indeed, Turkey's economy gained significantly from its membership in the Western alliance. Based on past trends, it can safely be asserted that the more Turkey integrates itself with the economic and political values and standards of the transatlantic community, the likelier it is that Turkey's economy will improve. In the past, including during the Cold War, Turkey experienced numerous financial crises that required bailouts from the IMF and credits from the World Bank. Turkey's membership in the transatlantic community and its strategic importance for the United States have, however, made it easier for Ankara to receive the financial support it needs and that otherwise might not have been available.[18]

Similar observations can also be made with regard to foreign direct investment (FDI) inflows into Turkey. FDI and other capital flows are considered critical to the country's economic development because of its chronically low savings rate, and they noticeably increased as Turkey's relationship with the EU deepened. In October 2005, responding to the question of how the EU accession negotiations benefited Turkey, the then foreign minister Abdullah Gül mentioned that interest rates were falling as confidence in Turkey increased, and that every one-percentage-point drop in the rates meant a saving of $2 billion for the country.[19] In 2011 the then minister responsible for relations with the EU, Egemen Bağış, also underlined the importance of integrating with the EU by drawing attention to its positive impact on Turkey's international image. As a result, according to Bağış, the entire economy picked up. In the tourism sector, to take one example, the number of visitors exceeded 30 million in 2011, generating over $30 billion in income. By contrast, when Turkey first applied for an association agreement with the European Economic Communities (EEC) in 1959, it saw fewer than 200,000 tourists annually, for an income derived from tourism of no more than $8 million.[20]

All these developments have furnished Ankara with considerable prestige and influence. Its G-20 membership is a striking example in this regard. As noted by Jacob Lew, the former U.S. treasury secretary, a decision was made at the 2009 G-20 Pittsburgh summit "to elevate the G-20 as the premier forum for international economic cooperation."[21] Turkey's continuously positive performance at the time despite the financial crisis of 2008 propelled it into the limelight—after it had spent an entire decade as a G-20 member with little global attention. Its G-20 membership also transformed Turkey into a contributor with a say in setting the agenda and the rules for the post crisis global economy instead of remaining a passive recipient of rules imposed by the leading powers.[22] As one Turkish expert put it, G-20 membership offered Turkey "an important opportunity for increasing its international standing."[23] With its strong economic and political performance, Turkey came to the fore in the region as a model to be emulated, especially in the Arab world.[24] According to public opinion surveys, Turkey's prospects for EU membership and its role as the EU's regional partner were the main reasons behind the Arab world's fascination with the improvements in the country.[25] The International Crisis Group also observed similar attitudes among Middle Eastern countries. Many would express their concerns about the fate of the region and their neighborhood as "Ankara started to turn its back on its EU accession process."[26]

Turkey's membership in the transatlantic community and the ensuing gains the country realized were also reflected in Turkey's growing soft power. One striking manifestation was the stunning popularity of

Turkish soap operas in its neighborhood but especially in the Arab world. Despite fatwas issued by religious authorities, who condemned the Western lifestyle depicted in these shows, a March 2009 survey of Saudi women above the age of fifteen revealed that more than 71 percent of respondents enjoyed Turkish TV series.[27] This is striking, because the programs depict Muslims leading a modern social life and engaging in romantic, sometimes adulterous affairs and present a way of life for women that is more liberal than the one Saudi women are used to. Many in the Middle East also viewed these TV series as an example of how a Western way of life could be compatible and exist in harmony with Islamic traditions. They showcased Turkey as democratic, liberal, and secular, yet still Muslim, and therefore as a bridge between the Arab and Western worlds—almost as a nation that many Arab citizens aspired to be a part of. The sharp uptick in the number of tourists to Turkey from its Middle Eastern neighbors, from 500,000 in 2002 to almost 4 million in 2015, and in the tourism revenues so generated is attributed to the publicity the TV series provided.[28]

WHAT TURKEY LOST THROUGH DISTRUST OF THE WEST

The many gains Turkey realized in the economic and political spheres from its close relations with and membership in the transatlantic community are often taken for granted or, worse, overlooked by skeptical narratives that fuel distrust of the West. The United States bears most of the brunt of this sentiment. Anti-Americanism has been rampant once again in Turkey, especially since the U.S. intervention in Iraq beginning in 2003. In the following years, politicians and the media, both secular and religious, struck an anti-American tone. According to one foreign commentator, this pervasive anti-American discourse went "farther than anything found in most of the Arab world's state-controlled press."[29] The situation was little improved with the election of President Obama in 2008: the "Obama bounce" was experienced at a lower level in Turkey than in any EU country, and allegations that the United States was behind the coup attempt of July 2016 have since sent relations between the two countries into a tailspin.[30] Considerable groundwork for this situation was dug not by any specific international incident, however, but by the persistent popularity of conspiracy narratives casting the United States in the role of destroyer of Turkish values, whether Muslim or secular.

Conspiracy Theories: The Enemy at the Gate

Rampant conspiracy theories are not unique to Turkey, though conspiracy theories in Turkey reflect that country's specific historical legacy. Conspiracy narratives in general oversimplify more complicated algorithms into trite, memorable formulas, which can become powerful tools in domestic politics.[31] In the context of international relations, conspiracy theories are invoked to unify the public against real or perceived threats. The struggle is generally presented as that of the "good" against the "bad"—an evil enemy that will have inevitably co-opted fifth columns, such as NGOs, political parties, intellectuals, liberals, and naïve though well-meaning nationals.[32]

In Turkey, conspiracy theories are driven by a narrative that blames the collapse of the Ottoman Empire on long years of economic, political, and military interventions by the West. The West of today is understood to correspond to the great powers of the nineteenth century, or *düveli muazzama* in Ottoman Turkish.[33] The trauma resulting from the collapse of the empire burned into the national consciousness a dread of what dangers might exist beyond the national boundaries, prompting fear of and wariness toward foreigners—or so the narrative goes.[34] In the twentieth century, and especially since the end of World War II, the crusade to weaken Turkey's greatness was spearheaded by the United States, the current *düveli muazzama*. The United States is seen, along with the EU, as part of the same, mutually interlocking "West" or Western civilization.[35]

These conspiracy theories have a number of key tenets. One of them is the notion that Turks have no friends other than fellow Turks and the corollary belief that Turks should never trust anyone else, especially the West. This axiom is strongly reflected in public opinion polls: approximately one-third of those surveyed in 2013, 2015, and 2016 by Kadir Has University in Istanbul believed that Turkey "does not have any close friends." Only Azerbaijan was perceived by most of the respondents as the "closest friend" (*dost*), whereas the United States was selected as a "*dost*" by only 5 percent of the respondents.[36] These results match those of a survey conducted in 2001, when one-third of the respondents indicated Turkey had "no best friend" in the international arena, implying that Turkey is simply a loner.[37] This mental disposition has helped bolster the claim that the West does not want a strong and successful Turkey.

Such a view prevails even among well-educated and seasoned world travelers. For instance, the late Kamran İnan, a former diplomat, a former member of parliament, and a former minister of foreign affairs, often argued that Western Europe and Germany "[felt] uncomfortable about Turkey getting stronger."[38] He infamously called for a Turkey that could stand up against and say no to the West.[39] A similar resentment toward the West bubbled up during the Gezi Park protests in June 2013. Erdoğan, one of his advisers, and the pro-government media argued that the protests had been instigated by Western actors to prevent Turkey from transforming itself into "a model for the world."[40] Lufthansa was included on the list of conspirators, with the claim that the German airline feared competition from its successful rival, Turkish Airlines, and the prospects of a third airport in Istanbul, which might divert passengers from Germany's transit hubs.[41] Conspiracy theories after the July 2016 coup attempt gained unprecedented ground as the government, the media, and the public in tandem attributed the whole affair to the United States. In a similar vein, a former head of the military intelligence alluded to the covert involvement of the United States and the EU when a bomb exploded near a soccer stadium in Istanbul in December 2016.[42] Such claims, however groundless and fantastical, would have been accepted at face value by most of the public.

Turkey's educational system, the national press, and the entertainment industry subscribe to and propagate this conspiratorial line of thinking. The aftermath of the U.S. invasion of Iraq, and especially the undignified treatment of Turkish soldiers by the U.S. military when the soldiers were taken into custody with sacks over their heads, provided material for a rash of anti-U.S. films and books. Moreover, the number of books with anti-Western conspiratorial themes has surged since the U.S. invasion of Iraq in 2003, many giving voice to nationalist perspectives of resistance against the West. Also popular are leftist books exposing the theme that Western powers, in collaboration with Islamists, aim to weaken Turkey's secular foundations, and works with an anti-Semitic tincture.[43] Social media exacerbate these conspiratorial narratives by ginning up a climate of frenzy, keeping them constantly alive and fresh.[44]

Conspiracy Theories: The Enemy Within

Another common feature of conspiracy theories are fifth columns, imagined internal enemies collaborating with external adversaries. The fear that there are fifth columns in society stems from the trauma of the collapse of the Ottoman Empire and the anxiety it fueled about "internal cohesion"—and again, a link with outsiders, especially the West, is an important part of the internal conspiracy narrative. As the political scientist Malik Mufti has written, it is suspected that "Western prescriptions for political liberalism, cultural pluralism and market economics" could easily mask "predatory intentions."[45] This phenomenon is referred to as the "Tanzimat syndrome," denoting the widely held belief that the political reforms adopted by the Ottoman government at the urging of the European powers in the latter part of the nineteenth century, which primarily aimed at improving minority rights, actually led to the empire's weakening and disintegration.[46] Throughout Turkey's history as a republic, both non-Muslim minorities and Kurds often have been labeled "internal enemies."[47] Yet it was not only these groups that entered into "insidious alliances" with external enemies.

Liberals, Westernized Turks, and civil society organizations with links to the West are often depicted as "internal enemies" by nationalists, leftists, and Islamists. NGOs involved in democracy promotion projects are depicted as "Soros's children," bent on promoting color revolutions.[48] Turkey-based German foundations were hit with bouts of accusations that their employees were conspiring against Turkey.[49] Prominent German companies with a longstanding presence in Turkey, such as BASF and Daimler, met a similar fate when a list appeared, around the time of the first year anniversary of the coup attempt, accusing them of supporting the coup perpetrators. The list was promptly withdrawn and the government embarked on damage control.[50] There is also the striking case of Orhan Pamuk. The then Turkish president, Ahmet Necdet Sezer, refused to congratulate him on winning the Nobel Prize in literature for having said, during an interview with a Swiss newspaper, that "thirty-thousand Kurds were killed here, 1 million Armenians as well. And almost no one talks about it." This statement was used as evidence to support allegations that Pamuk "had insulted Turkishness," and he was accordingly indicted in 2005. His Nobel Prize in 2006 was interpreted as an emblem of his willingness to serve "Western interests."[51] Turkish Islamists, too, have resorted to similar methods and have accused pro-Western and liberal secular groups of being involved in the Gezi Park protests against the Turkish government.[52] In the latter half of 2016, as the Turkish economy began to contract and the currency lost considerable value against the U.S. dollar, Western-oriented businesses were attacked in the media for not responding to the government's call to invest their savings, then held in U.S. dollars, in Turkish lira.[53] In an alarming move, according to some reports, the government was urged to let the Turkish Stock Exchange collapse as a way to punish these business owners.[54]

In turn, Islamists, including Erdoğan himself, have faced accusations from secularists for conspiring with the West to transform Turkey into a "moderate Islamic" country in line with the George W. Bush administration's Greater Middle East and North Africa project, intended to prevent terrorism by improving democracy and educational opportunities in those areas.[55] Islamists have also charged each other with pursuing an agenda that would better serve the interests of the West than those of anyone else. The National Outlook (Millî Görüş) movement, represented by the Welfare Party (Refah Partisi) and then its successor, the Felicity Party (Saadet Partisi), were critical of the AKP leadership for building closer relations with the EU, which they considered to be a Christian club of nations.[56] The legendary late leader of both the Welfare Party and the Felicity Party, Necmettin Erbakan, accused the AKP of succumbing to imitating the West and exposing itself to exploitation by Zionism.[57] Simultaneously Islamists, including some from the ranks of the AKP, have asserted that the objective of the West and the United States was to colonize the Muslims, and warned that pious people should not fall prey to such designs.[58] Even İsmet İnönü, Turkey's president from 1938 to 1950, has been implicated in these conspiracy theories: the leftists found him guilty of betraying the legacy of Atatürk and surrendering Turkey to the mercies of an imperialist United States after the end of World War II.[59] Other prominent leaders, such as Adnan Menderes, Süleyman Demirel, and Turgut Özal, have also been accused of serving the interests of Western imperialism, the United States, and NATO.

The Politicization of Conspiracy Theories: Digging an East-West Divide

Turkish politicians have not been too keen on dispelling these conspiracy theories. On the contrary, they have often employed them toward their own ends, at public and governmental levels. In fact, this guides how the government assesses ebbs and flows in international affairs, and informs the decisionmaking apparatus.[60] Hewing to such beliefs, however, creates situations that test the bounds of reason and limits the impact Turkey could have on the world stage.

Different opinions obtain on what holds back the leadership from acknowledging that political developments may not be necessarily triggered by wild conspiracies. The most widely held explanation points to the Sèvres syndrome, which encapsulates the notion that, beginning in the dying years of the Ottoman Empire, European powers had aspired to push Turks out of Europe, and Europe took advantage of the empire's collapse to fragment the Anatolian regions into smaller states with the objective of subjugating them.[61] This narrative gained ground as incessant wars in the latter part of the nineteenth century and the early twentieth century took their toll on the Ottoman state and society, eventually leading to complete disintegration. The terms of the Sèvres Treaty signed with the Ottoman Empire in August 1920, from which the syndrome takes its name, strengthened this view.[62] Had it been implemented, the Sèvres Treaty would have carved two states, Armenia and Kurdistan, out of the territory of modern-day Turkey and partitioned the country into spheres of influence mandated by Britain, France, Greece, and Italy. Only a small part of Anatolia around Ankara, with a narrow strip along the Black Sea, would have been set aside for the successor state to the Ottoman Empire. Those who pay lip service to the Sèvres syndrome frequently quote the then British foreign minister Lord Curzon, who applauded the treaty as a matchless opportunity for expelling Turks from Europe and Constantinople.[63] The disinclination to trust the word of foreigners at face value was a reality for the founders of the Turkish Republic and would continue down the generations, along with a readiness to protect the country at all costs in what was perceived to be an anarchic world.[64] In the eyes of those who still subscribe to this notion, the West's calls for Turkey to improve its democracy and its record on civil and minority rights are efforts to undermine the country's territorial unity and political cohesion.[65]

The Sèvres syndrome figured prominently in the 1990s, a decade marked by intense Western criticism of Turkey for the flaws in its democratic edifice.[66] A striking case in point was the angry response given by the Turkish president Süleyman Demirel to the French minister of foreign affairs Alain Juppe in 1995 at the latter's suggestion that Turkey should find a political solution to its Kurdish problem. Demirel asserted that Juppe's remarks proved that the West was intent on creating a Kurdish state in Turkey. Despite his earlier favorable disposition toward the West, as well as his staunch support for Turkey's EU membership prospects, Demirel still claimed that the Copenhagen criteria on minority rights would only stoke the fires of separatism in Turkey.[67] The fear was that such reforms risked transforming Turkey into an "ethnic hell," not unlike Yugoslavia or Iraq.[68] This line of thinking persists to this day.

Yet, as Demirel's dilemma sets out, those who subscribe to the Sèvres syndrome still hope for a Turkey that would be accepted as a part of the West. For instance, General Yaşar Büyükanıt, former deputy chief of the Turkish general staff, in 2007 remarked that allowing Kurdish politicians—or in his words, the foot soldiers of the PKK—into the Turkish parliament would only set the conditions for a ploy to resurrect the Sèvres Treaty.[69] However, in an earlier address to a large gathering of military officers and civilians in 2003, he had opined that the Turkish military could not stand in the way of Turkey's EU membership, since it would fulfill Atatürk's chief mission of Turkish modernization.[70] (Atatürk's guiding objective was to catch up with "contemporary civilization," which he equated with Europe.) Even in the aftermath of the independence struggle waged against the West, the republican elite still believed that, by becoming a part of Europe, Turkey would remain a secular and a modern nation-state. Hence Europe (or the West) was a source of both inspiration and insecurity—a notion that still underpins this dilemma.[71] At the heart of the dilemma lies the tension between liberal democratic values, represented by the Copenhagen political criteria, on the one hand, and the traditional notions of sovereignty and territorial integrity dating from the days of the establishment of the Turkish republic in 1923 on the other. What emerges is a curious situation in which those who harbor mistrust toward the West seek "Westernization without the West."[72]

While Islamists also believe the West wants a weakened Turkey, they look at it through the lenses of religion rather than as a matter of the sovereignty of the nation-state. Islamists focus on the West as a Christian power, an enemy of the Ottoman Empire that in the past sought to drive Islam and Islamic civilization out of the European geography and still poses a threat to modern-day Turkey. Accordingly, Christian Europe is on a crusader's mission against Muslim Turkey that it seems hell-bent on winning. This view is accompanied by a deep-seated resentment of Westernization, which is construed as part of a European and Jewish or Zionist conspiracy to weaken Islam.[73] In Erbakan's narrative, the Sèvres Treaty, combined with the Lausanne Treaty of 1923 establishing the Turkish Republic, are construed to be part of a conspiracy to put into effect the "Grand Israel Project" (Büyük İsrail Projesi).[74] Adherents to this line of Islamist thinking have exercised considerable influence over a leading cadre of AKP and National Outlook members, who have extensively stressed this theme.[75]

In the early years of the AKP administration, the West was not publicly resented at the executive level, nor was it portrayed as the absolute other. Instead, what distinguished the AKP from its predecessor, the Welfare Party, was its commitment to Turkey's joining the EU. It wanted to construct a "Muslim and democratic identity" that would place "Turkey in a different civilization (read: Islamic) and yet in harmony with western civilization."[76] In this sense, Erdoğan stood in stark contrast to the Welfare Party's leader Erbakan, who viewed the EU as an exclusively Christian assemblage of countries, into which Turkey could never truly integrate. However, the commitment to constructing and sustaining harmonious relations with the West began to erode as Turkey's democracy weakened, and conspiracy theories resumed a prominent place in public discourse. Against this background, once a power struggle broke out between Erdoğan and his former political ally Fetullah Gülen, it became common practice for AKP supporters to denounce the Gülenists for collaborating with the United States and the West against Turkey.[77]

Another variant of anti-Westernism is a by-product of the left-wing politics of the 1960s and 1970s, which emerged in the aftermath of the military intervention in Turkish politics and the coup d'état of May 27, 1960. According to this interpretation, Turkey suffers from imperialist subjugation, which it can break out of only through revolution, greater state involvement in the economy, and rejection of membership in any constellation of Western states, especially NATO.[78] Advocates of this view have sometimes been referred to as left Kemalists. At times they have gone so far as to propose that İnönü had misconstrued or outright betrayed Atatürk's policy by aligning Turkey with the West after World War II and adopting a multiparty system later.[79] They entertained considerable hostility toward capitalism and the West but were less suspicious of the Soviet Union.[80] Anti-American protests were rampant across the country in the 1960s, especially protests against the presence of U.S. military bases. Different leftist circles called for a closer association with the Soviet Union or nonaligned countries and generously praised the regimes of Hafez al-Assad in Syria, Gamal Nasser in Egypt, and Muammar Gaddafi in Libya.[81] Indeed, there seemed to be little love lost for democracy. What they aspired to instead was a revolutionary regime modeled after Baathism. In the 1990s, anti-Westernism made a comeback. It was partly a reaction against deepening relations with the EU, but also a denunciation of U.S. involvement in Iraq and subsequent U.S. efforts to bring democracy to the Middle East.

Historical Roots of Resistance to the EU

The origins of the resistance to the EU stretch back to the late 1960s, when the debates over deepening the Association Agreement with the EEC were taking place. As the government entered into negotiations, posters went up bearing such slogans as "Six capitalist countries to exploit the Turkish people" and "They're the Partners, We're the Market." The conviction was that Turkey would eventually become a colony of the European Common Market.[82] In the 1970s, Islamists successfully blocked Turkey's further integration with the EEC.[83] The EU-related political reforms of the early 2000s triggered a new form of resistance. This time, those in resistance were the "neonationalists"— left-leaning nationalists and hard-core secularists with a Eurasian vocation, known as *ulusalcı*.[84] They viewed the reforms with suspicion and interpreted calls to improve human rights and democracy as plots to weaken Turkey. These neonationalists also resented the EU's support for the AKP and did not applaud the leadership's mission to refashion Turkey as an example for the Middle East of how Islam could be reconciled with democracy. Turkey's willingness to play a role in implementing the set of proposals put forward in the George W. Bush administration's Greater Middle East Initiative was construed as evidence of the West's intentions to erode secularism and Atatürk's values, and thus to exploit the country in collaboration with the Islamists.[85]

According to the proponents of this vision, the future of Turkey lay either in Eurasia or—echoing the sentiments of their predecessors from the 1960s and 1970s—among the ranks of the third world countries. A case in point was the virulent and surprising manner in which the secretary-general of the National Security Council, General Tuncer Kılınç, at an international military conference in Istanbul in March 2002 declared that the EU was a "Christian Club" and that it was a "neocolonialist force determined to divide Turkey." He proposed that Turkey should abandon its bid for EU membership and seek closer relations with Russia and Iran[86]—a line of thinking traditionally referred to as Eurasianism and known to enjoy strong support in the ranks of the Turkish military.[87] Another manifestation of this occurred coincidentally during the visit of the Turkish chief of general staff, Yaşar Büyükanıt, to the United States. Vladimir Putin's speech at the 2007 Munich Security Conference, deeply critical of the West, was briefly posted on the general staff's website.[88] Ironically, once the AKP's relations with the EU and the United States started to sour, especially after the Gezi Park protests of 2013, Erdoğan began to advocate the idea of membership in the Russian- and Chinese-dominated Shanghai Cooperation Organization (SCO).[89]

EUROPEAN SKEPTICISM TOWARD TURKEY

The other face of Turkey's deep skepticism over the West's intentions with respect to Turkey was the EU's hesitation in accepting Turkey into its ranks. The EU had only reluctantly extended candidate status to Turkey in 1999. The decision reflected a balance between those in the EU who believed in a multicultural definition of Europe based on shared values, represented largely by Social Democrats, and those who saw the EU primarily as a cultural bloc defined by a Judeo-Christian ethos, represented largely by Christian Democrats.[90] It was the latter perspective that had prevailed in the Luxembourg European Council decision of December 1997 excluding Turkey from the upcoming round of enlargement, one that would eventually bring the Central and East European states, as well as Cyprus and Malta, into the EU. The climate with regard to Turkey changed in 1998 with the rise of a German coalition government of the Social Democrats and the Green Party. The new chancellor, Gerhard Schröder, along with his coalition partner, Joschka Fischer, urged an approach to the EU's enlargement from a perspective that sought to "emphasize the significance of political and economic criteria in the process rather than religious and cultural factors underlined by the previous Christian Democrat government."[91] Along with other Social Democrat parties in the EU, this coalition's support for Turkey's further integration culminated in the adoption of the Helsinki European Council decision in December 1999.

Turkey did embark in good faith on an impressive set of economic and political reforms that gathered pace and intensity from 2003 on, including the decision to support the unification of Cyprus. A coalition of political, business, and civil society actors championed these reforms.[92] Public support for EU membership reached its peak in 2004, with 73 percent of those surveyed expressing favorable views of the EU.[93] But soon the mood in Europe once more turned against Turkey. Former French president Giscard D'Estaing aggressively argued that Turkey, which was not part of Europe, could cause the EU to "implode" if actually admitted into the EU. A Dutch politician, also a former European commissioner, went further, claiming that Turkish membership would mean the Islamization of Europe.[94] Similar attitudes were registered in public opinion surveys in Europe.[95] It is no wonder that the Independent Commission on Turkey, composed of European advocates of Turkish membership in the EU, felt the need to draw attention to the powerful effect of this trend on Turkish leaders, who were increasingly concerned that "the closer Turkey gets to EU membership, the more the resistance grows in Europe."[96]

These concerns manifested themselves more starkly when the European Council met in Luxembourg in October 2005 to start accession talks with Turkey. The terms were less than satisfying, since negotiations had to be "an open-ended process, the outcome of which cannot be guaranteed beforehand," and the ultimate decision would have to remain contingent on the EU's "absorption capacity."[97] With respect to the introduction of possible derogations to labor mobility, agricultural subsidies, and structural funds, many Turks expressed the belief that their country was being discriminated against and treated differently compared with previous candidates.[98] The Negotiation Framework presented to Turkey did not contain the more favorable conditions that were set out in the rubric handed to Croatia, which suggested to "the Turkish elite and public that a 'second-class membership' was being envisaged for Turkey."[99]

The accession talks inflicted the greatest damage on Turkey-EU relations. Work stretched on, with little progress made. The proposal of a "privileged partnership" instead of full membership, in line with the Christian Democrats' stand vis-à-vis Turkey and supported by Angela Merkel, would hamper Turkey-EU relations even further.[100] Only in the context of the socialist government in France under François Hollande, and subsequently with the European-Turkey migration deal arranged in 2016, did the accession process pick up some pace. Turkey's bid remains hostage to the Cyprus problem, and a careful reading of the signs suggests that a breakthrough on the fate of the island's reunification or a change in Turkey's policy concerning Cyprus does not loom on the horizon.[101] This was proven by the failure of the most recent intense round of UN-led negotiations held in Switzerland in July 2017.[102] With the introduction of emergency rule in Turkey after the July 2016 coup attempt, the extent of the clampdown on the opposition and the contestation over the results of the April 2017 referendum have effectively put the EU accession process on hold.

With the uptick in anti-Turkish sentiment and discourse across Europe, the AKP could not sustain a pro-EU discourse.[103] The EU in turn began to lose its electoral attractiveness for the AKP,[104] as support levels fell to 40 percent in 2007, reaching its lowest level of 38 percent in 2010. Pro-EU coalitions in Turkey also weakened, while the Euroskeptic parties saw their base of appeal broaden.[105] It was against this background of waning interest in the transatlantic community that Erdoğan's policies became increasingly authoritarian. When Erdoğan addressed the Fourth General Congress of the AKP in 2012 and detailed his vision for Turkey for the next decade, he barely mentioned the EU—a stark departure from past practice.[106]

Thus the setbacks to the gains from the period of democratization and reforms in 1999–2005 rapidly overwhelmed public sentiment and redirected Turkey's interest away from European integration. An important opportunity to anchor Turkey in the West by means of the EU mechanism slipped away. There was a brief moment when it looked as if there were those in Europe, especially in social democratic Europe, who accepted Turkey as a part of Europe and focused more on shared values, diverging from the Christian Democrats' practice of defining Europe in terms of culture or geography. Their conception of Europe carved out a place for Turkey.[107] In turn, a coalition in Turkey, one that included the AKP, wished to frame Turkey as a part of the European self based on shared democratic values; it was also intent on playing down the traditional conspiracy theories.

The moment of visualizing joining with the other on the basis of shared values did not last long; as Turkey's EU accession process encountered problems, the above coalitions underlining such a disposition very quickly disintegrated.[108] This strengthened the hand of those Turks who were skeptical of the country's integration with Europe and the West in general, and triggered an iterative process that pushed the sides further apart. As early as 2005, when accepting a literary award in Germany, Orhan Pamuk had warned that "the fueling of anti-Turkish sentiment in Europe is stoking an anti-European, indiscriminate nationalism in Turkey."[109] As a result of this tug of war, neither side could benefit from the many opportunities awaiting them in the wings. As the Independent Commission on Turkey had warned at the start of the accession process, its failure "could result in a serious crisis of identity in Turkey, leading to political upheaval and instability at the Union's doorstep."[110]

CONCLUSION

The gains that Turkey realized from its affiliation with the West were significant. Turkey's NATO membership and close relationship with the United States ensured territorial integrity during the Cold War and greater regional influence afterward. Further integration with the EU played a key role in the emergence of Turkey as a model country in its neighborhood. The democratization process ignited by the prospects of an EU membership—however distant that may now be—resulted in Turkey gaining soft power, which it skillfully leveraged in its new role as a mediator in Middle East conflicts. The signing of the customs union agreement with the EU and the subsequent domestic reforms were instrumental in transforming Turkey into a functioning market economy. The rise in GDP and per capita income was significant between 2003 and 2013, a period that also saw a substantial increase in FDI inflows and revenues from tourism. Its inclusion in the G-20 summits confirmed Turkey's newfound status as one of the leading economies in the world. As indicated by public opinion surveys, as well as by the interest in Turkish popular culture in the Arab world, Turkey had become an object of fascination, a country not only to be reckoned with but also to be emulated by the nations in the neighborhood.

Despite these gains, anti-Westernism and anti-Americanism still persists through all levels of Turkish society, which leads the public and the leadership to downplay the value of being anchored in the transatlantic fold. Various conspiracy theories continue to stoke anti-Western sentiment, reinforcing the saying that Turks have no friends other than fellow Turks. Attributing blame to the West for Turkey's internal problems is a regular practice in Turkish politics and has been used masterfully by Erdoğan in particular. His reaction to the Gezi protests in 2013, and more recently to the terror attacks that have shaken the country since 2015, was punctuated by salvos aimed at Western countries—powers that sought to undermine Turkey's rise as an important power, in his view. An emphasis on the role of internal enemies, meaning minority groups as well as Western-oriented, liberal Turks, is another part of the narrative. On the other hand, Erdoğan and his Islamist circle have themselves faced charges, mainly leveled by secular groups, that they have colluded with the West to undermine the secular nature of the Turkish Republic.

The historical and ideological veins that nourish the various conspiracy theories that abound in Turkey have instilled a certain paranoia with regard to foreign elements, both inside and outside Turkey, supposedly working to the detriment of the country. Skepticism as to the intentions of the West, and especially the United States, continues to shape the thinking and policies of successive leaders. In this light, the rising demands from Turkey's ethnic minorities are contorted into efforts to break up the country's territorial integrity. The increasing ethnic consciousness among some of the minorities in Turkey, most notably the Kurds, is perceived as a function of Western machinations, and this view is held by a number of academics as well as military and state officials, including those who support Turkey's transatlantic vocation.

In contrast to the perception of Westernization as an instrument to weaken Islam, which informed the ideology behind the founding of the AKP, Erdoğan's initial stand in favor of harmonizing relations with the West was an anomaly. In light of Turkey's recent drift away from the principles of the international liberal order, this is obviously no longer his position.

The EU's half-hearted support for Turkey's membership—the other face of the medallion—can be read as the manifestation of negative attitudes that run deep in the EU, regardless of Turkey's resolve to meet the political and economic criteria for membership. These negative attitudes, which have their counterpart in the Turkish demos, are substantially intertwined with the EU's understanding of its own "self" and the rather persistent view, occasionally mitigated by far-sighted leadership, of Turkey as the other. Some EU members' belief that the union is a cultural organization has made it difficult for the EU and Turkey to come together on the basis of shared values in addition to shared geopolitical strategies. In both Turkey and the EU, however, some sectors of the populace have sought to forge bonds through an understanding of shared values, but their efforts do not constitute majority opinion. Ultimately, the contentious relation between the EU and Turkey can be understood as a function of Turkey being "embedded in an identity interaction in which Turkey occupies a 'liminal' position with respect to the European collective identity."[111]

The fracture lines in the Turkey-EU relationship arising from disparate, and evolving, notions of self and other have been fueled by a deep-seated mistrust of the West on the part of Turkey, coupled more recently with the discourse and policies adopted by the AKP. These have further distanced Turkey from its transatlantic allies and strengthened Europe's reluctance to see Turkey as part of "us." The fault lines in this troubled alliance remain deep, complicating further the prospects of overcoming them.

CHAPTER SIX

The Politics of Regression

AFTER THE IMPRESSIVE STEPS taken toward liberal democracy in the first decade of the Justice and Development Party's (AKP's) governance, the world looked increasingly to Turkey as a model for reconciling Islam with democracy. These hopes were not to materialize, however. Instead the country is now, in 2017, making the news mostly for the increasingly authoritarian tendencies of its regime, and its democratic ambitions—still favored by a large part of the populace—are on life support.[1]

The downturn did not happen suddenly. Long before the Gezi protests of May and June 2013, the secular, Western-oriented segments of the society had already begun to raise their voice against some of the policies of the AKP that they saw as an unmistakable sign of a growing intolerance for diversity and individual freedoms. The manner in which the peaceful parts of protests were crushed left little room for optimism. From there on, the pillars of liberal democracy—freedom of expression and the right to peaceful protest—steadily deteriorated. The media found itself under growing siege, and access to the internet was frequently interrupted. In the summer of 2017 access to Wikipedia remained blocked since the authorities shut down the service in April.[2] Repeat national elections held in November 2015 were questioned as to how "free and fair" they were. The situation worsened especially after the coup attempt in July 2016, which was perpetrated by a renegade group of officers and their civilian allies. The introduction and now periodic extensions of a state of emergency on the heels of the coup attempt have made it impossible to hope for a return of the rule of law any time soon. In the meantime, a much-contested referendum in April 2017 opened the way for constitutional amendments that promise to give Erdoğan unprecedented executive powers while doing away with most of the checks on his or the AKP's authority.

Turkey's sharp swerve from its stumbling path toward a liberal democracy and affiliation with Western institutions has hardened the fault lines between Turkey and the transatlantic community. Relations with the United States have been made much more complex since the coup attempt. Many in Turkey accuse the United States of harboring the alleged mastermind of the coup attempt, Fethullah Gülen, a Muslim cleric in self-exile in Pennsylvania. The weak response from the EU in support of Erdoğan and his party after the coup attempt also remains a sore spot in the relations with both the Union and some of the member states. Erdoğan's growing authoritarianism and populist anti-European rhetoric did not make matters any easier. As such, Turkey surely does not project the image of a country that adheres to the ideals and principles around which members of the transatlantic community are expected to converge.

Several undercurrents prepared the ground for Turkey's retreat from its previous liberal aspirations. Both internal and external dynamics played a role in steering the country on its new course, toward increasing authoritarianism. In light of the violence that followed the collapse of the peace process with the Kurdistan Workers' Party (PKK), it is hard to hope for any improvement in the near future. The situation took a turn for the worse after the detention of many Kurdish deputies as part of the broader purges conducted in the aftermath of the coup attempt. The turmoil in the Middle East has hit Turkey hard, and not only because of the burden of providing for close to 3 million refugees from Syria and Iraq. Dwindling trade with the region and a drop in tourism revenues because of Islamic State (IS) and PKK terrorism have had an adverse effect on the economy. Moreover, the long commitment to the EU ideal seems to have simply disappeared from the government's agenda. After years of striving to narrow the fault lines with the West, Turkey is now growing further away from the values that have long constituted the international liberal order.

THE EROSION OF LIBERAL DEMOCRACY: EFFECTS ON TURKISH-WESTERN RELATIONS

The erosion of Turkey's brief encounter with liberal democracy was an incremental process. The first signs began to appear as early as 2004, even as the positive results in the economic, political, and sociocultural spheres as a result of Turkey's deepening engagement with the transatlantic community were starting to be fully felt. An example of early tightening was the government's decision to criminalize adultery, which came just weeks ahead of the EU's December 2004 meeting to decide whether to open accession negotiations with Turkey. The initiative was led by Recep Tayyip Erdoğan, then prime minister, and catered to the AKP's narrow conservative base, with little regard for his earlier promises to keep the state out of private life. The proposal failed in the face of strong opposition from Turkish women's organizations and certain European circles.[3] In the mid-2000s a number of prominent personalities, such as Hrant Dink, Orhan Pamuk, and Elif Şafak, faced prosecution on charges of denigrating Turkish identity under a vague law infamously open to interpretation. There were also complaints with respect to the actual implementation of minority rights, adopted as part of the EU-required reforms. These problems were flagged by the European Commission in its annual progress reports as early as 2006 and 2007, though at the time they were attributed primarily to resistance from state institutions and the lack of a truly independent judiciary.[4] The reports followed a pattern: they included recommendations for reforms in Turkey; if those recommendations were adopted, due recognition followed; if not, persisting problems, such as "pressures on the press and electronic media," continued to be raised in successive years.[5]

Criticism from the EU would steadily increase, particularly with respect to freedom of expression and freedom of the media. It reached a certain peak in 2012, which precipitated considerable friction with and pushback from the government. The then minister of EU affairs, Egemen Bağış, expressed his displeasure with the European Commission's report for that year by accusing the EU of purposefully lodging unfair criticisms to weaken the government's bid for membership.[6] On another occasion, the AKP's response was telegraphed in a dramatic move by Burhan Kuzu, a law professor turned parliamentary deputy, who threw the progress report into a trash bin on live TV.[7] In hindsight, it is possible to see these reactions as indications of a growing disregard for freedom and diversity rather than as petulant outbursts. The turning point came with the Gezi Park protests in May and June 2013. The protests did not remain limited to Gezi Park itself and instead spread to cities across the country and became, according to political scientist Cihan Tuğal, the biggest spontaneous revolt in Turkish history.[8] They were a common reaction to a set of policies that had been incrementally curtailing individual freedoms and represented a no vote to Erdoğan, who, in the eyes of the protesters, had gone back on his promise to respect people's way of life, regardless of religion, ethnicity, or gender. Not surprisingly, the majority of those gathered at Gezi Park, at least in the initial, peaceful stages of the protest, were well-educated, nonpolitical, middle-class youths, concerned for their personal liberties before anything else.[9]

The Gezi protests were preceded by a string of statements and practices on the part of the AKP that caused concern among large segments of the population. Erdoğan's call for women to have at least three children may have resonated with his base, but it raised alarms among those who wished the state not to intervene in private life.[10] And oppressive rhetoric by the government continued after the protests. A remark by the then deputy prime minister Bülent Arınç that virtuous women should refrain from laughing in public, for example, drew even stronger criticism as the manifestation of a mental disposition in conflict with the ideals of a modern state and society.[11] Erdoğan publicly expressed disapproval of co-ed dorm arrangements, calling them contrary to "democratic conservative values."[12] Of particular economic impact was a new ban on serving and consuming alcohol in public. Prior to Gezi, growing restrictions on the consumption of alcohol had deepened the debate over individual freedoms. The ban on the consumption of alcohol in public space limited the ability of many restaurants to use outdoor space, as was the practice in popular districts of Istanbul, areas mostly frequented by secular, liberal, Western-oriented Turks.[13] The image of quaint, narrow streets lined with tables where people freely enjoyed a glass of *rakı* along with *mezes* started to disappear, and along with it the touristy charm of whole neighborhoods and the economic gains they had long provided for the entertainment sector.

Infringements on individual freedoms extended to New Year celebrations, a practice long established as part of the larger modernization and westernization project adopted in the early years of the republic. Mehmet Görmez, director of religious affairs, an entity under the oversight of the prime minister, stated in December 2012 that decorating and illuminating trees for the occasion would be frowned on by his institu-

tion. The proximity of New Year's Eve to Christmas and images of Santa
Claus popping up in carefully dressed shop windows were clearly a concern to Görmez, but his denouncement was contrary to the more tolerant stand taken by the directorate a decade earlier. Back in 2003 his
predecessor, Ali Bardakoğlu, had also opposed the idea of adopting some
of the customs attached to Christmas by Muslims. He was careful at the
same time to distinguish New Year's Eve festivities as a separate universal
secular practice. This was common to all cultures, and therefore it should
be perfectly acceptable for the Muslims to celebrate the coming of a new
year and the hope that it symbolized.[14] By December 2016 the whole
discussion had reached such a pitch that even expatriate communities in
Istanbul were made uncomfortable marking Christmas. Reports that the
German teachers at an elite high school teaching a joint curriculum with
Germany had been asked not to expose their Turkish Muslim students
to any Christmas-related activity caused a stir.[15]

THOSE WHO GATHERED AT Gezi Park in June 2013 were bothered not
only by what they saw as the government's encroachment on individual
liberties. They were also raising their voices as concerned witnesses to
the increasing pace of large-scale construction that seemed to be sweeping the country. News that an expansive office and residence complex
was being constructed for Erdoğan's use as presidential palace in Ankara
had received considerable public attention. What struck a chord, especially among secular segments of society, was that the immense project
was set to take over a site of significance in republican history, a wooded
farm built by Atatürk near Ankara and symbolizing Turkey's early efforts
to modernize its agriculture. The cost of the project came under scrutiny,
and its extravagant size and style—designed to spread over 22.5 acres
of land and featuring more than 1,100 rooms fitted with the latest
technology—drew criticism.[16] Furthermore, the new construction of such
a lavish building for the president's use was seen by many as an attempt to
do away with an important association in the public mind. The relatively
modest residence that had served the presidents until then was situated on
top of a hill in Ankara overlooking the entire city; the name of the hill,
Çankaya, had come to stand for the authority and prestige of the Turkish
state. The decision to leave the former site was therefore criticized as an
assault on the legacy of the founders of the Turkish Republic.

Both the government's rhetoric and its action seemed to confirm the
perception that the country was now pursuing a rapid course toward

Islamization, marking a wholesale abandonment of a Western, liberal and secular ideal and the inculcation of conservative Islamist values among younger people by way of the educational system. Erdoğan's statement in 2012 that he aspired to raise a devout generation was not well received by secular groups.[17] (He would subsequently repeat the same words on numerous occasions.) The accompanying promise that his leadership would nevertheless protect the rights of all citizens, devout and atheist alike, was far from convincing. One particular reason was an awareness of Islamist policies shaping the educational system. The number of religious high schools (*imam hatip*) was on the rise from its 2004 level, when 453 schools in this category registered 90,000 students. By 2014 the number of schools had increased to 952 and served almost half a million students, with an especially sharp increase after 2013.[18] According to Al-Monitor reports, the content of the educational material in secular schools also began acquiring an increasingly Islamic tone.[19] Evolution was again at the center of debate through the first half of 2017 when the government put forward a new curriculum that would completely scrap any mention of it in school texts. A Turkish commentator interpreted the development as a win for the religious conservative camp in the AKP that considered Darwin's theory as corrosive of religious faith and advocated that young generations be protected from such "harmful" ideas.[20] The new curriculum was finally adopted in June 2017 for the upcoming school year with an AKP member of the parliamentary education commission celebrating it by announcing, "There's no use in teaching mathematics to a child who doesn't know jihad."[21] The remark symbolizes the extent of departure from a reason- and science-based educational approach that had characterized the perspective of the founding fathers of the Turkish republic and their Western vocation.

The growing importance attributed to Islamization of Turkish society and its transformation away from the founding values of the republic is also revealed in Erdoğan's reaction when he called Gezi protesters *"çapulcus"* (marauders), a term that evoked persisting tensions from the late Ottoman era through Turkey's republican history. The construction project that was at the center of the conflict involved the revival of an Ottoman-era military building, the Halil Pasha Artillery Barracks (Topçu Kışlası), that once stood on the site of Gezi Park. This was also where the mutineers of the 1909 revolt, a group consisting of military units and part of the religious establishment, had gathered when they rose up against the government of the Committee of Union and Progress (CUP), or Young Turks. The perception that the CUP was leading anti-Islamic policies had triggered the uprising; its objective was to restore the *ancien régime* of Sultan Abdulhamid, the Ottoman ruler who had skillfully appealed to religious sensitivities and pan-Islamism before being sidelined from power.[22] The revolt was eventually crushed by the Action Army (Hareket Ordusu), but its memory would linger on, lending itself to various, conflicting interpretations in history writing.

In the version of Necip Fazıl Kısakürek, deeply revered in the ranks of the National Outlook (Millî Görüş) religio-political movement and a mentor for Erdoğan, the mutineers were "true soldiers of Islam." The units loyal to the CUP government, the forces that ended the uprising, were, he said, no more than a bunch of *çapulcus*.[23] Insofar as both Atatürk and İnönü were members of the Action Army, it would have been hard to miss Kısakürek's salvo directed at the founding fathers of the republic.[24] In a fascinating coincidence, Erdoğan, just a few days before he saw fit to call the Gezi Park protesters marauders, had praised Kısakürek in his speech to the AKP group in parliament. The occasion was the thirtieth anniversary of his death. Erdoğan proudly remembered having been his follower and advocated that youth needed to be informed about him and his thinking. Perhaps it was this fresh link that prompted Erdoğan to use a discourse that would reach beyond Gezi to strike at the Western and secular orientation that the founders of the Turkish republic had given to the future of the country. The symbolism also involved the very fact that the park that Erdoğan sought to demolish was a landmark of the era associated with İnönü, the leader who spearheaded single-party rule and was known for his strict secularism. Erdoğan's contempt for the founders were contained in a thinly veiled attack on Atatürk and İnönü when he referred to them as "two drunks" (*iki ayyaş*).[25]

THE GÜLENISTS AND THE COUP ATTEMPT

Erdoğan's obvious distaste for Kemalism and the Kemalist legacy (generic terms used to refer to the ideas and policies of Mustafa Kemal Atatürk and his colleagues who founded the Turkish Republic as well as their disciples) was seen by the opposition as a counterrevolution to the republican project of secularization and enlightenment.[26] What they viewed as outright Islamization Erdoğan called normalization, a process whereby the government simply accommodated to the preferences of a large majority. The legislation that aimed to regulate social behavior in accordance with Islamic principles can be considered the "top-down" aspect of Islamization. Secularist groups were also concerned about what they perceived as a growing intolerance for nonreligious ways of life. The phenomenon was to be captured in the phrase "neighborhood pressure" (*mahalle baskısı*), which emphasized the role of the pious groups, not the state, in restricting the living space of those who preferred a nonreligious way of life, hence "bottom-up" Islamization.[27] The trend had already been recorded through the findings of two important public surveys conducted in 1999 and 2006 as well as subsequent ones.[28]

This was accompanied by a growing societal antisecularist streak that extended at times to an outright defense of sharia law, as can be found in some of the columns that appeared in pro-government newspapers. There were reports of public demonstrations with calls for the reinstatement of the caliphate and a return to Asr-ı Saadet, the golden age of Islam.[29] According to a former adviser to Abdullah Gül, this was a manifestation of "soft Salafization," an outcome of "Turkey's strategy of supporting the Salafi factions in Syria, and its huge public relations machinery that praised the fighters, and in a way, normalized Salafism in the eyes of many ordinary, pious Sunni Turks."[30] Despite the declining numbers after a series of terrorist attacks in Turkey, the percentage of those who did not view IS as a threat remained surprisingly significant: the figure was 16.2 percent and 13.6 percent in 2015 and 2016, respectively, among voting age respondents.[31] This would correspond to roughly 9.2 million and 7.7 million voters, and—with the caveat that these figures should be taken cautiously—suggests an approximate idea of the degree of sympathy for the values represented by IS or Islamic extremists in Turkey.[32]

The drift away from the letter and spirit of EU reforms and liberal democracy continued. Repression of the media increased, especially after December 2013, following the eruption of a corruption scandal. Members of the cabinet and even Erdoğan's family came under suspicion as a number of voice tapes suddenly surfaced that contained what appeared to be potentially incriminating evidence.[33] Since then it has become much clearer that this was part of an attempt to undermine Erdoğan and his government rather than to address the issue of corruption per se.[34] The perpetrators, it is now thought, were the Gülenists, members of a religious and social movement named after its founder, Fethullah

Gülen, once a close ally of Erdoğan before their fallout. To a large public, Gülen's organization was known, at least until the July 2016 coup attempt, as a religiously motivated initiative dedicated to fostering tolerance and interfaith dialogue. In contrast to the National Outlook tradition of Necmettin Erbakan, once the leader of numerous Islamist parties including the Welfare Party (Refah Partisi), it put a greater emphasis on Turkish nationalism as opposed to pan-Islamic solidarity.[35] The web of schools it established in more than 100 countries received high praise from many corners, both secular and Islamic, as an effective venue for promoting Turkish language and culture around the world.[36] Bülent Ecevit, for example, a former prime minister known for his secularist sensitivity, was one of the supporters of Gülen's educational initiative. At one point the movement was even considered a critical player that could help Islam reconcile with the secular state and contribute to Turkey's democratization.[37] The Gülenists' abundant human capital, product of his movement's long standing commitment to education, political clout, and presence within the state bureaucracies such as the judiciary, police and even the military, made them an ideal ally for the AKP and Erdoğan in the early years of their rule. They shared a common interest in weakening the influence of the Kemalist establishment, often equated with especially the Turkish military but also the judiciary and other state institutions, such as the Ministry of Foreign Affairs, to "achieve the freedom to live a faith-based life in a staunchly secular state."[38] Erdoğan allowed the Gülenists' long-standing aspiration to increase their influence in state bureaucracies at large but also in the military to grow.[39] The military in Turkey together with the judiciary was long regarded as exercising a kind of guardianship over elected civilian governments to prevent departures from secularism and the founding principles of the Turkish Republic. The AKP and the Gülen movement popularized the term "tutelary regime" to capture the nature of this undemocratic form of guardianship and their objection to it.[40]

The alliance of the Gülenists and the AKP reached a peak during the judicial proceedings conducted against hundreds of members of the police corps, judiciary, military, academia, and the media on the charge of plotting against the government. The sheer scale of the proceedings as well as the trials that ensued, that of the Ergenekon network and that of the "Sledgehammer" (*Balyoz*) plot being the most notable, did not stop stunning the public or observers from the beginning in 2007 to the conclusion of the last court cases in 2013. The whole episode came to an end with draconian sentences handed down to more than 250 defendants.[41] The initial reaction from many quarters was to see the trials as part of a legitimate action by the Turkish government to thwart any attempt to overthrow an elected government by the "tutelary regime." The trials were for the most part considered a natural process on the path to democratization. The EU also stated an opinion along those lines, referring to the trials as "an opportunity for Turkey to strengthen confidence in the proper functioning of its democratic institutions and the rule of law."[42]

A cloud of suspicion soon settled over the whole affair, however. It did not take long for questions to emerge with respect to the handling of the investigations and the conduct of the proceedings. There were also doubts as to whether the rights of the defendants had been preserved. As early as 2011 Dani Rodrik, a Harvard University economist who had gained firsthand familiarity with the process, drew attention to the political nature of the trials. In a *Financial Times* article he pointed out that "[Turkey] is headed towards becoming a Middle Eastern version of Russia, with the media and courts increasingly becoming tools of political manipulation."[43] The warning went unheeded. The trials struck at the heart of the opposition and effectively destroyed many centers of secularist resistance to the AKP and its vision for an Islamist-leaning "new Turkey."[44] Positions, especially military ones, thus vacated by the members of the secularist establishment were quickly filled by Gülenists sympathetic to the AKP government.[45] This came on top of a years-long, if not decades-long, campaign to place members of the movement into Turkish bureaucracy, mainly in the police force and the gendarmerie, as well as the judiciary. The expression "parallel state" gained popularity to represent the project that was driven by a conviction on the part of Gülen that the state was "the most important institution in the promotion, as well as in the 'defense,' of his religious vision and movement from enemies within the security establishment."[46] A prominent conservative Turkish columnist, Taha Akyol, called this a process driven by the goal to achieve complete "control of the state."[47]

The political nature of the trials became more evident with the breakup of the alliance between the government and the Gülen movement, especially after the corruption allegations of December 2013. Erdoğan wasted no time distancing himself from the whole process and turning on the Gülen movement early in 2014 as a vicious power struggle became public.[48] The wind had turned so quickly and so drastically that one of his advisers saw no contradiction in claiming the above court rulings—once supported by the AKP—to be a "plot against their own country's national army."[49] Eventually the victims were released from prison when their convictions were overturned on appeal. As one of the former defendants, a two-star general, noted, this became possible because of the power struggle that erupted between the government and the Gülenists.[50] The tension increased in May 2016 when the government declared the Gülen movement a terrorist group, naming it the Gülenist Terror Organization (Fethullahçı Terör Örgütü, or FETÖ). This was followed by the elimination, in a speedier fashion than before, of those suspected to be close to the movement from the ranks of the police corps as well as the judiciary. There was talk of more to come.[51]

A similar cleansing, this time within the military, was deemed imminent by the Gülenist camp. This perception has come to be widely recognized as the main reason for the coup attempt of July 2016. As of this writing, the backstory as to who exactly was involved and what actually happened remains somewhat unclear.[52] However, in Turkey there is a strong consensus among observers that it was instigated by Gülenist civilians in close coordination with their high-ranking military collaborators.[53] One prominent Turkish journalist has convincingly argued that many of the plotters were the very officers who had stepped into the positions of their former colleagues, sentenced to long prison terms at the end of the Ergenekon and Sledgehammer trials.[54] Furthermore, as the trials of those accused of the coup attempt gathered pace in the summer of 2017, more background details are emerging from indictments and court proceedings, but the full picture will take a while to emerge.[55] Others have proposed that the Gülenists did not act alone and that the coup was the product of a coalition that included other anti-Erdoğan groups within the military.[56] The leader of the Republican People's Party (CHP), Kemal Kılıçdaroğlu, argued that what had happened was actually a "controlled coup" to justify government repression.[57] The true picture of what actually transpired will take some time to emerge as the trials of the main suspects, which started in May and July 2017, unfold over time.[58]

The night of July 15, 2016, witnessed large numbers of Turks coming out into the streets to block the coup attempt. Some of them had responded to the call of the president, the same Erdoğan who had not hesitated to label anyone who took to the streets during the Gezi protests a *çapulcu*. More significant, part of the popular resistance against the putschists that night came about even before Erdoğan appeared on TV screens; it was the result of spontaneous actions organized through social media and mosque networks.[59] The threat of a coup was also alarming to the opposition. All the political parties, including the Kurdish Peoples' Democratic Party (HDP), stood up for the elected government despite their differences. In the meantime, Erdoğan saw his popularity rating reach an unprecedented 68 percent.[60] These developments were reason enough for some observers to start nurturing the hope that this might help the country revitalize its weakened democracy. A commentary in the *Financial Times* argued that "the crisis offers Mr Erdoğan an opportunity to return to the moderate style that served him well in the early years of his premiership, when Turkey's economy and society thrived in an environment of greater tolerance."[61]

The announcement of a state of emergency, and the accompanying suspension of judicial oversight, brought an abrupt end to this optimism. A massive purge followed that targeted not only any individual or institution suspected of being implicated in the coup attempt or of having ties to the Gülen organization. Tens of thousands of public officials, among them schoolteachers, legislators, and academics, were detained within a span of a few months. Thousands of others were detained, mostly on curiously vague charges, while several news outlets and businesses—some run by the Gülenists, others thought to be somehow connected to the movement—were taken over by the government.[62] The media sustained their share of the repression too, leading Rod Nordland of the *New York Times* to argue that Turkey had become "the world's biggest jailer of journalists," outstripping China.[63] At the time of writing, July 2017, these measures had not yet been opened to judicial appeal, perpetuating concerns about the rule of law and the rights of the innocent.[64] The situation has been aggravated by Erdoğan's repeated attempts to reintroduce capital punishment, which was taken off the books in 2004—ironically, by his own government.[65] Another issue that has caused alarm for many is the growing number of reports of torture, a practice that successive AKP governments were openly proud to have eradicated.[66] It is not surprising that the leader of the main opposition party, Kemal Kılıçdaroğlu, argued early in October 2016 that Turkey had become a "semi-open prison," and when the police raided the long-standing opposition paper *Cumhuriyet*, he went on to accuse the government of trying to build a Baathist regime in Turkey.[67] In June 2017 he set out on a long march from Ankara to Istanbul calling for "justice" that culminated in a huge rally in July 2017 attended by hundred thousands of protesters.[68] This, however, did not seem to have impressed Erdoğan, who accused the CHP of giving support to terrorism and undermining national unity. He instead called for the continuation of the state of emergency as long as necessary. In sum, the coup attempt further aggravated Turkey's drift away from liberal democracy and the accompanying political, economic, and social miracles.

THE KURDISH ISSUE AND THE RETURN OF VIOLENCE

Another area that has suffered visible setbacks was to efforts to improve the situation of the Kurdish minority in Turkey and resolve the conflict between the PKK and the Turkish state. The positive climate that had built up through Erdoğan's striving for a peaceful resolution of the problem had already begun to erode before the coup attempt. The turning point had been the siege of Kobane by IS during the summer of 2014. Turkey's reluctance to intervene on the side of the Kurdish forces in this fight, which took place mere yards from the Turkish side of the Turkey-Syrian border, was not well received by Kurds. The situation provoked deep mistrust of the Turkish state among Kurds and should be counted as one of the main factors that undermined the peace process.[69] The protests that erupted in Kurdish-populated towns in southeastern Turkey were violently repressed by the government, leading to tens of deaths. The eventual decision to open the Turkish border to allow the Peshmerga from the Kurdistan Regional Government to come to the defense of Kobane did not improve the climate. Instead, a personal feud broke out between Erdoğan and the leader of the HDP, Selahattin Demirtaş, during the run-up to the June 2015 national elections. The latter's fierce opposition to Erdoğan's ambitions to transform Turkey's parliamentary system into an executive presidential system added to general Kurdish resentment of the government and earned the HDP enough votes to enter parliament. The results cost the AKP the majority it had enjoyed for many years (see figure 4-1).[70]

The events that followed the June 2015 elections further distanced Turkey from its course toward a liberal democracy. The country found itself in a state of increasing instability as the parties failed to form a coalition government, while a new round of violence swept across the southeastern regions. The explosion of an IS bomb in the Kurdish town of Suruç, across from Kobane on the other side of the border, was followed by the PKK declaring an end to the cease-fire that had been in place since 2013. In the face of this fast-worsening situation, Erdoğan's response was to call for repeat elections, while seeking to expand his electoral basis on a fierce rhetoric of nationalism. His strategy of presenting AKP rule as the key to stability paid off in the elections, which took place on November 1, 2015. The AKP received close to 50 percent of the vote total, winning a comfortable majority to form a government on its own. The HDP, on the other hand, barely entered parliament: the number of seats it held fell from eighty in June to fifty-nine. Most important, the repeat elections were soon followed by further escalation of violence when Kurdish militant youth closely associated with the PKK instigated an armed rebellion in Kurdish populated towns in southeastern parts of Turkey. The attempt seemed much inspired by developments across the border in Syria where the Kurdish Democratic Union Party (PYD) was expanding its territorial control and developing closer relations with the U.S. in the fight against IS.

The bitter confrontation between Kurdish militants and Turkish security forces took its toll in death and destruction, turning the urban landscape in the Kurdish-populated areas into displays of war violence, not unlike the scenes from Iraq and Syria.[71] This, however, gave Erdoğan an opportunity to scuttle the peace process, "resecuritize" the Kurdish question, isolate Demirtaş, and peel off conservative Kurdish votes from the HDP.[72] Furthermore, parliament lifted the immunities of a number of Kurdish deputies while dismissing or arresting the elected mayors of a string of Kurdish-populated cities, including Diyarbakır, the largest one.[73] The actual detention of Demirtaş and his HDP coleader, Figen Yüksekdağ, evoked images from another dark period in 1994 when Kurdish deputies had again been dragged out of the Turkish parliament. The 1990s is also being invoked in the context of fears of "disappearances and extrajudicial executions" as security authorities resort to methods that many hoped had been left behind for good.[74] These developments also suggested how far politics in Turkey had changed in the course of just a few years, how the pendulum had swung from peaceful aspirations, from the language of hope and compromise, to instability and a situation exacerbated by the venom of populist, nationalistic rhetoric.[75]

END OF THE RAPPROCHEMENT WITH THE ARMENIAN COMMUNITY

Relations with other minorities, the Armenian community in particular, were another area in which the AKP government regressed from its earlier liberal approach. The thaw of the mid-2000s did continue for some time, though not without certain setbacks. Parliamentary resolutions in a number of Western countries recognizing Ottoman actions against the Armenians as genocide drew a strong reaction from Erdoğan, who in turn threatened to deport more than 100,000 illegal immigrants from Armenia. The connotation of the term "deportation" was not lost on the Armenian community at large.[76]

The same year, on the other hand, also witnessed the holding of the first religious service in a landmark Armenian church in Van after a decades-long interruption. This had been made possible following a massive restoration initiated by Erdoğan's government. During a speech to mark the occasion, then Minister of EU Affairs Egemen Bağış proudly announced that the service was a sign of an increasingly liberal and tolerant Turkey that was overcoming its taboos. Efforts made by the government to ensure the return of Armenian properties that had once been confiscated by the state also earned the government praise during this period. A more significant step toward a thaw came from Erdoğan in 2014, on the eve of the ninety-ninth anniversary of April 24, the date commemorated by Armenians as the start of deportations. In an unexpected gesture, going further than any other Turkish politician had in republican history, Erdoğan described the events of 1915 as "inhumane," and referred to the episode as "our shared pain." His conciliatory remarks included a message of condolence to the grandchildren of those who lost their lives during what he called "mass killings," and he referred to "our shared pain" in remembering the large number of Muslims who were also killed during World War I.[77]

The following year brought additional pressure on the Turkish government as the approaching centenary led to growing international interest in the issue. A number of Western countries, including the European Parliament, called on Turkey to come to terms with this dark episode in its history; some passed resolutions that recognized the events of 1915 as genocide. Turkey reacted by recalling its ambassadors. When Pope Francis used the same term, Prime Minister Ahmet Davutoğlu accused him of belonging to an "evil gang" working against Turkey's interests.[78] The government, in the meantime, sought to draw the world's attention to another chapter in Ottoman history, one that evoked heroism rather than shame. The year 2015, being also the centenary of the Gallipoli battles where the Ottoman army had succeeded in repulsing a massive Allied attack on the Dardanelles and the surrounding peninsula, presented an opportunity for the Turkish government to draw international attention. This was also aided by the fact that the commemoration was attended, as in previous years, by several heads of state and dignitaries from Western countries. The Turkish government held the official centennial ceremony on the Gallipoli peninsula on April 24 instead of April 25, which was the day historically observed in the British Commonwealth. Clearly, this was seen as a maneuver to divert attention from the commemoration programs highly publicized by the Armenians around the world, and it is questionable whether it produced any positive effects.[79] Relations with Armenia remained tense; as for the situation at home, the positive atmosphere that had emerged with the opening of the churches in 2010 has been replaced by disappointment and concern as services were again suspended, on the ground of a deteriorating security situation in Turkey's southeast.[80]

A similar situation exists with regard to other minority groups in Turkey. The banning in 2016 of the annual religious service at the Sümela Monastery near Trabzon is a case in point. The site, which is of historical significance to the Greek community, had opened its doors to worshippers in 2010, after a hiatus of eighty-eight years.[81] The government based its decision on the ground that the restoration project at the monastery had not been finished and constituted a safety hazard for visitors.[82] Media reporting that ancient religious properties belonging to the small Assyrian community in Turkey were being confiscated by local authorities in the southeastern regions of Turkey and being turned over to the Department of Religious Affairs engendered concerns as well as contradicted Erdoğan's reassurances from 2013.[83] The LGBT community also suffered a similar setback in June 2016 and 2017 when it was banned from holding a parade in Istanbul. The preparations for "Istanbul Pride" attracted the ire of radical Islamic and nationalist groups, who threatened to attack parade participants, which led the authorities to officially cancel the march. Those who showed up nevertheless were forcefully dispersed and some detained.[84] Interestingly, it was again under AKP rule, in 2003, that the LGBT community had been granted permission to hold a parade, the first time ever. Yet, after more than ten years their request to hold the parade was being fiercely rejected by the authorities. By 2016 they had lost those small gains, and the whole episode revealed a situation in which the government elected to punish people under threat while the aggressors went unpunished. Creating a safe environment for the exercise of a basic civil right had ceased to be of concern and interest for the government.[85]

THE ECONOMY TAKES A HIT

The retreat from liberal democracy inevitably affected the performance of the Turkish economy. According to the International Monetary Fund (IMF), the Turkish economy grew at an average annual rate of 4.8 percent between 2002 and 2015, putting Turkey considerably ahead of Argentina, Russia, and Brazil, as well as the world average annual rate of 2.8 percent.[86] The dynamism and growth performance of the Turkish economy had made it the darling of the world. Erdoğan had promised to put Turkey among the top ten economies of the world by 2023, the centenary of the establishment of the Turkish Republic. Instead, the growth rate of the economy slowed significantly, and Turkey experienced a contraction of 1.8 percentage points in the third quarter of 2016, the first time since 2009.[87] The rebound in exports helped the economy recover and complete the year with a 2.9 percent overall growth rate. However, this was significantly lower than the 4.1 percent growth rate experienced by emerging market and developing economies as outlined by the IMF for the end of 2016.[88] The coup attempt also adversely affected the economy and contributed to the erosion of the national currency against the U.S. dollar.[89]

Nevertheless, the economy did recover in the first quarter of 2017, registering an impressive growth rate of 5 percent. Although Deputy Prime Minister Mehmet Şimşek expected this performance to continue throughout the rest of the year, such optimism has been subdued beyond government circles.[90] Economists, for instance, have attributed this growth to expansionary measures, especially making abundant cheap credit available to businesses and consumers during the run up to the constitutional referendum in April, as well as improving global conditions that helped boost Turkish exports.[91] They highlight how these policies have not actually helped to improve productivity, and that this is manifested in persistent high unemployment and inflation rates.[92]

The government had attributed the poorer performance in 2016 primarily to "geopolitical challenges" and slow growth rates in Europe. As much as the first quarter of 2017 projected a promising picture, there are fundamental structural problems facing the Turkish economy. They are closely associated with the deteriorating quality of governance, particularly with respect to accountability and transparency in business deals. The very regulatory bodies that were once recognized as central to Turkey's economic recovery from the 2001 financial crisis have seen their independence under constant challenge if not erosion. The loss of the "EU anchor" has also undermined confidence in the economy aggravated by the growing instability and repression in the country. Many in Turkey, including serving ministers as well as former president Gül, have pointed out the urgent need to end the "war on the market economy," boost the rule of law, and upgrade democracy to help energize the Turkish economy.[93] This deteriorating investment climate is also complicated by growing governmental interference with the economy and business. Many businesses were confiscated for their alleged connection to the coup attempt and the Gülen movement without due process of law, which has forged an inhospitable investment climate and eroded investors' trust in the Turkish government.[94] This climate was further exacerbated when a controversial list with the names of hundreds of German companies surfaced in July 2017, accusing them of having similar links. Not surprisingly, FDI flows into the country dropped by 30 percentage points, to $12 billion in 2016 from $17.5 billion in 2015, suggesting falling international confidence in the Turkish economy.[95] Clearly, earlier commitment to policies supportive of a liberal market economy has faded. As put by an American academic, Erdoğan, like Putin, prefers "to use the power of the state to reward business leaders who are loyal and to punish anyone who gets in the way," creating a situation in which "statism would trump capitalism."[96] Finally, there are also internally driven structural causes behind the slowdown in the economy and Turkey's failure to transform its industrial sector into a high-tech one.[97] The government's education policies, which increasingly focus on religiosity, are failing to provide the human capital needed to help this transformation.[98] Not surprisingly, the World Bank warned in 2014 that Turkey was at risk of being caught in a middle-income trap unless it introduced reform and encouraged innovation.[99]

DRIVERS OF REGRESSION

Just as it is difficult to pinpoint any single moment as the start of the political and economic downturn that afflicted Turkey, it would also be too narrow to attribute the situation to a single factor. A deterioration in EU-Turkish relations can, however, be cited as one important reason. In the academic literature there is considerable agreement that the EU's engagement of Turkey was "not necessarily the principal explanatory variable of Turkey's domestic transformation, but represent[ed] a fundamental explanatory variable."[100] The same argument applies in the opposite direction, suggesting that the EU's weakening interest in Turkey's bid for membership was an important factor contributing to the reversals in the reform process.[101] As two Turkey experts have noted, "Many Turks felt that if the EU was not serious about the accession negotiations, there was no reason why they should be."[102] One point that needs to be noted, in all fairness, is the commitment demonstrated by Erdoğan on the path to fulfilling the requirements for accession even as the EU began to show signs of wavering support amid calls for a privileged partnership rather than full membership. The prime minister had expressed his resolve then by saying that "if the promises are not kept, then we will name the Copenhagen criteria as Ankara criteria and continue our own way."[103] Reforms did continue after the "golden age of Europeanization" of 2002–05, but with weakening commitment and enthusiasm, in a form that has been fittingly termed "loose Europeanization."[104]

Loose Europeanization was partially the outcome of a decline in the trust invested by AKP supporters in the social legitimacy of the EU. To put it bluntly, the EU did "not make the news anymore," or, as stated by Minister for EU Affairs Egemen Bağış, the EU did not "sell" to the public.[105] According to one expert, this was not unexpected, considering the divisions that existed between Turkey and the EU member countries across the lines of identity and religion; in this sense, the AKP's initial resolve to join the EU was even described as "irrational."[106] Hence it is not surprising that Erdoğan hardly mentioned the EU in his address to his party at the Fourth Regular Congress in October 2012.[107] The goal of membership was number sixty on the list of sixty-three priorities cited in the document listing the AKP's vision for 2023, the centennial of the Turkish Republic. Clearly, this marked a sharp contrast to the position held in 2002.[108]

It was, in fact, the promise of improvements in utilitarian issues, such as the free movement of labor, and the expectation of economic benefits that made it possible for the AKP to ensure support among its base for EU membership.[109] The EU was also seen by the party's elite as a vehicle that could not only help loosen the grip of state control over religion and weaken "assertive secularism" but also bolster the legitimacy of their rule. A critical issue in that context was the ban on the wearing of headscarves in universities. The European Court of Human Rights' ruling in *Leyla Sahin v. Turkey* in 2004, that the banning of headscarves in Turkish universities did not violate the European Convention on Human Rights, was also a factor contributing to the loss of enthusiasm for the EU, even though the court is not part of the EU. Hence, Eurofatigue and Euroskepticism returned quickly to the ranks of the AKP.[110]

Other domestic political factors also contributed to the loose Europeanization, which eventually slackened into further disassociation from EU ideals. One indication of weakening interest can be found in Erdoğan's speeches to the Turkish parliament. His references to the EU fell almost to a trickle beginning roughly right after the 2007 elections.[111] This is not surprising in light of the decisive win with 47 percent of the votes (see figure 4-1) that the AKP achieved and the boost in confidence both the party and its leader realized as a result. The perception of EU membership as a kind of insurance policy against the military and secular establishment began to wane from that point on. Furthermore, the decisive win had come on the heels of the Turkish military's "e-memorandum," issued in an effort to preempt Abdullah Gül, then the minister of foreign affairs and cofounder of the AKP, from being elected president by parliament. This was accompanied by mass protests by secularists and parts of the Turkish civil society fearful of a hidden agenda that aspired to Islamize the country.

The main opposition party, the CHP, in the meantime continued to pursue its policy of resistance to reforms, especially the one aiming to lift the ban on female students wearing headscarves from attending universities.[112] Many CHP supporters were also less than forthcoming on some of the EU reforms that AKP was trying to get through. A former CHP deputy could not help wondering where Turkey's democracy might have been today if "my hard-line colleagues had been less impertinent toward Erdoğan, and more accommodating of AKP's reform initiatives when they were compatible with the EU acquis."[113] The government's attempts to prepare a new constitution to replace the one dating from the military intervention of 1980 also failed in the face of a polarized political climate in parliament. The country projected an image of a highly polarized one trapped in a *Kulturkampf*.[114] In the meantime, the AKP barely weathered an attempt to have the party closed down, just as its predecessors such as Refah and others had been. However, in July 2008 the Constitutional Court ruled on a technicality against the charge that the AKP was involved in "anti-constitutional activities intended to undermine the secular character of the Turkish Republic."[115]

THE AKP'S GROWING HEGEMONY AND THE EMERGENCE OF "NEW" TURKEY

Overcoming and surviving these challenges clearly sharpened Erdoğan's political ambitions in favor of a more authoritarian form of governance and enabled the AKP to gradually establish a hegemony in Turkish politics.[116] There began a marked slowdown in the reform process, as the European Commission noted in its 2008 progress report. There also emerged signs of interference with the freedom of the media when, in response to growing criticism, the press accreditation of several journalists who covered the prime ministry was rescinded. That step led *The Economist* in November 2008 to describe Erdoğan as "increasingly autocratic."[117] The following years only brought more pressure on the media as several news outlets critical of the government became targets of tax investigations and exclusion from public tenders.[118] One prominent Turkish columnist writing as early as in November 2009 warned that Turkey was facing the risk of slipping into "civilian tyranny."[119]

However, these developments did not in any way undermine the popularity of Erdoğan and the AKP among the electorate. In 2010 the government was able to push through, with an impressive majority of 58 percent of votes, constitutional amendments meant to help end the tutelary regime. This outcome has been seen as an important step toward the AKP consolidating its power, enabling the government to enhance its control of the judiciary (to the detriment of the rule of law) and opening the way to "Erdoğan's majoritarian drift."[120] The Ergenekon and Sledgehammer indictments also weakened, in these years, the judiciary and the military, institutions that had long been regarded as prepared not only to defend secularism but also to check the power of the AKP. The "death blow" to the tutelary regime came with the April 2017 constitutional referendum, discussed below, that adopted amendments bringing the military and bureaucracy under the tighter control of the new executive presidency and hence Erdoğan.[121]

This drift became even more pronounced when Erdoğan adopted an increasingly majoritarian view of democracy once the AKP received close to 50 percent of the votes at the 2011 national elections. This result would send Turkey down a path of a highly centralized, executive form of democracy.[122] Critical to this process was Erdoğan's conception that the vote was "a mandate to refashion the country according to his own values,"[123] which also explains his growing eagerness for a presidential system equipped with broad and unchecked powers. The opportunity to push for this came in August 2014 when, in contrast to past practice, the Turkish electorate went to the voting booth to directly elect a president. During the run-up to the elections, Erdoğan made it clear that he would seek the transformation of Turkey's parliamentary system into a presidential one and declared that until then, he would behave like one, irrespective of constitutional restrictions.[124] This would be a form of government where the ballot box would be the only instrument of accountability and democratic legitimacy, without the checks and balances associated with a liberal democracy.[125] Erdoğan won the presidential election with close to 52 percent of the votes, de facto amassing executive authority into his hands.

Ironically, the coup attempt of July 2016 was to Erdoğan a "gift from God," as he put it. It proved to be an opportunity to tighten his grip on power. Hopes that the support he received against the putschists might lead to efforts to revitalize democracy could not be entertained for long. Instead, Erdoğan adopted a very populist and nationalist discourse, arguing that Turkey was facing internal and external enemies that required unity and a powerful executive at the helm of the state to defeat them. In an ironic manner, he even adopted a narrative associating himself with Atatürk by calling the struggle ahead a "second national liberation war."[126] Erdoğan worked closely with Devlet Bahçeli, the leader of the Nationalist Action Party (MHP), and got the parliament to adopt a package of amendments to the constitution that sought to transform Turkey from a parliamentary system into a presidential one.[127] The amendments were submitted to a referendum in April 2017 and passed by a tight vote of 51.4 percent in favor and 48.6 percent against. Once these amendments take effect in 2019, they will enable the current president, Recep Tayyip Erdoğan, to enjoy dramatically enhanced executive powers with very limited checks and balances. The position of prime minister will disappear, and ministers appointed by Erdoğan from outside the parliament will form the executive cabinet. (Currently, the cabinet is composed of members of parliament.) He will also enjoy considerable influence over the composition of the judiciary and higher echelons of the state bureaucracy. Erdoğan will then be able to stay at the helm of government until 2029, if he continues to win the popular vote for two terms. If parliament calls for snap elections toward the end of his second term, his presidency could be extended until 2034. Should that happen, the current president will have been in power for more than three decades, a tenure unprecedented in Turkish republican history.

The report prepared by the Organization for Security and Cooperation in Europe monitoring team noted that the "referendum took place on an unlevel playing field and the two sides of the campaign did not have equal opportunities. Voters were not provided with impartial information about key aspects of the reform, and civil society organizations were not able to participate."[128] Supporters who voted yes were the ones who enjoyed overwhelming access to the media, while critics—whether politicians, journalists, or others—were muzzled, and some detained, through the various provisions of the state of emergency rule. Notably, even the prime minister, a staunch Erdoğan loyalist, remarked that the country never had a chance to discuss the proposed amendments.[129] The referendum was more a popularity contest for Erdoğan than an informed vote on the content of the proposals. This was also accompanied by allegations of voting irregularities that cast an additional shadow on the legitimacy of the results, leaving the country once more deeply divided. Metropolitan centers such as Ankara, Antalya, Istanbul, and İzmir—three of which are governed by AKP mayors—as well as all the provinces along the Aegean and Mediterranean coasts voted no, as did many of the Kurdish-populated southeastern regions of Turkey. The yes votes came largely from along the Black Sea coast, including Erdoğan's home province, and the conservative parts of central and eastern Anatolia.

It is against this background that the Parliamentary Assembly of the Council of Europe (PACE) expressed its concerns about the state of democracy in Turkey and decided to restart monitoring Turkey, a process it had relaxed in 2004 in response to reforms adopted by the new AKP government in power.[130] Turkey thus became the first country to be returned to monitoring after exiting it and now finds itself in the same league as Albania, Armenia, Azerbaijan, Bosnia-Herzegovina, Georgia, Moldova, Serbia, Russia, and Ukraine. The degree of regression is further accentuated by the fact that only a few years earlier Turkey's minister of foreign affairs, Mevlüt Çavuşoğlu, had served as the president of PACE.[131] The PACE decision followed by the European Parliament one that recommended to the European Commission and EU member states to formally suspend Turkey's membership talks if the constitutional amendments were implemented unchanged.[132]

FROM MUSLIM DEMOCRATS TO ONE-MAN RULE

A number of domestic developments have facilitated Erdoğan's con-solidation of power over the years and the gradual erosion of Turkish democracy. The manner in which he pushed out many of his colleagues, including some of AKP cofounders, is particularly important.[133] These included party members deeply committed to AKP's original political agenda, and they once represented diverse interests within the party, ranging from center right to liberals and the Kurdish minority. A case in point is Abdullah Gül. Gül, throughout his political career, first as a brief caretaker prime minister for Erdoğan and then as minister of foreign af-fairs from 2003 to 2007, and subsequently as president until 2014, rep-resented a more liberal political perspective tolerant of diversity. This was reflected, for example, in his remarks in October 2009 when he ar-gued that a modern democracy needs to provide guarantees for "the free-dom and rights of those who think differently from the majority." He went on to underline the importance of cherishing diversity and not in-sisting on one standard to fit all.[134] When the Gezi Park protests erupted, he called for moderation and urged the police to be more sensitive in dealing with protesters.[135] Protests and demonstrations, he said, were "a natural part of democracy." He also revealed a fundamental disagree-ment with Erdoğan's notion of majoritarian democracy by noting that true democracy "does not only mean elections."[136] The two clashed over Twitter: Erdoğan promised to "wipe out" the service, while Gül held that "websites should only be blocked if courts found that they had violated personal privacy."[137] Not surprisingly, as Gül's term of office as president was coming to an end, Erdoğan made sure he could not return to poli-tics in the ranks of the AKP.[138] The AKP party congress to elect a new leader and prime minister once Erdoğan became president was held one day before Gül completed his presidential term of office, effectively pre-venting him from competing for these positions.

Ahmet Davutoğlu, who became the party leader and served as prime minister after Erdoğan, experienced a similar fate. Davutoğlu was forced to resign in May 2016 amid growing disagreements with Erdoğan. Davutoğlu's position had been uncompromising with regard to the impeachment of the ministers and AKP deputies implicated in the corruption scandal of 2013. Also, as a former academic, he had displayed a more favorable disposition on the issue of the freedom of expression; in particular, his defense of academics who had signed a statement critical of the government's handling of the Kurdish issue late in 2015 had not been in line with Erdoğan's stance.[139] His willingness to explore the prospects of a coalition government with the leading opposition party after the AKP lost the majority in the June 2015 elections and his lukewarm support for the presidential system were additional sources of tension with Erdoğan. Davutoğlu's readiness to work with the West, his willingness to jump into the limelight during the process, as happened when he brokered an immigration deal with the EU in March 2016, is reported to have irritated Erdoğan. This also came on the heels of growing criticism of his Syria policy, and Davutoğlu's premiership ended in what is reported to be a forced resignation.[140] The AKP elected Binali Yıldırım, an Erdoğan loyalist, as replacement. Yıldırım proved to constitute less of a threat to Erdoğan and implemented his political agenda with rigor.

Having assured his own future as an elected president, Erdoğan insisted on the application of a party bylaw that no elected official could run for the same elected office for more than three terms. This reportedly enabled him to replace former deputies with handpicked candidates, including his own son-in-law, for the ill-fated elections of June 2015, as well as the repeat one in November 2015. The composition of the AKP parliamentarians has since become more political-Islam oriented, especially compared to the profile of the deputies from the 2002 and 2007 elections. In between elections the party has grown homogenized, with a larger proportion of the deputies coming from the National Outlook background. The AKP's center-right, liberal, and "conservative democrat" members either have been purged or have quit the party.[141] Though there were more than seventy official founders of the party back in 2001, representing a very diverse background, the names of thirteen, in a typical example of rewriting history, have been removed from the current official list of founders on the AKP website.[142] A case in point is that of Yaşar Yakış, a retired diplomat who also served as the minister of foreign affairs in the early months of the first AKP cabinet and played a critical role in Turkey's EU accession process, including as one of the Turkish representatives at the convention for establishing a constitution for Europe in 2003. He defined himself as "not even an Islamist or conservative, but rather a staunch democrat,"[143] and saw himself ejected from the party in March 2016 after serving two terms in parliament. The stated cause was having links to the Gülen movement, but he was better known for his virulent criticisms of governmental policies on a range of issues, from its attacks on freedom of expression and crumbling relations with the West to the regime's vision for Syria, where he had once served as a diplomat.

Erdoğan's growing authoritarianism is also explained as a function of weak opposition on the political scene. The CHP faces the brunt as the largest opposition party in the parliament and has been criticized, along with its leader, Kemal Kılıçdaroğlu, for failing to come up with a convincing party program and a vision to win votes. Instead, the party has remained divided within itself between those wanting to pursue a liberal democratic pro-EU agenda and those who have tried to maintain a more nationalist and hard-line secularist posture. The latter group was especially effective under the party's previous leadership and had approached the AKP's EU orientation with suspicion and resisted some of the key reforms.[144] Though the party has since moved toward a relatively more liberal position, it has failed to receive more than 27 percent of the votes. It was actually the leader of the HDP, Selahattin Demirtaş, who somewhat unexpectedly emerged as a popular leader, especially during the run-up to the June 2015 elections, with a program focused on liberalism and diversity that succeeded in winning more than 13 percent of the votes. Demirtaş's vision and the challenge he mounted to Erdoğan's aspiration to transform Turkey into a presidential system earned him considerable support among both liberal Turks and conservative Kurds, who traditionally voted for the AKP.[145] However, against the background of the return of PKK violence, Erdoğan was able to convince an important part of the electorate that only he could deliver stability and security to Turkey, thus weakening the HDP's base of support. Furthermore, the AKP, by exploiting the HDP's liberal and secular image among conservative Kurdish circles, succeeded in peeling away some of the Kurdish votes as well.[146]

In the meantime, growing government control over the media has hampered the efforts of the opposition parties to make their voice heard. The 2015 election campaign and the run-up to the referendum in 2017 were marked by complaints about unequal media time for the opposition and intimidation. Compared to the past, concerns have multiplied over how free and fair Turkish elections can be held up to be. Since the coup attempt in July 2016, the situation has worsened; *Cumhuriyet*, one of the few remaining opposition newspapers and also closely associated with the CHP, has seen its offices raided and some of its journalists detained. Their trial received considerable international attention. *The Economist* highlighted the absurdity of accusing one of the journalists,

Ahmet Şık, who had been tried during the Ergenekon and Sledgehammer trials for exposing the Gülen movement's efforts to run a "parallel state," this time for aiding the Gülenists.[147] Many Kurdish newspapers and TV stations have also been shut down on the grounds of antiterrorism charges. Similarly, Demirtaş was first stripped of his parliamentary immunity, together with a number of his colleagues, then later detained, again on the grounds of supporting the PKK and its terrorist activities. He risks 142 years of imprisonment.[148] Under these circumstances, it would be difficult to blame the opposition for lack of effectiveness and absence of vision. Instead these developments are seen by commentators as manifestations of Erdoğan's ambition to take Turkey on a journey of ever greater "conservativism and authoritarianism," as well as nationalism and anti-Westernism.[149]

One last factor that can help explain the rise of Erdoğan as an authoritarian leader is Turkey's political culture and the nature of its party politics. The Turkish electorate since 1950 has participated in eighteen national and thirteen local elections with quite impressive voter turnouts, often well above 80 percent.[150] There is general recognition of the Turkish electorate's attachment to democratic elections. This is also supported by public opinion surveys. However, these surveys also reveal that Turkish public opinion is much less attached to the civil liberties associated with liberal democracy, such as freedom of expression and the media, and prefer to sacrifice them in favor of stability and order.[151] Over the last few decades the Turkish public has shifted to the right and become more religious in its political preferences.[152] Furthermore, Turkish political party politics is such that, independent of ideology, the party leader commands enormous authority and power. This applies also to the social democrat CHP: its supporters "are no different in their acceptance of an authoritarian, strong leader than are supporters" of the MHP or the AKP.[153] The CHP is recognized for its deep attachment to secularism yet has shown a disturbing "lack of any genuine understanding of or commitment to individual freedom."[154]

When combined with the "low tolerance of deviance" observed in Turkish society, this creates a climate conducive to obedience.[155] In the case of the AKP, this even led a former adviser to Erdoğan to complain about the lack of institutionalization in the party and the need for Erdoğan to intervene and regulate mundane issues at the lowest level within the party.[156] This is not particular to Erdoğan. As a commentator noted, "Turkey has never had a liberal leader."[157] Erdoğan fits well the profile of what a scholar of Turkish studies has called the tradition of "bigman" leadership and its accompanying "bigman" politics, which allow little room for pluralism.[158] This may also explain why a Pew survey conducted in 2013 found that preference "for democracy over powerful leader" at 67 percent was lower than in many other Muslim countries, such as Lebanon (81 percent), Kosovo and Tajikistan (76 percent each), and Tunisia (75 percent), not to mention most sub-Saharan African countries (average 70.4 percent).[159] These characteristics of Turkish politics and public opinion have clearly facilitated Erdoğan's task of consolidating his power and authority.

Since his election as president, Erdoğan, who once was the face of reform in Turkey and a symbol of its encounter with liberal democracy, has first transformed his party into "a single-man party" and Turkey into "a single-man regime."[160] This reality was symbolically captured by one of his presidential advisers, just as in May 2016 Davutoğlu was addressing his AKP colleagues and toying with the idea of resignation, who passed around a note that read "Turkey=RTE=AK Party."[161] Such a single-man regime is also one reason why commentators have noted parallels between Erdoğan's rule and that of Vladimir Putin.[162] Interestingly, Erdoğan's entourage nowadays increasingly refers to him as *"reis"* (chief) and his rule as *"reiscilik."* Such a conception of leadership is in line with Erdoğan's mentor Kısakürek's ideal leader, the *Başyüce*. This is an authoritarian leader that, in the words of one Turkish academic who has studied Kısakürek's works very closely, enjoys "discretion to do what they think is best without much regard for what people want."[163] This is what makes him, in the words of one commentator, an "imperial president" that is someone who aspires for total control and cannot stand any challenger to his popularity.[164] His successful efforts to transform Turkey into a presidential system can be read as an exercise no more than formalizing a de facto situation that does not appear likely to stop the regression away from democracy, let alone a "liberal" one. Instead, it is "a new form of democracy that the West neither likes nor understands: an authoritarian regime that exalts the will of the majority."[165]

CONCLUSION

When the AKP embarked on democratic reforms soon after it came to power in 2002, it was perceived as anomalous that a political party with Islamist roots should strive for more democracy. That it also brought Turkey closest to EU membership prospects seemed like a significant paradox.[166] At the helm of his government, Erdoğan gave Turkey a taste of liberal democracy; for a brief period, there seemed to be a promise that the country could finally be at ease with its ethnic, religious, and political diversity and become anchored in the transatlantic community. The improvements made in this direction eroded fast, however. Again under Erdoğan, Turkey drifted into a politics of regression that has expanded the fault lines with respect to the tenets and values of this community. Erdoğan's form of government and personality cult have become much more closely associated with the ways of Russia's Putin, president of a country where media freedom is restricted, the opposition is suppressed, and civil liberties are ignored.[167] It is no wonder that Freedom in the World 2017 reports Turkey as a country where civil liberties and the rule of law have declined substantially, placing it just after Central African Republic and barely ahead of Gambia.[168] In the summer of 2017, it would be difficult to argue that Turkey adheres to the principles that sustain the international liberal order.

Ironically, Erdoğan has declared the day of the coup attempt is to be celebrated as Democracy and National Unity Day.[169] Yet the country is deeply divided.[170] The starkest division is the one between conservative religious supporters of Erdoğan, who have been mobilized by his populist nationalism and anti-Westernism, and those who disagree with him. The two are roughly of equal size, as the result of the constitutional referendum of April 2017 revealed. Supporters of Erdoğan are promised a Turkey defined by the precepts of the National Outlook, which emphasizes political Islam, is uncomfortable with secularism, and is uneasy with women's and minority rights. Erdoğan's electorate perceives the West as an existential threat that constantly seeks to prevent Turkey from becoming strong and to undermine its potential to lead the Muslim world. It is a vision that rejects the legacy of the founders of the Turkish Republic and their Westernization agenda, symbolized in the name of Atatürk. The resentment of Atatürk and what he has come to represent is so deeply entrenched that a senior adviser to Ahmet Davutoğlu, is reported to have remarked, "Secularists live with Atatürk's corpse. . . . We need to carry Mr. Atatürk to his grave again."[171]

This resentment is also directed toward Westernized and secular citizens of Turkey. One conservative columnist in a pro-government paper went so far as to advocate that "Westernized Turks" should simply "get out" and stop being an obstacle to the Islamization of the country.[172] Turkey's long-standing identity crisis is therefore likely to persist as Turkey seems set to remain the "prototypical torn country," as suggested by the prominent American political scientist Samuel Huntington almost three decades ago.[173] Accordingly, Turkey's existential problem originated in the fact that its elite was secular and Western-oriented while its conservative religious masses adhered to Islam and belonged to the Islamic civilization. Indeed, one of the failures of past governments was to soften the harsher aspects of secularism and become more inclusive and allow greater room for expression of religious as well as ethnic and political diversity.

This kind of rigidity had caused the fault lines with the transatlantic community to harden in the pre-AKP period. The party's accession to power and Erdoğan's reforms were meant to overcome this division. But Turkey has instead swung to the opposite extreme, from one form of regime that failed to become inclusive of its pious citizens and ethnic minorities, most notably the Kurds, to another that automatically labels its critics and opponents as traitors, terrorists, or agents of the West. The discourse is increasingly similar in content, with the main difference being that the "old" Turkey emphasized adherence to secularism while the "new" Turkey emphasizes adherence to Islam. Both rest on a vision that disregards the other side of society, and both passionately try to impose the "right" way of life on the entire population with scant tolerance for diversity.[174]

This is extremely worrying for Turkey's future as a stable and prosperous country. Yet, as Hüsamettin Cindoruk, a former speaker of the Turkish parliament and a veteran of Turkish politics, argues, it is only within a democracy that the challenges of governance faced by Turkey can be addressed. This leads him to retain some hope for the future return of democracy to Turkey.[175] Only then will it be possible to see whether Turkey can once again play a constructive role in helping to sustain the international liberal order. In the meantime, as a former U.S. ambassador to Turkey put it, Erdoğan "wants a Turkey where he is the undisputed, unchallenged decider without the constraints of a normal democratic system . . . and he wants to render the opposition incapable of challenging him and to exercise clear power over them."[176] Hence, the people of Turkey are set to live in a country that has indisputably become "Erdoğan's Turkey" where "Erdoganism" is going to rule, at least for the near future.[177] As discussed in the next chapter, Turkish foreign policy followed a similar pattern as its domestic politics. Initially, under the AKP Turkey adopted a very constructive and pragmatic foreign policy with its neighborhood and the West. However, in due course these relations, both with many of its neighbors and the West, became troubled.

CHAPTER SEVEN

Turkey's Foreign Policy

The Rise and Fall of Soft Power

TURKISH FOREIGN POLICY UNDER the Justice and Development Party (AKP) and Erdoğan has followed a course similar to the government's trajectory in domestic politics—an ascending curve, driven by early promises and gains, and a sharp downward turn as the approach hardened and the rhetoric grew bitter. Soon after it came to power in 2002, the AKP acted in a remarkably forthcoming manner to tackle some of Turkey's long-entrenched problems. It gave fresh impetus to Turkey's EU membership bid. Building energetically on the work of earlier governments, it improved relations with the neighboring countries of Greece, Syria and Iraq, and delivered critical support to the 2004 UN initiative in Cyprus to unify the island. Another example of positive outreach occurred in relation to Armenia, an especially important development in light of the acrimonious history between the two countries. These early initiatives were famously captured by the expression "zero problems with neighbors," coined by Ahmet Davutoğlu while serving as adviser to the minister of foreign affairs, Abdullah Gül, from 2003 to 2007. Better relations with the countries in its region granted Turkey the ability to deal with "all parties" in various conflicts.[1] With continuing democratic reforms, a stronger economy, and closer integration with the EU, Turkey began gaining recognition for its soft power and was touted as a model, especially for countries struggling with the question of whether Islam could ever be reconciled with democratic principles and a liberal economy.[2]

This period of hope and expectations would be cut short as Turkey found itself heading toward a state of problems with almost everyone in its neighborhood and beyond. There seems to be a consensus that Turkey's backsliding from the early gains in foreign policy under the AKP occurred as the country's commitment to democratic reforms began to weaken and its relations with the EU cooled.[3] The parallel between the drift away from democratic principles at home and the erosion of Turkey's soft power abroad also became obvious, especially after the AKP came to power a second time in 2007.[4] In due course, skepticism arose as to whether Turkey could truly become a model for the Arab Spring countries.[5] The contradiction between the idea of Turkey as a source of inspiration, on the one hand, and the reality of an increasing number of journalists detained on the other was not missed by anyone. Growing authoritarianism in the aftermath of the Gezi Park protests in 2013 elicited harsher criticism from the West, also leading to the conclusion that the last days of the Turkish model had come.[6] Finally, these developments coincided with a visible turn away from pragmatism to an increasingly ideologically driven foreign policy.

By then the zero-problems policy had become irrelevant. As Turkey became embroiled in the Syrian civil war, it started to face growing criticism for lending support to radical Islamist groups. The repercussions of this policy were manifold, leading not only to a deterioration in relations with Turkey's own allies in the West but also to conflicts with the allies of the Assad regime, Iraq, Iran, and Russia. Turkey's withdrawal of ambassadors from a string of countries in the region and elsewhere strengthened the perception that Turkey was becoming increasingly isolated on the world stage. The growing number of Syrian refugees entering through Turkey's southern border had in the meantime developed into a colossal problem for the government. The spillover effects of the Syrian chaos also emerged in the form of terrorist attacks emanating from the self-styled Islamic State (IS) and the Kurdish Workers' Party (PKK). The cost of Turkey's involvement in Syria was rapidly becoming dire, both politically and economically.

Symbolically, the final recognition of the bankruptcy of Turkish foreign policy came in May 2016, when Davutoğlu resigned as prime minister. Binali Yıldırım, who replaced him, was quick to state that from then on, the regime's intent would be to "increase the number of our friends" and "decrease the number of our enemies."[7] Thereafter Turkish foreign policy began to show signs of pragmatism, the overtures to Israel and Russia being illustrative. As for Syria, there was a tentative softening of the demand for regime change and a distancing from the more radical Islamist groups fighting the Assad government. Relations with the West remained tense, however, as Erdoğan continued to blame the whole bloc for the instability across the Middle East and beyond, expressing particular ire for the support given to the Kurdish Democratic Union Party (PYD) and Kurdish fighters of the Popular Protection Units (YPG). His rhetoric continued to chip away at the effectiveness of the latest pragmatic turn in foreign policy.

The AKP's conduct of foreign policy from the turn of the twenty-first century to the time of writing can be discussed in three distinct periods. The first period covers the initial years between 2002 and 2009, when the government pursued a course in line with the international liberal order, expanding on its predecessors' efforts to work toward greater regional cooperation and deeper integration with the EU. Foreign policy during this time was under the leadership of Abdullah Gül and his successor, Ali Babacan, while Davutoğlu served as an adviser. The second period, from 2009 to 2016, was marked by Davutoğlu's growing aspirations to shape the regional order in the Middle East, first as minister of foreign affairs and then as prime minister. Davutoğlu's departure from government in May 2016 ushered in a new era characterized in particular by a hesitant turn toward pragmatism in Turkish foreign policy, the third period.

The argument developed here distances itself from the widely held view that Davutoğlu was the éminence grise of Turkish foreign policy and that dealing with Turkish foreign policy was equivalent to dealing with Davutoğlu.[8] It also takes issue with the opinion that his foreign policy marked a distinct break from established statecraft. Instead, a certain degree of continuity existed between the conduct of Turkish foreign policy by leaders such as Turgut Özal, Hikmet Çetin, and İsmail Cem and their AKP successors, Abdullah Gül and Ali Babacan. Gül became especially recognized as a leader who worked closely with the establishment in forging the AKP's foreign policy during his tenure.[9] A distinct departure from preceding statecraft did not occur until after the Arab Spring, when Erdoğan and Davutoğlu became increasingly involved in the internal dynamics of the Arab countries.

All this should not distract from Davutoğlu's legacy, however.[10] No other minister of foreign affairs in Turkish republican history has received the kind of media attention or academic interest extended to him. It would not be wrong to see his policy practices, statements, and writings—which constitute a rich body—as amounting to a Davutoğlu doctrine or paradigm (see the appendix for details). Finally, even though Turkey remains integrated with the transatlantic community, its domestic problems and the volatility along its borders are likely to keep its foreign policy in a state of unpredictability.

THE YEARS OF OPTIMISM: 2002–09

The AKP's first dramatic foreign policy challenge came with the U.S. invasion of Iraq in 2003. Soon after its rise to power, the AKP government found itself under pressure from the United States to allow U.S.-led coalition troops to transit Turkey and help U.S. efforts to open a northern front in its war in Iraq. Protracted negotiations with the United States under the premiership of Abdullah Gül did lend themselves to a deal.[11] But this was far from being adopted wholeheartedly by the party leadership or its body of delegates. Gül preferred that the crisis be resolved through dialogue and diplomacy. He was particularly concerned that support for a Western-led action against Muslims might undermine his government's credibility among neighboring Muslim countries as well as AKP voters at home.[12]

Gül and his team were also mindful of the EU's reaction, as they were heavily engaged in a process they hoped would lead to the start of accession negotiations. They were conscious of the need to alleviate concerns the French leadership had expressed, such as fear that allowing a pro-U.S. Turkey into the EU would be equivalent to accepting a Trojan horse in their midst. There were also massive protests in Europe against an invasion of Iraq, and the British parliament had taken a stand against it. Hence Gül, together with Davutoğlu as his foreign policy adviser, embarked on a last-minute "active diplomacy for peace" with Iraqi leadership to avoid a military disaster. In contrast, Erdoğan, who had to remain outside the cabinet while completing a political ban handed down before the elections, was more favorably disposed to support the U.S. plan. He saw it as a tool to guarantee a place for Turkey at the eventual negotiation table for a post-Saddam Iraq.[13] In the end, the deal that would have helped the United States open a northern frontier fell apart in the Turkish parliament.[14] In many ways the decision was not surprising: in Turkey as elsewhere in Europe, public opinion was strongly against any form of military intervention in Iraq.[15]

The United States nevertheless went ahead with the invasion despite the major logistical challenges that arose from Turkey's rejection of access. This provoked deep resentment toward Turkey; as a long-standing observer put it, it had "a shattering impact" on Turkey's relations with the United States.[16] Yet Turkey's stance earned it considerable popularity in Europe and across the Arab world. Turkey would eventually use this position to play a constructive role in Iraq by persuading certain Sunni groups to participate in the 2005 parliamentary elections and getting them to support the federal constitutional arrangement that came into being afterward. Similarly, Turkey's relations with the Kurdistan Regional Government (KRG) also began to improve from 2008 on, reaching a high point when Davutoğlu became the first Turkish minister of foreign affairs to visit the KRG in 2009, a move planned as part of a broader trip to Iraq.[17] Furthermore, the AKP's ability to prove its independence from the United States would contribute, in due course, to the image of Turkey as a model for the region that would be acknowledged by Obama.

Possibly the most significant legacy of AKP's foreign policy in this particular period will be remembered as the effort put into winning a date for EU accession talks to start. Undoubtedly, a combination of domestic reforms and the constructive discourse adopted by Erdoğan, which reiterated Turkey's position as a strong ally of the West, had been critical to this positive advance. Another important factor was Gül's ability and willingness to work closely with the foreign policy establishment and especially its top diplomats, a practice that in a few years would be abandoned as Turkish foreign policy lost its pragmatism and became more ideological. For Erdoğan too, the decision came as a relief. As he stated to an excited crowd on his return from the EU meeting, "Turkey has taken a great leap forward. We've overcome our greatest obstacle on our EU journey in the past forty years."[18]

The same period witnessed Turkey's increasing engagement with its neighborhood, in particular with the Middle East.[19] The government focused on improving relations with all neighbors, but some exchanges attracted more attention than others. In 2004 Vladimir Putin and Bashar al-Assad became the first leaders of Russia and Syria, respectively, to visit Turkey. Subsequently Erdoğan hosted Assad and his family for a vacation in Turkey amid deepening relations between the two countries.[20] Similarly, in January 2007 Erdoğan visited Lebanon, where he also met with the leaders of Christian and Shia communities after Turkey agreed to send troops to join the United Nations Interim Force in Lebanon (UNIFIL) earlier that year, almost three decades after UNIFIL's original establishment. (Turkey's participation had traditionally been opposed by the Armenian communities in Lebanon, and that Turkish troops were now accepted speaks to how much the AKP had changed Turkey's image.) The effort to foster better relations with Armenia and the growing thaw with respect to broaching the topic of the Armenian genocide in Turkey were also important in diffusing protests from members of the Armenian community in Lebanon. Even if the effort to improve relations with Armenia failed,[21] the government nevertheless enabled Armenian nationals to travel relatively freely to Turkey, and allowed some volume of trade with Armenia to take place through Georgia. Very quickly the focus on encouraging greater regional trade and movement of people became the most visible aspect of Turkey's engagement of its neighborhood, earning Turkey the label "trading state."[22]

Turkey's modest support for democratization efforts in the Middle East was also noticeable. On a number of occasions Erdoğan and Gül addressed the importance of democracy for the region and the Muslim world, as well as the need to recognize the Turkish experience as evidence of the compatibility of Islam with democracy. In his speech at Harvard University in January 2003, Erdoğan argued that EU accession would not only strengthen democracy in Turkey but also help promote it in the Middle East. He even quoted from Thomas Jefferson when he invited "those in the West and in the Middle East who say that democratization is not possible in that region to 'doubt a little of their own infallibility.' "[23] Gül also sounded keen on the issue of democracy. He urged his fellow Muslim colleagues at an Organization of Islamic Cooperation (OIC) meeting in Tehran "to first put our house in order" and pay greater attention to human rights and women's rights, and encouraged greater transparency in governance.[24] Strikingly, however, the Turkish emphasis always rested on setting an example; putting in place an elaborate program for democracy promotion or regime change was not part of the agenda.

Yet the intense diplomatic and economic engagement directed toward the neighborhood, in particular the Middle East, raised questions in Western circles. The issue was whether Turkey was shifting its axis and orienting itself away from the West and toward the East. Many disagreed with this perspective. The members of the Independent Commission on Turkey argued that "it would be wrong to see Turkey's intensified relationship with its eastern neighbors as an 'Islamic' foreign policy, even if President Gül and Prime Minister Erdoğan have been more open towards the Middle East than earlier generations of Turkish policy-makers."[25]

Some commentators attributed these policies to pragmatism, while others saw them as the gradual Europeanization of Turkish foreign policy.[26] The logic behind this paradoxical analogy was that Turkey's policies were no different from EU efforts to create a "ring of friendly and well governed countries" around the EU.[27] Some even pointed to Turkey as an agent "doing the European Neighborhood Policy for the EU."[28] A contrasting view held that Turkey's orientation signaled a search for alternatives to EU, which was an outcome of weakening engagement by the EU. A term that gained traction in this respect was "soft Eurasianism."[29] In any event, after Davutoğlu became minister of foreign affairs in May 2009 and the Arab Spring erupted in 2011, Turkish foreign policy began to change in fundamental ways, first incrementally, then with vigor, as its main architect sought to fulfill his dream of changing the course of the "river of history" (see the appendix for details).

THE RISE AND FALL OF THE "DAVUTOĞLU DOCTRINE": 2009–16

After Davutoğlu became minister of foreign affairs in 2009, he supported the policies pursued by his predecessors—some of which he had helped formulate while serving as adviser. This did not mean, however, that his conduct at the helm of Turkish foreign policy was entirely in harmony with the spirit of zero problems with neighbors or dictated by pragmatic considerations alone. A case in point is the angry exchange between Erdoğan and the Israeli president Shimon Peres at the 2009 World Economic Forum in Davos, just before Davutoğlu was appointed minister, an encounter that shocked the global audience. The discussion had turned to the Israeli military's incursions into the Gaza Strip, and Erdoğan stormed out of the panel in protest, vowing never to return to the forum, after having said to Peres, "When it comes to killing, you know very well how to kill."[30] Such a clash was clearly undiplomatic; it was also an early hint of the swerve in Turkish foreign policy away from pragmatism. The timing of the incident, which fell right before important local elections, provided Erdoğan with the opportunity to galvanize his base. At home he was received as the "Davos Fatihi" (Conqueror of Davos) and exploited his rift with Peres to whip up anti-Semitic feelings, a sure method to mobilize populist votes.[31] In the meantime, his popularity in the Arab world was also boosted, as suggested by the number of Palestinian babies named after him.[32] In hindsight, this incident marked a turning point in Turkish foreign policy, which saw the gradual entry of domestic considerations and ideological issues.

This emerging trend was further clarified when a diplomatic crisis erupted in Israeli-Turkish relations following a commando raid by the Israeli Defense Forces on a Gaza-bound Turkish aid ship. The deadly attack on the *Mavi Marmara* occurred as it was about to break the Israeli blockade of the Gaza Strip in May 2010. The flotilla in which the ship was sailing was organized and led by the Humanitarian Relief Foundation (IHH), a Turkish NGO with a strong anti-Israeli agenda that had been given permission to carry humanitarian assistance to Gaza. Prior warnings by the Israeli authorities had fallen on deaf ears among the Turkish administration, which stated its reluctance to interfere with what it saw as a civil society initiative. This stand contrasted with the spirit of mediation adopted until then—the very spirit that had made it possible for Erdoğan to host both Shimon Peres and Mahmoud Abbas, the president of the Palestinian Authority in 2007, and to facilitate indirect talks between Israel and Syria until just before the Davos incident. It also clashed with the pragmatic approach that Erdoğan had displayed on prior occasions domestically. Only earlier in the year he had defended a contract given to an Israeli company against criticism from the ranks of the AKP by saying that "money has no religion, nationality or ethnicity" and that a deal deemed beneficial to Turkey could be made with any country.[33]

The position taken against Israel was defended by both Davutoğlu and Erdoğan on ethical, humanitarian, and principled grounds. However, these arguments were found by many to be inconsistent with the conduct of relations with other countries. For example, Erdoğan would later dismiss allegations of genocide against the Sudanese president Omar Hassan al-Bashir on the grounds that "a Muslim can never commit genocide."[34] His government also remained silent in the face of human rights violations and repression in Bahrain, and again when Saudi Arabia, together with the UAE, militarily intervened in the country to suppress the Arab Spring protests. The case of Bahrain was particularly striking because it involved a Shiite majority seeking improved governance in an autocratic Sunni monarchy, and Turkey's silence engendered accusations of sectarianism.[35] The government's position conflicted with both the spirit and the letter of Davutoğlu's claim in 2012 that "if the ruler were a Muslim who oppressed Christians in Syria, we would equally be against him/her."[36]

Similarly, the silence over the heavy-handed suppression of the Green protests after the 2009 Iranian presidential elections was notable.[37]

There were no words of criticism when Saudi and UAE air forces began pounding Yemen starting in March 2015. This was also the case with the Russian bombing of civilian targets in Syria in 2016. Commentators have also drawn attention to the irony of Erdoğan's silence over the Russian bombing of a UN aid convoy near Aleppo in September 2016, just days after he had lambasted the West for lack of response to ease the plight of Syrian refugees.[38] The bombings of hospitals, schools, and residential neighborhoods, according to an Indian commentator, were no different from the punctual bombardment of Gaza by Israel. Both displayed a disregard for human life and international law.[39]

Erdoğan's stand on Israel was indeed quite popular nationally and regionally.[40] However, the position taken by Erdoğan and the AKP on Israel cannot solely be explained by populism and the desire to uphold ethical principles. A better explanation can be found in the ideology that had guided both Erdoğan and Davutoğlu all along. Davutoğlu viewed the regional order in the Middle East as a function of Western designs. In relation to Israel in particular, he had used the term "geopolitical tumor" and referred to Israel as "a state that is politically foreign to that geography."[41] This was in line with the views of the National Outlook (Millî Görüs) movement, which traditionally rejected relations with Israel to avoid alienating Turkey's "Muslim brothers."[42]

Pragmatism and Economic Integration

In contrast to these developments, Davutoğlu continued to support earlier efforts under Gül and Babacan to encourage greater economic integration with Turkey's neighborhood. As foreign minister, he became a keen advocate of regionalism and encouraged the expansion of visa liberalization and free trade arrangements with Arab countries. Previously the focus had been more on the former Soviet and Balkan countries. In October 2009 Erdoğan announced the first such agreement with Syria, referring to the Schengen visa regime in the EU as an example. As he stated playfully, his objective was to work toward a "Shamgen visa," a pun on Şam, the Turkish word for Damascus.[43] In an effort to deepen and institutionalize this kind of engagement with the region, by 2012 Davutoğlu had negotiated the establishment of High-Level Strategic Cooperation Councils with thirteen countries, mostly in Turkey's immediate neighborhood.[44] Davutoğlu aspired to see "the free movement of goods and people taking place in a vast area stretching from the city of Kars in eastern Turkey to the Atlantic, and from Sinop on the Black Sea coast to the Gulf of Aden."[45] The Quartet High-Level Strategic Cooperation Council, which involved Turkey, Syria, Lebanon, and Jordan, was especially ambitious since it aspired to no less than the establishment of a free trade area among the four.[46] This kind of economic engagement became critical in terms of connecting the neighborhood into the global economy. It also helped expand the realm of liberal and open markets.

In Davutoğlu's words, Turkey was ready to act as an "economic engine" of growth for the neighborhood.[47] Not surprisingly, Turkey's overall trade with neighboring countries (Armenia, Azerbaijan, Bulgaria, Georgia, Greece, Iran, Iraq, Moldova, Romania, Russia, Syria, and Ukraine) saw a massive increase, from a mere U.S. $8.6 billion in 2002 to $92 billion in 2012. The number of nationals from the neighborhood entering Turkey reached almost 11.5 million in 2012, whereas the figure had remained at 3.5 million in 2002.[48] Domestically, this kind of pragmatic engagement especially served the interests of the Anatolian Tigers, keen to trade with Turkey's neighborhood.[49] Increased trade did bring higher levels of employment as well as wealth to these cities and provinces. In turn, the AKP's average votes in these provinces were generally higher than the national average in 2002, 2007, and 2011.[50]

The Arab Spring raised hopes that other countries in the region would follow in Turkey's footsteps. However, in due course Davutoğlu introduced a politically ambitious agenda that aspired to a great deal more—a complete change in the regional order. In his opinion, the Arab Spring, together with the euro crisis, represented the third major geopolitical earthquake since the end of the Cold War and the collapse of the Soviet Union and the events of 9/11. He expected the protests in the Arab world to have a profound impact on the regional as well as the global order.[51] This was very quickly conceptualized by Davutoğlu and academics close to him as a development that would help Turkey fulfill its role as a "central country" (the concept is discussed in the appendix) in replacing the Western-imposed order in the Middle East. It was defined as an opportunity to bring Turkey into an "intracivilizational" solidarity with the Arab Spring countries. Islam would be the tie that united them all. Turkey would become "the spokesperson of the Islamic world in the international system."[52] Simultaneously, this was seized on as the moment that would finalize Turkey's domestic transformation from the "old" Turkey to a "new" Turkey led by the AKP. The Arab Spring was thus hailed "as the guarantee of this 'new' Turkey" and was considered "an indistinguishable part (*ayrılmaz parçası*) of Turkey," and both transformations would mutually reinforce each other.[53]

The Turkish government's support for regime change in Tunisia and Egypt was enthusiastic. Erdoğan became one of the first world leaders to call on Mubarak to heed the demands for change. He offered Turkey's experience under his leadership as the best example of how democracy had changed the destiny of a people.[54] In the case of Libya, his position evolved somewhat hesitantly, partly because of his close relationship with Muammar Gaddafi, from whom he had only a few weeks earlier received a human rights award.[55] There was also concern for extensive Turkish businesses, especially in the construction sector, and the presence of 25,000 expatriates in the country. Once they were evacuated, Turkey did cooperate closely to ensure the success of the NATO operation. Its role was well received among the Libyans, and large crowds embraced Davutoğlu during his subsequent visit to Benghazi in April 2011.

The government extended substantial political and economic support to particularly Egypt and Tunisia. It was keen to help consolidate the rule of the Muslim Brotherhood in the former and the Ennahda party in the latter, with both of whom the AKP had a long-standing relationship. The Egyptian president Mohamed Morsi and the Ennahda leader Rachid Ghannouchi were among the guests of honor at the 2012 AKP congress, for example. They were joined by Khaled Mashal, then head of Hamas, and Tariq Hashimi, the exiled vice president of Iraq; all were considered to be part of the broader Muslim Brotherhood movement in the Middle East.[56] More conspicuous than their presence, however, was the absence at the same event of Shia leaders or representatives from the Palestinian Authority. This led to speculations of sectarianism.[57] Davutoğlu objected energetically to any suggestion that the AKP might have a preference for the Sunnis and the Muslim Brotherhood. He argued that his party would have supported any elected leader in these countries.[58] But his objections were ineffective in muting criticisms of sectarianism. The appearance of Mashal and Ghannouchi at the AKP's electoral rallies in the run-up to the 2015 general elections without a semblance of sectarian balance among the invitees made him much less convincing.[59]

Sliding into the Syrian Quagmire

Turkey approached the Arab Spring with wider aspirations. The euphoria of the moment gave Davutoğlu hope that he could begin to seek greater integration of the region. He introduced his plan for a "Grand Restoration" (Büyük Restorasyon) in an impassioned speech that largely drew on the religious, cultural, and historical ties that united Muslims across the Middle East. His mission would be to overcome the borders that divided them and bring an end to an order imposed by Western powers in history.[60] He argued that the Arab Spring would culminate in the closing of a "historical parenthesis" opened by colonial forces and the Cold War.[61] In this new era, according to him, the peoples of the region would once again interconnect with one another, as they did in the Ottoman times, and matters would return to the "natural flow of history."[62] The word is not used in his pronouncements, but the new order he had in mind appears to resemble a caliphate that would bring together the Islamic *ummah* (community).

Turkey would lead this process. However, how it would proceed in this undertaking remained ambiguous, even puzzling, because Davutoğlu did not seem to envision a change in the existing borders in the Middle East.[63] Apparently, the new order was to have come about as a result of the Arab Spring, producing a belt of countries led by Muslim Brotherhood regimes. These would have been regimes in ideological solidarity with an AKP-led Turkey and prepared to defer to its leadership.[64] That notion was also implied in Davutoğlu's remarks that Turkey would be returning to the geography from which it had been separated by the post–World War I order.[65] This exceptionally ambitious turn in Turkish foreign policy did not go unnoticed by the outside world. A Washington, D.C.–based think tank observed that "Ankara did everything to boost the Muslim Brotherhood, seeking to build a pro-Turkish Sunni crescent from Egypt to northern Iraq across Gaza and Syria."[66]

This vision and the bold aspiration to reconstruct history died a slow and destructive death in Syria. It was driven by an uncompromising policy of supporting regime change and by the conviction that Turkey would be able to lead this change. In an address to the Turkish parliament on Syria in April 2012, Davutoğlu declared that Turkey would lead, but at the same time it would also be a "servant" to an emerging "new" Middle East.[67] The main opposition, the Republican People's Party (CHP), warned loudly that "meddling in the internal affairs of its neighbors, instigating war and taking part in regional conflicts" was unrealistic and untenable and that it would adversely affect "Turkey's stature, reliability and claims to regional leadership."[68] These warnings were confidently dismissed as holdover attitudes from an era in which

Turkey could not go beyond acting as a timid player on the world stage. But in fact, Davutoğlu's policy would eventually lead Turkey to a dead end, isolated from its neighbors.[69] It would also bring about his own downfall.

Entrapment in Syria started with Davutoğlu's failure in his attempt in August 2011 to persuade Assad to accept reforms and share power with the Muslim Brotherhood–dominated opposition.[70] Subsequently Erdoğan severed Turkey's relations with the Assad regime and lent its open support to the Syrian opposition, which was in line with the approach of most Western governments, including the U.S. government. The Assad regime defied all predictions that it would collapse quickly. Instead the conflict turned first into a civil war, then into a wide-ranging conflict involving a multitude of external actors. Radical jihadist groups were also drawn into the quagmire. In the hope of expediting the end of the Assad regime, Turkey, together with Saudi Arabia and Qatar, provided these groups shelter, medical treatment, and arms.[71]

The failure to foresee the gradual involvement of Iran and Russia on the side of the regime, and the reluctance of the Obama administration to enforce its "red lines" pulled Turkey further into the chaos. The situation was aggravated in June 2014 when IS burst onto the scene by occupying Mosul, where it took hostage the entire personnel of the Turkish consulate. It then quickly spread into a good part of Syria, including areas close to the Turkish border. Unfortunately, Davutoğlu's "principled position"—that the transition sparked by the Arab Spring would not be "as bloody and painful as was the case in some countries in the Balkans"—ran into the unpredictability of history and war. His ambition to make Turkey "run . . . in front of history, rather than follow behind" also proved too high to achieve owing to the complexity of the situation and the realities on the ground.[72]

This situation left Turkey facing accusations of falling short of preventing the flow of foreign fighters and equipment into the ranks of IS and other extremist groups.[73] Turkey earned the reputation of having become a "jihadi highway" or a "rat line." It also drew criticism from the international community as a country that explicitly or inadvertently contributed to the jihadist groups that came to dominate the Syrian opposition.[74] Furthermore, Turkey also became subject to the evolving conflict between IS and Syrian Kurds that was epitomized by the siege of Kobane, the Kurdish town on the Turkish border that sustained heavy IS attacks during the summer and fall of 2014. Turkey's growing involvement in Syria's conflict led to warnings that Turkey it-self risked becoming another Syria. It was insistently noted that the country might eventually suffer from the spillover effects of the war next door, similar to what had happened in Pakistan when it became ex-posed to violence perpetrated by the Taliban.[75] One former member of the Turkish parliament called it the "creeping Pakistanization of Tur-key."[76] The relevance of these warnings became obvious when a wave of terror shook the country, starting with the July 2015 IS attack on the southeastern town of Suruç.

The Price of "Precious Loneliness"

Turkey's relations with Egypt also suffered as the Arab Spring turned into winter. The July 2013 military coup against Mohamed Morsi trig-gered great resentment among AKP supporters; the government was quick to present the turmoil as yet another consequence of the ill-designed, Western-imposed order in the region. Erdoğan and several leading politicians from his party adopted the four-finger "Rabia" ges-ture to express solidarity with those who risked their lives in Cairo's Rabia Square while protesting against Morsi's overthrow.[77] The sign later became the symbol of continued commitment to the cause of the Muslim Brotherhood in Egypt. Indignant over what he described as as-sault on a democratically elected government, Erdoğan bitterly criticized the international community, targeting especially Western countries, for not living up to democratic principles. As relations with the new govern-ment in Egypt deteriorated, the Turkish ambassador in Cairo was ex-pelled.[78] The government responded with a policy of hosting Muslim Brotherhood members in Istanbul, where they were allowed to run propaganda, on radio and TV, against the government in Egypt. The incendiary language that marked some of these programs raised con-cern, leading to efforts by an opposition deputy in the Turkish parlia-ment to investigate the matter.[79]

A similar situation occurred with regard to Iraq amid accusations and counteraccusations of sectarianism.[80] Both countries reached a point where they had to summon the other's ambassador, and Turkey reduced its representation in Iraq. The move was part of an emerging pattern of withdrawing ambassadors from a growing list of countries. There would be mounting criticism. This is the point at which Davutoğlu's signature policy of zero problems with neighbors began to be increasingly referred to as "zero neighbors without problems." This was also accompanied by arguments that there was a "Sunnification" of Turkish foreign policy, which greatly undermined Turkey's once praised ability to talk to all parties in its neighborhood.[81] Turkey's resulting loss of prestige and soft power was reflected in its failure to be reelected as a nonpermanent member of the UN Security Council in 2014. The motion was rejected by a very large margin, in striking contrast to the majority vote that only six years earlier had granted Turkey the same seat.[82]

The government did not relent in the face of growing criticism at home and abroad. The memorable phrase "precious loneliness" began to circulate vigorously. Turkey was alone because it alone had sought to maintain a noble standard in foreign policy; it was Turkey alone that had held ethical standards above self-interest and realist considerations.[83] However, many commentators, including Yaşar Yakış, a former AKP minister of foreign affairs and a retired ambassador with extensive experience in the Middle East, criticized these policies. He asserted that the loneliness was a sign of a leadership that had replaced a realistic approach to foreign policy with an ideologically driven one.[84] Davutoğlu remained unyielding and continued to stand behind his policies after he became prime minister in September 2014.[85] This culminated in closer cooperation between Turkey and its Gulf allies, Qatar and Saudi Arabia, especially after the arrival of the new Saudi king in January 2015. They jointly supported rebel groups in northern Syria and parts of Aleppo.[86] Turkey's efforts to push back IS from its southern border would not start before June 2015, however. At the same time, Turkey tried to block the westward advance of the Syrian Kurdish forces that, worryingly from Ankara's perspective, aspired to unify Kurdish-held enclaves along the Turkish border. The success of the Turkish- and Gulf-supported rebels in expanding the areas under their control, particularly in Aleppo, triggered Russia's direct military intervention in September 2015, adding another layer of complexity.[87]

Shortly thereafter, when Turkey shot down a Russian warplane in November, Russia suspended all cooperation with Turkey and imposed economic sanctions, with severe consequences in terms of Turkish exports to Russia; Russian tourism to Turkey, a major source of revenue, especially for coastal towns, also came to a halt. This was followed by reciprocal threats: when Russia cut the route from Aleppo to Turkey, Erdoğan responded by hinting at a possible Turkish military intervention in Syria, which triggered in turn a suggestion from the Russian side that it might consider resorting to the use of tactical nuclear weapons.[88] At the same time, Turkey faced a security situation within the country that was worsening by the day and accompanied by growing criticism of Davutoğlu's Syria policy. Calls were made for the AKP to abandon its ideologically driven policies aimed at reordering the Middle East and to recognize instead that there was no historical parenthesis to close.[89]

Surveys by Kadir Has University showed that those who found Turkey's Middle East and Syria policies to be "unsuccessful" or "neither successful nor unsuccessful" increased between 2013 and 2016.[90] Furthermore, Turkey's trade with the region exhibited a sharp decline in the face of growing resentment of Turkey, especially in Egypt and Iraq. Turkish exports to the Arab Middle East and to Russia fell by 11 percent and 40 percent, respectively, from 2014 to 2015.[91] The status that Turkey had once had as a successful trading state was withering away.[92] Similarly, Turkey's prestige and soft power efficacy in the Arab world seemed to be eroding as well. In 2011 a think tank close to the government had proudly stated that according to a survey conducted by the University of Maryland, Turkey was perceived in the Arab World to be playing a constructive role, while Prime Minister Erdoğan was selected as the most admired world leader.[93] Another survey in 2016 disclosed sharply contrasting findings: favorable Arab public opinion toward Turkey had declined significantly, with the biggest declines seen in Saudi Arabia (from 74 percent to 35 percent), Iraq (from 80 percent to 30 percent), and Lebanon (from 83 percent to 56 percent) compared to just a year earlier.[94]

The turn of events was well captured by a former under-secretary of the Turkish Foreign Ministry: the government had "misjudged Muslim Brotherhood's coming to power in Egypt as a sign of an irreversible regional trend and engaged in regime change in Syria," but this policy had "boomeranged" and multiplied Turkey's problems.[95] By May 2016 it had become obvious that precious loneliness could no longer be held out as guidance for policy.[96] The effort to affect the flow of the "river of history" turned out to be an unrealistically ambitious undertaking. Davutoğlu had obviously not taken heed of international relations scholar Raymond Aron's warning: that men and women often write history without knowing what they write.[97] Davutoğlu's forced resignation from the cabinet as prime minister was therefore no surprise to anyone and was thought to have been at least partly brought on by his foreign policy in Syria.[98] After all, he had long been known as "the owner of the intellectual property rights" of this policy.[99] Ironically, as Davutoğlu was leaving, Assad was still in power, in defiance of Davutoğlu's prediction in August 2012 that there were "not years but months possibly just weeks" remaining to Assad's regime.[100] The foreign policy that has since emerged is still in the making, with some signs that the pendulum is moving once again toward a more pragmatic approach.

A RETURN TO PRAGMATISM OR MERE CONFUSION? 2016–PRESENT

A degree of pragmatism crept into Turkish foreign policy soon after the departure of Davutoğlu. This was reflected in the new prime minister Binali Yıldırım's remarks that Turkey needed "to increase the number of friends and reduce the number of enemies."[101] Shortly thereafter Erdoğan sent a letter to Vladimir Putin expressing regret over the downing of the Russian plane and seeking to reconstitute Russian-Turkish relations. The announcement of the normalization of relations between Israel and Turkey followed. Yet along with this preference for pragmatism there have also been times when populist and ideological considerations have made a comeback.

Relations with Russia further improved when Putin was quick to lend his support to Erdoğan after the coup attempt of mid-July. The two sides were also able to reach a modus vivendi that allowed Turkey to mount a military intervention in parts of northern Syria to fight both IS and the PYD, as well as to create a safe zone for civilians fleeing the hostilities and destruction in eastern Aleppo. Implicit in this deal appeared to be an acceptance that Turkey's focus would no longer be on toppling the Assad regime.[102] However, the cooperation with Russia went forward in a rather surreal fashion, with each side maintaining its support for opposing parties in the war of proxies. The limits of Turkey's ability to affect outcomes in Syria over the head of Russia were revealed on at least three occasions, with the desire to see Assad removed always waiting in the wings. The first had to do with some remarks by Erdoğan, who, in an attempt to rally his supporters, appalled by the situation in Aleppo, argued that the Turkish military had entered Syria "to end the rule of the tyrant al-Assad who terrorizes with state terror."[103] After some prodding by Russia, he had to walk back this statement just hours before the foreign ministers of the two countries were due to meet in Turkey to negotiate a cease-fire in Aleppo.[104]

The second incident took place within weeks, when an off-duty Turkish police officer shot dead the Russian ambassador in Ankara in protest of Russian involvement in Aleppo. Neither side wanting another round of tension, they forged ahead with the planned talks in Moscow. This resulted in a deal that ensured, together with Iran, the evacuation of East Aleppo and the withdrawal of defeated rebels further north into areas still controlled by the opposition. The deal and the withdrawal of Turkish-supported rebels from Aleppo became a bitter reminder that Russia, to some extent together with Iran, had now become the power shaping outcomes in Syria. The military reality on the ground favoring Russia and the regime forced the Turkish government to once again reconsider its position on Assad. This was noted by Mehmet Şimşek, deputy prime minister, when he recognized that "a settlement without Assad is not realistic" since the "facts on the ground have changed dramatically."[105]

The third occasion occurred after the U.S. president Donald Trump in April 2017 ordered a missile attack on a Syrian air base from which the planes that had mounted a chemical attack on civilians in the province of Idlib had taken off. The government was quick to lend its support and repeat its hope for further steps from the United States to ensure the departure of Assad.[106] However, it was evident during the meetings between Erdoğan and Trump in Washington, D.C., the following month that the United States remained focused on defeating IS; hence Russia's ongoing position as the main broker on the ground. Clearly, the issue of the future of Assad will continue to torment the government in Turkey, caught between the hope that the Trump administration might be won over and the reality imposed by Russia and the Astana process, which Turkey has been part of since December 2016. This dilemma was captured succinctly by a Turkish security analyst who remarked that "there is a struggle for power between Russia and the United States over the future of Syria and Turkey is stumbling back and forth between the two."[107]

Another issue on which the Turkish government remains caught between pragmatism and the call of populism has to do with relations with Israel. Improved relations with Israel caused resentment in Islamist circles in Turkey, which protested the swift pace of the reconciliation process.[108] Not surprisingly, the strongest reaction came from the IHH, the organizers of the ill-fated expedition to bring humanitarian assistance to the Gaza Strip. They objected to the normalization of relations with Israel, which they called an untrustworthy partner. Erdoğan's pragmatism overrode objections in this matter: he hit back at the IHH, arguing that he had not been consulted about the expedition and that turning the whole affair into a big show had not been wise after all.[109]

In fact, the pragmatic side of Erdoğan had been at work all along, since even at the height of tensions with Israel he had never tampered with the free trade agreement between the two countries. Throughout the crisis, Turkish exports to Israel continued to grow, increasing by almost 26 percent between 2012 and 2016. This is in some contrast to overall Turkish exports to the rest of the world for the same period increasing by less than 6 percent. This also stands out considering the fall in Turkish exports to Arab countries of 20 percent during the same period.[110] Erdoğan appears to maintain an interest in the prospect of transporting Israeli natural gas to Europe via Turkey, a development that would help turn Turkey into an energy hub and also boost its ailing economy.[111] Yet, while calling for a peaceful resolution to the Palestinian problem, it is not unusual for Erdoğan to resort to inflammatory language. He has not refrained, for example, from accusing Israel of conducting racist policies or attacking its government over a plan to regulate the volume of the call for prayers from mosques in Jerusalem as well as access to the Al-Aqsa Mosque.[112]

Rhetoric Despite Diplomacy with the West

Populist and ideological priorities trumping pragmatism are also reflected in Erdoğan's tendency to continue to pursue Davutoğlu's agenda for a "post-Western international order," at least at the rhetorical level. This in turn has engendered confusion over Turkey's long-term strategic orientation as Erdoğan maintains a virulent discourse targeting the West, the United States in particular. The theme of one of his talks, for example, was the issue of internal fighting among fellow Muslims, which he traced back to a grand conspiracy put in place by the West a century ago. It was "them," "the rivals of Islam," who had helped erect, through the conflicts they fomented all along, "walls of fear" between Turkey and its neighbors to the east and south. It was again through their machinations, Erdoğan reasoned, that the Muslim world was left facing the scourge of extremist groups such as IS, Boko Haram, or al Shabaab.[113]

Erdoğan has not spared the UN either. In his address to the General Assembly in 2014, he expressed criticism for the veto power held by the five permanent members of the Security Council. The phrase he employed then, "the world is bigger than five," has since turned into a slogan, a byword for the role he fashioned for himself as "the voice of the rest."[114] Erdoğan's vexation with the UN is partly a function of that body's inability to resolve the Syrian conflict and partly owing to the absence of any Muslim country among the permanent members of the Security Council.[115] This has not prevented him from seeking to join the Shanghai Cooperation Organization (SCO), dominated by China and Russia, two of the five UN powers he resents. Instead, he employs the SCO membership card to express his dissatisfaction with the West and whenever he feels vulnerable to EU criticism of his domestic policies. For example, after the European Parliament recommended that accession talks with Turkey be suspended, he indignantly accused the EU of dragging its feet for fifty-three years on the matter of Turkey's accession.[116] He argued that pursuing EU membership was futile and suggested instead that Turkey would do better by going along with the SCO.[117] The likelihood of the SCO pressing Erdoğan over the issue of democracy and human rights is not high, and this may be one factor that makes the option attractive.

That this kind of posturing over the SCO and against the West "leaves Turkey looking unpredictable and untrustworthy in the eyes of its Western allies" should not come as a surprise.[118] Furthermore, such a stand conflicts with Turkey's economic, military, and political ties to the West, which creates confusion internally as well as externally. Erdoğan complained in April 2016 to NATO secretary general Jens Stoltenberg about the need to increase NATO's presence in the Black Sea as a measure to counterbalance Russia's massive military buildup in the region.[119] He repeated the same point at the NATO Warsaw Summit in July and at the ministerial meeting in October the same year, which had in fact succeeded his reconciliation with Putin.[120] Clearly, it is difficult to see how membership in the SCO would be compatible with membership in NATO. The matter is also complicated by the emergence in Ankara, since the coup attempt in July 2016, of an influential "Russian lobby" advocating a rupture of relations with the EU and a reduction of the ties to NATO.[121]

Even Erdoğan's own government seems to be confused by these swings. Former deputy prime minister and government spokesman Numan Kurtulmuş sought to calibrate Erdoğan's remarks by saying that the SCO option did not mean breaking off ties with other countries.[122] The Turkish minister of foreign affairs, Mevlüt Çavuşoğlu, nuanced the notion that Turkey "was "tilting toward Russia" by claiming that Turkey maintained its "principled position" over the territorial integrity of Ukraine and Georgia.[123] The vulnerability of Turkey's national security interests to Russian expansionist tendencies must have been in their minds when they made these statements.

Relations with the EU

Mehmet Şimşek, another deputy prime minister, has consistently referred to the importance of Turkey's relations with the EU and its membership perspective as an anchor for the country.[124] The economy minister, Nihat Zeybekçi, has taken a similar line and has been especially supportive of modernizing the customs union between the EU and Turkey.[125] Those who have been inspired by Brexit have in turn suggested that Turkey can coordinate more closely with the UK to create a synergy that would help negotiate a new broader relationship with the EU in place of membership.[126] However, not all in Turkey agree with the notion of a "soft exit" from the traditional EU accession process. Vocal business and civil society groups such as the Economic Development Foundation (İKV), the Turkish Industry and Business Association (TÜSİAD), and the Turkish Enterprise and Business Confederation (TÜRKONFED) have continued to advocate energetically for EU accession as an anchor for Turkish democracy and economic growth.[127] These positions are partly shaped by the economic realities that make the EU Turkey's most important trading and economic partner, especially now that it has lost business with Russia and the post–Arab Spring Middle East.[128] However, they are also shaped by a deep conviction in parts of Turkish civil society that it is only Turkey that aspires for EU membership and through it anchors itself in the international liberal order that will enjoy prosperity and stability.

The pragmatic trend that began to evolve in the AKP, however, does not seem to have reined in Erdoğan's inclination to resort to populist discourse whenever he sees it fit. His frequent threats to the EU that he could "open the flood gates of Syrian refugees" should be understood more as a tool to serve his own domestic agenda than as a stick to beat Europe with. In a recent instance—clearly a damage control effort in the wake of the European Parliament's recommendation—he accused the EU of not abiding by the terms of the migration deal reached in March 2016.[129] According to the deal, Turkey was to receive financial assistance and support for sped-up accession talks in return for the measures that it committed to taking to improve the lot of Syrian refugees in Turkey. In contrast to his rhetoric, in practice the Turkish government has by and large kept its end of the bargain, continuing to host close to 3 million Syrian and other refugees, while the flow of refugees into Greece has remained at only a fraction of the peak numbers from 2015.[130]

This, however, does not hide the fact that EU-Turkish relations have hit their lowest point in years. The EU's failure to respond to the coup attempt promptly and lend support to the government led to resentment in Turkey, aggravated by the European Parliament's recommendations in November 2016 to suspend Turkey's membership negotiations. This was followed by Erdoğan's accusations of Nazism directed against the governments of Germany and the Netherlands during the run-up to the constitutional referendum in April 2017, when AKP politicians were denied the possibility of addressing the Turkish diaspora in both countries. However, an element of realism and pragmatism appears to persist. The European Council, the body representing member states, did not suspend Turkey's accession talks. Instead it decided in December 2016 and reiterated in May 2017 that no new chapters would be opened in the accession process as long as the Turkish government continued to maintain a state of emergency rule, which it had introduced after the coup attempt, and remained on the monitoring list of the Council of Europe.[131] The remark by the EU minister Ömer Çelik that the "EU process is a necessity of politics, not romanticism" captures well the focus on "interests" rather than the once highly touted "shared democratic values."[132] Erdoğan's unexpected reference, on Europe Day, May 9, to EU membership being a "strategic target" for Turkey could have not been driven by considerations other than pragmatic ones, especially in light of his practice of blowing "hot and cold toward Europe."[133] However, such pragmatism does not hide the fact that the prospect of relations returning to where they stood in the early years of Erdoğan's rule appears to be slim.

The chances have become even slimmer after an exchange of bitter recriminations between Turkey and Germany, following the detention of German nationals for allegedly aiding terrorism.[134] The blacklist of foreign companies, which included hundreds of German names, also did not help matters, even if the government promptly denied the existence of such a document and assured the companies that their investments were and would remain safe. Needless to say, this further tarnished Turkey's image in Europe, even leading to calls that the EU should impose sanctions on the Turkish government and suspend pre-accession aid as well as the negotiations on upgrading the customs union until rule of law was reestablished.[135] European Commission President Jean-Claude Juncker was reluctant to take such steps, but still remarked that "Turkey is moving away from its self-imposed obligation to become a member of the European Union almost every minute. It's not the European Union that joins Turkey, but it's Turkey joining the European Union."[136] It is more likely that the two sides will try their best to maintain a modicum of a relationship and avoid becoming the party to end the accession process.

Relations with the United States

U.S.-Turkish relations have also been affected by the contradiction between Erdoğan's anti-American rhetoric and Turkey's national security needs. The primary source of this rhetoric is Erdoğan's deep disillusionment with the Obama administration's reluctance to enforce its self-declared "red lines" against the Assad regime. In turn, this undermined the construction of a Middle East in line with Davutoğlu's vision, a deficit that would be further aggravated by the July 2013 military coup against Egypt's Mohamed Morsi. In Syria, however, once the presence of extremist groups increased and IS emerged, Turkey's differences with the United States became even deeper. Tactical cooperation at the level of supporting moderate rebel groups could not hide the profound conflict between Turkey's continued determination to bring about a defeat of Assad and U.S. priorities evolving in the direction of defeating IS. The conflict became especially aggravated when the United States began to cooperate more closely with the Syrian Kurds as the YPG became one of the more successful forces in fighting IS. Turkey's decisions to join the international coalition fighting IS, to tighten its border to prevent the flow of foreign fighters and logistical support to IS, and to grant the United States, in July 2015, access to the Incirlik military base to strike at IS forces did not improve the situation. The resentment persisted and in December 2016 led Erdoğan to cry to the United States, "We are your NATO ally!" and "How on earth can you support terrorist organizations and not us?"[137] In the summer of 2017 tension between the United States and Turkey further escalated when officials from both sides accused each other of supporting terrorist organizations in Syria.[138]

Yet Erdoğan's remarks came simultaneously with his spokesman İbrahim Kalın seeking greater U.S. support for Turkish troops, which faced growing challenges in fighting IS.[139] This was accompanied by news that it was the Turkish side in particular that had expressed interest in having U.S. participation in the January 2017 meeting of the Astana process.[140] It was not until May 2017 that the Trump administration finally sent a representative to such a meeting. By then the Astana process appeared to be moving toward discussing the future of Syria, not just the implementation of the cease-fire agreement of 2016. These brief examples suggest that despite all the anti-American rhetoric, there is a recognition that Turkey needs to work with the United States as a strategic ally to balance the asymmetric relationship that Turkey finds itself in with Russia. This reality is captured by Kurtulmuş's remarks, "We have a strained relationship with the United States at the moment but I don't think it will last long. I think this tension will soon be eased," and his observation that Turkey looked forward to working with the new administration. Interestingly, he went on to acknowledge Russia's "enormous power" in Syria, adding, "We also believe the U.S. will also have to accompany us if the Turkish-Russian partnership reaches a point [in a Syrian peace deal]."[141] Hence, it is not surprising that Erdoğan personally called on the United States to participate in the Astana talks in June 2017.[142]

The issue of the future of Syria is a highly delicate matter, fraught with difficulties and challenges. Clearly, Turkey does not wish to face Russia and Iran alone. It needs to work with the United States, but the Trump administration's willingness to cooperate with Russia on Syria adds an additional layer of complication. This may well explain why Erdoğan is generally recognized to have returned to Turkey with empty hands from his meeting with Trump in May 2017. He failed to change the U.S. policy on arming the Syrian Kurds or gain support for his long-standing ambition to see Assad removed from power.[143] He was also unsuccessful in advancing his agenda to have Fethullah Gülen extradited to Turkey. Saudi and other Gulf state governments' decision in June 2017 to break off relations with Qatar, a close ally of Erdoğan, on the heels of Trump's visit to Saudi Arabia further complicated matters for Turkish foreign policy in the Middle East.

Improving relations with the United States will indeed be a challenge for the government when Erdoğan's anti-American rhetoric has had such a deep impact on Turkish public opinion. According to a survey from July 2017, those that perceived the United States as a threat to Turkey increased by more than twenty percentage-points between 2016 and 2017 (from 44.1 percent to 66.5 percent), while those that identified Russia as a national threat decreased by almost fifteen points (from

34.9 percent to 18.5 percent). At the same time, however, 61.8 percent of those surveyed supported Turkey's NATO membership in 2017 (though this figure was higher at 73.6 percent in 2016).[144]

However, independent of such a result, the declaration by an AKP deputy that NATO was a terrorist organization threatening Turkey rather than protecting it is a stark reminder of the lasting impact of Erdoğan's rhetoric.[145] Under these circumstances the government has an uphill battle to overcome the consequences of the barrage of anti-American and anti-Western rhetoric that has dominated the airwaves especially since the July 2016 coup attempt. Giving pragmatic foreign policies toward the United States and the EU a chance will be difficult. This will be further complicated by the adverse impact that the regression of democracy in Turkey is having on relations with Turkey's transatlantic allies. Trump appears not to be affected by such considerations and seems comfortable ignoring human rights and rule of law issues. However, this is unlikely to be the case with the U.S. Congress. The furor that erupted over Erdoğan's security guards' attack on protesters in Washington, D.C., is likely to cast a long shadow over relations between the two countries for some time to come. That Erdoğan apparently looked on approvingly provoked congressional protests, especially from Senator John McCain, who called for the expulsion of the Turkish ambassador.[146] Arguments by Turkish officials that the security detail was only trying to protect Erdoğan and accusing the Washington, D.C., police force of not doing its job are unlikely to change matters. As a former Turkish ambassador to Washington observed, "such an event has never occurred in the history of Turkish diplomacy."[147] The incident will remain in the public memory for a long time as a reminder of the extent to which Turkey under Erdoğan has drifted away from shared transatlantic values. However, there is also the reality that both sides, Turkey on one side and the United States and EU on the other, need each other in facing the mounting security challenges emanating from Turkey's neighborhood, both in the north and in the south.

Relations with Russia

Erdoğan's policy toward Russia is characterized by conspicuous contradictions. Russian-Turkish relations entered a positive trend beginning in the late 1990s, especially in the economic and energy realms. The two sides would become partners in the "axis of the excluded" that came into being as a result of the tensions that both Turkey and Russia experienced with the West in the mid-2000s, over issues such as the EU accession process and U.S. intervention in Iraq in the case of the former, and over "color revolutions" for the latter.[148] They also shared a common interest in limiting U.S. access to the Black Sea and in further expanding bilateral economic relations. The complete lifting of visa requirements for each other's nationals in 2010 symbolized the extent of the bilateral engagement between the two countries. A High-Level Strategic Cooperation Council was also set up in 2010 to institute regular summits between leaders and cabinet level meetings.

However, there are fundamental contradictions in the relationship. Erdoğan's aspiration to see Russia as a "strategic ally" and even to seek Putin's support in becoming a member of the SCO does not converge with his own interests in Syria. Russia served as a convenient partner to an Erdoğan that increasingly sought to become part of an alternative world order, and both sides succeeded in "compartmentalizing" their relations from their deepening differences over Syria and Crimea.[149] However, the limits of such an approach became starkly evident when the fact that the two countries supported opposing sides in the Syrian conflict led Turkey to shoot down a Russian fighter plane in November 2015, an act that elicited severe economic sanctions from Putin against Turkey. Erdoğan's letter of apology to Putin in June 2016 and maneuvers to mend relations can be partly explained by the obvious cost of these sanctions to the Turkish economy but also by Russia's decisive military superiority in Syria. The latter became especially conspicuous when Turkey could launch its long awaited cross-border military intervention (called Euphrates Shield) into northern Syria in August 2016 only with Russian acquiescence and was compelled to declare its completion in March 2017 once the operation ran up against Russian-supported regime forces and Kurdish groups near the towns of Al-Bab and Manbij.[150]

Erdoğan now faces a Russia that is militarily stronger than when both countries belonged to the axis of the excluded a decade ago. With a reconstituted naval force, Russia now commands a more powerful presence in the Black Sea. Then the chief of Russia's general staff, Valery Gerasimov, in September 2016 did not hesitate to remind Turkey that the naval balance of force had indeed changed dramatically in favor of Russia.[151] However, so far this state of military asymmetry does not appear to have induced Erdoğan to see the value of an alliance with the West as a way to offset the threat posed by Russia. Instead, Erdoğan at his summit with Putin in May 2017 cozied up to Russia by expressing interest in purchasing an S-400 long-range air defense system.[152] However, a Turkish defense expert noted the dilemma in the efforts of a NATO member to plug a weakness of its air force resulting from the purges of F-16 pilots after the coup attempt in 2016 with Russian equipment.[153]

However, it is not difficult to identify major sources of potential future conflict. One source above all concerns Syria. That Turkey has worked closely with Russia in reaching and sustaining a cease-fire agreement and an agreement on de-escalation zones in Syria is no guarantee that their interests will converge as the parties to the conflict seek a political solution for the longer term. Erdoğan appears resigned to Assad remaining in power, but only reluctantly, and this is also no guarantee that he will maintain this position all the way through. He will have to consider the resentment within his own political base about the Russian upper hand in Syria; this is a sentiment manifested most strikingly when an off-duty police officer assassinated the Russian ambassador to Turkey while shouting that he did so in revenge for Russia's actions in Aleppo. Reports from the January 2017 negotiations in Moscow on a new Syrian constitution also point to deep disagreements over the form of the future regime.[154] Russia's reluctance to see Islamic law as a basic source of legislation is expected to raise concern for Erdoğan. The early indications that Putin is actually entertaining a federal form of government for Syria—clearly a green light for the Kurdish minority in northern Syria to establish territorial autonomy along the Turkish border—are likely to test the viability of Russian-Turkish relations.[155] These differences may explain why Erdoğan briefly reentertained his ambition to see Assad removed when Trump ordered a missile attack on a Syrian airbase in April 2017.

Beyond Syria, there is also an uneasy and deepening Turkish dependence on Russia in the energy realm. Furthermore, in recent years, not only have Turkish exports to Russia been falling, but Turkey has also consistently been running a major trade deficit with Russia. Unlike before, the current level of Russian tourism and remittances from Turkish businesses in Russia are no longer sufficient to compensate for the gap. The observation by a Russian commentator that "Erdogan may think Putin is his ally, but instead, Turkey is falling far deeper under Moscow's influence than even Erdoğan may realize"[156] may find an attentive ear in Ankara. In that case, there may emerge room for greater pragmatism in Turkey's relations with not just the United States and NATO but with the EU as well. Turkish decisions to tighten a ban on shipping from Crimea

and revamp relations with Ukraine, including in the area of defense cooperation as well as trade, may be early signs of a renewed effort to achieve
better balance in the asymmetric Russian-Turkish relationship.[157]

CONCLUSION

Davutoğlu's forced resignation in May 2016 brought an element of pragmatism to Turkish foreign policy but did not completely end the era of
ideologically driven policies and the practice of allowing domestic politics to shape foreign policy. Improved relations with Russia and Israel,
the change of position on a future for Syria that may permit the Assad
regime to remain in power, and the cooperation with Russia and Iran
for a cease-fire in Syria largely attest to this turnaround. However, it is
not clear what kind of an end game might emerge from this picture, especially in light of Turkey's current military presence inside Syria. Uncertainty over the U.S. position beyond its determination to defeat IS
constitutes another major challenge. Erdoğan's disappointment over U.S.
support for the YPG has been playing into his anti-Western rhetoric, yet
he also recognizes the need to cooperate with the United States if he is to
balance the deeply asymmetric power relationship he finds himself in
with Putin's Russia over Syria and the broader region. His request for
the extradition of Fethullah Gülen from the United States remains a
thorny issue.[158] Erdoğan's anti-EU vitriolic continues at the same time,
accompanied by his periodic calls for Turkey to distance itself from the
EU and to join instead the SCO.

   This kind of oscillation and the accompanying rhetoric leads to confusion over the strategic orientation of Turkish foreign policy and undermines the global community's confidence in Turkey. It also signals a
major shift from established Turkish statecraft. This is not to say that
Turkey never had any disagreements with the West; however, previous
contestations saw Turkey nonetheless determined to pursue its basic strategic Western orientation and its aspiration for EU membership, which
was not questioned before an ideologically driven agenda took precedence in the conduct of foreign affairs.

   It is very difficult to say what the future holds for Turkish foreign
policy. Early signs of pragmatism since the departure of Davutoğlu are
evident, as is a growing readiness to work with the United States and the
EU despite the virulent anti-Western rhetoric. In the meantime, Erdoğan
has become the undisputed strongman of Turkey. The new constitution

will give the president the right to appoint the top leadership of the Ministry of Foreign Affairs and the diplomatic corps. Hence Turkish foreign policy will indeed be shaped by Erdoğan's priorities and preferences for the foreseeable future and will remain caught between the pragmatism called for by mundane realism and ideological considerations. The latter will always be tempting in keeping his domestic political base mobilized. In the meantime, traditionally pro-Western actors such as the Ministry of Foreign Affairs and the military establishment have already, as one close observer of Turkish foreign policy noted, "turned into non-players and marginal bookkeepers."[159]

Nonetheless, Turkey remains deeply tied to the West institutionally and economically, and still relies on NATO for its own national security in a highly volatile neighborhood. The Turkish leadership is likely to continue to pursue a rhetoric critical of the West as long as the direction of the international order remains unclear. In the short term, this stance may serve Erdoğan's domestic political agenda and help consolidate his one-man rule. On the other hand, his aspiration for closer ties with Eurasia at the expense of throwing aside Turkey's potential EU membership prospects does not seem realistic. In the longer run, the chaos in Turkey's neighborhood and the pressing need to ensure internal security and revive the economy may lead Erdoğan to seek improvements in relations with Turkey's transatlantic partners. One great unknown is the future status of the transatlantic community, especially the role of the United States, and the relationship that emerges with adversaries such as China, Russia, and Iran. In a period marked by a shifting international order, Turkish foreign policy might remain adrift and confused, caught between the legacy of Davutoğlu and emerging Eurasian temptations.

CHAPTER EIGHT

Turkey's Future in the Transatlantic Alliance

Three Scenarios

GREAT UNCERTAINTY FACES TURKEY. Its Western vocation seems to be in hiatus, and its place in the transatlantic alliance is weakening. This is occurring in parallel with the uncertainty that currently engulfs the international liberal order. It is not clear whether present and future U.S. administrations will remain committed to safeguarding the pillars of this order—free trade, common defense under NATO, respect for territorial integrity, the promotion of democratic values, and a host of other norms. It is also not clear how the European Union will manage the unending arrival of migrants and refugees, adjust to the challenges of Brexit, or negotiate rising populist and nationalist sentiments in its member states. On the borders of the EU, Russia's territorial ambitions will be difficult to check. There are also many challenges emanating from the turmoil in the Middle East. Indeed, the post–World War II international order put in place by the United States and its transatlantic allies now increasingly appears to be more and more "out of order."[1]

The question of where Turkey will stand and what it will do to protect and support this order will be critical. So far, Turkey has not stepped forth as a stalwart ally. Its recent trajectory has not been promising: from its high point of being touted as a model of democracy and economic stability for the region, Turkey has sunk into an abyss of instability. The hope that it would succeed in marrying Islam with liberal democratic principles has long been dashed. The fault lines between Turkey and the West have been accentuated by a poorly thought-out U.S. policy in the region, especially with respect to Syria and Iraq; Turkey's entrenched suspicion of Western agendas and its belief that it is basically trying to operate in a friendless world; and Europe's persistent othering of Turkey. Nonetheless, Turkey formed an important element of the transatlantic alliance in the past, and securing its anchor should be a matter of high priority to Europe and the United States. In this regard, the categorical observation by retired U.S. ambassador James F. Jeffrey— "We could not have won the Cold War, had Turkey gone under or even better [remained] neutral—it's that simple. And Turkey could not have remained a sovereign, independent state, had we not supported it in the beginning of the 1940s. And in the post–Cold War mess . . . short of Colombia, North Korea and the South China Sea, almost all of our conflicts, Georgia, Ukraine, Bosnia, Kosovo, Iran nukes, Syria, Gaza . . . they all involved Turkey and we could not have done the things we did had Turkey been uncooperative or opposed to it—it's that simple"—is very revealing and still valid.[2] It would not be wrong to claim that today's international disorder would perhaps be less of a disorder without the tug of war between a disillusioned and skeptical Turkey and a Western alliance that has largely failed to adopt policies to dispel this distrust.

MAKING A NEW TURKEY

The Gezi Park protests of June 2013 and their violent suppression by Turkish security forces surfaced the tensions, instability, and authoritarian turn in Turkey's political life that had been simmering subterraneously. The regressive trend in Turkey, marked by a deterioration in civil liberties, the almost complete loss of an independent judiciary, vastly reduced freedom for the media, economic decline, and increased restrictions on minorities, has been closely associated with Erdoğan's actions and aspirations. Though the role of regional and international developments in Turkey's present difficulties cannot be denied, it is also obvious that Turkey's domestic and foreign policymaking has been increasingly enmeshed with Erdoğan's outlook and ambitions.

Domestic Policy

"Erdogan's journey"—so dubbed by a *Foreign Affairs* columnist— since his early conduct in office has taken a distinctly conservative and authoritarian tone, with little tolerance for dissent and diversity.[3] Disturbing practices reminiscent of the 1990s, which included stripping

Turkish nationals of their citizenship, have been reintroduced.[4] Following the coup attempt in July 2016, an ever-growing number of people have been purged from their jobs, detained, and even had their properties confiscated with little regard for due legal process.[5] The reintroduction of capital punishment is being called for with fervor. The coup attempt helped him justify the introduction of a state of emergency, and its renewal ever since, that further centralized executive decision making in his hands by suspending judicial oversight over his decisions. A wave of terror attacks by the Kurdistan Workers' Party (PKK) and the Islamic State (IS) has shaken the country, giving Erdoğan additional leeway to justify his repressive policies. The referendum of April 2017 introduced constitutional amendments to eliminate the traditional checks and balances that underwrite a democracy. The supervisory role of the parliament will be reduced, the office of the prime minister will be abolished, and the president will enjoy considerable leverage over the judiciary. Erdoğan will be able to appoint his ministers directly, without any confirmation process, and to appoint and dismiss all high-ranking bureaucrats. The new constitution opens the way for Erdoğan to rule single-handedly until 2029 and possibly to 2034, which would make him the longest-serving president in Turkish republican history, well ahead of Atatürk, who ruled from 1923 to 1938. As an astute observer of Turkey noted, Erdoğan's governing philosophy is fast becoming Turkey's new "official ideology," replacing that of Kemalism, and is also centered on a cult of personality.[6]

Erdoğan's authoritarian and strong man streak needs to be seen against the background of a political culture that has yet to produce liberal-minded politicians and a public broadly receptive to it. Authoritarianism is not unique to the AKP; the other parties and their constituencies, including the main social democratic opposition party the Republican People's Party (CHP), not to mention the right-wing Nationalist Movement Party (MHP), all suffer in varying degrees from the same condition. Turkish democracy is a "democracy without democrats,"[7] deeply shaped by a long-standing authoritarian political culture and conservative social values that dictate obedience to state authority accompanied by an absence of broad-based support or any commitment to civil liberties. This also constitutes "the foundation on which the AKP rests."[8] Not surprisingly, the few truly "conservative democrats" among the founders and supporters of the AKP saw themselves being purged in due course. Ironically, under the "new sultan," the "silent revolution" once led by the AKP ended up "devouring its own children."[9]

The autocratic turn in Turkey has unfolded in parallel with widening divisions with the West that are also accentuated by the erosion of secularism. The constitutional amendments of April 2017 do not contain any provisions against the secular nature of the Turkish state. However, the line between advocating conservative values and implementing sharia is likely to become narrower, while the challenges to the basic values of the republic will continue to increase. This is accentuated by the view among some Islamists in Turkey that democracy and Islam cannot be compatible because one is based on the electoral will of the individual while the latter is based on divine law.[10] Turkey's still relatively stable legal system may not be able to protect civil liberties against the AKP's restrictive initiatives for much longer, as was once safely predicted in 2012.[11] The question of whether or not Turkey is moving in the direction of becoming an Islamic state is likely to produce further debate. In the meantime, the bigger agenda than Islamization for Erdoğan and the AKP seems to have been the restructuring of the traditional republican state. The party paid particular attention to staff the state with people committed to its cause, with little regard for meritocracy. The AKP's declared objective was to "normalize and democratize" Turkish politics by undoing the "tutelary regime"—the centerpiece of it being the Turkish military, along with the judiciary and a good part of the state bureaucracy—which was seen as inhibiting democracy. However, efforts to dismantle this regime did not bring a "normalized and democratized" state apparatus. Instead, the current system ironically seems to have adopted the logic and habits of the old "deep state," one with little democratic accountability and scrutiny.[12]

Finally, at a time when established democracies are witnessing the rise of populist leaders, Erdoğan's Turkey is seen as setting the standard, even for the United States.[13] The decisive test of whether Turkey will indeed become a model of authoritarian populism for the rest of the world, and even established democracies, to emulate will depend on how politics in post-referendum Turkey unfolds. The tight outcome of the referendum is a constant reminder that close to one-half of the Turkish electorate is restless about a one-man authoritarian rule. The fact that from now on, winning a national election will require a minimum of 50 percent plus one vote, instead of the lower percentages that used to ensure governing majorities in parliament for the AKP, is likely to make the system much more open to change.[14] This might require Erdoğan to abandon his recent practice of mobilizing voters through divisive, identity-based politics and return to the AKP's "factory settings" to win hearts and minds beyond his immediate base. In a different scenario, he might risk seeing a new leader from the ranks of the AKP or the opposition emerging with the promise of a less polarized and freer Turkey. This, however, would call for truly free and fair elections, the minimum sine qua non of democratic politics.

Foreign Policy: Toward Zero Neighbors without Problems

Turkey's backsliding from democratization efforts at home was paralleled by the loss of its soft power status abroad. The zero problems with neighbors policy pursued by the AKP in its initial years, though much in line with the work and vision of previous governments, had been carried out with more vigor. Particularly impressive during Abdullah Gül's tenure was the overhauling of Turkey's long-standing policy on Cyprus by lending support to the UN's unification plan for the island. Turkey's outreach to Armenia also marked a significant moment after decades of deadlock between the two countries. In the Middle East, Turkey's efforts not only helped improve political relations in the region but also increased commercial and cultural integration. In parallel, there was also an emphasis on maintaining a constructive relationship with both the United States and the EU. Turkey even gave modest support to democracy promotion projects, expanded its peacekeeping operations, and assumed a greater role in humanitarian and development assistance projects. As some observers remarked, Turkey could be seen as running the European Neighborhood Policy to build a "ring of friends" on behalf of the EU.[15] In short, Turkey looked solidly anchored in the international liberal order and actively contributing to its strengthening.

This picture began to change soon after Ahmet Davutoğlu was named minister of foreign affairs in 2009. His initial policies, based on pragmatism and soft power, gradually revealed a more ambitious objective once the Arab Spring erupted. Davutoğlu and his circle took a more assertive position in the region, guided by a pan-Islamist ideology that predicted the Muslim Brotherhood coming to power across the region. The expectation that the Muslim Brotherhood would readily welcome an AKP-led Turkish leadership prompted them to advocate for a "post-Western international order" for the region (discussed in chapter 7 and the appendix). Despite the chaos that followed, Davutoğlu resisted altering course. Turkey, against all advice and resistance from many circles—the diplomatic corps, the military leadership, even former deputies and ministers of the AKP—became embroiled in the Syrian war and the domestic conflicts of Arab countries. Becoming an open party to an intra-Arab conflict and persistently seeking regime change marked a major deviation from Turkey's traditional statecraft. A long-established precept of Turkish foreign policy, believed to have originated in Atatürk's instructions to Numan Menemencioğlu, secretary general of the Ministry of Foreign Affairs in the 1930s (and subsequently, during most of World War II, as minister of foreign affairs), is not to become involved in the internal affairs of Arab countries.[16] This precept began to be widely articulated as Davutoğlu's policies came under increasing criticism, not only by the opposition but also within the ranks of his own party. A remark by Numan Kurtulmuş, a former deputy prime minister—"I am one of those who believe our policy on Syria made big mistakes"—is very revealing.[17] After Davutoğlu's resignation as prime minister in May 2016, a degree of realism and pragmatism began to replace his "imperial fantasy."[18]

However, this does not mean that Turkey is likely to return to its traditional statecraft. It is even doubtful whether the current Turkish leadership would revert to its own party's "factory settings" in foreign policy, as in Gül's era. Even if such a return were sought and were possible, it is doubtful whether Turkey can enjoy the goodwill and trust of its neighbors once again and serve as a model for the region. The days when Turkey was regarded "as a source of inspiration for political reform" seem to be long gone. This may well explain why Rachid Ghannouchi made the point of mentioning Tunisia as an inspiration for the region rather than Turkey, as he had so often done in the past, and cautioned against the dangers of succumbing to a majoritarian understanding of democracy.[19] The comment by Yaşar Yakış, the first minister of foreign affairs of the AKP, that "Tunisia was inspired by Turkey, and now we have to be inspired by Tunisia," should therefore not come as a surprise.[20]

The future course of Turkish foreign policy defies any prediction. Signs of pragmatism in the efforts of reconciliation with Russia, Israel, and to some degree Iraq are evident. Turkey has also revealed a discreet willingness to work with the United States and the EU, despite the virulent anti-Western rhetoric of Erdoğan. What is also clear is that Turkey's foreign policy is likely to be shaped by Erdoğan's priorities and preferences in the foreseeable future. Turkish foreign policy is likely to oscillate between the pragmatism called for by mundane realism, on the one hand, and the ideological impulses of "new" Turkey, steeped in political Islam and rising nationalism, on the other. Advocates of traditional statecraft—those who have managed to survive in the Ministry of Foreign Affairs—and the more realist members of the military top brass are likely to call for the former. They would also be joined by the business community, which needs export markets and foreign direct investment. The emphasis for these groups is likely to be on the need to repair relations with Western allies, especially at a time of such uncertainty in the world. There will also be those in the military and the entourage of the Turkish president who will stoke skepticism toward both the EU and the United States while seeking to deepen relations with China, Russia, and Eurasia. They will continue to question the value of Turkey's NATO membership and advocate for its exit. Yet, geopolitical realities in the region as well as Turkey's national security needs will mitigate their efforts. After all, once a country is out of NATO, it would be very difficult to get back in, especially for a country that is failing to keep its commitments to the democratic standards that is required of member-states.[21] These contradictory forces will lend considerable uncertainty as well as volatility to Turkish foreign policy and will generate challenges for Turkey's relations with the West. As a former under-secretary of the Ministry of Foreign Affairs remarked, "Engaging in endless rhetoric, having spats with Turkey's traditional allies and zigzagging between major powers may appeal to some in today's polarized Turkey but they can no longer be presented as a coherent, national interest-based foreign policy."[22] Time will tell whether this advice is heeded.

FUTURE SCENARIOS

Three basic scenarios for Turkey's future relations with the West present themselves. As someone at least theoretically likely to be in power and shaping Turkey's foreign power until 2034, Erdoğan is central to each scenario.

In the first scenario, Erdoğan walks back his party's domestic political agenda to the early days of his reign. Every sign currently points to his aspiration for an authoritarian, personalized system of power, yet Erdoğan does have a long track record of pragmatism and a demonstrated ability to make U-turns. More liberal policies that respect personal and religious freedoms are in his tool kit. Reinstating the rule of law and various freedoms would eliminate much of the tension and simmering resentment being directed toward Erdoğan.

Politically, relaunching the peace process with the Kurds would help Turkey heal a long-bleeding wound. Together with a renewed commitment to the Ankara criteria, this would help reenergize the coalition of liberals, Kurds, and conservative democrats and would soften the current *Kulturkampf* in the country. Such a domestic agenda would also go far toward reviving EU-Turkish relations, which need not take the form of immediately reactivating Turkey's membership bid. The focus would be on deepening bilateral economic and societal relations and on injecting life into the harmonization process, with eventual accession deferred to a later date. A greater strategic dialogue on foreign and security policy issues would help reconstitute mutual trust but also assist Turkey to resume its zero-problems policy in foreign affairs.

These measures would help rebuild Turkey's soft power and prestige in its neighborhood. From a newly grounded base, Turkey could return to a constructive role in managing the many problems of the region, especially in war torn Syria and Iraq as well as the unsettled Cyprus conflict. Restoring a modicum of peace and stability in Turkey's neighborhood would be a "win-win" for all involved. European (and other) recognition of Turkey's positive steps would be expected to improve the investment climate in the country and help resuscitate the economy. In turn, in such a Turkey the rest of the transatlantic community would find a solid partner to address the many challenges facing Turkey's neighborhood. Finally, for this scenario to be sustainable, a peaceful transition of power from Erdoğan to a new leader, mediated through free and fair elections, would eventually be necessary. The improving climate for democracy would help narrow the fault lines in Turkey's relations with its transatlantic allies and move the country to a more important position in the liberal international order.[23]

This optimistic scenario, unfortunately, does not look likely. It seems somewhat unrealistic to expect Erdoğan to overcome his majoritarian understanding of democracy and his increasingly authoritarian and confrontational ways. Should that situation continue to persist, the possibility of a more macabre scenario emerges, one that points toward a conclusive abandonment of the institutions underpinning the global liberal order.

In such a case—the second scenario—Erdoğan would continue to mobilize his nationalist and Islamist supporters, only more aggressively. He would employ antipluralist rhetoric reinforcing the notion that he alone represented the will of the people (the 50 percent plus one vote bogey) and that anyone who criticized him posed a threat to the well-being of society at large.[24] He would continue to maintain the state of emergency imposed after the July 2016 coup attempt and use it to repress his critics. Conspiracy narratives involving the West would abound. These policies and the accompanying purges, along with the practice of staffing bureaucracies based on loyalty, would continue to weaken state capacity and the ability of the judiciary to deliver justice. This kind of othering and the absence of the rule of law would further polarize the country and fuel societal tension.

In such a scenario, the Kurdish problem would persist and defy resolution. In the aftermath of the coup, Erdoğan has detained, imprisoned, and purged officials of the leading Kurdish political party, the People's Democratic Party (HDP), under the terms of a loosely defined anti-terror law, with little regard for their being elected officials, representing millions of votes. The main difference from the 1990s, when Kurdish deputies saw their immunities lifted and were imprisoned, is that this familiar picture is compounded many times by the chaos reigning next door in Syria. The conflict has been spilling over into Turkey as members of IS and their sympathizers have perpetrated acts of terrorism that have traumatized Turkish society and adversely affected the economy.

The weakening of the main institutions of the country—its military, police force, and the judiciary—is a major obstacle in Turkey's fight against terrorism. This is compounded by concerns that Erdoğan mistrusts and fears the military as a long standing republican institution and is said to be raising his own army.[25] The security situation and the erosion of the rule of law at one point even led to worries that Turkey might become yet another failed state.[26] Coupled with growing repression and polarization of society this "could catapult Turkey into a terrible civil war."[27] Though these may be exaggerated, it is not difficult to envisage a situation under which Turkish citizens would be found among the ranks of refugees and irregular migrants fleeing to Europe as security, stability and the economy in the country deteriorates.[28] This eventuality would not be surprising and is not without precedent: there was a period back in the 1980s and 1990s when large numbers of Turkish nationals, particularly leftists and Kurds, did seek asylum in Europe. Today, there are growing reports of an "exodus" of talented Turks from the country.[29] A Turkey that loses its well-educated and Westernized human capital and is racked by internal problems would be far from able to help stabilize an already difficult neighborhood, nor could it be a model of democracy and economic prosperity. Quite the contrary: it would be an exporter as well as an instigator of instability, aggravating the chaos in the region. The lack of security and the crumbling institutions would also undermine an already strained international liberal order.

It is under this scenario that Erdoğan, in a moment of populist frenzy, could break completely with the West and abandon institutions central to the international liberal order. Erdoğan has on numerous occasions already entertained the idea. He has advocated abandoning the bid for EU membership and instead joining the Shanghai Cooperation Organization (SCO), which would presumably require leaving NATO. Since the coup attempt, he has frequently called for the reintroduction of capital punishment, which would put Turkey's membership in the Council of Europe, the very institution that symbolizes Turkey's European vocation, in serious jeopardy.[30] Or, as a result of the blatant human rights violations Turkey has accumulated, the country could be suspended from membership in the European Court of Human Rights (ECHR). Historically, Turkey is among the countries that have faced the largest number of cases at the EHCR. However, even in the worst of times the notion of exiting the court has never seriously been entertained. This could change if a future Turkey under Erdoğan abandoned its Western vocation.

The third and most likely scenario is a return to a situation reminiscent of the 1990s, with Erdoğan leading a Turkey that limps from one crisis to another and with a fragile economy deeply stuck in a middle-income trap. It would be a Turkey run by an oppressive leader who also continued to enjoy significant electoral support by keeping the country in a state of constant tension and by channeling large subsidies to his loyal base. The latter would lead to the abandonment of the AKP's long-standing budgetary discipline and weaken Turkey's financial standing while providing additional fodder for blaming the West for the ills of the country. Nevertheless, Erdoğan would still display an element of pragmatism. The geopolitical reality on the ground and the need to prevent the instability in Syria from spilling over into Turkey even more than it has would drive this pragmatism. He would grudgingly find a way of distancing himself from regime change in Syria and from the establishment of an Islamic-oriented form of government in that country. This would require cooperating with Russia and Iran, and possibly with the U.S. administration. If Russia and Assad were to resort to the same scorched-earth policies they followed in eastern Aleppo in 2016 toward remaining opposition-controlled regions, such as the one in Idlib, it would be more difficult for Erdoğan to keep his Islamist base in Turkey under control, and also to maintain improved relations with Russia. In contrast, such relations would be critical to maintaining some economic cooperation with Russia, especially in the energy realm, and encouraging much-needed Russian tourism to return to Turkey.

Most poignantly, under scenario three the taste of liberal democracy that Turkey experienced in the early days of AKP rule would be recognized as an anomaly. Whatever democracy might be permitted in the country would be *demokrasi*, Erdoğan style, characterized by populism, majoritarianism, and a mixture of Islam and intolerant Turkish nationalism.[31] In this "new" Turkey, liberals, Kurds, and secularists would have to resign themselves to a socially and politically conservative, if not oppressive, environment. There would remain large question marks with respect to the independence of the judiciary and a level playing field in the economy. The "new" Turkey would also be hostile to the legacy of the "old" Turkey and its Western orientation, and would ignore the best years of the AKP when Turkey was most integrated into the international liberal order and touted as a model of governance. However, as Shadi Hamid, an expert on Islam and the Middle East, has noted, international criticism and a "dimming of the Turkish model" is a small price for Erdoğan to pay in return for putting into place a system of governance that ensures "religious Turks will always have to be catered to, no matter who is running for office."[32]

Though the picture is daunting, scenario three is the most likely to eventuate. Structural factors such as geopolitical, institutional, and national security considerations and economic ties would break the temptation to leave NATO and completely rupture relations with the EU. However, it would be unrealistic to expect in EU-Turkey relations a scenario that could go beyond improving the customs union between the two sides.[33] In any event, Erdoğan's ideological preferences and longing for a post-Western international order would continue to raise questions about Turkey's relationship with the West and its place in the transatlantic community. Hence, under this scenario, the fault lines between Turkey and the West would be expected to persist and deepen, while whatever relationship survives would be strictly transactional.

ERDOĞAN AND THE AKP have been in power now for more than fifteen years, since the AKP came to power in November 2002 (Erdoğan became prime minister in March 2003). Erdoğan will soon have served more years as head of the Turkish state and government than Atatürk did as the founder of the Turkish Republic. However, as much as Erdoğan has become synonymous with Turkey, Turkey is still bigger than Erdoğan.[34] The test will come when the nation prepares for a transition to a post-Erdoğan Turkey. It is very difficult to predict who could lead such a transition. Though some in the AKP did not welcome the constitutional referendum and the idea of turning the Turkish parliamentary system into one-man rule,[35] it is not clear whether a reformist movement favoring greater democracy and closer relations with the EU would emerge from the ranks of the AKP. The emergence of a leader from the ranks of the opposition looks even less likely. The "long march" for "justice" from Ankara to Istanbul in June and July 2017, led by the leader of the main opposition party, Kemal Kılıçdaroğlu, received large public support, but whether this can be turned into an electoral success in the next national elections in 2019 is not certain. Ultimately, barring the frightening prospects of civil chaos, it is a long-standing Turkish expectation that "those who came through the ballot box, will go through the ballot box (*sandıkla geldiler, sandıkla giderler*)," in other words, it normally should be through the ballot box that the next leader should be decided.[36] This of course assumes respect for the minimum prerequisite of a democracy: free and fair elections. Time will tell whether this is indeed respected and "new" Turkey's remaining link to the international liberal order is sustained.

RECOMMENDATIONS

Turkey has been a member of the transatlantic community for more than seven decades, and its economy is largely integrated with that of the West. Though the association has at times been fraught with difficulties and not free of crises, it is important to protect the minimum democratic and economic gains achieved so far by Turkey through its connection to the West. How this might be accomplished is a challenge, in light of the volatility in Turkey's region and the uncertain future of the international liberal order itself. Nonetheless, some recommendations can be forwarded for the EU, the United States, and Turkey.

Despite the deepening setbacks to Turkish democracy, continuing to engage Turkey rather than abandoning it is of paramount importance. Turkey has a long tradition of electoral democracy and, despite the recent trend toward de-democratization, can return to it. Democratization is not always a linear process with a clear yes/no outcome; rather, it is best understood as a continuous struggle for improvement. Therefore, it is important that both the EU and the United States continue to support the process in Turkey and keep its EU membership prospects alive, whatever the challenges might be.

The EU should recognize that its reluctance to truly embrace Turkey accounts for part of the regressive trend in the country. Some EU member states' regard of Turkey as too culturally different provoked profound resentment, which was exploited by opponents of reforms and EU membership for populist ends. Erdoğan's response to advocates of EU membership at a meeting organized by the Turkish Industry and Business Association (TÜSİAD) in May 2017 is telling: "It is not that we were received with open arms by the EU, that we then turned them down."[37] He challenged the EU to engage Turkey fairly and honorably rather than keep it waiting at its door—a suggestion that Erdoğan is still open to the possibility of constructive engagement. However, during a BBC interview he argued that the EU was wasting Turkey's time and that the EU was not indispensable to Turkey, then quickly qualified that "we will continue being sincere with the EU for a little more time."[38]

One way for the EU to demonstrate its readiness to accept Turkey would be to become more convincing that visa liberalization for Turkish nationals will indeed be honored once the terms are met. This is a long-standing issue between the two sides. EU nationals have long been able to enter Turkey freely without a reciprocal arrangement that would benefit Turks traveling to Europe. Visa restrictions on Turkish nationals were introduced in the early 1980s in reaction to the military coup. Lifting these restrictions had long been on the agenda but was not acted on until March 2016, when it was incorporated into the migration deal between the EU and Turkey in a somewhat transactional spirit. However, the introduction of the state of emergency after the coup attempt and the increasingly poor chemistry between the two sides complicated matters. Resolving the visa issue would help diffuse Turkey's sense of exclusion and would bring significant economic benefits to both the EU and Turkey. This is especially the case if at the same time the customs union between the two sides is modernized and upgraded, not only leading to an expansion in trade into new sectors but also obliging Turkey to adopt reforms. Ultimately, these would be reforms that would help stop the erosion of the rule of law and encourage both transparency and accountability. Such an engagement would also help slow down what has become labelled as "de-Europeanization", a process that is undoing the EU reforms that AKP had put into place to make Turkey a more "liberal democracy" and a dynamic market economy, and allow the protection of at least some of the gains for the future.[39]

Relieving Turkey of some part of the burden of caring for the now more than 3 million Syrian and other refugees also appears urgent. Erdoğan has repeatedly complained that Turkey carries most of this burden alone, and that it needs the support of the EU and the United States. He has a point. Protecting refugees is an international responsibility, and burden sharing can take the form of both financial assistance and resettlement, both of which are incorporated into the migration deal Turkey reached with the EU in March 2016. The EU should redouble its efforts to make sure the agreement's mechanisms and provisions are working effectively. Recruiting U.S. interest in attending to the needs of refugees and improving security cooperation with Turkey will be critical in making sure that refugees—especially the younger and more impressionable refugees—do not get swept into the recruitment networks of extremist groups.

In a similar vein, the United States would be well advised to adopt a more sensitive attitude toward Turkey's national security concerns. In the past, the United States pursued policies that left the Turkish side deeply disappointed that its concerns and interests were not always adequately considered. The U.S. invasion of Iraq and its aftermath, for example, undermined the safety of Turkish nationals and affected trade with Turkey's regional trading partners. More recently, the U.S. decision to work closely with the PYD to fight IS in Syria without due consideration for Turkish interests has not been well received in Ankara. U.S. actions and behaviors around issues of concern to Turkey are jeopardizing any prospect of finding a long-term solution to the chaos in Syria and the instability in the Middle East through bilateral cooperation.

With respect to security matters, Turkey is in a neighborhood with a notorious geopolitics; the security challenges along its borders are overwhelming. NATO has been the key vehicle for Turkey to ensure its defense and provide a strong anchor to the West. The failed 2016 coup has already institutionally distanced Turkey from NATO. Turkey has been an invaluable and loyal NATO ally, and ways should be found to engage Turkey in NATO operations. While it would be unrealistic to expect a more active Turkey in operations against Russia in the Black Sea or the Baltics, Turkey could play a role in NATO-led efforts in the Mediterranean, for example by monitoring illegal migration or helping to stabilize Libya. However, assuaging Turkey's concerns about defense capabilities against ballistic missiles will be the most critical challenge going forward. Turkey's uncertainty over whether the Article 5 provisions of the NATO treaty will be upheld is fueling doubt, especially in the context of the proliferation of ballistic missile capabilities in the region. This, coupled with insensitivity toward Turkey's national security concerns, is driving Turkey to seek closer military cooperation with China and Russia, which cannot be in the interest of the transatlantic community. The United States taking Turkey's security concerns seriously and finding a way to mitigate its feeling of abandonment will be as critical as reminding Erdoğan that NATO members are expected to adhere to the democratic standard of its membership.[40]

This is important also from a geostrategic perspective. Keeping Turkey anchored in the transatlantic community will be critical in terms of protecting the international liberal order and managing challenges to it. The cost of losing Turkey to the other side would be detrimental to the interests not only of the United States but also of the West at large. The situation is better in the matter of trade. Unlike most of its neighbors, Turkey has no gas or oil to export and must maintain a competitive economy that is open to foreign trade. The EU is Turkey's paramount trading partner, and upgrading the customs union is going to be critical in keeping Turkey engaged in the institutions of the international liberal order. However, the United States could help too. Currently the United States enjoys an important trade surplus with Turkey, and the only way to expand U.S. exports to Turkey would entail having fair trade between the two countries such that Turkey could expand its exports. Such trade expansion could also work as a policy to encourage reform in Turkey in return for greater market access to the United States. In this way trade policy, especially when combined with an upgrade of the EU-Turkey Customs Union, could become an important vehicle to enhance the rule of law and governance in Turkey as well as strengthen Turkey's ties to the international liberal order.

For these recommendations to be most effective, Turkey will need to do its share too. Most important, Turkey must recognize that anger, fury, and ideologically driven slogans, as much as they may serve populist causes, do not help solve Turkey's problems or those in its neighborhood. The problems of its region are entrenched, and making progress on them will require good will and trust, not confrontation. Reviving the letter and the spirit of the zero-problems policy of the AKP's earlier foreign policy would help. The experiences of past statecraft can help guide

Turkey toward a recovery of its standing in its region and in global relations.

For this to happen, a certain degree of self-understanding will be required. Turkey enjoyed its greatest influence and prestige when its relations with the West were good and Turkey was well integrated into the transatlantic community. Indeed, two former undersecretaries at the Turkish ministry of foreign affairs are correct in observing that "what earned us prestige internationally was our democracy and economy much more than our military."[41] It was Turkey's promising performance in these two areas that had endowed it with abundant soft power in the Muslim world and beyond. Patience, pragmatism, and a commitment to liberal democratic governance and the rule of law should help Turkey recover its soft power and prestige. This would also enable Turkey and its transatlantic allies to address more openly the many grievances that have accumulated on both sides. Turkey would also be on better footing to develop its relations with states outside the transatlantic community, such as those in the Middle East, Russia, China, and beyond.

Erdoğan appears to be adopting a more pragmatic approach to foreign policy, though leaving behind an ideological agenda and Ahmet Davutoğlu's dream of a post-Western international order will be difficult. Here the West must understand that Turkey today is not yesterday's Turkey; the leadership is not keen to uphold "old" Turkey's Western orientation, believing rather that Turkey belongs to a different civilization from the West. In the near term, it is uncertain in which direction the leadership will steer the country; however, a full return to a liberal democracy trajectory is desired but not very likely. Turkey at best will be an electoral democracy in which civil liberties are likely to remain constrained. However, keeping Turkey engaged in the transatlantic community will be important in terms of sustaining the parts of Turkish society that are committed to a Western vocation and liberal democratic values. In the longer run, this is what would help Turkey's return to the fold. Abandoning Turkey would neither serve the interests of the transatlantic community, nor Turkey or the stability of Turkey's neighborhood.

The pendulum-like nature of Turkey's foreign policy, at times distancing itself from the West and then returning to it, may be expected to continue. The course would still resemble "Turkish Gaullism," but without the strong base of confidence it enjoyed in 2011, when the notion was first introduced.[42] It is likely to harden into a foreign policy run on self-interest, driven by a strong sense of nationalism, shaped by an

Islamic worldview, and articulated in a confrontational mode directed against the West. The basis of relations with the West and the EU is likely to be strictly transactional, somewhat in line with the nationalist tendencies surfacing in both the United States and parts of the EU. The aspiration to see Turkey as part of a liberal and democratic transatlantic community may well have to wait for recent political developments to play out, and the duration of the wait is unknown. The challenge now is for these longtime allies—Turkey, the EU, and the United States—to work out a relationship that can still help maintain a modicum of security, stability, and prosperity in Europe and in Turkey's neighborhood. Time will tell whether this might be achievable without nurturing a sense of common values, a "we-ness" that could strengthen each other's position. In any event, the "new" Turkey will be even more challenging to deal with than the "old" one.

The Davutoğlu Doctrine

AHMET DAVUTOĞLU IS WIDELY seen as the author of the Justice and Development Party's (AKP's) foreign policy and someone whose name became synonymous with Turkish diplomacy during his years in office. The ideas expressed in his publications and public speeches, starting from the early days of his academic career and continuing through his term in office, amount to no less than a doctrine. His constant presence on the diplomatic stage led some to compare him to Henry Kissinger, though Davutoğlu has claimed to be more of a person of ideals and principles than with Realpolitik.[1]

Davutoğlu's conduct of foreign policy owed a great deal to the ideas he formulated during his academic career in the 1990s at a Malaysian university as well as at two Turkish universities. Many of the expressions he introduced to the field, such as "zero problems with neighbors," or his descriptions of Turkey as a "central," "wise," and "order-building" country, are recognized internationally.[2] As a result, he is seen by many as the person who singlehandedly "constructed the theoretical and intellectual background of Turkish foreign policy in the AK Party era," in *The Economist*'s estimation.[3] Davutoğlu has indeed left a heavy imprint on the way Turkey conducted its foreign affairs in the past decade, and his concerns while in office continue to drive Turkey's agenda.

The reality, however, is much more complex than the slogans he promulgated.

During Davutoğlu's time in office as minister of foreign affairs and prime minister, May 2009 to May 2016, when he had to resign, his ambitious political agenda sought to reorient Turkish foreign policy away from its established statecraft and assumed for Turkey a capacity to alter the regional order in the Middle East by riding the Arab Spring wave. This was accompanied by an effort to restructure the Turkish foreign policy establishment as part of a larger project by the AKP to craft a new national identity for Turkey. However, once the Arab Spring turned sour and the region became embroiled in chaos, his agenda collapsed. Turkey was left, ironically, with only problems with neighbors and the dust of his ambitious dreams.

FROM PRAGMATIC VISIONARY TO IDEOLOGICAL VICTIM

Davutoğlu's transition from academia to the ranks of the AKP occurred soon after the party's 2002 electoral victory, when he became the foreign policy adviser to Abdullah Gül, then serving as prime minister.[4] In 2009 Erdoğan appointed him minister of foreign affairs, later chairman of the AKP, and, after the August 2014 presidential elections, prime minister—the highest office Davutoğlu would achieve.

The initial years of Turkish foreign policy under Gül received broadly positive recognition from the international community. Turkey's election in 2008 by a large margin to a seat on the UN Security Council as nonpermanent member was evidence of this recognition, for Turkey had not served on that body since 1961. Once Gül became president, in 2007, and Ali Babacan stepped into the post of foreign minister, Davutoğlu's influence as adviser became much more pronounced. During this period Davutoğlu was still concerned to foster regional cooperation in the South Caucasus, the Balkans, and especially the Middle East, through pragmatic and incremental policies. He promoted the concept of economic interdependency with neighboring states as a way to achieve greater security and stability for the region as well as for Turkey. He was cognizant of the importance of the European integration project as a recipe for success in conflict resolution and did not hesitate to refer to it as a model to emulate. He argued that Turkey's opening up to the East should be understood in that light and compared Turkey's engagement of countries in its neighborhood, and especially in the Middle East, to Germany's "Ostpolitik" of the late 1960s.[5] He also advanced quite liberal institutionalist ideas. He defended the importance of multilateralism in international relations and proposed that international organizations have the capacity to teach states norms whereby states could achieve more stable international relations.[6] He urged for Turkey's active participation in international forums and organizations as an important aspect of his policy of multilateralism to promote constructive relations with neighbors and regions beyond.[7] Finally, his was a unique voice in arguing that Turkish security could be better served by extending freedoms and democracy both in Turkey and abroad.[8]

Though Davutoğlu's "Ostpolitik" did not necessarily represent a novel turn in Turkish diplomacy—the notion of expanding relations with the neighborhood had originated in the 1980s and 1990s, when Turgut Özal was in power, and was pursued by İsmail Cem as minister of foreign affairs before the AKP came to power—Davutoğlu understood regional integration, especially in the Middle East, from a different perspective, as a way to transcend the borders imposed by the Western powers on what used to be Ottoman territory. His aspiration was to make once more available to subsequent generations a geography that had historically been accessible to earlier generations.[9] This interest foreshadowed some of his bolder policies that would emerge as he felt increasingly secure in his role at the helm of the Ministry of Foreign Affairs. Thus he welcomed the Arab Spring as an event signaling a change of course of the "river of history,"[10] as he called it, and an opportunity to establish a "post-Western international order" in the Middle East, to be led by Turkey.[11] His agenda, to close what he described as a "parenthesis" in Middle Eastern history that represented a Western-imposed order,[12] got Turkey embroiled in the Arab Spring, which subsequently turned into a winter and plunged Turkey into the ensuing chaos in Syria.

Thus the ideational answer to the question of how Turkey fell from its promising heights into the quagmire of chaos and insecurity that reigns in the Middle East lies at least partly in Davutoğlu's foreign policy doctrine, often associated with his magnum opus, *Stratejik Derinlik* (Strategic Depth).[13] Parallel insights come from the rich body of his academic publications stretching back to the early 1990s, as well from the ideas and concepts he formulated and expressed during his years in government.

DAVUTOĞLU'S DOCTRINE AS EXPRESSED IN *STRATEJIK DERINLIK*

Davutoğlu's performance as the main figure behind Turkish foreign policy for more than a decade has been well studied, but there seems to be little agreement on the exact nature of the considerations—ideological, pragmatic, or realistic—that drove Davutoğlu.[14] A number of studies have stressed his vision of Turkey as a "central country" that should take on a proactive role in the reshaping of its region and the world beyond, on its way to becoming a global actor.[15] Others have described Davutoğlu as a civilizational visionary motivated by the aspirations of uniting the *ummah*, the broader Islamic world, under Turkey's leadership, in the hope of having a say in the formation of a new international order.[16] One line of scholarship has attributed the AKP's policies closely associated with Davutoğlu to a functionalist approach to international relations aimed at enhancing Turkey's interests by supporting peace and interdependency in its neighborhood.[17] The view that Turkish foreign policy in those early years was experiencing "Europeanization," or falling increasingly in line with EU Common Foreign and Security Policy declarations, and gaining a soft power role in world politics similar to the EU's, has also been expressed.[18] More recently there has been the suggestion that Davutoğlu's foreign policy, particularly after the Arab Spring, was driven by purely realist considerations that emerged in response to external developments.[19] Finally, Davutoğlu's *Stratejik Derinlik* has come under critical scrutiny as the blueprint of his doctrine.[20] In the words of a prominent scholar, Baskın Oran, it exposes a synthesis of typical realism and romanticism, the product of a deep nostalgia for the leadership position once held by the Ottomans over an entire Islamic civilization.[21]

Stratejik Derinlik departs from the premise that traditional Turkish foreign policy was encumbered by a defensive or rather a passive approach.[22] Prone to metaphors, Davutoğlu once described Turkey as a body with "big biceps but an empty stomach" and "a weak heart full of fears instead of courage to develop a vision." This would no longer be the case under his leadership, Davutoğlu claimed. Speaking in 2012, he argued that Turkey was now in a position where it could "embrace the lands that were lost between 1911 and 1923"[23]—a reference to the period when the preceding Ottoman state was gradually disintegrating. At the time, Davutoğlu, together with Erdoğan, was expecting the imminent collapse of the Assad regime in Syria, and Erdoğan predicted they would soon be able to pray at the famous Umayyad Mosque in Damascus, a comment revealing a religious longing beyond a straightforward interest in a more representative government.[24] The expectation was for a new government led by the Muslim Brotherhood opposition, as had been the case in Egypt, Libya, and Tunisia after the Arab Spring. This vision foresaw the emergence of a new Middle East united by the Muslim Brotherhood, which would in turn defer to Turkish leadership.[25]

Davutoğlu made it clear that he was looking forward to a future where, by the centenary of the Turkish republic in 2023, "we will be united with our brothers" in the territories once dominated by the Ottoman Empire.[26] The roots of such bold statements can be found in *Stratejik Derinlik*, as audacious in its content and claim as the title suggests.[27] The strategic worldview advanced in the book is based on the premise that Turkey, as the natural heir to the Ottoman Empire, is entitled to see the geography formerly ruled by the Ottomans as its hinterland. According to Davutoğlu, this was no different from the policy pursued by Britain, France, and Russia in the aftermath of World War I, and Turkey should have seized the opportunity that emerged in the post–Cold War era to do the same by reconnecting with former Ottoman lands. The book also contains an important criticism of the precedence given to relations with the EU: Davutoğlu argues that such a policy would hinder Turkey from growing into a role beyond that of being simply "a market and tourism destination for Europe."[28] Instead, he writes, Turkey's central country position should be exploited to formulate a "multidimensional and multilayered" foreign policy, a concept that envisages relations developed simultaneously with a range of foreign policy actors and on a range of issues.[29]

The concept of *lebensraum,* despite its infamous misapplication by Hitler, is another theme central to Davutoğlu's thinking.[30] His strategic worldview borrows heavily from the classic scholars of geopolitics, such as Halford Mackinder, Karl Haushofer, Nicholas John Spykman, and Alfred Thayer Mahan, who seem to have impressed on Davutoğlu the idea of a state as essentially expansionist and bent on creating regional and civilizational hegemony wherever and whenever possible. Therefore, he reasons, Turkey risks facing encroachment on its interests, even on its territory, unless it turns its gaze to its long-neglected "hinterland"—a term rarely used outside Davutoğlu's writings. For reasons of identity, history, and culture, Davutoğlu sees Turkey destined "to play an extended international role" in its hinterland.[31] Davutoğlu believes that only in this way can Turkey become a subject of history, capable of shaping it rather than remaining a passive actor.[32] Despite all the focus on the concept, though, the borders of lebensraum are left undefined in Davutoğlu's writings. He does seem to have a rough geographic area in mind, as he argues that the defense of Turkey in the West "starts at the Adriatic Sea and Sarajevo," extends in the east to "the Northern Caucasus and Grozny," and continues in the south to the Middle East, particularly Iraq and Syria.[33] Similarly, Davutoğlu never specifically identifies Turkey's "civilizational basin"[34] beyond his frequent references to an Ottoman imperial hinterland.[35] In *Stratejik Derinlik* the frequent references to "cultural ties" need to be read as referring to communities and geographies involving the common experience of belonging to the same Islamic civilization. Yet it is the Arab Middle East that receives particular attention.

The perspective that emerges from *Stratejik Derinlik* has led many to link Turkish foreign policy under Davutoğlu's stewardship to neo-Ottomanism.[36] There is enough evidence in his book and other writings, however, to suggest that his vision for Turkey is also defined by a dominant Islamic civilizational perspective.[37] Overall, the basic premise in Davutoğlu's thinking seems to be that culture, religion, and civilization are the main factors that shape world politics, hence the image he conveys of being an ardent believer in "civilizational geopolitics."[38] Thus Davutoğlu objects to Turkey being considered part of a "Western polity" in a "Westphalian international order" based on nation-states.[39] Instead, he foresees Turkey as part of a new order to be shaped by a group of "non-Western civilizations," which he expects to emerge in the near future.

In Davutoğlu's thinking, the hegemonic position held by the Europe-centered civilizational world is doomed to weaken, and this explains his hope for a nascent order that would be represented by "the rest"—the Chinese, Indians, Africans, Latin Americans, and most notably the Muslims.[40] While rejecting "Huntingtonian theories of inevitable civilizational conflict," he argues that it is "high time that we have a global conversation and commit our various selves to a new grand bargain concerning the economic, political, and cultural order" in global governance.[41] Davutoğlu's aspiration is to shape this new international order by getting Turkey to lead the "reunification of the Islamic world" and become the "spokesperson of the Islamic world."[42] This also sits well with Davutoğlu's missionary zeal to see Turkey as an "order-building" country.[43] Erdoğan's emphasis on Turkey as an "indispensable nation," a power with the will and potential to contribute to the making of "a global order based on justice, equality, and transparency," clearly converges with this perspective.[44]

Salient to Davotoğlu's emphasis on the importance of the Middle East for Turkey is the conviction that the collapse of the Ottoman Empire was not the result of the loss of its territory in the Balkans but of the "lands of the Middle East inhabited by a Muslim majority" falling outside imperial domination.[45] He sees the "geopolitical disintegration of the Muslim community" as a function of the nation-state system imposed by the West, and forwards Turkey as the only power that could overcome the divisions in the Islamic world and ensure unity.[46] He is reported to have "detested the importation of the nation-state order in the Islamic world"[47] in a way that resonates with the ideas of a former generation of Islamist authors in Turkey, most notably Sezai Karakoç and Necip Fazıl Kısakürek. Their legacy was a resentment against a world based on nation-states, which they believed was a machination designed by the West to keep the *ummah* divided and weak. This was accompanied by the belief that only Turkey could reunite it in the form of a "Grand Islamic Federation."[48] This conviction clearly places Turks at the center of Islam. It is based on the teaching among Islamists in Turkey that it was the Turks who succeeded in spreading Islam from its origins in the Hejaz, where it would otherwise have remained a local religion.[49]

The influence of these ideas was central to how Davutoğlu imagined Turkey's potential to acquire additional clout on the global stage. This pan-Islamist agenda and ambition, hence, are critical to understanding Turkish foreign policy under Davutoğlu's leadership after the Arab Spring. They help clarify, on the one hand, the grounds for a discourse of dissent toward the Western-led international order[50] and, on the other, the support lent to radical Islamist groups to ensure regime change in Syria.

DAVUTOĞLU'S DOCTRINE AND TRADITIONAL TURKISH STATECRAFT

Stratejik Derinlik is also a virulent critique of traditional Turkish foreign policy, questioning the premises on which the founders of the republic sought to build a national identity. From Davutoğlu's perspective, Turkish foreign policy had been conducted for a long time without a dynamic strategic vision in place.[51] This, argues Davutoğlu, is an "inevitable by-product of an elite that chose to be associated with a civilization [meaning Western] that does not correspond to the political culture of the broader society."[52] Indeed, the Turkish foreign policy that emerged with the founding of the republic in 1923 is generally recognized to have been shaped by "Westernism" (*Batıcılık*) and "status quoism" (*statüko-culuk*).[53] This policy was closely linked to the process of nation building, an effort inspired not only by the emerging Turkish nationalism at the time but also by an understanding of modernization in the model of the West. The term "Westernism" can be read to capture the notion of identification and not just orientation. Secularism was a major orientation and constantly reinforced by a discourse that favored a break from the Ottoman tradition and its emphasis on religious principles.

The first-generation republican elite consisted of former Ottoman bureaucrats, diplomats, and military officers who had seen and fought in successive wars, witnessed great power interventions, and, understandably, erred on the side of caution.[54] The foreign policy narrative they developed focused on Turkey as a "Westphalian polity" based on a "secular-nationalist" identity.[55] This is precisely why advocates of traditional statecraft would have regarded interfering in the internal affairs of a neighboring country, let alone supporting violent Islamist groups in their effort to overthrow a regime, "absolutely unimaginable" and a threat to national security.[56] Their perspective was also accompanied by an institutionalized relationship that started taking shape with the transatlantic community in the aftermath of World War II and saw the consolidation of Turkey's place in the West, especially during the Cold War.[57] Turkish foreign policy was, in fact, in a constant state of evolution and contestation during this time. Particularly toward the end of the Cold War and in its immediate aftermath, Turkish statecraft became exposed to at least two distinct worldviews as represented by Turgut Özal and İsmail Cem (discussed in chapter three). Their common denominator was the emphasis they both put on a more active involvement in Turkey's neighborhood, both economically and politically, and the need to become more assertive but at the same time maintain Turkey's Western vocation and EU membership ambition.[58]

RESTRUCTURING TURKISH NATIONAL IDENTITY AND FOREIGN POLICYMAKING

It is against this background that Davutoğlu's initial foreign policy vision emerged, with its critical view of traditional Turkish foreign policy. He advocated replacing the dominant elite discourse and its accompanying policies, and even mocked them once in office.[59] Davutoğlu argued that traditional statecraft alienated Turkey from communities in the Middle East, which once enjoyed civilizational and historical links to the Ottomans, while simultaneously reducing Turkey to adopting policies indexed to the global powers.[60] He criticized Özal for failing to "treasure Islamism as the only valid ideological legacy of the Ottoman Empire" and likened him to a Tanzimat pasha, a direct reference to their eager efforts to develop friendships "with strong Western countries."[61] In his writing, the failure to solidify these links and to nurture ways to secure a leadership role for Turkey in the region was nothing less than an act of "denial of the self."[62] In its place, he envisaged a "new" Turkey and openly challenged the traditional national project that "emphasized the unitary, secular character of the Turkish nation-state, and displayed a staunch commitment to a Western anchor for Turkish identity and foreign policy."[63] He reconceptualized Turkey's foreign policy (along with Turkey's national identity) into one that placed an emphasis on its Islamic foundations. İbrahim Kalın, a close colleague of Davutoğlu and then serving as an undersecretary at the office of the prime minister, also highlighted this ideational reorientation. At a conference in Istanbul in October 2012, at the height of the Arab Spring, he argued unequivocally that Turkey did not belong to Western civilization but to the Islamic world. This led a former EU representative present at the conference to conclude, "To my knowledge, this is to date the clearest public, on-the-record expression of Turkey's inclination to challenge its 89-year old anchorage to the West and, perhaps, question its drive towards the EU too."[64]

Another instance of a sharp break with Turkey's traditional Western orientation came to the fore as Erdoğan confronted a group of former Turkish ambassadors who did not agree with his undiplomatic conduct at Davos. Erdoğan responded to their criticism by invoking the term *"monşer,"* which became a buzzword in his clash with the foreign policy establishment. The term is one of affection and respect in its original French, *"mon cher,"* but to the Turkish ear it has multiple connotations. Principally, it evokes Westernization in the most negative sense. It conjures up the image of a stock character from the late Ottoman era, a man who displays a foolish admiration for Western manners, especially in his preference for addressing his fellows in the French style, *mon cher.* In current usage the term conjures up snobbish behavior, the kind that is usually attributed to those educated in the Western style, fluent in foreign languages but detached from the realities of their own country.[65]

This single word, *monşer*, was strong enough to express Erdoğan's displeasure not only with a group of diplomats but also with the long tradition they represented. He shared Davutoğlu's criticism that Turkish foreign policy had been too timid and insecure and said that as a politician, he would take it upon himself to defend and get what was right for Turkey without worrying about what others might think.[66] The tension with the diplomatic corps escalated further when, in June 2010, a large group of former diplomats issued a public statement critical of Erdoğan's style and his government's foreign policy. There was particular concern that the government was deviating "from Turkey's traditional, Western-orientated foreign policy," which, the diplomats stipulated, was based on an alliance with the United States, membership in NATO, and the prospect of EU membership.[67]

The confrontation was also part of a broader *Kulturkampf.* Erdoğan and the AKP were wary of the military, the judiciary, and the civilian bureaucracy becoming potential threats to their rule. Those bodies had intervened in politics several times in recent history and toppled a number of democratically elected governments. With his party in charge as a majority government, Erdoğan seized the opportunity to curtail the traditional power of the bureaucracy, eliminate "the perpetrators of the status quo," in his words, and bring an end to what he called a "tutelage" over the national will as represented by him. Erdoğan saw these ambassadors—and much of the Ministry of Foreign Affairs, for that matter—as part of an apparatus that would fight hard not to yield to the rule of his party. In contrast, the signatories to the statement represented the concern that the AKP initiatives were aimed at a "civilian dominance" under the guise of democratization, and that the party was transforming Turkey into a state governed in accordance with Islamic values.[68]

It was against this background that Davutoğlu introduced legislation to significantly restructure the Ministry of Foreign Affairs and expand its ranks. The new legislation was introduced in July 2010. In line with Davutoğlu's ambitions to transform Turkey into a global actor, the law stipulated the creation of new departments and areas of specialization within the ministry, as well as an increase in Turkish diplomatic representation abroad.[69] These provisions were, by and large, welcomed by the establishment since the need to relieve the burden of an already overstretched diplomatic corps was clear.[70] However, the new law ushered in a set of practices that clashed with the established norms of the Ministry of Foreign Affairs. As an example, ambassadors were from then on to represent not only the Turkish state but also the government. Another arrangement that drew criticism was the possibility of appointing personnel from outside the ministry. As one long-standing commentator on Turkish foreign policy and domestic politics reflected, "No one was against reform within the ministry, but many feared that these changes were part of the AKP's strategy to replace the republican/old-guard/secular establishment with a new/conservative/Islamist establishment."[71]

The law also introduced a new recruitment policy that aimed, on paper at least, to "give all bright graduates a chance to enter the ministry and . . . break the elitist and status-related approach of the old school." Critics, however, feared that tempering with a system based on meritocracy would "facilitate the entrance of the AKP's own cadres into the foreign ministry (e.g., through political appointments and the recruitment of theology graduates) and tighten its grip over the foreign policy-making process."[72] After the July 2016 coup attempt one-third of the 1,202 diplomats in the ministry were purged, including four ambassadors who had played a critical role in the diplomats' recruitment.[73] Ironically, an important cadre of those purged had been recruited during Davutoğlu's term in office and were alleged to have had connections to the Gülen movement, overwhelmingly considered by most of the Turkish public to have been behind the 2016 coup attempt.[74]

IT IS POSSIBLE TO speak of two Davutoğlu doctrines. The first one was characterized by pragmatism and shaped by the early years of the AKP's foreign policy under Gül. Developed in coordination with the foreign policy establishment, it can be regarded as the continuation of an evolving statecraft. It was this policy that earned for Turkey its election to the UN Security Council and that was adopted by Davutoğlu during his tenure as adviser and in his initial years as minister. With the Arab Spring, the more ideological side of Davutoğlu's doctrine came to the fore. It reflected a determination to achieve a post-Western order for the Middle East and must be understood in conjunction with the domestic political agenda of putting in place a "new" Turkey and a new national identity.

It also coincided with disregarding a major established practice in Turkish foreign policy of not interfering in the domestic affairs of third countries, let alone becoming actively involved in regime change, especially through violence. It is difficult not to draw a connection between this particular version of Davutoğlu's doctrine and the quagmire that Turkey has been dragged into in Syria, as well as a connection between disregarding noninterference and the many conflicts raging in the region. The failure of this version of Davutoğlu's doctrine when compared with the earlier and more pragmatic one was symbolically captured in Turkey's failed bid to be reelected to the UN Security Council in 2014. Davutoğlu had to resign from his post as prime minister in early May 2016, and his foreign policy appears to have played an important role in that turn of events. However, the more ideological aspects of his doctrine's legacy still shape Turkish foreign policy. This is especially evident in the case of the Turkish government's resolute support in June 2017 for Qatar, in line with its commitment to the Muslim Brotherhood and against Qatar's neighbors, who see the brotherhood as a terrorist organization threatening their national security. Another example is the Turkish government's support for President Trump's decision to hit a Syrian military base in April 2017 as punishment for Syria's use of chemical weapons, even though the latter action only momentarily engendered the hope that this might signal a policy of the American administration to bring the al-Assad regime to an end.

Notes

CHAPTER 1

1. G. John Ikenberry, *Liberal Leviathan: The Origins, Crisis and Transformation of the American World Order* (Princeton University Press, 2011), 29.

2. George C. McGhee, "Turkey Joins the West," *Foreign Affairs*, July 1954.

3. İsmail Soysal, "The Influence of the Concept of Western Civilization on Turkish Foreign Policy," *Foreign Policy* 6, nos. 3–4 (1977), 3–5.

4. Charles Krauthammer, "The Unipolar Moment," *Foreign Affairs*, September 18, 1990.

5. Ikenberry, *Liberal Leviathan*, 17.

6. Ann Bernstein, "The Democratic Alternative from the South: India, Brazil and South Africa," in *Democracy Works* (London: Legatum Institute; Johannesburg: Centre for Development and Enterprise, 2014) (www.cde.org.za/wp-content/uploads/2014/09/Dem_Works_FinalReport2014.pdf); and Anne-Marie Slaughter and John Ikenberry, "Democracies Must Work in Concert," *Financial Times*, July 10, 2008.

7. Larry Diamond, *The Spirit of Democracy: The Struggle to Build Free Societies throughout the World* (New York: Henry Holt, 2009); and Theodore Piccone, *Five Rising Democracies and the Fate of the International Liberal Order* (Brookings Institution Press, 2016).

8. Kemal Derviş, "Convergence, Interdependence, and Divergence," *Finance and Development* (IMF) 49, no. 3 (September 2012) (www.imf.org/external/pubs/ft/fandd/2012/09/pdf/dervis.pdf).

9. *Arab Human Development Report 2002* (New York: United Nations Development Program, Regional Bureau for Arab States, 2002). (http://hdr.undp.org/sites/default/files/rbas_ahdr2002_en.pdf). For a discussion, see "How the Arabs Compare: Arab Human Development Report 2002," *Middle East Quarterly* 9, no. 2 (Fall 2002), 59–67.

10. Robin Wright, "U.S. Readies Push for Mideast Democracy Plan," *Washington Post*, February 28, 2004; and Tamara Cofman Wittes, "The New U.S. Proposal for a Greater Middle East Initiative: An Evaluation," Middle East Memo, no. 34, Brookings, May 10, 2004 (www.brookings.edu/research/papers /2004/05/10middleeast-wittes).

11. Robert Kagan, *The World America Made* (New York: Vintage Books, 2013); Bruce Jones, *Still Ours to Lead* (Brookings Institution Press, 2014); Michael Beckley, "China's Century? Why America's Edge Will Endure," *International Security* 36, no. 3 (Winter 2011/12), 41–78; and Fareed Zakaria, *The Post-American World* (New York: W. W. Norton, 2009).

12. Christopher Layne, "The End of Pax Americana: How Western Decline Became Inevitable," *The Atlantic*, April 26, 2012; and Martin Jacques, *When China Rules the World: The End of the Western World and the Birth of a New Global Order* (London: Penguin Books, 2010).

13. Marco Lo Duca and Livio Stracca, "The Effect of G20 Summits on Global Financial Markets," European Central Bank Working Paper, no. 1668 (April 2014).

14. Charles A. Kupchan, *No One's World: The West, the Rising Rest, and the Coming Global Turn* (Oxford University Press, 2012).

15. Thomas J. Wright, *All Measures Short of War: The Contest for the Twenty-First Century and the Future of American Power* (Yale University Press, 2017), 28–29.

16. Marc Lynch, *The New Arab Wars: Uprisings and Anarchy in the Middle East* (New York: Public Affairs, 2016).

17. Shadi Hamid, *Temptations of Power: Islamists and Illiberal Democracy in the Middle East* (Oxford University Press, 2014).

18. Vali Nasr, *The Dispensable Nation: American Foreign Policy in Retreat* (New York: First Anchor Books, 2014).

19. Rachid Ghannouchi, "Tunisia Shows There Is No Contradiction between Democracy and Islam," *Washington Post*, October 24, 2014; Sayida Ounissi and Monica Marks, "Ennahda from Within: Islamists or 'Muslim Democrats'? A Conversation," Project on the U.S. Relations with the Islamic World at Brookings, Rethinking Political Islam Series, March 2016 (www.brookings.edu /research/papers/2016/03/ennahda-islamists-muslim-democrats-ounissi); and Monica Marks, "Tunisia's Unwritten Story," Century Foundation, March 14, 2017 (https://tcf.org/content/report/tunisias-unwritten-story/).

20. Peter Baker, Mark Lander, David E. Sanger, and Anne Barnard, "Off-the-Cuff Obama Line Put U.S. in Bind on Syria," *New York Times*, May 4, 2013. See also the relevant sections in Jeffrey Goldberg, "The Obama Doctrine," *The Atlantic*, April 2016. See Rick Brennan, "Withdrawal Symptoms: The Bungling of the Iraq Exit," *Foreign Affairs*, November/December 2014; Michael Weiss and Hassan Hassan, *ISIS: Inside the Army of Terror* (New York: Regan Arts, 2013); and Martin Indyk, Kenneth Lieberthal, and Michael O'Hanlon, *Bending History: Barack Obama's Foreign Policy* (Brookings Institution Press, 2012).

21. António Guterres, "Open Briefing on the Humanitarian Situation in Syria," speech delivered at the United Nations Security Council, 7433th Meeting, New York, April 24, 2015 (www.unhcr.org/en-us/admin/hcspeeches /553a3fc39/united-nations-security-council-7433th-meeting-open-briefing -humanitarian.html). For a discussion of the protracted crisis, see Elizabeth Ferris and Kemal Kirişci, *The Consequences of Chaos: Syria's Humanitarian Crisis and the Failure to Protect* (Brookings Institution Press, 2016).

22. Jackson Janes, "A Reason to Be Rattled," American Institute for Contemporary German Studies, June 1, 2016 (www.aicgs.org/issue/a-reason-to-be -rattled/); Carlo Bastasin, "Closed Borders Will Make Europe Collapse," *Order from Chaos* (blog), Brookings, April 29, 2016 (www.brookings.edu/blogs/order -from-chaos/posts/2016/04/29-european-borders-nationalization-bastasin); and William Drozdiak, *Fractured Continent: Europe's Crises and the Fate of the West* (New York: W. W. Norton, 2017).

23. Shibley Telhami, "American Attitudes on President Trump's Early Policies," *Order from Chaos* (blog), Brookings, May 11, 2017 (www.brookings.edu /research/american-attitudes-on-president-trumps-early-policies/); and Elizabeth Ferris, "The Disastrous Ripple Effects of Trump's Executive Action on Refugee Resettlement," *Order from Chaos* (blog), Brookings, January 26, 2017 (www.brookings.edu/blog/order-from-chaos/2017/01/26/the-disastrous-ripple -effects-of-trumps-executive-action-on-refugee-resettlement/).

24. Fiona Hill, "Understanding and Deterring Russia: U.S. Policies and Strategies, Testimony before the U.S. House of Representatives," February 10, 2016 (www.brookings.edu/research/testimony/2016/02/10-us-strategy-russia-hill).

25. Steven Pifer, *The Eagle and the Trident: U.S.-Ukraine Relations in Turbulent Times* (Brookings Institution Press, 2017), 277–314.

26. "In the Kremlin's Pocket," *The Economist*, February 14, 2015; and Luke Harding, "We Should Beware Russia's Links with Europe's Right," *The Guardian*, December 8, 2014.

27. David J. Lynch, "Key Findings of US Agencies' Report on Russia Election Interference," *Financial Times*, January 6, 2017; and Uri Friedman, "Russia's Interference in the U.S. Election Was Just the Beginning," *The Atlantic*, April 26, 2017.

28. George W. Bush, "A Europe Whole and Free: Remarks to the Citizens of Mainz," U.S. Diplomatic Mission to Germany, May 31, 1989. On Russia's intentions, see Janusz Bugajski, *Dismantling the West: Russia's Atlantic Agenda* (Washington: Potomac Books, 2009).

29. Kılıç Kanat and Kadir Üstün, "U.S.-Turkey Realignment on Syria," *Middle East Policy* 22, no. 4 (Winter 2015), 88–97. In 2014, Erdoğan is reported to have said that the Kurds were his top concern and that removing Assad ranked second, while IS came only third. Adam Entous, Greg Jaffe, and Missy Ryan, "Obama's White House Worked for Months on a Plan to Seize Raqqa: Trump's Team Took a Brief Look and Decided Not to Pull the Trigger," *Washington Post*, February 2, 2017.

30. For "pool of blood," see "Turkey's Erdoğan Denounces US Support for Syrian Kurds," *BBC News*, February 10, 2016. For "desperate predicament," see

Liz Sly, "Turkey's Increasingly Desperate Predicament Poses Real Dangers," *Washington Post*, February 20, 2016.

31. Robert Ford, "The Fatal Flaw in Trump's ISIS Plan," *The Atlantic*, May 11, 2017; and Aslı Aydıntaşbaş and Kemal Kirişci, "The United States and Turkey: Friends, Enemies, or Only Interests," Turkey Project Policy Paper, no. 12, Brookings, April 2017 (www.brookings.edu/research/the-united-states -and-turkey-friends-enemies-or-only-interests/).

32. "Turkey Back under Euro Monitoring after 13 Years, Government Furious," *Hürriyet Daily News*, April 24, 2017.

33. Kemal Kirişci, "Democracy Diffusion: The Turkish Experience," in *Turkey and Its Neighbors: Foreign Relations in Transition*, ed. Ronald H. Linden et al. (Boulder, Colo.: Lynne Rienner, 2011).

34. The Turkish Economic and Social Studies Foundation (TESEV) ran a series of public opinion surveys to gauge perceptions of Turkey between 2010 and 2013. For the most recent publication, see Mensur Akgün and Sabiha Şenyücel Gündoğar, "The Perception of Turkey in the Middle East 2013," TESEV Foreign Policy Programme, January 2014 (http://tesev.org.tr/wp-content/uploads /2015/11/The_Perception_Of_Turkey_In_The_Middle_East_2013.pdf).

35. Rania Abouzeid, "Why Turkey's Erdoğan Is Greeted Like a Rock Star in Egypt," *Time*, September 13, 2011.

36. Cengiz Çandar, "Turkey's Foreign Policy Reset Will Not Be Easy," Al-Monitor, December 1, 2013; and Abbas Djavadi, "Turkey's Foreign Policy: From 'Zero Problems' to 'Nothing but Problems,' " Radio Free Europe and Radio Liberty, June 6, 2016.

37. At one point between between April 2015 and May 2016, nine such ambassadors had been recalled home. See "Seven World Capitals Now without Turkish Ambassadors," *Hürriyet Daily News*, April 23, 2015; "Turkey Recalls Ambassador to Bangladesh after Execution of Nizami," *Daily Sabah*, May 12, 2016; and Philip Oltermann and Constanze Letsch, "Turkey Recalls Ambassador after German MPs' Armenian Genocide Vote," *The Guardian*, June 2, 2016.

38. Kemal Kirişci, "Is Turkish Foreign Policy Becoming Pragmatic Again?," *Order from Chaos* (blog), Brookings, July 11, 2016 (www.brookings.edu/blogs /order-from-chaos/posts/2016/07/11-pragmatic-turkish-foreign-policy-kirisci).

39. Retired ambassador Uğur Ziyal, former assistant secretary of the Turkish Ministry of Foreign Affairs, interview by the author, Ankara, May 18, 2016.

40. Semih İdiz, "UN Vote Confirms Turkey's Waning Influence," Al-Monitor, October 17, 2014 (http://www.al-monitor.com/pulse/originals/2014/10/turkey -united-nations-security-council-vote.html).

41. "Turkey Not 'Lonely' but Dares to Do So for Its Values and Principles, Says PM Adviser," *Hürriyet Daily News*, August 26, 2013.

42. Güler Yılmaz, "Has Turkey Lost its Weight in the Region?," Al-Monitor, September 3, 2013; " 'Precious Loneliness' of Turkey or Sublimation of a Failure?," *Hürriyet Daily News*, April 19, 2013; Aaron Stein, "Turkey's New Foreign Policy: Davutoğlu, the AKP and the Pursuit of Regional Order," *Whitehall Papers* 83, no. 1 (2014) (www.tandfonline.com/doi/pdf/10.1080/02681307.2014.989694).

43. Author's interview with Hikmet Çetin, Ali Tuygan, Yaşar Yakış, and Uğur Ziyal, May 18, 2016, Ankara. See also Gün Kut, "Türk Dış Politikasında Çok Yönlülüğün Yakın Tarihi: Soğuk Savaş Sonrası Devamlılık ve Değişim," in *Siyasetin Bilimi*, ed. Pınar Uyan Semerci, Boğaç Erozan, and Nihal İncioğlu (Istanbul: İstanbul Bİlgi Üniversitesi Yayınları, 2015), 181.

44. Referred to in Ruşen Çakır, "Erdoğan: Demokrasi tramvayında ihtiraslı bir yolcu," *Vatan*, November 6, 2012 (www.gazetevatan.com/rusen-cakir -491426-yazar-yazisi-erdogan--demokrasi-tramvayinda-ihtirasli-bir-yolcu/).

45. Calire Berlinski, "How Democracies Die: Guilty Men," *American Interest*, April 24, 2017. For the state of ongoing purges in Turkey, see https:// turkeypurge.com/. As of July 31, 2017, the website had reported almost 146,000 people sacked from their jobs, 122,756 detentions, almost 57,000 arrested, more than 8,570 academics dismissed from their positions, and 270 journalists arrested.

46. Bobby Gosh, "Erdoğan's Moment," *Time*, November 28, 2011.

47. Timur Kuran, "Turkey Electoral Dictatorship," Project Syndicate, April 10, 2014 (www.project-syndicate.org/commentary/timur-kuran-warns -that-recent-local-elections-will-reinforce-recep-tayyip-erdo-an-s-authoritarian -turn).

48. Abbas Djavadi, "Erdogan and Putin: Two Sides of the Same Coin," *Turkey Notebook* (blog), Radio Free Europe and Radio Liberty, June 13, 2016; and Anne Applebaum, "Erdogan, Putin and the Strongman Ties That Bind," *Washington Post*, August 11, 2016. For similarities between Erdoğan's policies and Putinism, see Fareed Zakaria, "The Rise of Putinism," *Washington Post*, July 31, 2014.

49. Tim Arango and Ceylan Yeğinsu, "Peaceful Protest over Istanbul Park Turns Violent as Police Crack Down," *New York Times*, May 31, 2013.

50. "The Next Sultan?," *The Economist*, August 16, 2014.

51. Dexter Filkins, "Turkey's Vote Makes Erdogan Effectively a Dictator," *New Yorker*, April 17, 2017.

52. Freedom House, *Freedom in the World 2017: Report on Turkey* (https:// freedomhouse.org/report/freedom-world/freedom-world-2017).

53. "Turkey ranks 155th in RSF's latest press freedom index, down by four points from last year," *Hürriyet Daily News*, April 26, 2017.

54. For reports of torture, see Suzy Hansen, "Inside Turkey's Purge," *New York Times*, April 13, 2017. Concerns about torture have been expressed by the United Nations Office for Human Rights Commissioner and Human Rights Watch too: "Torture: UN Expert Calls on the Turkish Government to Live Up to Its 'Zero Tolerance' Policy," December 2, 2016 (www.ohchr.org/EN /NewsEvents/Pages/DisplayNews.aspx?NewsID=20977#sthash.dk4pGndd .dpuf); and Human Rights Watch, "Turkey," in *World Report 2017* (www.hrw .org/world-report/2017/country-chapters/turkey).

55. One commentator on Turkish foreign policy sees a direct relationship between the rise of authoritarianism in Turkey and Turkey's involvement in the Arab Spring: Behlül Özkan, "Yeni-Osmanlıcılık ve Pan-İslamcılık," in *Türkiye'de*

Yeni Siyasal Akımlar, ed. Deniz Yıldırım and Evren Haspulat (İstanbul: Kolektif, 2016), 448.

56. Jacob Poushter, "Support from Turkey's Erdoğan Drops Sharply in Middle East," Pew Research Center, July 30, 2014 (www.pewresearch.org /fact-tank/2014/07/30/support-for-turkeys-erdogan-drops-sharply-in-middle -east/).

57. "Does Turkey Still Belong in NATO?," *New York Times*, March 29, 2016.

58. Robert Pearson and Gregory Kist, "Turkey's Dangerous Dance with Radicalism," *Politico*, January 13, 2016.

59. White House, "Remarks by President Obama to the Turkish Parliament," press release, Office of the Press Secretary, April 6, 2009 (www.whitehouse.gov /the-press-office/remarks-president-obama-turkish-parliament).

60. Fareed Zakaria, "Inside Obama's World: The President Talks to Time about the Changing Nature of American Power," *Time*, January 19, 2012.

61. Goldberg, "The Obama Doctrine."

62. Ufuk Ulutaş, "Obama'nın Dış Politika Mirası," January 17, 2016 (www. setav.org/obamanin-dis-politika-mirasi/). Davutoğlu too took a critical view of Obama's performance and expressed his disappointment in an interview after he left office: Ahmet Davutoğlu, "From Obama to Trump: The Lessons, the Challenges," *Middle East Eye*, February 2, 2017.

63. "Turkey Is Sliding into Dictatorship," *The Economist*, April 15, 2017; and Editorial Board, "Erdogan's Ugly Win Could Cause All Kinds of Problems—Even for Him," *Washington Post*, April 18, 2017.

64. Samuel P. Huntington, "The Clash of Civilizations?," *Foreign Affairs*, Summer 1993. See also Samuel P. Huntington, *The Clash of Civilizations and the Remaking of World Order* (New York: Simon and Schuster, 2011), 144–49.

65. Selim Deringil, "The Turks and 'Europe': The Argument from History," *Middle Eastern Studies* 43, no. 5 (2007).

66. Yalçın Akdoğan, "The Meaning of Conservative Democratic Political Identity," in *The Emergence of a New Turkey*, ed. Hakan Yavuz (University of Utah Press, 2006), 59. The author of this article subsequently served as deputy prime minister of Turkey from 2014 to 2016.

67. Author's interview with Taha Akyol and Yusuf Müftüoğlu, June 29, 2016, Istanbul, and telephone conversation with Mustafa Akyol, April 28, 2017.

68. Author's interviews with Yusuf Müftüoğlu, Sedat Ergin and Murat Yetkin, Istanbul, June 29, 2016.

69. Hayrettin Kahraman, "İslam, demokrasi ve Medine Vesikası," *Yeni Şafak*, May 29, 2014 (www.yenisafak.com/yazarlar/hayrettinkaraman/islam -demokrasi-ve-medine-vesikas%C4%B1-53922).

70. Çiğdem Yasemin Ünlü, "Amerikanvari Seçim Sonu Konuşmalarının Milli Bir Örneği Olarak 'Balkon Konuşmaları': 2014 Cumhurbaşkanlığı Seçimi Konuşması Üzerine Retoriksel Bir Analiz," *İletişim Dergisi*, December 2015 (http://iletisimdergisi.gsu.edu.tr/article/view/5000163646/5000147646).

71. Ahmet İnsel, "Vesayet Rejiminin Sonu ve Sonrası," *Birikim*, March–April 2010, 5 and 251–52. On the meaning of "tutelage," sometimes also called

"tutelary" and "national will" for Erdoğan, see Mustafa Akyol, "Erdoganism [noun]: From "National Will" to "Man of the Nation," an Abridged Dictionary for the Post-Secular Turkish State," *Foreign Policy*, June 21, 2016.

72. The full picture of what transpired on that fateful night has yet to emerge, but for a discussion of the background and the coup itself, see Aslı Aydıntaşbaş, "The Good, the Bad and the Gülenists: The Role of the Gülen Movement in Turkey's Coup Attempt," European Council on Foreign Relations, September 23, 2016 (www.ecfr.eu/publications/summary/the_good_the_bad_and_the _gulenists7131); and Dexter Filkins, "Turkey's Thirty-Year Coup," *New Yorker*, October 17, 2016. See also Mustafa Akyol, "Who Was behind the Coup Attempt in Turkey?," *New York Times*, July 22, 2016.

73. Author's interviews with Ünal Çeviköz, June 26, 2016; with Yusuf Müftüoğlu, Sedat Ergin, and Murat Yetkin, June 29, 2016, Istanbul; and with Hikmet Çetin, Ali Tuygan, Yaşar Yakış, and Uğur Ziyal, May 18, 2016, Ankara.

74. For a detailed discussion on the meaning of *dava*, see Nihal Bengisu Karaca, "AK Parti'nin 'dava'sı," *Habertürk*, May 25, 2016 (www.haberturk.com /yazarlar/nihal-bengisu-karaca/1244323-ak-partinin-davasi).

75. Zeynep Gürcanlı, "AK Parti Kongresi'nde ağır konuklar," *Gündem*, September 30, 2012 (www.hurriyet.com.tr/ak-parti-kongresinde-agir-konuklar -21588818). Thirty-seven foreign dignitaries were present at the Assembly. Author's interviews with Ünal Çeviköz and Behlül Özkan, respectively June 26 and July 1, 2016, Istanbul.

76. "Israeli President Addresses Turkish Parliament," *New York Times*, November 13, 2007.

77. Author's interviews with Ünal Çeviköz, June 26, 2016, Istanbul; and Hikmet Çetin, Ali Tuygan, Yaşar Yakış, and Uğur Ziyal, May 18, 2016, Ankara.

78. Ibid.

79. Davutoğlu's strategic depth doctrine is laid out in his book, *Stratejik Derinlik: Türkiye'nin Uluslararası Konumu* (İstanbul: Küre Yayınları, 2014). The book was originally published in 2001. See the discussion in the appendix to this book.

80. Özkan, "Yeni-Osmanlıcılık ve pan-İslamcılık"; Behlül Özkan, "Turkey's Islamists: From Power-Sharing to Political Incumbency," *Turkish Policy Quarterly* 14, no. 1 (Spring 2015), 71–83; and Malik Mufti, "The AK Party's Islamic Realist Political Visions: Theory and Practice," *Politics and Government* 2, no. 2 (2014), 28–42.

81. "Dışişleri Bakanı Sayın Ahmet Davutoğlu'nun Diyarbakır Dicle Üniversitesi'nde Verdiği 'Büyük Restorasyan: Kadim'den Küreselleşmeye Yeni Siyaset Anlayışımız' Konulu Konferans," March 15, 2013 (www.mfa.gov.tr /disisleri-bakani-ahmet-davutoglu_nun-diyarbakir-dicle-universitesinde -verdigi-_buyuk-restorasyon_-kadim_den-kuresellesmeye-yeni.tr.mfa).

82. Kemal Öztürk and Kemal Fırık, "Rabaa Sign Becomes the Symbol of Massacre in Egypt," Anadolu Agency, August 16, 2016 (http://aa.com.tr/en /turkey/rabaa-sign-becomes-the-symbol-of-massacre-in-egypt/225250). See also the interview with Davutoğlu in the *Middle East Eye*.

83. This close cooperation is recounted in detail by Hasan Cemal, "En uzun gün ve AB'den tarih," *Milliyet*, December 19, 2004.

84. German Marshall Fund of the United States, *Transatlantic Trends 2010* (German Marshall Fund of the United States, 2010). (http://trends.gmfus.org /files/archived/doc/2010_English_Key.pdf).

85. Calculated based on data available at www.tradingeconomics.com/turkey /gdp-per-capita. When GDP per capita (in purchasing power parity) is factored in, the change in percent for the same years is from 43 percent to 50 percent.

86. Ayhan Şimşek, "Turkey: 25 Years in EU's Waiting Room," *Deutsche Welle*, April 14, 2012.

87. Semih İdiz, "AKP Finally Acknowledges Its Foreign Policy Failures," *Hürriyet Daily News*, June 2, 2016.

88. "Bush Rebuff to Chirac over Turkey," CNN, June 29, 2004.

89. For a current survey on America's global image, see Richard Wilke, "America's Global Image," Pew Research Center, June 28, 2017 (http://www .pewglobal.org/2017/06/28/americas-global-image/). For a comprehensive table that traces how America's image changed in the Middle East, see the Pew Research Center's Global Indicators Database, specifically responses to the question, "Do you have a favorable or unfavorable view of the U.S.?," last updated August 2015 (www.pewglobal.org/database/indicator/1/group/6/).

90. See slides 33 and 34 in a PowerPoint slide deck available from Kadir Has Üniversitesi, "Türk Dış Politikası Kamuoyu Algıları Araştırması," May 18, 2016, Istanbul (www.khas.edu.tr/news/1367). The corresponding figures for the same survey taken in 2017 were 64.5 percent and 81.4 percent; see slides 31 and 33 in a PowerPoint slide deck available from Kadir Has Üniversitesi, "Public Perceptions on Turkish Foreign Policy," July 20, 2017, (www.khas.edu.tr/news/1588). The significant difference can, at least partly, be attributed to the association of the U.S. with the coup attempt in the eyes of the Turkish public.

91. "Conspiracy Theories in Turkey: After the Coup, Turkey Turns against America," *The Economist*, July 18, 2016.

92. Ted Piccone, "Tillerson Says Goodbye to Human Rights Diplomacy," *Order from Chaos* (blog), Brookings, May 5, 2017 (www.brookings.edu/blog /order-from-chaos/2017/05/05/tillerson-says-goodbye-to-human-rights-diplomacy /); and Philip Rucker, "Trump Keeps Praising International Strongmen, Alarming Human Rights Advocates," *Washington Post*, May 2, 2017.

93. Mark Lander, "Trump Congratulates Erdogan on Turkey Vote Cementing His Rule," *New York Times*, April 17, 2017.

94. Gökhan Bacık, "Turkey and the BRICS: Can Turkey Join the BRICS?," *Turkish Studies* 14, no. 4 (December 2013), 758–73; and Soner Cagaptay, "Defining Turkish Power: Turkey as a Rising Power Embedded in the Western International System," *Turkish Studies* 14, no. 4 (December 2013), 797–811.

95. Cagaptay, "Defining Turkish Power," 808.

96. These statistics were calculated based on data available on the TUIK (Turkstat) website. See remarks by the Hoteliers Federation of Turkey

(TÜROFED), Osman Ayık, in Burak Coşan, "Turkish Tourism Players Warn of Bigger Losses in 2017," *Hürriyet Daily News*, June 23, 2016.

97. Mehmet Şimsek, Deputy Prime Minister, recognized at the end of 2015 the estimated cost of loss of Russian tourism to be around U.S. $9 billion: "Mehmet Şimşek'ten Rusya İtirafı: '9 Milyar Dolar,'" *Cumhuriyet*, December 7, 2015.

98. "Wave of Terror Attacks in Turkey Continue at a Steady Pace," *New York Times*, January 5, 2017.

99. In the words of a former Turkish Navy commander and a former Turkish ambassador to Moscow, "The conflict with Russia has reminded us of the value of NATO membership." Conversation with the author, Washington, D.C., March 31, 2016.

100. Ünal Çeviköz, "Varşova Zirvesi'nin tarihi önemi," *Hürriyet*, July 10, 2016.

101. This point was made by most of the participants at a private meeting organized by the Strategic Studies Center in Ankara, October 11, 2016. The meeting was held under Chatham House rules.

102. Author's conversation with a retired Turkish colonel, February 27, 2017, Washington, D.C.

103. "Getting into Bed with a Bear," *The Economist*, February 16, 2017.

104. Henri Barkey, "Putin and Erdogan's Marriage of Convenience," *Foreign Policy*, January 11, 2017.

105. See slide 35 in a PowerPoint slide deck available from Kadir Has Üniversitesi, "Public Perceptions on Turkish Foreign Policy," July 20, 2017 (www.khas.edu.tr/news/1588).

106. Piccone, *Five Rising Democracies*.

CHAPTER 2

1. Rajan Menon and S. Enders Wimbush, "Is the United States 'Losing' Turkey?," Hudson Institute White Paper Series (Spring 2007); Owen Matthews, "Who Lost Turkey?," *Newsweek*, December 11, 2006; Laura Batalla Adam, "Turkey's Foreign Policy in the AKP Era: Has There Been a Shift in the Axis?," *Turkish Policy Quarterly* 11, no. 3 (Fall 2012), 139–48; Ian O. Lesser, "Beyond Suspicion: Rethinking U.S.-Turkish Relations," *Insight Turkey* 9, no. 3 (2007); Nick Danforth, "How the West Lost Turkey," *Foreign Policy*, November 25, 2009; and Svante Cornell, "Axis Shift," Policy Notes, no. 3 (Washington Institute for Near East Policy, January 2011), 3–6.

2. Ömer Taşpınar, "Rise of Turkish Gaullism: Getting Turkish-American Relations Right," *Insight Turkey* 13, no. 1 (2011), 11–17; Ziya Öniş, "Multiple Faces of the 'New' Turkish Foreign Policy: Underlying Dynamics and a Critique," *Insight Turkey* 13, no. 1 (2011), 47–63; and Kemal Kirişci, Nathalie Tocci, and Joshua Walker, "A Neighborhood Rediscovered: Turkey's Transatlantic Value in the Middle East," Brussels Forum Paper Series (Washington: German Marshall Fund of the United States, March 2010).

3. Henri Barkey, "Turkish-American Relations in the Post-War Era: An Alliance of Convenience," *Orient* 33, no. 3 (1992), 447–64.

4. Füsun Türkmen, *Kırılgan İttifaktan "Model Ortaklığa": Türkiye-ABD İlişkileri* (İstanbul: Timaş Yayınevi, 2012).

5. For a succinct analysis of Soviet threats by the Turkish minister of foreign affairs of the late 1940s, see Necmeddin Sadak, "Turkey Faces the Soviets," *Foreign Affairs*, April 1949.

6. Reported in Selim Deringil, *Turkish Foreign Policy during the Second World War: An "Active" Neutrality* (Cambridge University Press, 1989), 180.

7. As reported in Baskın Oran, "Dönemin Bilançosu [1945–1960: Batı Bloku ekseninde Türkiye—1]," in *Türk Dış Politikası: Kurtuluş Savaşından Bugüne Olgular, Belgeler, Yorumlar (1919–1980)*, vol. 1, ed. Baskın Oran (İstanbul: İletişim Yayınları, 2001), 491.

8. George S. Harris, *Troubled Alliance: Turkish-American Problems in Historical Perspective, 1945–1971* (Washington: American Enterprise Institute for Public Policy Research, 1972), 15–20.

9. Sadak, "Turkey Faces the Soviets."

10. Deringil, *Turkish Foreign Policy during the Second World War.*

11. Ibid., 179.

12. Bernard Lewis, "Foreword," in *Turkey: America's Forgotten Ally*, ed. Dankwart A. Rustow, (New York: Council on Foreign Relations Press, 1989), ix.

13. This reasoning was clearly articulated by Atatürk in an interview he gave to the French journalist Maurice Pernot on October 29, 1923, the very day on which he would also proclaim Turkey a republic: *Atatürk'ün Söylev ve Demeçleri*, 3 vols., 3rd ed. (Ankara: Türk İnkılap Tarihi Enstitüsü Yayınları, 1981), 68. See also Yücel Güçlü, *Eminence Grise of the Turkish Foreign Service: Numan Menemencioğlu* (Ankara: Ministry of Foreign Affairs of the Republic of Turkey, May 2002), 30–31; and Metin Tamkoç, *Warrior Diplomats: Guardians of the National Security and Modernization of Turkey* (University of Utah Press, 1976).

14. The term "Kemalist" is a widely used, but also at times abused, term in Turkey. In this book it is used to refer to the founders of the Turkish Republic as well as to those adhering to the founding principles of Turkey, which include secularism as an organizing principle for law and politics. It should be noted at the same time that not all "Kemalists" are necessarily pro-Western (see chapter 5).

15. Ekavi Athanassopoulou, *Turkey-Anglo-American Security Interests, 1945–1952: The First Enlargement of NATO* (London: Frank Cass, 1999), 220.

16. Ibid., 130.

17. The actual vote was "404 to 0, with one abstention." George C. McGhee, "Turkey Joins the West," *Foreign Affairs*, July 1954. See also Gencer Özcan, "Ellilerde 'Dış' Politika," in *Türkiye'nin 50'li Yılları*, ed. Mete Kaan Kaynar (İstanbul: İletişim Yayınları, 2016).

18. For in-depth discussions of the period, see Bernard Lewis, *The Emergence of Modern Turkey* (Oxford University Press, 2002); and Feroz Ahmad, *The Making of Modern Turkey* (London: Routledge, 1994).

19. Lewis, *The Emergence of Modern Turkey*, 304–08. For a firsthand discussion of these demands, see Ahmet Emin Yalman, "The Struggle for Multi-Party Government in Turkey," *Middle East Journal* 1, no. 1 (January 1947); and Ahmet Emin Yalman, *Turkey in My Time* (University of Oklahoma Press, 1956).

20. Yalman, "The Struggle for Multi-Party Government in Turkey," 8. See also Feroz Ahmad, *The Turkish Experiment in Democracy, 1950–1975* (Boulder, Colo.: Westview Press, 1977).

21. Quoted in Ahmad, *Making of Modern Turkey*, 102.

22. The six principles, republicanism, nationalism, populism, etatism, secularism, and reformism, were first adopted by the Republican People's Party in 1931. The sextet is often presented as the basis of Kemalism, referring to the ideology of the founder of modern Turkey. Tarık Zafer Tunaya, *Türkiye'de Siyasi Partiler: 1859–1952* (İstanbul: Arba Yayınları, 1995 [1952]); and Mete Tunçay, *Türkiye Cumhuriyeti'nde Tek-Parti Yönetimi'nin Kurulması (1923–1931)* (Ankara: Yurt Yayınları, 1981).

23. Deringil, *Turkish Foreign Policy during the Second World War*, 19.

24. Ibid., 12–13.

25. Oran, "Dönemin Bilançosu [1945–1960: Batı Bloku ekseninde Türkiye—1]," 489–90.

26. Ibid., 497.

27. Harris, *Troubled Alliance*, 36.

28. Oran, "Dönemin Bilançosu [1945–1960: Batı Bloku ekseninde Türkiye—1]," 496.

29. Harris, *Troubled Alliance*, 38; William Hale, *Turkish Foreign Policy since 1774* (London: Routledge, 2012), 84–85; and Paul Kubicek, "Turkey's Inclusion in the Atlantic Community: Looking Back, Looking Forward," *Turkish Studies* 9, no. 1 (March 2008), 21–35. Similar but much shorter-lived resistance also faced Turkey's bid for membership in the Council of Europe. Turkey was not initially invited to become a founding member of the council. Kubicek, "Turkey's Inclusion in the Atlantic Community," 25.

30. Kubicek, "Turkey's Inclusion in the Atlantic Community," 26; and Hale, *Turkish Foreign Policy since 1774*, 85–86.

31. Mustafa Aydın, "Determinants of Turkish Foreign Policy: Historical Framework and Traditional Inputs," in "Seventy-Five Years of the Turkish Republic," special issue, *Middle Eastern Studies* 35, no. 4 (October 1999), 152–86. See also Faruk Sönmezoğlu, "II. Dünya Savaşı Döneminde Türkiye'nin Dış Politikası: 'Tarafsızlık'tan NATO'ya," in *Türk Dış Politikasının Analizi*, ed. Faruk Sönmezoğlu (İstanbul: Der Yayınları, 1994), 79–87.

32. Hale, *Turkish Foreign Policy since 1774*, 87.

33. Deringil, *Turkish Foreign Policy during the Second World War*, 3. For Atatürk's foreign policy as described by his long-serving minister of foreign affairs, see Tevfik Rüştü Aras, *Atatürk'ün Dış Politikası* (İstanbul: Kaynak Yayınları, 2003).

34. Şadi Koçaş, *Atatürk'ten 12 Mart'a—Anılar* (İstanbul: Doğuş Matbaası, 1977), 193.

35. Nasuh Uslu, *The Turkish-American Relationship between 1947 and 2003: The History of a Distinctive Alliance* (New York: Nova Science Publishers, 2003), 1. Uslu calls it "a perfect honeymoon period." Bruce R. Kuniholm, "Turkey and NATO: Past, Present and Future," *Orbis* 27 (1983), 421–45, 424.

36. Between 1948 and 1964, Turkey received about U.S. $2.5 billion in military assistance (Hale, *Turkish Foreign Policy since 1774*, 89). Turkey's GDP in 1952 was just under U.S. $5 billion (Oran, "Dönemin Bilançosu [1945–1960: Batı Bloku ekseninde Türkiye—1]," 487).

37. Duygu Sezer, "Turkey's Security Policies," in *Greece and Turkey: Adversity in Alliance*, ed. Jonathan Alford (London: Gower, 1984), 73. Khrushchev is reputed to have blamed Stalin for having "succeeded in frightening the Turks right into the open arms of the Americans": Bruce R. Kuniholm, "Turkey and the West since World War II," in *Turkey between East and West: New Challenges for a Rising Regional Power*, ed. Mastny Vojtech and R. Craig Nation (Boulder, Colo.: Westview Press, 1997), 45.

38. Harris, *Troubled Alliance*, 56; and F. Stephen Larrabee, *The Troubled Partnership: U.S.-Turkish Relations in an Era of Global Geopolitical Change* (Rand Corporation, 2010), 1.

39. Sezer, "Turkey's Security Policies," 63.

40. Hale, *Turkish Foreign Policy since 1774*, 91–95; Melek Fırat and Ömer Kürkçüoğlu, "Orta Doğu'yla İlişkiler," in *Türk Dış Politikası*, vol. 1, 617–34.

41. Fırat and Kürkçüoğlu, "Orta Doğu'yla İlişkiler," 621, 634–35. See a detailed analysis in Eyüp Ersoy, "Turkish Foreign Policy toward the Algerian War of Independence (1954–62)," *Turkish Studies* 13, no. 4 (2012), 683–95.

42. Melek Fırat, "Yunanistan'la İlişkiler," in *Türk Dış Politikası*, vol. 1, 731.

43. Hale, *Turkish Foreign Policy since 1774*, 89–90.

44. Malik Mufti, *Daring and Caution in Turkish Strategic Culture: Republic at Sea* (London: Palgrave Macmillan, 2009), 30.

45. Oran, "Dönemin Bilançosu [1945–1960: Batı Bloku ekseninde Türkiye—1]," 486–94.

46. Harris, *Troubled Alliance*, 80–83.

47. Dilek Barlas and Serhat Güvenç, "Turkey and the Idea of a European Union in the Inter-War Years, 1923–39," *Middle Eastern Studies* 45, no. 3 (2009), 425–46.

48. Çağrı Erhan and Tuğrul Arat, "AET'yle ilişkiler," in *Türk Dış Politikası*, vol. 1, 808–53.

49. Quoted in Mehmet Ali Birand, *Türkiye'nin Büyük Avrupa Kavgası: 31 Temmuz 1959'dan 17 Aralık 2004'e* (İstanbul: Doğan Yayıncılık, 2005), 131.

50. Quoted in ibid., 132. The quotation can also be found in Alessandro Albanese Ginammi, "Le origini dell'integrazione della Turchia nella CEE dal punto di vista italiano (1957–1963)" [The origin of the EEC-Turkey integration from the Italian perspective (1957–1963)] (Ph.D. diss., European University of Rome, 2017).

51. The agreement in Article 28 notes that parties would "examine the possibility of the accession of Turkey to the Community." For a discussion of the

negotiations leading to the agreement and its terms, see Erhan and Arat, "AET'yle ilişkiler," 808–53. See also Selim İlkin, "A History of Turkey's Association with the European Community," in *Turkey and the European Community*, ed. Ahmet Evin and Geoffrey Denton (Opladen: Leske and Budrich, 1990).

52. Sezer, "Turkey's Security Policies," 63.

53. Çağrı Erhan, "ABD ve NATO'yla ilişkiler," in *Türk Dış Politikası*, vol. 1, 681–715.

54. Donald L. Haffner, "Bureaucratic Politics and 'Those Frigging Missiles': JFK, Cuba and US Missiles in Turkey," *Orbis* 21, no. 2 (Summer 1977), 307–32.

55. George E. Gruen, "Ambivalence in the Alliance: U.S. Interest in the Middle East and the Evolution of Turkish Foreign Policy," *Orbis* 24 (1980), 363–79, 369.

56. For a discussion of the "letter," its content and impact, see Süha Bölükbaşı, "The Johnson Letter Revisited," *Middle Eastern Studies* 29, no. 3 (1993), 505–25; and Erhan, "ABD ve NATO'yla ilişkiler," 685–92.

57. Deringil, *Turkish Foreign Policy during the Second World War*, 154.

58. Harris, *Troubled Alliance*, 116–17.

59. Uslu, *The Turkish-American Relationship between 1947 and 2003*, 85. The interview was published in its Turkish original in Mehmet Ali Kışlalı, "Batı ittifakı yıkılır," *Milliyet*, April 17, 1964.

60. İlhan Üzgel, "TDP'nin oluşturulması," in *Türk Dış Politikası*, vol. 1, 79.

61. Gencer Özcan, "Altmışlı Yıllarda 'Dış' Politika," in *Türkiye'nin 60'lı Yılları*, ed. Gencer Özcan (İstanbul: İletişim Yayınları, 2017), 217–57.

62. Oran, "Dönemin Bilançosu [1960–1980: Göreli Özerklik—3]," in *Türk Dış Politikası*, vol. 1, 669–70. See also Özcan, "Altmışlı Yıllarda 'Dış' Politika."

63. Mufti, *Daring and Caution*, 40.

64. Erhan, "ABD ve NATO'yla ilişkiler," 694. Demirel's government could not escape being accused by a leading leftist intellectual of serving the U.S. to make Turkey an American colony; see Harris, *Troubled Alliance*.

65. Erhan, "ABD ve NATO'yla ilişkiler," 689–90.

66. Hale, *Turkish Foreign Policy since 1774*, 109; and Oran, "Dönemin Bilançosu [1960–1980: Göreli Özerklik—3]," 679. Also, as Oran points out, arguments about leaving NATO died down once the Soviet navy started to cruise around the Mediterranean and Soviet tanks rolled into the streets of Prague.

67. Harris, *Troubled Alliance*, 143.

68. Mufti, *Daring and Caution*, 39.

69. Ibid., 36–41: Mufti associates the "left Kemalist" movement with the spirit behind the 1960 military intervention and notes that adherents of this movement have been less suspicious of the Soviet Union than the "right Kemalists," who have been more open to cooperation with the United States, but underlines how Kemalists of both types have been very pro-independence, with a strong aversion to foreign entanglements. See also Tanıl Bora, *Cereyanlar: Türkiye'de Siyasi İdeolojiler* (İstanbul: İletişim, 2017), 162–64.

70. Emirhan Yorulmazlar, "The Role of Ideas in Turkish Foreign Policy: The JDP-Davutoğlu Paradigm and Its Role after 2002" (Ph.D. diss., Boğaziçi University, 2015), 48.

71. Bülent Ecevit, "Turkey's Security Policies," in *Turkey and Greece: Adversity in Alliance*, ed. Jonathan Alford (London: Gower, 1984), 138.

72. Oran, "Dönemin Bilançosu [1960–1980: Göreli Özerklik—3]," 674.

73. Erhan and Arat, "AET'yle ilişkiler," 845.

74. Elena Calandri, "A Special Relationship under Strain: Turkey and the EEC, 1963–1976," *Journal of European Integration History* 15 (2009), 57–76, 68.

75. Quoted in ibid., 75.

76. Necmettin Erbakan, *Türkiye ve Ortak Pazar* (İzmir: İstiklal Matbaası, 1971). These ideas were also repeated in *1991 Genel Seçimi Refah Partisi Beyannamesi*, 168.

77. For a commentary recalling these remarks, see Güneri Civaoğlu, "Top zinadan döndü," *Milliyet*, September 24, 2004. For Tansu Çiller's critical remarks, see also *Türkiye Büyük Millet Meclisi Genel Kurul Tutanağı* 20. Dönem, 3. Yasama Yılı, 38. Bileşim, January 6, 1998.

78. Hale, *Turkish Foreign Policy since 1774*, 118.

79. Ömer Karasapan, "Turkey's Armament Industries," *MERIP Middle East Report* (January–February 1987), 27–31.

80. Henry Barkey, *The State and the Industrialization Crisis in Turkey* (Boulder, Colo.: Westview Press, 1990).

81. İhsan D. Dağı, "Democratic Transition in Turkey, 1980–83: The Impact of European Diplomacy," *Middle Eastern Studies* 32, no. 2 (April 1996), 124–41.

82. Gökçen Alpkaya, "İnsan Hakları Konusu," in *Türk Dış Politikası: Kurtuluş Savaşından Bugüne Olgular, Belgeler, Yorumlar (1980–2001)*, vol. 2, ed. Baskın Oran (İstanbul: İletişim Yayınları, 2010), 191–95.

83. For the full text of the opinion, see Commission of the European Communities, Sec. (89) 2290, "Commission Opinion on Turkey's Request for Accession to the Community" (Brussels, December 1989).

84. Commission of the European Communities, "Press Conference by Mr. Matutes on Membership of Turkey to the Community" (Brussels, December 1989; ref. BIC/89/393).

85. İlhan Üzgel, "ABD ve NATO'yla ilişkiler," in *Türk Dış Politikası*, vol. 2, ed. Oran, 63. On April 24 each year Armenians around the world annually commemorate the mass atrocities that were perpetrated against them by the Ottoman Empire during World War I. Most historians put the number of Armenians who perished at between 1 million and 1.5 million and consider the events to have been genocide. Turkish authorities, however, have contested these figures and rejected the use of the term genocide. The official Turkish position instead attributes the deaths and displacements to the broader context of the war, during which many Muslims and Turks also perished. The United States is home to the largest Armenian community outside Armenia itself and the issue of recognizing the genocide by the U.S. Congress and the White House regularly comes up. For a discussion of the genocide issue see Thomas de Waal, *Great Catastro-*

phe: Armenians and Turks in the Shadow of Genocide (Oxford University Press, 2015).

86. Ziya Oniş, "The Political Economy of Export-Oriented Industrialization in Turkey," in *Turkey: Political, Social and Economic Challenges in the 1990s*, ed. Çiğdem Balım (Leiden: Brill Academic Publishers, 1995).

87. For a coverage of the "democracy" issue in the early years of U.S.-Turkish relations, see Nicholas Danforth, "Malleable Modernity: Rethinking the Role of Ideology in American Policy, Aid Programs, and Propaganda in Fifties' Turkey," *Diplomatic History* 39, no. 3 (2015), 477–503. See also George Kennan, *Memoirs: 1925–1950* (Boston: Little, Brown, 1967), 411–12.

88. Hakan Yılmaz, "American Perspectives on Turkey: An Evaluation of the Declassified US Documents between 1946–1960," *New Perspectives on Turkey* 25 (Fall 2001), 77–101, 78.

89. Ibid.

90. Danforth, "Malleable Modernity."

91. Larrabee, *Troubled Partnership*, 1. For a detailed study of Turkey's contribution to NATO security, see Serhat Güvenç, *NATO'da 60 yıl: Türkiye'nin Transatlantik Güvenliğine Katkıları* (İstanbul: İstanbul Bilgi Üniversitesi Yayınları, 2013).

92. Hale, *Turkish Foreign Policy since 1774*, 120.

93. Saadet Değer, "The Economic Costs and Benefits of U.S.-Turkish Relations," in *Europe after an American Withdrawal: Economic and Military Issues*, ed. Jane M. O. Sharpe (Oxford University Press, 1990), 247.

94. See "Turkey's Rising Soft Power," special issue, *Insight Turkey* 10, no. 2 (2008).

95. Senem Aydın-Düzgit and Nathalie Tocci, "Transforming Turkish Foreign Policy: The Quest for Regional Leadership and Europeanization," *CEPS Commentary*, November 2009; Kemal Kirişci, "Comparing the Neighborhood Policies of Turkey and the EU in the Mediterranean," in *Turkey: Reluctant Mediterranean Power*, ed. Meliha Benli-Altunışık, Kemal Kirişci, and Nathalie Tocci, Mediterranean Paper Series 2011 (Washington: German Marshall Fund of the United States, February 2011), 21–44.

96. Independent Commission on Turkey, "Turkey in Europe: Breaking the Vicious Circle," 2009; International Crisis Group, "Turkey and the Middle East: Ambitions and Constraints," ICG Europe, no. 203, April 7, 2010 (www.crisisgroup.org/en/regions/europe/turkey-cyprus/turkey/203-turkey-and-the-middle-east-ambitions-and-constraints.aspx).

97. Türkmen, *Kırılgan İttifaktan "Model Ortaklığa."*

CHAPTER 3

1. Mustafa Aydın, "Foucault's Pendulum: Turkey in Central Asia and the Caucaus," *Turkish Studies* 5, no. 2 (Summer 2004), 1–22, 2.

2. "Süleyman Demirel, Top Turk," *The Economist*, July 22, 1999. For Demirel's own words, see *Cumhuriyet*, February 24, 1992.

3. Malik Mufti, "Daring and Caution in Turkish Foreign Policy," *Middle East Journal* 52, no. 1 (1998), 32–50.

4. İlhan Üzgel, "ABD ve NATO'yla İlişkiler," in *Türk Dış Politikası: Kurtuluş Savaşından Bugüne Olgular, Belgeler, Yorumlar (2001–2012)*, vol. 3, ed. Baskın Oran (İstanbul: İletişim Yayınları, 2013), 315.

5. This was noted, for example, in "Star of Islam: A Survey of Turkey," *The Economist*, December 14, 1991. See also R. Craig Nation, "The Turkish and Other Muslim Peoples of Central Asia, the Caucasus, and the Balkans," in *Turkey between East and West: New Challenges for a Rising Regional Power*, ed. Vojtech Mastny and R. Craig Nation (Boulder, Colo.: Westview Press, 1996).

6. Armağan Emre Çakır, *The United States and Turkey's Path to Europe* (London: Routledge, 2016), chaps. 9–11; and Andrew Mango, "Turkish Model," *Middle Eastern Studies* 29, no. 3 (1993), 726–57.

7. Sabri Sayari, "Turkey, the Changing European Security Environment and the Gulf Crisis," *Middle East Journal* 46, no. 1 (1992), 9–21, 10–11.

8. For a discussion of Özal's stance verging on the "daring" and resistance to it from the advocates of "caution" in Turkish foreign policy, see Malik Mufti, *Daring and Caution in Turkish Strategic Culture: Republic at Sea* (Basingstoke: Palgrave Macmillan, 2009), 58–84. See also Sayari, "Turkey, the Changing European Security Environment and the Gulf Crisis." For an account of the resignation by the then chief of staff himself, see Necip Torumtay, *Orgeneral Torumtay'ın Anıları* (İstanbul: Milliyet Yayınları, 1994).

9. Kemal Kirişci, " 'Provide Comfort' and Turkey: Decision Making for Refugee Assistance," *Low Intensity Conflict and Law Enforcement* 2 (Autumn 1993).

10. For a discussion of the Kurds and their quest for a state, see Denise Natali, *The Kurds and the State: Evolving National Identity in Iraq, Turkey, and Iran* (Syracuse University Press, 2005); and David McDowall, *A Modern History of the Kurds*, 3rd ed. (London: I.B. Tauris, 2004).

11. Joel Peters, *Pathways to Peace: The Multi-Lateral Arab-Israeli Peace Talks* (London: Royal Institute of International Affairs, 1996); and Kemal Kirişci, "The Future of Turkish Policy toward the Middle East," in *Turkey in World Politics: An Emerging Multiregional Power*, ed. Barry Rubin and Kemal Kirişci (Boulder, Colo.: Lynne Rienner, 2001), 101.

12. Meliha Benli Altunışık, "Turkish Policy toward Israel," in *Turkey's New World: Changing Dynamics in Turkish Foreign Policy*, ed. Alan Makovsky and Sabri Sayari (Washington: Washington Institute for Near East Policy, 2000); and Gencer Özcan and Ofra Bengio, "The Decade of the Military in Turkey: The Case of the Alignment with Israel in the 1990s," *International Journal of Turkish Studies* 7, nos. 1–2 (2001), 90–110.

13. Mahmut Bali Aykan, "The Palestinian Question in Turkish Foreign Policy from the 1950s to the 1990s," *International Journal of Middle East Studies* 25, no. 1 (February 1993), 94–102.

14. Richard D. Asmus, Larry Diamond, Mark Leonard, and Michael McFaul, "A Transatlantic Agenda for the Promotion of Democracy in the Broader Middle East," *Washington Quarterly* 28, no. 2 (Spring 2005), 7–21; and Hüse-

yin Bağcı and Bayram Sinkaya, "The Greater Middle East Initiative and Turkey: The AKP's Perspective," in *The Importance of Being European: Turkey, the EU and the Middle East*, ed. Nimrod Goren and Nachmani Amikan (Jerusalem: European Forum at the Hebrew University, 2007), 165–77. For specific contributions to democracy promotion projects, see Kemal Kirişci, "Democracy Diffusion: The Turkish Experience," in *Turkey and Its Neighbors: Foreign Relations in Transition*, ed. Ronald H. Linden et al. (Boulder, Colo.: Lynne Rienner, 2011), 157–64; and Burak Akçapar, *Turkey's New European Era: Foreign Policy on the road to EU Membership* (Lanham, Md.: Rowman and Littlefield, 2007), 107–08.

15. Thomas Straubhaar, "Turkey as an Economic Neighbor," in *Turkey and Its Neighbors*; and Kemal Kirişci, Nathalie Tocci, and Joshua Walker, *A Neighborhood Rediscovered: Turkey's Transatlantic Value in the Middle East*, Brussels Forum Papers Series (Washington: German Marshall Fund of the United States, March 2010).

16. Juliette Tolay, "Migration and Changes in Turkish Foreign Policy," in *Turkey and Its Neighbors*.

17. Bülent Aras, "Davutoğlu Era in Turkish Foreign Policy," *Insight Turkey* 11, no. 3 (2009), 127–42.

18. Sayari, "Turkey: Changing European Security Environment and the Gulf Crisis," 18.

19. Berdal Aral, "Dispensing with Tradition? Turkish Politics and International Society during Özal Decade 1983–1993," *Middle Eastern Studies* 37, no. 1 (2001), 72–88, 76.

20. İsmail Cem, *Turkey in the New Century: Speeches and Texts Presented at International Fora (1995–2001)* (Nicosia: Rustem, 2001), 2.

21. Ibid., 22 and 26.

22. Ibid., 20–21.

23. For a discussion of this topic, see Gün Kut, "Türk Dış Politikasında Çok Yönlülüğün Yakın Tarihi: Soğuk Savaş Sonrası Devamlılık ve Değişim," in *Siyasetin Bilimi*, ed. Pınar Uyan Semerci, Boğaç Erozan, and Nihal İncioğlu (İstanbul: İstanbul Bilgi Üniversitesi Yayınları, 2015), 158–87; and Meliha Altunışık, "Worldviews and Turkish Foreign Policy in the Middle East," *New Perspectives on Turkey* 40 (April 2009), 169–92.

24. Author's interviews with Hikmet Çetin, Ali Tuygan, Yaşar Yakış, and Uğur Ziyal, May 18, 2016, Ankara, and with Abdullah Gül, May 20, 2016, Istanbul. Gül's readiness to work closely and constructively with the Ministry of Foreign Affairs was greatly appreciated, according to "one highly experienced career diplomat": Gerald MacLean, *Abdullah Gül and the Making of the New Turkey* (London: OneWorld, 2014), 238–39.

25. For a discussion of the conflict, see Thomas de Waal, *Black Garden: Armenia and Azerbaijan through Peace and War* (New York University Press, 2003).

26. Şule Kut, "Turkish Policy towards the Balkans," in *Turkey's New World*, 82.

27. There were, though, allegations that Turkey was supplying weapons to Bosnians in violation of UN sanctions, as reported in İlhan Üzgel, "The Balkans: Turkey's Stabilizing Role," in *Turkey in World Politics*, 66.

28. Paul Flenley, "Russia and the EU: The Clash of New Neighborhoods," *Journal of Contemporary European Studies* 16, no. 2 (August 2008), 189–202.

29. William Hale, *Turkish Foreign Policy since 1774* (London: Routledge, 2012), 206.

30. Serhat Güvenç and Soli Ozel, "NATO and Turkey in the Post–Cold War World: Between Abandonment and Entrapment," *Journal of Southeast European and Black Sea Studies* 12, no. 4, (December 2012), 533–53, 539.

31. "Turkey and Armenia: Opening Minds, Opening Borders," Europe Report 199 (International Crisis Group, April 14, 2009), 1–2 (https://d2071 andvip0wj.cloudfront.net/turkey-and-armenia-opening-minds-opening -borders.pdf). See also Fiona Hill, Kemal Kirişci, and Andrew Moffatt, "Armenia and Turkey: From Normalization to Reconciliation," *Turkish Policy Quarterly* (Winter 2015), 132–33.

32. Instead the then prime minister Süleyman Demirel argued that "Turkey would not act alone" and added that "foreign policy decisions cannot go along with street level excitement." *Turkish Daily News*, April 14, 1993.

33. Aydın, "Foucault's Pendulum," 13.

34. For detailed coverage of the diplomacy leading to the protocols and then the eventual failure to put them into effect, see Thomas de Waal, *Great Catastrophe: Armenians and Turks in the Shadow of Genocide* (Oxford University Press, 2015), 214–34.

35. Hill, Kirişci, and Moffatt, "Armenia and Turkey," 135–36.

36. European Commission Director-General for Trade, "European Union, Trade in Goods with Armenia," April 11, 2016, 8 (http://trade.ec.europa.eu /doclib/docs/2006/september/tradoc_113345.pdf).

37. For the strategic significance of the BTC, see Richard Morningstar, "From Pipe Dream to Pipeline: The Realization of the Baku-Tbilisi-Ceyhan Pipeline," Belfer Center Event Report (Belfer Center, Harvard Kennedy School, May 8, 2003) (http://belfercenter.ksg.harvard.edu/publication/12795/from_pipe_dream _to_pipeline.html). For TANAP, see Gareth Winrow, "Realization of Turkey's Energy Aspirations: Pipe Dreams or Real Projects?," Turkey Project Policy Paper, no. 4, Brookings, April 2014, 10.

38. Cavid Veliyev, "From Alliance to Integration: The Turkey-Azerbaijan-Georgia Triangle," *Eurasia Daily Monitor* 11, no. 46 (March 2014).

39. Hikmet Çetin, "The Security Structures of a Changing Continent: A Turkish View," *NATO Review* 40, no. 2 (April 1992). See also similar views expressed by a Turkish diplomat: Ünal Çevikoz, "European Integration and New Regional Cooperation," *NATO Review* 40, no. 3 (1992).

40. Mustafa Aydın, "Regional Cooperation in the Black Sea and the Role of Institutions," *Perceptions: Journal of International Institutions* 10 (Autumn 2005) (http://sam.gov.tr/tr/wp-content/uploads/2012/01/Mustafa-Ayd%A6-n .pdf), 57–83.

41. "UN Mission's Summary Detailed by Country," December 31, 2016 (www. un.org/en/peacekeeping/contributors/2016/dec16_3.pdf). Currently (May 2017), Turkey is contributing 146 military personnel to nine UN operations (MINUSMA,

MINUSTAH, MONUSCO, UNAMID, UNIFIL, UNMIK, UNMIL, UNMISS, and UNSOM). International Institute of Strategic Studies, *The Military Balance: The Annual Assessment of Military Capabilities and Defense Economics* (London: Routledge, February 2016), 150: Turkey contributes 905 personnel to five NATO missions (Operation Resolute Support, Operation Ocean Shield, KFOR, and two missions on the Mediterranean Sea). For a discussion of Turkey's involvement in peacekeeping, see Tarık Oğuzlu and Uğur Güngör, "Peace Operations and the Transformation of Turkey's Security Policy," *Contemporary Security Policy* 27, no. 3 (2006), 472–88.

42. Cem Say and Günter Seufert, "Turkey in Afghanistan: A Successful but Difficult Partner," *SWP Comments* 28 (May 2016), 4. For Turkey's development policies, see also Saban Kardaş, "Turkey's Regional Approach in Afghanistan: A Civilian Power in Action," SAM Papers 6 (Ankara: Center for Strategic Research, April 2013) (http://sam.gov.tr/wp-content/uploads/2013/04/SAM_paper_ing_06_int.pdf).

43. Reported in Serhat Güvenç, *NATO'da 60 Yıl: Türkiye'nin Transatlantik Güvenliğine Katkıları* (İstanbul: Istanbul Bilgi Üniversitesi Yayınları, 2013), 55.

44. Kemal Kirişci, "New Patterns of Turkish Foreign Policy Behaviour," in *Turkey: Economic, Political and Foreign Policy Challenges for the 1990s*, ed. Çiğdem Balım (Leiden: E. J. Brill, 1995), 18–19.

45. Ted Piccone, *Five Rising Democracies and the Fate of the International Liberal Order* (Brookings Institution Press, 2016), 182. See also Reşat Bayer and E. Fuat Keyman, "Turkey: An Emerging Hub of Globalization and Internationalist Humanitarian Actor?," *Globalizations* 9, no. 1 (2012).

46. "Turkey to Host Landmark World Humanitarian Summit," Turkish Cooperation and Coordination Agency, June 5, 2016 (www.tika.gov.tr/en/news/turkey_to_host_landmark_world_humanitarian_summit-22648). According to "Global Humanitarian Assistance Report 2016," June 7, 2016 (www.globalhumanitarianassistance.org/wp-content/uploads/2016/07/GHA-report-2016-full-report.pdf), Turkish humanitarian assistance amounted to $3.1 billion and was spent mostly on Syrian refugees in Turkey (pp. 45–46).

47. Republic of Turkey, Ministry of Foreign Affairs, "Turkey's Development Cooperation: General Characteristics and the Least Developed Countries Aspect" (Ankara, 2011) (www.mfa.gov.tr/turkey_s-development-cooperation.en.mfa).

48. Ahmet Davutoğlu, "Turkey's Humanitarian Diplomacy: Objectives, Challenges and Prospects," *Nationalities Papers: The Journal of Nationalism and Ethnicity* 42, no. 6 (2013), 865–70, 866.

49. Mark Bradbury, "State-building, Counterterrorism and Licensing Humanitarianism in Somalia," briefing paper (Feinstein International Center, Tufts University, September 2010), 4.

50. "Suicide Bomb Kills Two in Mogadishu ahead of Visit by Turkish President," *The Guardian*, January 22, 2015.

51. Kathryn Achilles, Onur Sazak, Thomas Wheeler, and Auveen Elizabeth Woods, *Turkish Aid Agencies in Somalia Risks and Opportunities for Building*

Peace (Istanbul: Safer World and Istanbul Policy Center, March 2015), 19. For another assessment of Turkey's efforts in Somalia, see Pınar Akpınar, "Turkey's Peacebuilding in Somalia: The Limits of Humanitarian Diplomacy," *Turkish Studies* 14, no. 4 (2014), 735–57.

52. Fulya Apaydın, "Overseas Development Aid across the Global South: Lessons from the Turkish Experience in Sub-Saharan Africa and Central Asia," *European Journal of Development Research* 24, no. 2 (2012), 261–82, 266.

53. Turkish Ministry of Foreign Affairs, "Turkey's Development Cooperation: General Characteristics and the Least Developed Countries Aspect."

54. Turkish Ministry of Foreign Affairs, "High-Level Comprehensive Midterm Review of the Implementation of the Istanbul Programme of Action for the Least Developed Countries" (Ankara, May 29, 2016) (www.mfa.gov.tr/high _level-comprehensive-midterm-review-of-the-implementation-of-the-istanbul -programme-of-action-for-the-least-developed-coun.en.mfa).

55. World Bank, coordinator, "G20 and Low Income Developing Countries Framework" (www.oecd.org/g20/topics/development/G20-Low-Income-Deve loping-Countries-Framework.pdf). For a discussion of the Turkish government's effort to include the interests of developing countries and Africa, see Ussal Sahbaz and Feride İnan, "Turkey and the G-20 Presidency: Implications for LIDCs and Africa," South African Institute of International Affairs, *Policy Insights* 19 (June 2015) (www.saiia.org.za/policy-insights/836-turkey-and-the-g-20 -presidency-implications-for-lidcs-and-africa/file), 1–8.

56. For the description of Turkey as a country in constant search of its identity, see Selim Deringil, "The Turks and 'Europe': The Argument from History," *Middle Eastern Studies* 43, no. 5 (2007), 709–23.

57. Bahar Rumelili, "Constructing Identity and Relating to Difference: Understanding the EU's Mode of Differentiation" *Review of International Studies* 30, no. 1 (January 2004), 27–47, 44.

58. Desmond Dinan, *Ever Closer Union: An Introduction to European Integration* (Boulder, Colo.: Lynne Rienner, 2010).

59. Heinz Kramer, "Turkey and the European Union: A Multi-Dimensional Relationship," in *Turkey between East and West*, 210.

60. William Hale and Gamze Avcı, "Turkey and the European Union: The Long Road to Membership," in *Turkey in World Politics*, 33–34; and Senem Aydın and Nathalie Tocci, *Turkey and the European Union* (London: Palgrave, June 2015), 94.

61. Hale, *Turkish Foreign Policy since 1774*, 177–78.

62. Its approval came after considerable lobbying by the Turkish government and civil society, as well as by EU governments particularly supportive of the customs union and the United States. The U.S. ambassador Stuart Eisenstadt was given the task of coordinating lobbying of the European Parliament. Eventually the European Parliament voted in support of the customs union, 343 to 149, with 113 abstentions. See Mehmet Ali Birand, *Türkiye'nin Avrupa Macerası (1959–1999)* (İstanbul: Doğan Kitap, 2000), 369–71. See also Stefan Krauss, "The European Parliament in EU External Relations: The Customs

Union with Turkey," *European Foreign Affairs Review* 5, no. 2 (2000), 215–37.

63. For a comprehensive assessment, see Kamil Yılmaz, "The EU–Turkey Customs Union Fifteen Years Later: Better, Yet Not the Best Alternative," *South European Society and Politics* 16, no. 2 (June 2011), 235–49; and World Bank, "Evaluation of the EU-Turkey Customs Union" (Washington: World Bank, 2014).

64. Bahadır Kaleağası and Barış Ornarlı, "Why Turkey Belongs to the Transatlantic Economy," *Congress Blog*, TheHill.com, March, 13, 2013 (http://thehill.com/blogs/congress-blog/foreign-policy/287675-why-turkey-belongs-to-transatlantic-economy#ixzz2ZEDc9sMg).

65. Director-General for Trade, European Commission, "European Union, Trade in Goods with Turkey," August 27, 2014.

66. Ahmet Sever, "Çiller: Tam üyelik," *Milliyet*, December 17, 1995.

67. Atilla Eralp, "Turkey and the European Union in the Post–Cold War Era," in *Turkey's New World*, 181.

68. Kramer, "Turkey and the European Union," 217–18. See also James Ker-Lindsay, "The Policies of Greece and Cyprus towards Turkey's EU Accession," *Turkish Studies* 8, no. 1 (2007), 71–83.

69. Aydın-Düzgit and Tocci, *Turkey and the European Union*, 184.

70. These are criteria that candidate countries need to meet to become members of the EU. They were adopted at the EU's Copenhagen summit in 1993. The political criteria require candidate countries to be democratic, to function according to the rule of law, and to respect minority rights. The economic criteria, on the other hand, require candidates to have a functioning market economy that can withstand the competitive pressures of the single market and be able to take on the obligations of membership, including the aim of economic and monetary union.

71. Kemal Kirişci, "The Kurdish Question and Turkish Foreign Policy," in *The Future of Turkish Foreign Policy*, ed. Lenore Martin and Dimitris Keridis (MIT Press, 2002). For the ECHR decision, see "Apo dosyasında kritik gün," *Milliyet*, November 30, 1999.

72. Ali Çarkoğlu and Kemal Kirişci, "The View from Turkey: Perceptions of Greeks and Greek-Turkish Rapprochement by the Turkish Public," *Turkish Studies* 5, no. 1 (2004), 117–53; and Ahmet Evin, "Changing Greek Perspective on Turkey: An Assessment of Post-Earthquake Rapprochement," *Turkish Studies* 5, no. 1 (2004), 4–20.

73. Aydın-Düzgit and Tocci, *Turkey and the European Union*, 36–37. What Turkey would need to do to "sufficiently" meet these criteria was laid out in the accession partnership document adopted by the EU in December 2000. In turn, Turkey adopted its first National Programme for the Implementation of the Acquis in 2001. All official EU documentation concerning Turkey's accession process can be accessed at http://ec.europa.eu/enlargement/candidate-countries/turkey/key_documents_en.htm. The corresponding documents in Turkish can be accessed at www.ab.gov.tr/?p=123&l=2.

74. Süheyl Batum, *Towards EU Membership: Political Reforms in Turkey* (Istanbul: TÜSİAD, 2012); and Ioannis N. Grigoriadis, *Trials of Europeanization: Turkish Political Culture and the European Union* (London: Palgrave Macmillan, 2009), 56–59.

75. Burhanettin Duran, "JDP and Foreign Policy as an Agent of Transformation," in *The Emergence of a New Turkey: Democracy and the AK Party*, ed. Hakan Yavuz (University of Utah Press, 2006).

76. A large body of literature examines Turkey's reform process and the workings of the EU conditionality principle, including Ergun Özbudun and Serap Avcı, *Democratization Reforms in Turkey, 1993–2004* (Istanbul: TESEV, 2004); Gamze Avcı and Ali Çarkoğlu, *Turkey and the European Union: Accession and Reform* (London: Routledge, 2012); and Susannah Verney and Kostas Ifantis, eds., *Turkey's Road to European Union Membership* (London: Routledge, 2009).

77. Ayse Aslıhan Çelenk, "The Restructuring of Turkey's Policy towards Cyprus: The Justice and Development Party's Struggle for Power," *Turkish Studies* 8, no. 3 (2007), 349–63.

78. International Crisis Group, "Cyprus: Reversing the Drift to Partition," January 10, 2008 (https://d2071andvip0wj.cloudfront.net/190-cyprus-reversing -the-drift-to-partition.pdf).

79. Ziya Öniş and Şuhnaz Yılmaz, "Greek-Turkish Rapprochement: Rhetoric or Reality?," *Political Science Quarterly* 123, no. 1 (2008), 123–49. For the Helsinki decision requirements on Turkey concerning Cyprus and Greece, see "Helsinki European Council: Presidency Conclusion," December 10 and 11, 1999, paragraphs 4 and 9b (www.europarl.europa.eu/summits/hel1_en.htm).

80. For an exhaustive study of U.S. involvement and support for Turkey's EU vocation from 1959 on, see Armağan Emre Çakır, *The United States and Turkey's Path to Europe* (London: Routledge, 2016). See also Nathalie Tocci, *Turkey's European Future: Behind the Scenes of America's Influence on EU-Turkey Relations* (New York University Press, 2012); Sabri Sayarı, "Challenges of Triangular Relations: The US, the EU and Turkish Accession," *South European Society and Politics* 16, no. 2 (June 2011), 251–63; and Morton Abramowitz, "The Complexities of American Policymaking on Turkey," in *Turkey's Transformation and American Policy*, ed. Morton Abramowitz (New York: Century Foundation Press, 2000).

81. Çakır, *The United States and Turkey's Path to Europe*.

82. Ibid., 10.

83. Quoted in "US Warned to Keep Out of Turkey's EU Talks," *Financial Times*, April 22, 2003.

84. "Angry Chirac Puts Bush in His Place," *The Guardian*, June 29, 2004.

85. Tocci, *Turkey's European Future*, 79–83.

86. In contrast to previous very brief visits by Eisenhower and George H. W. Bush, Bill Clinton spent five long days and also visited areas of Turkey that had been hit by the August and November earthquakes. He was greatly appreciated by the public for mixing with ordinary people and is remembered to this

day for holding up a baby who had survived the devastation of the earthquake and who grabbed his nose. James Gerstenzang, "Clinton Visits Turkish Quake Victims," *Los Angeles Times*, November 17, 1999.

87. This thought was expressed as early as 1998 by then secretary of state Strobe Talbott: "U.S.-Turkish Relations in an Age of Interdependence," *Policy-Watch* 344 (Washington Institute for Near East Policy, October 16, 1998) (www.washingtoninstitute.org/policy-analysis/view/u.s.-turkish-relations-in-an -age-of-interdependence). The speech extracted in the cited paper was delivered in memory of the late Turgut Özal at the Washington Institute for Near East Policy.

88. Independent Commission on Turkey, "Turkey in Europe: More Than a Promise?," September 16, 2014 (http://www.independentcommissiononturkey .org/pdfs/2004_english.pdf).

89. William Clinton, "Remarks by President Clinton to the Turkish Grand National Assembly," November 15, 1999 (www.presidency.ucsb.edu/ws/?pid =56935).

90. Independent Commission on Turkey, "Turkey in Europe: Breaking the Vicious Circle," September 2009 (www.independentcommissiononturkey.org /pdfs/2009_english.pdf).

91. Füsun Türkmen, *Kırılgan İttifaktan "Model Ortaklığa": Türkiye-ABD İlişkileri* (İstanbul: Timaş Yayınları, 2012), 167.

92. Alan Makovsky, "The New Activism in Turkish Foreign Policy," Policy Analysis (Washington Institute for Near East policy, Winter/Spring 1999) (www .washingtoninstitute.org/policy-analysis/view/the-new-activism-in-turkish -foreign-policy).

93. Ziya Öniş, "Turkey and the Middle East after September 11: The Importance of the EU Dimension," *Turkish Policy Quarterly* 2, no. 4 (Winter 2003), 84–85. Öniş distinguishes between "coercive" and "benign" regional powers. The former are more likely to use force in their foreign policy and hence can be a source of insecurity and instability in its neighborhood. In contrast, a benign power adopts a more constructive role and promotes a network of economic and political relations.

94. Şükrü Elekdağ, "2½ War Strategy," *Perceptions: Journal of International Affairs* 1, no. 1 (March–May 1996), 1–12. For the quotation, see Mufti, "Daring and Caution in Turkish Foreign Policy," 34.

95. Abramowitz, *Turkey's Transformation and American Policy*, 15.

96. "Gulf Crisis Continues to Inflict High Cost on Turkey," *Hürriyet Daily News*, January 17, 2001 (www.hurriyetdailynews.com/gulf-crisis-continues-to -inflict-high-cost-on-turkey.aspx?pageID=438&n=gulf-crisis-continues-to -inflict-high-cost-on-turkey-2001-01-17).

97. Mahmut Bali Aykan, "Turkey's Policy in Northern Iraq, 1991–1995," *Middle Eastern Studies* 32, no. 4 (1996), 343–66; and Füsun Türkmen, "Anti-Americanism as a Default Ideology of Opposition: Turkey as a Case Study," *Turkish Studies* 11, no. 3 (September 2010), 329–45, 341. For examples of accusations that Washington was trying to weaken Ankara, see Baskın Oran, *"Kalkık*

Horoz": *Çekiç Güç ve Kürt Devleti* (Ankara: Bilgi Yayınevi, 1996), and Ümit Özdağ, *Türkiye-PKK ve Kuzey Irak* (Ankara: Avrasya Dosyası Yayınları, 1999).

98. In Turkey, polls revealed that 88 percent of the public was against the war, and almost two out of three respondents thought Turkey should stay out of it. Aylin Güney, "An Anatomy of the Transformation of the U.S.-Turkish Alliance: From 'Cold War' to 'War on Iraq,'" *Turkish Studies* 6, no.3 (2003), 341–59, 348.

99. MacLean, *Abdullah Gül and the Making of the New Turkey*, 231–37.

100. Güney, "An Anatomy of the Transformation of the U.S.-Turkish Alliance," 350. Gürkan Zengin, *Hoca: Türk Dış Politikasi'nda 'Davutoğlu Etkisi,'* *2002–2010* (İstanbul: İnkilap, 2014), 128–30.

101. Füsun Türkmen, "Anti-Americanism as a Default Ideology of Opposition," 341.

102. For Turkey's resistance to the notion of Kurdish independence, especially in the context of Iraq, see Asa Lundgren, *The Unwelcome Neighbor: Turkey's Kurdish Policy* (London: I. B. Tauris, 2007); and Henri Barkey, "Turkey and Iraq: The Perils (and Prospects) of Proximity," Special Report 141 (United States Institute of Peace, July 2005).

103. The Turkish military felt that for this reason, "Turkey would be better off inside the American tent than outside." Quoted in Hale, *Turkey Foreign Policy since 1744*, 166.

104. Henri J. Barkey, "Turkey's New Engagement in Iraq Embracing Iraqi Kurdistan," Special Report 237 (United States Institute of Peace, May 2010); and Soner Cagaptay and Tyler Evans, "Turkey's Changing Relations with Iraq: Kurdistan Up, Baghdad Down," *Policy Focus* 122 (Washington Institute for Near East Policy October 2012) (www.washingtoninstitute.org/uploads /Documents/pubs/PolicyFocus122.pdf).

105. Tocci and Walker, "Turkey and the Middle East," in *Turkey and Its Neighbors*, 45; Türkmen, *Türkiye-ABD İlişkileri*, 261–62.

106. Gönül Tol, "Turkey's KRG Energy Partnership," *Foreign Policy*, January 29, 2013.

107. "US Soldiers with YPG Insignias Unacceptable, Says Turkish FM," *Hürriyet Daily News*, May 27, 2016. See also Pinar Tremblay, "Turks Question Loyalties after Picture Emerges of US Soldiers with YPG Patches," Al-Monitor, June 7, 2016.

108. Missy Ryan, Thomas Gibbons-Neff, and Karen DeYoung, "In Blow to U.S.-Turkey Ties, Trump Administration Approves Plan to Arm Syrian Kurds against Islamic State," *Washington Post*, May 9, 2017.

109. George W. Bush, "Remarks at Galatasaray University in Istanbul," June 29, 2004 (American Presidency Project, University of California) (www.presidency.ucsb.edu/ws/?pid=64397).

110. "Powell'dan gaf: Türkiye Islam cumhuriyeti," *Radikal*, April 2, 2004. The Turkish president at the time, Ahmet Necdet Sezer, in response argued that "Turkey is neither an Islamic republic, nor an example of moderate Islam."

Quoted in "Crisis between Civilizations," *Turkish Daily News*, October 2, 2004.

111. Oran, *Türk Dış Politikası*, vol. 3, 269. This conviction actually made its way into the indictment advocating closure of the governing AKP in 2008. See Jenny White, *Muslim Nationalism and the New Turks* (Princeton University Press, 2014), 52.

112. Christiane Amanpour, "Exclusive Interview with Recep Tayyip Erdogan," CNN, September 7, 2012.

113. Anthony Faiola and Souad Mekhennet, "In Turkey, a Late Crackdown on Islamist Fighters," *Washington Post*, August 12, 2014; and Tim Arango and Eric Schmitt, "A Path to ISIS, through a Porous Turkish Border," *New York Times*, March 9, 2015. David Phillips, "Research Paper: ISIS-Turkey Links," *Huffington Post*, November 9, 2014.

114. Aslı Aydıntaşbaş, "The Tragedy of Modern Turkey," *Wall Street Journal*, July 4, 2016.

115. Murat Yetkin, "Syria Policy a 'Source of Many Sufferings' for Turkey," *Hürriyet Daily News*, August 19, 2016 (www.hurriyetdailynews.com/syria-policy-a-source-of-many-sufferings-for-turkey.aspx?pageID=449&nID=103003&NewsCatID=409); and Murat Yetkin, "Turkey's Syria Policy Changes: With or without Assad," *Hürriyet Daily News*, August 16, 2016 (http://www.hurriyetdailynews.com/turkeys-syria-policy-changes-with-or-without-assad.aspx?pageID=449&nID=102881&NewsCatID=409).

116. "Turkey Recalls Ambassador over Genocide Resolution," CNN, October 11, 2017; and "Turkey Recalls Envoy to U.S. over Panel's 'Genocide' Vote," CNN, March 5, 2014.

117. Thomas de Waal, "The G-Word," *Foreign Affairs*, January–February 2015, 2. For the most recent statement, see White House, "Statement by the President on Armenian Remembrance Day," news release, Office of the Press Secretary, April 24, 2017 (www.whitehouse.gov/the-press-office/2017/04/24/statement-president-donald-j-trump-armenian-remembrance-day-2017).

118. Philip Oltermann and Constanze Letsch, "Turkey Recalls Ambassador after German MPs' Armenian Genocide Vote," *The Guardian*, June 2, 2016; and "Turkey Withdraws Ambassador from France," *Spiegel Online*, December 22, 2011.

119. "International Affirmation of the Armenian Genocide," ArmenianGenocide.org (www.armenian-genocide.org/current_category.7/affirmation_list.html).

120. Maclean, *Abdullah Gül and the Making of the New Turkey*, 228–29.

121. George Kyris, "The Cyprus Problem: Failure of a Catalyst," in *Turkey and the European Union: Facing New Challenges and Opportunities*, ed. Fırat Cengiz and Lars Hoffmann (London: Routledge, 2014), 18–19.

122. Aydın-Düzgit and Tocci, *Turkey and the European Union*, 48.

123. Kyris, "The Cyprus Problem," 19–21. See also Hakan Yılmaz, "Euroscepticism in Turkey: Parties, Elites, and Public Opinion," *South European*

Society and Politics 16, no. 1 (March 2011), 185–208, 194. He argues that after the "AKP government" had "boldly changed the official Turkish policy on Cyprus," the absence of a solution on the island that contributed to the AKP losing its "initial zeal and determination regarding Turkey's EU accession" contributed to a slowdown in the reform process.

124. Kadir Üstün and Kılıç Buğra Kanat, "Turkish-American Relations in the AK Party Decade," SETA Policy Brief, January 2012, 235.

125. Philip C. Bleek and Aaron Stein, "Turkey and America Face Iran," *Survival* 54, no. 2 (2012), 27–38.

126. Daniel Dombey, "US Issues Arms Deal Ultimatum to Turkey," *Financial Times*, August 10, 2010.

127. Mustafa Kibaroğlu, "Turkey's Place in the 'Missile Shield,'" *Journal of Balkan and Near Eastern Studies* 15, no. 2 (2013), 223–36.

128. Tom Shanker, "U.S. Hails Deal with Turkey on Missile Shield," *New York Times*, September 15, 2011.

129. Mustafa Kibaroğlu and Selim Sazak, "Why Turkey Chose, and Then Rejected, a Chinese Air-Defense Missile," *Defense One*, February 3, 2016 (www.defenseone.com/ideas/2016/02/turkey-china-air-defense-missile /125648/). Author's interview with official from Roketsan, March 2016, Istanbul.

130. Üstün and Kanat, "Turkish-American Relations in the AK Party Decade," 233.

131. Gün Kut, "Türk Dış Politikasında Çok Yönlülüğün Yakın Tarihi" in *Siyasetin Bilimi*, 183.

132. Sabri Sayarı, "Turkish-American Relations in the Post–Cold War Era: Issues of Convergence and Divergence," in *Turkish-American Relations: Past, Present and Future*, ed. Mustafa Aydın and Çağrı Erhan (London: Routledge, 2004), 91–106.

133. Aydın-Düzgit and Tocci, *Turkey and the European Union*, 116.

CHAPTER 4

1. Francis Fukuyama, "The End of History?," *National Interest* (Summer 1989) (https://ps321.community.uaf.edu/files/2012/10/Fukuyama-End-of-history -article.pdf).

2. On the broader theme of post–Cold War chaos affecting Turkey internally, see Ali Çarkoğlu and Ersin Kalaycıoğlu, *The Rising Tide of Conservatism in Turkey* (New York: Palgrave, 2009), 144. For a succinct study of three decades of political and economic developments in Turkey since 1980, see Kerem Öktem, *Turkey since 1989: Angry Nation* (London: Zed Books, 2011).

3. The eleven governments and thirteen foreign ministers are identified in Baskın Oran, "Dönemin Bilançosu—1990–2001: Küreselleşme Ekseninde Türkiye," in *Türk Dış Politikası: Kurtuluş Savaşından Bugüne Olgular Belgeler ve Yorumlar*, vol. 2, ed. Baskın Oran (İstanbul: İletişim Yayınları, December 2001), table 1, "Dönemin Yönetimi," 203.

4. Çarkoğlu and Kalaycıoğlu, *The Rising Tide of Conservatism in Turkey*. For a detailed analysis of the polarization and tension between these two groups of "Turks," see Jenny White, *Muslim Nationalism and the New Turks* (Princeton University Press, 2013).

5. Interestingly, Zakaria notes that Turkey "is not a full-fledged democracy" (80) and goes on to observe that Turkey "is a flawed but functioning liberal democracy" on 127 in Fareed Zakaria, *The Future of Freedom: Illiberal Democracy at Home and Abroad* (New York: W. W. Norton, 2007). In his classic "The Rise of Illiberal Democracy," *Foreign Affairs*, November/December 1997, where he discusses illiberal democracy in the 1990s, Zakaria does not raise the case of Turkey at all.

6. Calculated from the table "1991–2001 Türkiye'nin Temel Ekonomik Göstergeleri," in Oran, "Dönemin Bilançosu—1990–2001: Küreselleşme Ekseninde Türkiye."

7. Çarkoğlu and Kalaycıoğlu, *The Rising Tide of Conservatism in Turkey*, 23. Late in 2000 the interest rate reached the incredible level of 2,000 percent. See Yakup Kepenek and Nurhan Yentürk, *Türkiye Ekonomisi* (İstanbul: Remzi Kitapevi, 2009), 593.

8. World Bank, World Development Indicators, "GDP Growth (Annual %)" (database and graphs) (http://data.worldbank.org/indicator/NY.GDP.MKTP .KD.ZG?locations=TR). Data were current as of July 11, 2017.

9. Oran, "Dönemin Bilançosu—1990–2001: Küreselleşme Ekseninde Türkiye," 216.

10. Öktem, *Turkey since 1989*, 84–121.

11. Doğu Ergil, *Doğu Sorunu: Teşhisler, Tespitler* (Ankara: TOBB, 1995).

12. Ironically, Kenan Evren, who was the leader of the 1980 military coup and subsequently the president of Turkey until 1989, and who played a central role in this ban, admitted many years later during an interview that banning the use of the Kurds' mother tongue was wrong. "Kürtçeye Ağır yasak koyduk Ama Hataydı," *Milliyet*, November 7, 2007.

13. In 2013 the author of the report reflected on how he was socially ostracized at the time for having written such a report: Fatih Vural, "Doğu Ergil: Benden annem bile utanmıştı," *Türkiye Gazetesi*, November 19, 2013 (www.turkiyegazetesi.com.tr/gundem/104236.aspx).

14. Bülent Tanör, *Türkiye'de Demokratikleşme Perspektifleri* (Istanbul: TÜSIAD, 1997).

15. "TÜSİAD'da Demokrasi Raporu çıkışı," *Dünya*, January 23, 2014.

16. Paul Kubicek, "The Earthquake, Civil Society and Political Change in Turkey: Assessment and Comparison with Eastern Europe," *Political Studies* 50, no. 4 (September 2002), 761–78.

17. Kemal Kirişci, "The Kurdish Issue in Turkey: The Limits of European Reform," *South European Society and Politics* 16, no. 2 (June 2011), 335–49, 340.

18. These included, for example, the lifting of capital punishment, ending emergency rule in Kurdish-populated parts of Turkey, and allowing the public

use of minority languages, including Kurdish. For a discussion of these early rounds of reforms, see Kemal Kirişci, "Turkey and the European Union: The Domestic Politics of Negotiating Pre-Accession," *Macalester International* 15, no. 10 (Spring 2005), 44–80.

19. Larry Diamond, *The Spirit of Democracy: The Struggle to Build Free Societies throughout the World* (New York: Henry Holt, 2008); and Max Fisher, "The Next 5 Emerging Economies That Will Change the World," *The Atlantic*, February 22, 2012.

20. Morton Abramowitz and Henri F. Barkey, "Turkey's Transformers: The AKP Sees Big." *Foreign Affairs* 88, no. 6 (2009), 118–28.

21. Soner Cagaptay, *The Rise of Turkey: The Twenty-First Century's First Muslim Power* (New York: Potomac Books, 2014).

22. Soli Özel, "After the Tsunami," *Journal of Democracy* 14, no. 2 (2003), 80–94.

23. Şerif Mardin's "Center-Periphery Relations: A Key to Turkish Politics," *Daedalus* 102, no. 1 (Winter 1973), 169–90, has long been used as a framework to explain politics in Turkey.

24. Ibid., 185; and Hakan Yavuz, *Islamic Political Identity in Turkey* (Oxford University Press, 2003), 60–62.

25. Metin Heper and E. Fuat Keyman, "Double-Faced State: Political Patronage and the Consolidation of Democracy in Turkey," *Middle Eastern Studies* 34, no. 4 (1998), 259–77. For a survey of religious discourse by political leaders, see F. Michael Wuthrich, *National Elections in Turkey: People, Politics and the Party System* (Syracuse University Press, 2015), 210–19.

26. For a discussion of the Turkish state's long-standing relationship with Islamic movements and their engagement, especially against the left, see Behlül Özkan, "Turkey's Islamists: From Power-Sharing to Political Incumbency," *Turkish Policy Quarterly* 14, no. 1 (Spring 2015), 71–83.

27. William Hale and Ergün Özbudun, *Islamism, Democracy and Liberalism in Turkey* (London: Routledge, 2010), xx. For a discussion of the "Turkish-Islamic synthesis" and its profound impact on Turkish politics, see Hugh Poulton, *Top Hat, Grey Wolf and Crescent* (London: Hurst, 1997), 181–87.

28. For a discussion of their teachings, see Burhanettin Duran, "Transformation of Islamist Political Thought in Turkey from the Empire to the Early Republic (1908–1960): Necip Fazıl Kısakürek's Political Ideas" (Ph.D. diss., Bilkent University, 2001) (www.thesis.bilkent.edu.tr/0001603.pdf); and Metin Gürcan, "Seventh Son of the East: Sezai Karakoç and His Doctrine of Revival," *Turkish Studies* 16, no. 1 (2015), 1–19. See also Burhanettin Duran, "Cumhuriyet Dönemi İslamcılığı," in *Modern Türkiye'de Siyasi Düşünce: İslamcılık*, ed. Murat Gültekingil and Tanıl Bora (İstanbul: İletişim Yayınları, 2005). For a comprehensive survey of Islamist ideologies in Turkey, see Tanıl Bora, *Cereyanlar: Türkiye'de Siyasi İdeolojiler* (İstanbul: İletişim, 2017), 415–511.

29. Yavuz, *Islamic Political Identity in Turkey*, 223–25; and İhsan Dağı, *Kimlik, Söyle ve Siyaset: Doğu-Batı Ayrımında Refah Partisi Geleneği* (Ankara: İmge Yayınları, 1998).

30. Carter Vaughn Findley, *Turkey, Islam, Nationalism and Modernity* (Yale University Press, 2010), 361.

31. Erbakan quoted in Wuthrich, *National Elections in Turkey*, 213.

32. Hasan Hüseyin Ceylan, *Erbakan ve Türkiye'nin Temel Meselleri* (Ankara: Rehber, 1996), 90.

33. Quoted from an October 1996 speech, in Hale and Özbudun, *Islamism, Democracy and Liberalism in Turkey*, 7.

34. Yavuz, *Islamic Political Identity in Turkey*, 225. For a broader discussion of his politics, especially when in power, see Haldun Gülalp, "The Poverty of Democracy in Turkey: The Refah Party Episode," *New Perspectives on Turkey* 21 (October 1999), 35–59.

35. Uğur Akıncı, "The Welfare Party's Municipal Track Record: Evaluating Islamist Municipal Activism in Turkey," *Middle East Journal* 53, no. 1 (Winter 1999), 75–94; Hakan Yavuz, "Political Islam and the Welfare (Refah) Party in Turkey," *Comparative Politics* 30, no. 1 (1997), 63–82; and Sabri Sayari, "Turkey's Islamist Challenge," *Middle East Quarterly* 3, no. 3 (September 1996), 35–43.

36. Öktem, *Turkey since 1989*, 106.

37. Findley, *Turkey, Islam, Nationalism and Modernity*, 357. The quotation is also mentioned in Meliha Benli Altunışık and Özlem Tur, *Turkey: Challenges of Continuity and Change* (London: Routledge, 2005), 59. Ersin Kalaycıoğlu, *Turkish Dynamics: Bridge across Troubled Lands* (London: Palgrave Macmillan, 2005), 157, reports the wording as "inject the vaccine of Sharia by force."

38. Gerassimos Karabelias, "Dictating the Upper Tide: Civil-Military Relations in the Post Özal Decade: 1993–2003," *Turkish Studies* 9, no. 3 (2008).

39. Zeyneb Çağlıyan İçener, "The Justice and Development Party's Conception of 'Conservative Democracy': Invention or Reinterpretation?," *Turkish Studies* 10, no. 4 (2009), 595–612, 596–97.

40. Nilgün Cerrahoğlu, "Veliaht Tayyip Erdoğan'a göre RP hepimizin partisi: 'Demokrasi amaç değil araçtır,' " interview, *Milliyet*, July 14, 1996.

41. Findley, *Turkey, Islam, Nationalism and Modernity*, 360.

42. Ruşen Çakır and Fehmi Çalmuk, *Recep Tayyip Erdoğan: Bir Dönüşümün Öyküsü* (Istanbul: Metis Kitap, 2001).

43. *AK Parti Kalkınma ve Demokratikleşme Programı* (Ankara: AK Parti Yayınları, 2002).

44. Hale and Özbudun, *Islamism, Democracy and Liberalism in Turkey*, 21.

45. Findley, *Turkey, Islam, Nationalism and Modernity*, 361. For a critical discussion of Kemalism, see Perry Anderson, "Kemalism," *London Review of Books* 30, no. 17 (2008). For a favorable discussion, see Suna Kili, "Kemalism in Contemporary Turkey," *International Political Science Review* 1, no. 3 (1980). For a discussion of different forms of Kemalism, see Bora, *Cereyanlar: Türkiye'de Siyasi İdeolojiler*, 156–70.

46. *AK Parti Kalkınma ve Demokratikleşme Programı*, 4–15. For a discussion of the two distinct forms of secularism, see Ahmet Kuru, "Passive and Assertive Secularism: Historical Conditions, Ideology Struggles, and State Policies

toward Religion," *World Politics* 59 (2007). See also Ahmet Kuru, *Secularism and State Policies toward Religion: The United States, France and Turkey* (Cambridge University Press, 2009). On its specific application to Turkey and the AKP's approach, see Ahmet Kuru, "Reinterpretation of Secularism in Turkey: The Case of the Justice and Development Party," in *The Emergence of New Turkey: Democracy and AK Parti*, ed. Hakan Yavuz (University of Utah Press, 2006).

47. For a list and discussion of these reforms, see World Bank, *Turkey's Transitions: Integration, Inclusion and Institutions* (Washington: World Bank, 2014), 37–41, including figure 1.9.

48. Ziya Öniş, "Political Economy of Turkey's JDP," in *Emergence of New Turkey*; and Sencer Ayata, "Patronage, Party, and State: The Politicization of Islam in Turkey," *Middle East Journal* 50, no.1 (Winter 1996), 40–56. For the term "Islamic Calvinists," referring to hard-working, money-making but pious entrepreneurs, see "Islamic Calvinists: Change and Conservatism in Central Anatolia," European Stability Initiative, September 19, 2005 (www.esiweb.org/pdf/esi_document_id_69.pdf).

49. Quoted in Hale and Özbudun, *Islamism, Democracy and Liberalism in Turkey*, 6.

50. "Gümrük Birliğini Tanımam," *Milliyet*, December 14, 1995.

51. Hale and Özbudun, *Islamism, Democracy and Liberalism in Turkey*, 24.

52. For a discussion of the notion of "Muslim democrats" in general and the AKP as a political party composed of Muslim democrats, see Vali Nasr, "The Rise of 'Muslim Democracy,'" *Journal of Democracy* 16, no. 2 (April 2005), 13–27. For an AKP-focused discussion, see Sultan Tepe, "Turkey's AKP: A Model 'Muslim-Democratic' Party?," *Journal of Democracy* 16, no. 3 (July 2005).

53. Nathalie Tocci, *The EU and Conflict Resolution: Promoting Peace in the Backyard* (Abingdon: Routledge, 2007), 69–70. See also Mustafa Aydın and Sinem A. Açıkmese, "Europeanization through EU Conditionality: Understanding the New Era in Turkish Foreign Policy," *Journal of Southern Europe and the Balkans* 9, no. 3 (2007), 263–74; and Senem Aydın-Düzgit and Nathalie Tocci, *Turkey and the European Union* (Palgrave, 2015), 32–37 and 160–75.

54. For a discussion of the details and the politics surrounding the adoption of these reforms, see Paul Kubicek, "The European Union and Grassroots Democratization in Turkey," *Turkish Studies* 6, no. 3 (2007), 61–77; and E. Fuat Keyman and Senem Aydın-Düzgit, "Europeanization, Democratization and Human Rights in Turkey," in *Turkey and the European Union: Prospects for a Difficult Encounter*, ed. Esra LaGro and Erik Knud Jorgensen (Basingstoke: Palgrave Macmillan, 2007). A complete list of all the reforms introduced by the AKP governments between 2002 and 2012 can be found in *The Silent Revolution: Turkey's Democratic Change and Transformation Inventory, 2002–2012* (Ankara: Undersecretariat of Public Order and Security Publications, November 2013) (www.kdgm.gov.tr/snetix/solutions/KDGM/resources/uploads/files/ingilizce.pdf).

55. Mehmet Ali Birand, *Emret Komutanım* (Ankara: Milliyet Yayınları, 1986); Fikret Bila, *Komutanlar Cephesi* (İstanbul: Detay Yayınları, 2007); and William Hale, *Turkish Politics and the Military* (London: Routledge, 1994).

56. Rabia K. Polat, "The 2007 Parliamentary Elections in Turkey: Between Securitization and De-securitization," *Parliamentary Affairs* 62, no. 1 (2009), 129–48.

57. Quoted in Findley, *Turkey, Islam, Nationalism and Modernity*, 361.

58. The growing environment of "open debate in Turkish society on a wide range of issues," including "issues traditionally perceived as sensitive," was acknowledged by European Commission Progress Reports on the adoption of the EU acquis; see, for example, Commission of the European Communities, "Turkey 2006 Progress Report," November 8, 2006, 4 (http://ec.europa.eu/enlargement /pdf/key_documents/2006/nov/tr_sec_1390_en.pdf); and Commission of the European Communities, "Turkey 2009 Progress Report," October 14, 2009, 19 (http://ec.europa.eu/enlargement/pdf/key_documents/2009/tr_rapport_2009 _en.pdf).

59. Kemal Kirişci and Gareth Winrow, *The Kurdish Question and Turkey: An Example of a Trans-State Ethnic Conflict* (London: Frank Cass, 1997); and Henri Barkey and Graham E. Fuller, *Turkey's Kurdish Question* (Lanham, Md.: Rowman and Littlefield, 1998).

60. For an in-depth analysis of this confrontation, see Aysegül Aydın and Cem Emrence, *Zones of Rebellion: Kurdish Insurgents and the Turkish State* (Cornell University Press, 2015).

61. A former chief of the Turkish General Staff, İlter Başbuğ, put the number of casualties at 32,000 militants, 6,500 security personnel, and 5,700 civilians since 1984: "Bir dönemin acı bilançosu," *Hürriyet*, September 16, 2008. For a more extensive study of casualties, see (Turkish Parliament) Türkiye Büyük Millet Meclisi, İnsan Hakları İnceleme Komisyonu, "Teror ve Şiddet Eylemleri Kapsamında Yaşam Hakkı İhlalleri İnceleme Raporu," 24. Dönem, 3. Yasama Yılı (2013).

62. The Internal Displacement Monitoring Centre puts the number of Kurds displaced between 1984 and 2005 at 954,000 to 1.2 million: "Turkey: Internal Displacement in Brief," December 31, 2013 (www.internal-displacement.org /europe-the-caucasus-and-central-asia/turkey/summary). However, much higher figures than these have also been cited. For a detailed discussion of the issue, see Ayşe Betül Çelik, "Resolving Internal Displacement in Turkey: The Need for Reconciliation," in *Displacement, Reconciliation and Justice*, ed. Megan Bradley (McGill-Queen's University Press, 2015), 195–222.

63. Mehmet Şimşek, former minister of finance, estimated the economic cost "over the last 30–40 years due to terrorism . . . [at] around $1 trillion overall." Quoted in Gümüş Kömürcüler, "What Is the Cost of Terrorism to Turkey's Economy?," *Hürriyet Daily News*, September 2, 2015. For an econometric study of the cost, see Fırat Bilgel and Burhan Can Karahasan, "The Economic Costs of Separatist Terrorism in Turkey," *Journal of Conflict Resolution* 61, no. 2 (March 2015), 457–79.

64. Reported in Kirişci and Winrow, *The Kurdish Question and Turkey*, 112–13.

65. An example of such a debate based on interviews held by Devrim Sevimay can be found in Devrim Sevimay, "Türkiye Kendi Modelini Arıyor: Şiddet Sona Ermeli," *Milliyet*, August 20, 2010. For a discussion of efforts to go beyond EU reforms, see Kirişci, "The Kurdish Issue in Turkey," 335–50.

66. Devrim Sevimay, "Şiddet Sona Ermeli," *Milliyet*, August 7, 2009.

67. Kadri Gürsel, "Ümit Pamir'in önerisi ışığında . . . Kürtlerden boşanmayı tartışabilmek," *Milliyet*, August 10, 2009.

68. "Cumhurbaşkanı Gül 'Kürdistan' dedi," *HaberTurk*, August 24, 2009 (www.haberturk.com/gundem/haber/136247-cumhurbaskani-gul-kurdistan -dedi).

69. The Kurdish opening was launched by the government to initiate a political dialogue with Kurds that would also involve the imprisoned leader of the PKK, Abdullah Öcalan. "Turkey and the Kurds: Peace Time?," *The Economist*, August 27, 2009. The process weakened when the PKK reneged on a cease-fire in late 2010. However, negotiations with Öcalan were eventually revived secretly and then continued publicly from 2013 through early 2015, when the process eventually collapsed. For a timeline, see "Kürt Meselesi: Adım Adım Çözüm Süreci," SETA, April 20, 2013 (www.setav.org/kurt-meselesi/). For an analysis of the "Kurdish opening" and the politics that led to its eventual collapse, see Ayşegül Aydın and Cem Emrence, "Two Routes to an Impasse: Understanding Turkey's Kurdish Policy," Turkey Project Policy Paper, no. 10, Brookings, December 2016 (www.brookings.edu/wp-content/uploads/2016/12/aydin-and -emrence-two-routes-to-an-impasse.pdf).

70. Quoted in Gerald MacLean, *Abdullah Gül and the Making of the New Turkey* (London: One World, 2014), 281.

71. For a brief discussion of the position of the Turkish state, see Thomas De Waal, *Great Catastrophe: Armenians and Turks in the Shadow of Genocide* (Oxford University Press, 2015), 163–67. See also Altay Cengizer, *Adil Hafızanın Işığında* (Istanbul: Doğan Kitap, 2014), for the notion of shared pain.

72. Tunç Aybak, "The Geopolitics of Denial: Turkish State's Armenian Problem," *Journal of Balkan and Near East Studies* 18, no. 2 (2016), 124–44 and 127, and Mneesha Gellman, "Remembering Violence: The Role of Apology in Turkey's Democratization Process," *Democratization* 20, no. 4 (2013), 771–94.

73. "Bilgi University Agrees to Host Conference," *Hürriyet Daily News*, September 24, 2005. The proceedings of the conference were published in *İmparatorluğun Çöküş Döneminde Osmanlı Ermenileri: Bilimsel Sorumluluk ve Demokrasi Sorunları, 23–25 Eylül 2005* (Istanbul: Bilgi Üniversitesi Yayınları, 2011).

74. "Justice Minister Çiçek: Conference on Armenians Like a Stab in the Back to Turkish People," *Hürriyet Daily News*, May 25, 2005.

75. Quoted in Sarah Rainsford, "Turkey Bans 'Genocide' Conference," *BBC News*, September 22, 2005.

76. Cited in Derya Sazak, "Ermeni tabusu," *Milliyet*, September 27, 2005.

77. Retired ambassador Volkan Vural had originally expressed these ideas to Neşe Düzel: "Volkan Vural: 'Ermeni ve Rumlar Tekrar Vatandaş Olsun,'" *Taraf*, September 9, 2008 (https://web.archive.org/web/20080913205241 /http://www.taraf.com.tr/yazar.asp?mid=1841). Same ideas were also expressed in "Diaspora'daki Ermenilere Çağrı Yapalım, Gelenlere Vatandaşlık Verelim," *Agos*, March 18, 2013 (www.agos.com.tr/tr/yazi/4589/diaspora-daki-ermenilere -cagri-yapalim-gelenlere-vatandaslik-verelim).

78. For a brief discussion of Hrant Dink and his legacy, see de Waal, *Great Catastrophe*, 185–93.

79. Benjamin Harvey, "Mass Protest at Editor's Funeral," *The Guardian*, January 24, 2007.

80. "Agos'un sözü: Allah affetsin," *Agos*, August 7, 2014 (www.agos.com.tr /tr/yazi/7737/agos-un-sozu-allah-affetsin); and Cengiz Çandar, "Erdogan Plays to Base Slighting Armenians," Al-Monitor, August 7, 2014 (www.al -monitor.com/pulse/originals/2014/08/candar-erdogan-ethnic-slur-armenians -insult-anti-semitism.html). Earlier in 1997, a former interior minister, Meral Akşener, was reported to have used the word "Armenian" in a derogatory sense as part of an insult that she intended for Abdullah Öcalan, the leader of the PKK.

81. Cengiz Aktar, "Turkish Civil Society: Driving the Politics of Memory," *Turkish Policy Quarterly* 13, no. 1 (Spring 2014) (http://turkishpolicy.com /article/Turkish-Society-Driving-the-Politics-of-Memory-Spring-2014-977), 79–86.

82. The full text is available at www.ozurdiliyoruz.com. The number of petitioners stood at just over 32,454 as of December 19, 2016. When last checked, on June 1, 2017, the website was no longer operational.

83. De Waal, *Great Catastrophe*, 178.

84. Recep Tayyip Erdoğan, "Democracy in the Middle East, Pluralism in Europe: The Turkish View," speech, Harvard University, Kennedy School of Government, January 30, 2003.

85. Recep Tayyip Erdoğan, "Başbakan Erdoğan'ın AK Parti Genişletişmiş İl Başkanları Toplantısı'nda Yaptığı Konuşmanın Tam Metni," January 14, 2011 (www.akparti.org.tr/site/haberler/basbakan-erdoganin-ak-parti-genisletilmis-il -baskanlari-toplantisinda-yapti/6945#1).

86. Kalaycıoğlu, *Turkish Dynamics*, 196.

87. Elizabeth Hurd-Shakman, "Negotiating Europe: The Politics of Religion and the Prospects for Turkish Accession," *Review of International Studies* 32, no. 3 (July 2006), 401–18, 415.

88. MacLean, *Abdullah Gül and the Making of the New Turkey*, 127–28; and Stephen Kinzer, "Head Scarf Puts Assembly in Turkey into Uproar," *New York Times*, May 3, 1999.

89. Kalaycıoğlu, *Turkish Dynamics*, 165.

90. José Casanova, "The Long, Difficult, and Tortuous Journey of Turkey into Europe and the Dilemmas of European Civilization," *Constellations* 13, no. 2 (2006), 234–47, 241.

91. Ergun Özbudun, "From Political Islam to Conservative Democracy: The Case of the Justice and Development Party in Turkey," *South European Society and Politics* 11, nos. 3–4 (2006), 543–57, 555.

92. Abdullah Gül, "Turkey's Role in a Changing Middle East Environment," *Mediterranean Quarterly* (Winter 2004), 1–7, 2. For the full text of the speech, see Abdullah Gül, *Horizons of Turkish Foreign Policy in the New Century* (Ankara: Foreign Office, 2007), 527–32.

93. Semih Idiz, "PM Erdoğan's Surprising Message in Cairo," *Hürriyet Daily News*, September 9, 2011.

94. Quoted in Piotr Zalewski, "Islamic Evolution: How Turkey Taught the Syrian Muslim Brotherhood to Reconcile Faith and Democracy," *Foreign Policy*, August 11, 2011.

95. Joerg Baudner, "The Domestic Effects of Turkey's EU Accession Negotiations: A Missed Opportunity for Europe?," in *Turkey and the European Union: Facing new challenges and opportunities*, ed. Fırat Cengiz and Lars Hoffmann (Abingdon: Routledge, 2014), 190.

96. Kemal Derviş, "Turkey and Europe: A New Perspective," in *Global Turkey in Europe: Political, Economic and Foreign Policy Dimensions of Turkey's Evolving Relationship with the EU*, ed. Senem Aydın-Düzgit et al. (Rome: Edizioni Nuova Cultura, 2013), 22. The average annual growth rate of the Turkish economy in constant domestic prices in the decade that started in January 2003 was 5.1 percent, in contrast to 1.2 percent for the EU.

97. World Bank, World Development Indicators, "GDP per capita (Current US$)" (database and graphs), accessed July 11, 2017, (http://data.worldbank.org /indicator/NY.GDP.PCAP.CD?locations=TR&year_high_desc=true). For a detailed analysis of Turkey's economic "miracle" as well as its shortcomings, see World Bank, *Turkey's Transitions*.

98. For his speech, see Recep Tayyip Erdoğan, "The Turkish Economy Meets EU Entry Criteria," *Huffington Post*, November 28, 2012.

99. Sinan Ciddi, "Kemalist Advocacy in a Post-Kemalist Era?," in *The Turkish AK Party and Its Leader: Criticism, Opposition and Dissent*, ed. Ümit Cizre (London: Routledge, 2016), 34.

100. In an interview, a prominent liberal columnist recognized that he had been misled by the AKP when he had enthusiastically supported them. İrfan Aktan, "Murat Belge: Sonuç Hayır Cephesi Açısından Müthiştir!," *GazeteDuvar*, April 23, 2017 (www.gazeteduvar.com.tr/yazarlar/2017/04/23/murat-belge -sonuc-hayir-cephesi-acisindan-muthistir/).

CHAPTER 5

1. For a literature discussing the image of Turkey as the other of Europe, see Iver B. Neumann and Jennifer M. Welsh, "The Other in European Self Definition: An Addendum to the Literature on International Society," *Review of International Studies* 17, no. 4 (1991), 327–48; Nilufer Göle, "Europe's Encounter with Islam: What Future?," *Constellations* 13, no. 2 (2006), 248–62;

José Casanova, "The Long, Difficult, and Tortuous Journey of Turkey into Europe and the Dilemmas of European Civilization," *Constellations* 13, no. 2 (2006), 234–47; Ingmar Karlsson, "The Turk as a Threat and Europe's Other," in *Turkey, Sweden and the European Union: Experiences and Expectations,* ed. Ingmar Karlsson and Annika Ström Melin (Stockholm: Swedish Institute for European Policy Studies, 2006), 6–13; and Hasan Köşebalaban, "The Permanent 'Other': Turkey and the Question of European Identity," *Mediterranean Quarterly* 18, no. 4 (2007), 87–111.

2. Şadi Koçaş, *Atatürk'ten 12 Mart'a—Anılar* (İstanbul: Doğuş Matbaası, 1977), 193. For more on these ideas, see also Gencer Özcan, "60'lı yıllarda 'dış' politika," in *Türkiye'nin 60'lı Yılları*, ed. Gencer Özcan (İstanbul: İletişim Yayınları, 2017), 217–57.

3. Mustafa Aydın, "Reconstructing Turkish-American Relations: Divergences versus Convergences," *New Perspectives on Turkey* 40 (Spring 2009), 125–46, 142.

4. Gürkan Zengin, *Hoca: Türk Dış Politikası'nda 'Davutoğlu Etkisi,' 2002–2010* (İstanbul: İnkilap, 2014), 71.

5. Gareth M. Winrow, "Turkish Policy towards Central Asia and the Transcaucasus," in *Turkey's New World: Changing Dynamics in Turkish Foreign Policy*, ed. Alan Makovsky and Sabri Sayari (Washington Institute for Near East Policy, 2000), 116–30.

6. William Hale, *Turkish Foreign Policy since 1774* (London: Routledge, 2013), 229.

7. For more details and a survey of Turkish mediation efforts in the 2000s, see Nathalie Tocci and Joshua Walker, "From Confrontation to Engagement: Turkey and the Middle East," in *Turkey and Its Neighbors: Foreign Relations in Transition*, ed. Ronald H. Linden et al. (Boulder, Colo.: Lynne Rienner, 2011), 51–54.

8. Ibid., 56.

9. Independent Commission on Turkey, "Turkey in Europe: More Than a Promise," September 2004, 17 (http://www.independentcommissiononturkey .org/pdfs/2004_english.pdf). The authors of the report remarked that "Turkish accession would considerably strengthen the Union's capabilities as foreign policy actor." In a similar vein, the Turkish minister of foreign affairs, Abdullah Gül, argued, "The message of reform, modernity, moderation, and integration represented by Turkey's EU membership will be spread to the wider international community." See Abdullah Gül, "Turkey's Role in a Changing Middle East Environment," *Mediterranean Quarterly* 15, no. 1 (Winter 2004), 1–7, 2.

10. Turkey met the Copenhagen political criteria "sufficiently" in 2004. Commission of the European Communities, "Regular Report on Turkey's Progress towards Accession," October 6, 2004 (http://ec.europa.eu/enlargement /archives/pdf/key_documents/2004/rr_tr_2004_en.pdf). It was also regarded as a "functioning market economy" in 2005. European Commission, "Turkey: 2005 Progress Report," November 9, 2005, 54. (http://ec.europa.eu/enlargement /archives/pdf/key_documents/2005/package/sec_1426_final_progress_report _tr_en.pdf).

11. Kemal Derviş, "Turkey and Europe, a New Perspective," in *Global Turkey in Europe: Political, Economic, and Foreign Policy Dimensions of Turkey's Evolving Relationship with the EU,* ed. Senem Aydın-Düzgit, Anne Duncker, Daniela Huber, E. Fuat Keyman, and Nathalie Tocci (Rome: Edizioni Nuova Cultura, 2013), 22.

12. World Bank, *Turkey's Transitions: Integration, Inclusion, Institutions* (Washington: World Bank, 2014).

13. World Bank, *Evaluation of the EU-Turkey Customs Union* (Washington: World Bank, 2014).

14. Turkey's per capita income in 2013 was at $10,700, and high-income level is defined as $12,600. World Bank, *Turkey's Transitions,* 29.

15. İzak Atiyas, "Economic Institutions and Institutional Change in Turkey during the Neoliberal Era," *New Perspectives on Turkey* 14 (Fall 2012), 45–69; Işık Özel, "The Politics of De-Delegation: Regulatory (In)dependence in Turkey, Regulation and Governance," *Regulation and Governance Forum* 6, no. 1 (2012), 119–29; and Galip Kemal Özhan, "The Growth Debate Redux," in *Growth, Convergence, and Income Distribution: The Road from the Brisbane G-20 Summit,* Think Tank 20, Brookings, November 2014 (www.guntramwolff.net/wp-content/uploads/2015/05/TT20-Nov-7-FINAL-Web-v2.pdf).

16. Daron Acemoğlu and J. Robinson, *Why Nations Fail: The Origins of Power, Prosperity and Poverty* (New York: Crown Business, 2012); and European Bank for Reconstruction and Development, *Stuck in Transition: Transition Report 2013* (London: EBRD, 2013).

17. World Bank, *Turkey's Transitions,* 19.

18. Aydın, "Reconstructing Turkish-American Relations," 141; Hale, *Turkish Foreign Policy since 1774,* 152; and Ziya Oniş and Şuhnaz Yılmaz, "Between Europeanization and Euro-Asianism: Foreign Policy Activism in Turkey during the AKP Era," *Turkish Studies* 10, no. 1 (March 2009), 7–24, 12.

19. Abdullah Gül, *Horizons of Turkish Foreign Policy in the New Century* (Ankara: Dış İşleri Bakanlığı Yayınları, 2007), 351.

20. "Bağış: AB ülkelerine ihtiyacımız yok," *Hürriyet,* June 1, 2011.

21. "Road to Hangzhou: Treasury Secretary Lew on What to Expect at the G20 Summit," Brookings event, August 31, 2016 (www.brookings.edu/wp-content/uploads/2016/09/20160831_lew_g20_transcript.pdf).

22. Ziya Öniş, "Multiple Faces of the 'New' Turkish Foreign Policy: Underlying Dynamics and a Critique," *Insight Turkey* 13, no. 1 (2011), 47–65, 55.

23. Hüseyin Bağcı, "The Role of Turkey as a New Player in the G20 System," in *G20: Perceptions and Perspectives for Global Governance,* ed. Wilhelm Hofmeister and Susanna Vogt (Singapore: Konrad Adenauer Stiftung, October 2011), 151.

24. Meliha Altunışık, "The Turkish Model and Democratization in the Middle East," *Arab Studies Quarterly* 27, no. 12 (Winter/Spring 2005), 45–63; and Meliha Altunışık, "The Possibilities and Limits of Turkey's Soft Power in the Middle East," *Insight Turkey* 10, no. 2 (2008), 41–54.

25. Mensur Akgün, Sabiha Şenyücel Gündoğar, Jonathan Levack, and Gökçe Perçinoğlu, eds., *Ortadoğu'da Türkiye Algısı 2010* (İstanbul: TESEV

Yayınları, February 2011), 14 (www.tesev.org.tr/tr/yayin/ortadoguda-turkiye
-algisi-2010); and Shibley Telhami, "Annual Arab Public Opinion Survey," 2011
(www.brookings.edu/wp-content/uploads/2016/06/1121_arab_public_opinion
.pdf).

26. International Crisis Group, "Turkey and the Middle East: Ambitions and
Constraints," Europe Report, no. 203 (ICG, April 7, 2010), ii (https://
d2071andvip0wj.cloudfront.net/203-turkey-and-the-middle-east-ambitions
-and-constraints.pdf).

27. Yousef al Sharif and Samir Saha, "Turkey's European Union Membership: The Arab Perspective. Notes from the Arab Media," in *Reflections on
EU-Turkey Relations in the Muslim World*, ed. Hakan Altınay, Gökçe
Tüylüoğlu, and Gülgün Küçükören (Istanbul: Open Society Foundation,
2009), 25.

28. Tülay Cetingülec, "Turkish Soap Operas Turn Istanbul into Paris of the
East," Al-Monitor, November 10, 2016 (http://www.al-monitor.com/pulse
/originals/2016/11/turkey-soap-operas-rescue-turkish-tourism.html).

29. Robert L. Pollock, "The Sick Man of Europe—Again," *Wall Street Journal*, February 16, 2005.

30. According to Kadir Has University surveys, on average almost 40 percent
of the respondents saw the United States as a threat in 2013, 2015, and 2016. See
slide 14 in a PowerPoint slide deck available from Kadir Has Üniversitesi, "Türk
Dış Politikası Kamuoyu Algıları Araştırması," May 18, 2016, İstanbul (www.
khas.edu.tr/news/1367).

31. Füsun Türkmen, *Kırılgan İttifaktan "Model Ortaklığa": Türkiye-ABD
İlişkileri* (İstanbul: Timaş Yayınevi, 2012), 244.

32. Doğan Gürpınar, *Komplolar Kitabı: Belki de Her Sey Göründüğü Gibi-
dir* (İstanbul: Doğan Kitap, 2014), 16.

33. The public and elite of modern-day Turkey, by virtue of the country's
mantle as the successor state to the Ottoman Empire, have inherited an accompanying narrative of the collapse. See Metin Heper, "Ottoman Legacy and
Turkish Politics," *Journal of International Affairs* 54, no. 1 (2000), 63–82; and
Frederick W. Frey, *The Turkish Political Elite* (MIT Press, 1965). For an analysis of how this narrative has been incorporated into a convincing conspiratorial
perspective on Western intentions to weaken Turkey, see Hakan Yılmaz, "Two
Pillars of Nationalist Euroscepticism in Turkey: Tanzimat and Sèvres Syn-
dromes," in *Turkey, Sweden and the European Union*, 29–40. For the history
of the collapse of the Ottoman Empire, see İlber Ortaylı, *İmparotorluğun en
Uzun Yüzyılı* (İstanbul: Timaş Yayınları, 2016); and Şükrü Hanioğlu, *A Brief
History of the Late Ottoman Empire* (Princeton University Press, 2010).

34. Malik Mufti, *Daring and Caution in Turkish Strategic Culture: Republic at Sea* (New York: Palgrave, 2009), 16.

35. Ziya Öniş and Şuhnaz Yılmaz, "Between Europeanization and Euro-
Asianism: Foreign Policy Activism in Turkey during the AKP Era," *Turkish
Studies* 10, no. 1 (March 2009), 7–24, 15.

36. Kadir Has Üniversitesi, "Türk Dış Politikası Kamuoyu Algıları Araştırması,"
slide 13.

37. Ali Çarkoğlu and Kemal Kirişci, "The View from Turkey: Perceptions of Greeks and Greek-Turkish Rapprochement by the Turkish Public," *Turkish Studies* 5, no. 1 (Spring 2004), 117–53, 125.

38. Quoted in Mufti, *Daring and Caution in Turkish Strategic Culture*, 160.

39. Kamran İnan, *Hayır Diyebilen Türkiye* (İstanbul: Timaş Yayınları, 1998).

40. Fiachra Gibbons, "Erdogan's Chief Adviser Knows What's behind Turkey's Protests—Telekinesis," *The Guardian*, July 13, 2013.

41. Ibid. Also Gürpınar, *Komplolar Kitabı*, 251–52.

42. "CIA'nın örtülü operasyonu," *Aydınlık*, December 12, 2016, (https://www.aydinlik.com.tr/turkiye/2016-aralik/cia-nin-ortulu-operasyonu); and Akif Beki, "Avşar Kızı'nın tepkisi mi Pekin Paşa'nın tepkisi mi," *Hürriyet*, December 13, 2016.

43. For a survey of these books and films, see Gürpınar, *Komplolar Kitabı*, 140–54.

44. Ibid., 147.

45. Mufti, *Daring and Caution in Turkish Strategic Culture*, 16.

46. Yılmaz, "Two Pillars of Nationalist Euroscepticism in Turkey," 29–40. Public opinion surveys link the less than enthusiastic support given by respondents to fundamental human and civil rights as manifestations of this "syndrome."

47. Dietrich Jung, "The Sèvres Syndrome: Turkish Foreign Policy and Its Historical Legacies," *American Diplomacy*, UNC.edu, 2003, 8 (http://www.unc.edu/depts/diplomat/archives_roll/2003_07-09/jung_sevres/jung_sevres.html).

48. Kemal Kirişci, "Democracy Diffusion: The Turkish Experience," in *Turkey and Its Neighbors*, 163.

49. Ersin Ramoğlu, "Alman vakıfları vatan hainleriyle," *Sabah*, October 21, 2014; and Serkan Üstüner, "En tehlikeli yapı: Alman vakıfları," *Haber 7*, March 1, 2016 (www.haber7.com/yazarlar/serkan-ustuner/1819072-en-tehlikeli-yapi-alman-vakiflari). See also the literature on the hypothesis that German foundations are involved in illegal activities in Turkey: Necip Hablemitoğlu, *Alman Vakıfları: Bergama Dosyası* (İstanbul: Pozitif Yayıncılık, 2016).

50. Connor Murphy, "Turkey Withdraws Blacklist of German Firms Accused of Financing Terrorism," *Politico*, July 24, 2017 (http://www.politico.eu/article/germany-turkey-erdogan-withdraws-blacklist-of-german-firms-accused-of-financing-terrorism/).

51. Karl Vick, "Turkey Charges Acclaimed Author," *Washington Post*, September 1, 2005; and Ömer Lütfü Mete and Mahir Kaynak, *Dünyayı Kimler Yönetiyor* (İstanbul: Timaş Yayınları, 2006), 196–97.

52. Yasin Aktay, "Gezi'deki Komplo ve Sosyoloji," *Yeni Safak*, June 22, 2013 (www.yenisafak.com/yazarlar/yasinaktay/gezideki-komplo-ve-sosyoloji-38264).

53. İlnur Çevik, "Big Business Has a Major Role to Play," *Daily Sabah*, December 6, 2016; and "TÜSİAD dövize suskun," *Sabah*, September 12, 2016.

54. Murat Yetkin, "Istanbul Terror Attacks Empower Ankara Scenarios," *Hürriyet Daily News*, December 14, 2016.

55. Erol Manisalı, *İslamcı Siyaset ve Cumhuriyet* (İstanbul: Derin Yayınları, 2006); and Yaşar Nuri Öztürk, *Allah ile Aldanmak* (İstanbul: Yeni Boyut, 2008). For similar observations and more examples, see Michelangelo Guida, "The Sevres Syndrome and 'Komplo' Theories in the Islamist and Secular Press," *Turkish Studies* 9, no. 1 (2008), 37–52.

56. Refah Partisi, *Tüzük ve Programı* (Ankara, 1985); and Saadet Partisi Programı (www.saadet.org.tr/program.pdf).

57. Reported in H. Bahadır Türk, *Muktedir: Türk Sağ Geleneği ve Recep Tayyip Erdoğan* (İstanbul: İletişim Yayınları, 2014), 200.

58. İbrahim Karagül, *Hesaplaşma Yüzyılı* (İstanbul: Timaş Yayınları, 2007).

59. Gürpınar, *Komplolar Kitabı*, 149–51.

60. Ibid., 195 and 264.

61. For a detailed discussion on the notion of "pushing Turks out of Europe" and the insecurity this has provoked, see Pınar Bilgin, "Securing Turkey through Western-Oriented Foreign Policy," *New Perspectives on Turkey* 40 (Spring 2009), 103–23; and Yılmaz, "Two Pillars of Nationalist Euroskepticism in Turkey."

62. The Sèvres Treaty was one of the five treaties imposed on the vanquished powers at the end of World War I. The other four were the Saint Germaine Treaty with Austria, Neuilly with Bulgaria, Trianon with Hungary, and Versailles with Germany.

63. Suat İlhan, *Avrupa Birliği'ne Neden Hayır* (İstanbul: Ötüken, 2002), 101. The author is a former three-star general and saw the prospects of Turkey's EU membership as a Western plot to undermine Turkey's territorial integrity and sovereignty. See also interview with the author in Mehmet Ali Kışlalı, "Emekli Korgeneral Suat İlhan: AB ilkelere aykırı," *Türkiye*, April 2, 2011 (www.turki yegazetesi.com.tr/yazarlar/mehmet-ali-kislali/103981.aspx).

64. For an exposé of this perspective, see Metin Tamkoç, *The Warrior Diplomats: Guardian of the National Security and Modernization of Turkey* (University of Utah Press, 1976).

65. Jung, "The Sèvres Syndrome"; and Yılmaz, "Two Pillars of Nationalist Euroscepticism in Turkey."

66. Baskın Oran, "Dönemin Bilançosu," in *Türk Dış Politikası: Kurtuluş Savaşından Bugüne Olgular, Belgeler, Yorumlar (1980–2001)*, vol. 2, ed. Baskın Oran (İstanbul: İletişim Yayınları, 2001), 235–36.

67. Kemal Kirişci, "The Kurdish Question and Turkish Foreign Policy," in *The Future of Turkish Foreign Policy*, ed. Lenore G. Martin and Dimitris Keridis (MIT Press, 2004), 296 and 300.

68. Ümit Özdağ, *Türk Sorunu* (Ankara: Kripto, 2010), 205 and 295.

69. "Büyükanıt: Meclis'te PKK Var," *Hürriyet*, December 11, 2007.

70. His full remark was "I state once again the views of the Turkish Armed Forces on this issue with capital letters; Turkish Armed Forces cannot be against the European Union because the European Union is the geo-political and geo-strategic ultimate condition for the realization of the target of modernization which Mustafa Kemal Atatürk chose for the Turkish nation." Yaşar Büyükanıt,

"Genelkurmay İkinci Başkanı Orgeneral Sayın Yaşar Büyükanıt'ın 'Küreselleşme ve Uluslararası Güvenlik' Konulu Açış Konusması," in *Küreselleşme ve Uluslararası Güvenlik: Birinci Uluslararası Sempozyum Bildirileri* (Ankara: Genelkurmay Basım Evi, May 2003).

71. Bilgin, "Securing Turkey through Western-Oriented Foreign Policy," 117.

72. Yılmaz, "Two Pillars of Nationalist Euroscepticism in Turkey," 37.

73. Doğan Gürpınar, "Turkish Radicalism and Its Images of the Ottoman Ancien Régime (1923–1938)," *Middle East Studies* 5, no. 3 (2014).

74. Reported in Bahadır Türk, *Muktedir*, 186.

75. Their works include Mehmet Akif Ersoy, *Safahat*, ed. Ertuğrul Düzdağ (İstanbul: Sütun Yayınları, 2011); Necip Fazıl Kısakürek, *Ulu Hakan* (İstanbul: Büyük Doğu Yayınları, 1998); Necip Fazıl Kısakürek, *İdeologya Örgüsü: Büyük Doğuya Doğru* (İstanbul: Kayseri Yüksek İslam Enstitüsü Talebe Derneği Yayınları, 1968); Abdurrahman Dilipak, *Cumhuriyet'e Giden Yol* (İstanbul: Beyan Yayınları, 1991); Kadir Mısıroğlu, *Lozan: Zafer mi? Hezimet mi?* (İstanbul: Sebil Yayınevi, 1971–75); and Cevat Rıfat Atılhan, *İslamı Saran Tehlike ve Siyonizm* (İstanbul: Aykurt Nesriyati, 1955). For a discussion of this Islamist intellectual tradition, see Burhanettin Duran, "Cumhuriyet Dönemi İslamcılığı," in *İslamcılık*, ed. Murat Gültekingil and Tanıl Bora (İstanbul: Iletişim Yayınları, 2005).

76. Meliha Altunışık, "Worldviews and Turkish Foreign Policy in the Middle East," *New Perspectives on Turkey* 40 (April 2009), 171–94, 188.

77. Ishaan Tharoor, "Turkey's Purge Marks Endgame in Islamist Civil War," *Washington Post*, August 6, 2016.

78. Doğan Avcıoğlu, *Türkiye'nin Düzeni: Dün-Bugün-Yarın* (İstanbul: Tekin Yayınevi, 1976); and Doğan Avcıoğlu, *Devrim ve Demokrasi Üzerine* (İstanbul: Tekin Yayınevi, 1997).

79. Avcıoğlu, *Devrim ve Demokrasi Üzerine*, 194; and Avcıoğlu, *Türkiye'nin Düzeni: Dün-Bugün-Yarın*, 516.

80. Mufti, *Daring and Caution in Turkish Strategic Culture*, 38 and 41.

81. Avcıoğlu, *Devrim ve Demokrasi Üzerine*, 6; and Hasan Cemal, *Kimse Kızmasın, Kendimi Yazdım* (İstanbul: Doğan Kitapçılık, 2015), 175–77. For a rare commentary that is critical of these perspectives and supportive of Turkey's Western vocation, see Emre Gönensay, "Fırtınalı Orta Doğu ve Türkiye," *Tercüman*, December 16, 1979. Gönensay subsequently served as minister of foreign affairs briefly in 1996; on the other hand, Cemal became a committed advocate of Turkey's EU vocation and liberal democracy.

82. Mehmet Döşemeci, *Debating Turkish Modernity: Civilization, Nationalism, and the EEC* (Cambridge University Press, 2013), 122–23.

83. See also Yılmaz, "Two Pillars of Nationalist Euroscepticism in Turkey," 191.

84. Emre Ersen, "The Evolution of 'Eurasia' as a Geopolitical Concept in Post-Cold War Turkey," *Geopolitics* 18, no. 1 (2013), 24–44, 31.

85. For details of these arguments, see Gürpınar, *Komplolar Kitabı*, 167–70; and Guida, "The Sèvres Syndrome and 'Komplo' Theories in the Islamist and Secular Press," 47–48.

86. "A General Speaks His mind," *The Economist*, March 14, 2002.

87. Author's interview with a U.S. military officer familiar with the Turkish military, who remarked, "Eurasianism is embeded in the DNA of Turkish Armed Forces," July 21, 2016, Washington, D.C. See also Emel Akçalı and Mehmet Perinçek, "Kemalist Eurasianism: An Emerging Geopolitical Discourse in Turkey," *Geopolitics* 14, no. 3 (2009), 550–69; and Şener Aktürk, "The Fourth Style of Politics as a Pro-Russian Rethinking of Turkey's Geo-political Identity," *Turkish Studies* 16, no. 1 (2015), 54–79.

88. Gencer Özcan, "Facing Its Waterloo in Diplomacy: Turkey's Military in Foreign Policy Making," *New Perspectives on Turkey* 40 (Spring 2009), 83–102, 94.

89. "Turkish PM Erdoğan to Putin: Take Us to Shanghai," *Hürriyet Daily News*, November 22, 2013.

90. Senem Aydın-Düzgit and Nathalie Tocci, *Turkey and the European Union* (London: Palgrave, 2015), 184–89.

91. Atila Eralp, "The Role of Temporality and Interaction in the Turkey-EU Relationship," *New Perspectives on Turkey* 40 (Spring 2009), 147–68, 156.

92. Ibid., 158.

93. Surveys on Turkish public opinion on EU membership between 2007 and 2014 can be accessed from German Marshall Fund, "Transatlantic Trends," 2007–2014 (http://trends.gmfus.org/archives/). For survey results from 2015, see German Marshall Fund, "Turkish Perceptions Survey," 2015 (www.gmfus.org/initiatives/turkish-perceptions-survey).

94. Elaine Sciolino, "European Public Uneasy over Turkey's Bid to Join Union," *New York Times*, October 2, 2004.

95. "EU's Talks with Turkey Opposed by Most Europeans," *Hürriyet Daily News*, September 9, 2005.

96. Independent Commission on Turkey, "Turkey in Europe: More Than a Promise," 15.

97. For the text of the document, see "Negotiating Framework," October 3, 2005 (http://ec.europa.eu/enlargement/pdf/turkey/st20002_05_tr_framedoc_en.pdf). See Hale's comments in his *Turkish Foreign Policy since 1774*.

98. Aslı Tosabay-Esen and H. Tolga Bölükbaşı, "Attitudes of Key Stakeholders in Turkey towards EU-Turkey Relations: Consensual Discord or Contentious Accord?," in *Talking Turkey in Europe: Towards a Differentiated Communication Strategy*, ed. Nathalie Tocci (Rome: Istituto Affari Internazionali, December 2008), 175–98, 195–96. Also see Senem Aydın-Düzgit, *Seeing Kant in EU's Relations with Turkey* (Istanbul: TESEV, 2006).

99. Senem Aydın-Düzgit and E. Fuat Keyman, "EU-Turkey Relations and the Stagnation of Turkish Democracy," in *Global Turkey in Europe*, 106.

100. For a discussion of discourses against Turkey's membership in France and Germany, see Hakan Yılmaz, "Turkish Identity on the Road to the EU: Basic Elements of French and German Oppositional Discourses," *Journal of Southern Europe and the Balkans* 9, no. 3 (November 2009), 293–305. See also

Hans Arnold, "Political Arguments against the Accession of Turkey to the European Union," in *European and Turkish Voices in Favour and Against Turkish Accession to the European Union*, ed. Christiane Timmerman, Sara Mels, and Dirk Rochtus (Brussels: Peilang, 2008).

101. Harry Tzimitras and Mete Hatay, "The Need for Realism: Solving the Cyprus Problem through Linkage Politics," Turkey Project Policy Paper, no. 9, Brookings, October 2016 (www.brookings.edu/wp-content/uploads/2016/10 /turkey_20161005_cyprus_problem.pdf).

102. Ioannis N. Grigoriadis, "Cyprus Negotiations Thwarted by Issues on Security and Guarantees," *SWP Comments* 27 (July 2017).

103. Eralp, "The Role of Temporality and Interaction in the Turkey-EU Relationship," 161.

104. Joerg Baudner, "The Domestic Effects of Turkey's EU Accession Negotiations: A Missed Opportunity for Europe?," in *Turkey and the European Union: Facing New challenges and Opportunities*, ed. Cengiz Fırat and Lars Hoffmann (London: Routledge, 2014), 187.

105. Yılmaz, "Two Pillars of Nationalist Euroscepticism in Turkey," 194.

106. Independent Commission on Turkey, "Turkey in Europe: The Imperative for Change," March 2014, 9 (www.independentcommissiononturkey.org /pdfs/2014_english.pdf). For the text of Erdoğan's speech, see "Başbakan Erdoğan'ın AK Parti 4. Olağan Büyük Kongresi konuşmasının tam metni," September 30, 2012 (www.akparti.org.tr/site/haberler/basbakan-erdoganin-ak -parti-4.-olagan-buyuk-kongresi-konusmasinin-tam-metni/31771#1).

107. It was colorfully demonstrated at the European Parliament, when, upon the approval of the European Commission's recommendation for the start of accession talks with Turkey, the deputies lifted banners with the words "evet," "yes," "ja," and "oui" inscribed on them. For the photograph, see the cover of Burak Akçapar, *Turkey's New European Era: Foreign Policy on the Road to EU Membership* (New York: AltaMira, 2007).

108. For discussions of a definition of Europe with Turkey, see Ingrid Kylstad, "Turkey and the EU: A 'New' European Identity in the Making?," LSE "Europe in Question" Discussion Paper 27, no. 210 (London School of Economics, 2010) (www.lse.ac.uk/europeanInstitute/LEQS%20Discussion%20 Paper%20Series/LEQSPaper27.pdf); José Casanova, "The Long, Difficult and Tortuous Journey of Turkey into Europe and the Dilemmas of European Civilization"; and Ingmar Karlson, "Turkey's Historical, Cultural and Religious Heritage: An Asset to the European Union?," in *European and Turkish Voices in Favour and against Turkish Accession to the European Union*, ed. Christiane Timmerman, Dirk Rochtus, and Sara Mels (Brussels: Peilang, 2008).

109. Quoted in Sarah Lyall, "Turkish Writer Wins Nobel Prize in Literature," *New York Times*, October 13, 2006.

110. Independent Commission on Turkey, "Turkey in Europe: More Than a Promise," 46.

111. Bahar Rumelili, "Constructing Identity and Relating to Difference: Understanding the EU's Mode of Differentiation," *Review of International Studies* 30, no. 1 (January 2004), 27–47, 44.

CHAPTER 6

1. "Turkey's Dangerous Path Away from Democracy," *New York Times*, March 29, 2017.

2. "Turkish Authorities Block Wikipedia without Giving Reason," *BBC News*, April 29, 2017.

3. Murat Yetkin, "Nereden Çıktı Bu 'Zina' Konusu?," *Radikal*, September 14, 2004. See also William Hale and Ergun Özbudun, *Islam, Democracy and Liberalism in Turkey* (New York: Routledge, 2010), 70–71.

4. See Commission of the European Communities, "Turkey 2006 Progress Report," Commission Staff Working Documents, November 8, 2006, 62 (http://ec.europa.eu/enlargement/pdf/key_documents/2006/nov/tr_sec_1390 _en.pdf); and Commission of the European Communities, "Turkey 2007 Progress Report," Commission Staff Working Documents, November 6, 2007, 15 (http://ec.europa.eu/enlargement/pdf/key_documents/2007/nov/turkey _progress_reports_en.pdf).

5. See, for example, Commission of the European Communities, "Turkey 2008 Progress Report," Commission Staff Working Documents, November 5, 2008, 19 (http://ec.europa.eu/enlargement/pdf/press_corner/key-documents /reports_nov_2008/turkey_progress_report_en.pdf).

6. "Avrupa Birliği Bakanı ve Başmüzakereci Sayın Egemen Bağış'ın Avrupa Komisyonu 2012 Türkiye İlerleme Raporu Değerlendirmesi," October 10, 2012 (www.ab.gov.tr/files/haberler/2012/sayin_egemen_bagis_in_2012_turkiye _ilerleme_raporu_degerlendirmesi_nihai_konusma.pdf).

7. "Burhan Kuzu AB Raporunu Böyle Çöpe Attı," *Hürriyet*, October 13, 2012.

8. Cihan Tuğal, *The Fall of the Turkish Model: How the Arab Uprisings Brought Down Islamic Liberalism* (London: Verso, 2016), 250.

9. Esra Ercan Bilgiç and Zehra Kafkaslı, *Gencim, Özgürlükçüyüm, Ne İstiyorum? #direngeziparkı Anketi Sonuç Raporu* (İstanbul: Bilgi Üniversitesi Yayınları, 2013) (www.bilgiyay.com/Content/files/DIRENGEZI.pdf). The protests turned violent when more politicized groups joined the protests and engaged in running battles with the police: Tola Sardan, "Gezi'de Kalanlar ve Farklı bir Analiz," *Milliyet*, November 25, 2013.

10. "Erdoğan: En Az Üç Çocuk Doğurun," *Hürriyet*, March 7, 2008.

11. Işıl Arslan and Mehmet İnan, "Arınç: Kadınlar Herkesin İçerisinde Kahkaha Atmayacak," *Hürriyet*, July 29, 2014.

12. "Başbakan Erdoğan Kız ve Erkek Öğrenci Aynı Evde Olmaz, Denetleyeceğiz," *Radikal*, November 4, 2013.

13. Alev Scott, "Is Pavement Café Ban a Step on the Road to Islamism?," *The Independent*, August 2, 2011.

14. It is possible to compare the attitude of the current director of religious affairs with his predecessors in the early 2000s: "Diyanet İşleri'nden Yılbaşı Fetvası," *Hürriyet*, December 30, 2013; and "Diyanet'ten Yılbaşı Eleştirisi," *InternetHaber*, December 26, 2012 (www.internethaber.com/dinayetten-yilbasi -elestirisi-488913h.htm). The contrast has also been noted by a conservative journalist; see Taha Akyol, *Hürriyet*, December 31, 2014.

15. Gülseven Özkan and Önder Öndeş, "İstanbul Lisesi'nde Noel Yasağı İddiası," *Hürriyet*, December 18, 2016; and "German School in Istanbul, Turkey 'Bans Christmas,'" *BBC News*, December 19, 2016.

16. Kadri Gürsel, "Erdoğan's $350M Presidential Palace," Al-Monitor, September 17, 2014 (www.al-monitor.com/pulse/en/originals/2014/09/turkey-Erdoğan-white-palace-presidential-residence.html).

17. For the statement and reaction from the secular opposition leader see "Dindar gençlik yetiştireceğiz," *Hürriyet*, February 2, 2012.

18. Ruşen Çakır, İrfan Bozan, and Balkan Talu, *İmam Hatip Gerçekleri: Efsaneler ve Gerçekler* (İstanbul: Tesev Yayınları, 2004); and Eğitim-Sen, "2015–2016 Eğitim-Öğretim İstatistikleri: Eğitimde Ticarileşme ve Dinselleşmesinin Temel Göstergeleri," March 22, 2016 (http://egitimsen.org.tr/2015-2016-egitim-ogretim-istatistikleri/).

19. Kadri Gürsel, "Erdoğan Islamizes Education System to Raise 'Devout Youth,'" Al-Monitor, December 9, 2014 (www.al-monitor.com/pulse/originals/2014/12/turkey-islamize-education-religion.html).

20. Mustafa Akyol, "What Is Turkey's Problem with Darwin?," Al-Monitor, January 20, 2017 (http://al-monitor.com/pulse/originals/2017/01/turkey-what-is-turks-problem-with-darwin.html#).

21. Patrick Kingsley, "Turkey Drops Evolution from Curriculum, Angering Secularists," *New York Times*, June 23, 2017; Samuel Osborne, "Turkish MP Says 'No Use in Teaching Maths to a Child Who Doesn't Know Jihad,'" *The Independent*, July 25, 2017. Osborne notes that "Jihad is often translated as 'holy war' in the context of fighters waging war against enemies of Islam; but Muslim scholars stress that it also refers to a personal, spiritual struggle against sin."

22. Erik Jan Zürcher, *Turkey: A Modern History* (London: I. B. Tauris, 2004), 96.

23. Fazıl Kısakürek, *Son Devrin Din Mazlumları* (İstanbul: Büyük Doğu Yayınları, 1969), 11 and 30.

24. For a comprehensive article on the episode as well as the influence of Kısakürek on Erdoğan's thinking, see Sean R. Singer, "Erdoğan's Muse: The School of Necip Fazıl Kısakürek," *World Affairs* 137, no. 4 (November/December 2013), 81–88.

25. "Tayyip Konuşmasında Atatürk'e Ayyaş Diyor," video, YouTube, May 29, 2013 (www.youtube.com/watch?v=Oj5u35OKZF8). "'Who Are the Two Drunks?,' Turkish Politicians Ask after PM's Remarks," *Hürriyet Daily News*, May 29, 2013.

26. Atatürk's body of ideas and policies are referred to as Kemalism, sometimes also called "*Atatürkçülük*" and often associated with the six arrows adopted by the CHP in 1931. However, since then a wide range of interpretations of Kemalism has emerged. For a comprehensive discussion of them, see Tanıl Bora, *Cereyanlar: Türkiye'de Siyasi İdeolojiler* (İstanbul: İletişim, 2017), 119–70.

27. Berna Turam, "Are Rights and Liberties Safe?," *Journal of Democracy* 23, no. 1 (January 2012), 109–18.

28. Ali Çarkoğlu and Binnaz Toprak, *Türkiye'de Din, Toplum ve Siyaset* (İstanbul: TESEV, 2006); see figure 5.5 on p. 75 for a broader range of surveys showing fluctuating levels of support for Islamization across time. See also Ali Çarkoğlu and Ersin Kalaycıoğlu, *The Rising Tide of Conservatism in Turkey* (New York: Palgrave Macmillan, 2009); and Hakan Yılmaz, "Conservatism in Turkey," *Turkish Policy Quarterly* 7, no. 1 (2008), 57–63.

29. For such public demonstrations, see Özgür Altuncu, Süleyman Kaya and Özgür Arslan, "İstanbul'un ortasında hilafet çağrısı!," *Sözcü*, June 19, 2015 (www.sozcu.com.tr/2015/gunun-icinden/istanbulun-ortasinda-hilafet-mitingi -863973/); and "AKP'li Üsküdar belediyesinin aracından hilafet çağrısı: Halifemizi seçmeliyiz," *Diken*, December 14, 2016 (www.diken.com.tr/akpli -uskudar-belediyesinin-aracindan-hilafet-cagrisi-halifemizi-secmeliyiz/). See also Mustafa Çelik, "Hilafet hayal değil hayattır," *Yeni Akit*, June 29, 2016 (www.yeniakit.com.tr/yazarlar/mustafa-celik/hilafet-hayal-degil-hayattir -15531.html).

30. Yusuf Muftuoglu, "How the 'Normalization' of Salafi Extremism Has Come Back to Haunt Turkey," *Huffington Post*, n.d. (http://www.huffington-post.com/yusuf-muftuoglu/salafi-extremism-turkey_b_10814254.html). On the rise of Salafism in Turkey, see also Ruşen Çakır, "Türkiye'de selefi cihatçılık neden ve nasıl güçleniyor?," Medyascope.tv, April 25, 2017 (http://medyascope. tv/2017/04/25/turkiyede-selefi-cihatcilik-neden-ve-nasil-gucleniyor/).

31. See slide 67 in a PowerPoint slide deck available from Kadir Has University, "Türkiye Sosyal-Siyasal Eğilimler Araştırması, 2016," January 18, 2017 (www.khas.edu.tr/news/1498).

32. These figures were calculated based on the number of registered voters (just above 56.9 million) before the November 2015 elections, made available by the Supreme Election Council of Turkey (www.ysk.gov.tr/ysk/content/conn /YSKUCM/path/Contribution%20Folders/SecmenIslemleri/Secimler /2015MVES/96-D.pdf).

33. Tim Arango, "Corruption Scandal Is Edging Near Turkish Premier," *New York Times*, December 25, 2013.

34. Hanefi Avcı, *Cemaatin İflası* (İstanbul: Tekin, 2015), 221.

35. Remarks made by Ömer Taşpınar at the conference, "Turkey and the Failed Coup: One Year Later," Washington Institute, July 13, 2017. The video recording of the conference can be accessed at www.washingtoninstitute.org /policy-analysis/view/turkey-and-the-failed-coup-one-year-later.

36. For a brief discussion of the movement and its politics, see Carter Vaughn-Findley, *Turkey, Islam, Nationalism and Modernity: A History, 1789–2007* (Yale University Press, 2010), 384–90.

37. Berna Turam, *Between Islam and the State: The Politics of Engagement* (Stanford University Press, 2007).

38. Ibid.; and Berna Turam, "Gülenology," *American Interest*, February 2, 2015 (www.the-american-interest.com/2015/02/02/glenology/).

39. "Is Erdoğan Right to Worry about the Gulen Movement?," Deutsche Welle, September 29, 2016 (www.dw.com/en/is-Erdoğan-right-to-worry-about

-the-gulen-movement/a-35918581). Erdoğan was warned by the Turkish National Security Council as early as 2004 about Gülenist infiltration of the military: "Kılıçdaroğlu Belgeyi Gösterdi, İsimleri Tek Tek Saydı: FETÖ'nün Miladını Buradan Kabul Edin," *Cumhuriyet*, February 17, 2017.

40. For a discussion of the nature of this regime, referred to as "tutelary" or "tutelage" regime, and its transformation under AKP rule, see Koray Caliskan, "Explaining the End of Military Tutelary Regime and the July 15 Coup Attempt in Turkey," *Journal of Cultural Economy* 10, no. 1 (2017), 97–111; and Ergun Özbudun, "Problems of Rule of Law and Horizontal Accountability in Turkey: Defective Democracy or Competitive Authoritarianism?," in *Democratic Consolidation in Turkey: Micro and Macro Challenges*, ed. Cengiz Erişen and Paul Kubicek (New York: Routledge, 2016).

41. Semih Idiz, "Turkey's Ergenekon Verdicts: Justice or Vengeance?," Al-Monitor, August 6, 2013 (www.al-monitor.com/pulse/originals/2013/08/ergenkon-military-coup-verdicts-revenge.html); and Dexter Filkins, "Show Trials on the Bosphorus," *New Yorker*, August 13, 2013.

42. Commission of the European Communities, "Turkey 2009 Progress Report," Commission Staff Working Documents, October 14, 2009, 7 (http://ec.europa.eu/enlargement/pdf/key_documents/2009/tr_rapport_2009_en.pdf).

43. Dani Rodrik, "A Sledgehammer Blow to Turkish Democracy," *Financial Times*, March 3, 2011. For a detailed discussion of the deeply problematic nature of the proceedings, see Dani Rodrik, "The Plot against the Generals," June 2014 (www.sss.ias.edu/files/pdfs/Rodrik/Commentary/Plot-Against-the-Generals.pdf); and Dani Rodrik and Pınar Doğan, *Balyoz Bir Darbe Kurgusunun Belgeleri Ve Gerçekler* (İstanbul: Destek Yayınevi, 2010). See also Gareth Jenkins, "Between Fact and Fantasy: Turkey's Ergenekon Investigation," Silk Road Papers, August 2009 (www.silkroadstudies.org/resources/pdf/Silk RoadPapers/2009_08_SRP_Jenkins_Turkey-Ergenekon.pdf).

44. Aslı Aydıntaşbaş, "The Good, the Bad and the Gülenists: The Role of the Gülen Movement in Turkey's Coup Attempt," European Council on Foreign Relations, September 2016, 4–6 (www.ecfr.eu/page/-/ECFR_188_-_THE_GOOD _THE_BAD_AND_THE_G%C3%9CLENISTS.pdf).

45. Ibid.

46. Omer Taspinar, "The Failed Coup and Turkey's Gulenist Predicament," *LobeLog* (blog), August 8, 2016 (lobelog.com).

47. Taha Akyol, "Devleti ele geçirmek," *Milliyet*, July 13, 2017.

48. Piotr Zalewski, "Erdogan Turns on Gulenists' 'Parallel State' in Battle for Power," *Financial Times*, May 6, 2014.

49. Quoted in Tim Arango, "Turkish Leader Disowns Trials That Helped Him Tame Military," *New York Times*, February 26, 2014.

50. Reported in Metin Gürcan, "What Turkey Can Learn from Coup Plot Case Dismissal," Al-Monitor, April 25, 2016 (www.al-monitor.com/pulse /originals/2016/04/turkey-ergenkon-coup-plot-case-dimissed-after-nine-years .html#ixzz4OPhflutn).

51. For a concise discussion of how relations between Erdoğan and Gülen broke down, leading to a power struggle between the two sides, see Soner

Cagaptay, *The New Sultan: Erdogan and the Crisis of Modern Turkey* (London: I. B. Tauris, 2017), 134–37.

52. Patrick Kingsley, "Mysteries, and a Crackdown, Persist a Year after a Failed Coup in Turkey," *New York Times*, July 13, 2017.

53. For two comprehensive discussions of the background and unraveling of the coup attempt, see Aydıntaşbaş, "The Good, the Bad and the Gülenists," and Dexter Filkins, "Turkey's Thirty-Year Coup," *New Yorker*, October 17, 2016. See also Mustafa Akyol, "Who Was behind the Coup Attempt in Turkey?," *New York Times*, July 22, 2016.

54. Sedat Ergin, "O Albaylar Gitti Darbeciler Geldi," *Hürriyet*, July 22, 2016.

55. Sedat Ergin, a columnist and former editor of the Turkish daily *Hürriyet*, is publishing a serial on the coup attempt based on indictments and court proceedings starting with "15 Temmuz ve Akıncı Üssü (1): Bir hava üssünde olağan şüpheliler" (*Hürriyet*, July 11, 2017). At the time of the completion of this book, it had reached fifteen columns; some of these columns were translated into English and published in *Hürriyet Daily News*.

56. See, for example, Gareth Jenkins, "Myths and Mysteries: Six Months On from Turkey's Curious Coup," TurkeyAnalyst.org, January 26, 2017.

57. "Coup inquiry turns into cover-up operation, says CHP head Kılıçdaroğlu," *Hürriyet Daily News*, May 30, 2107.

58. Metin Gurcan, "Turkey Trial Seeks to Account for Six Critical Hours during Coup," Al-Monitor, May 30, 2017 (www.al-monitor.com/pulse/originals/2017/05/turkey-trial-to-uncover-what-happened-failed-coup-night.html#ixzz4ilzHknnx).

59. H. Akin Unver and Hassan Alassaad, "How Turks Mobilized against the Coup," *Foreign Affairs*, September 14, 2016.

60. Onur Ant, "Erdoğan's Approval Ratings Soars in Turkey Following Coup Attempt," Bloomberg, August 11, 2016.

61. "Turkey Faces Risk of Institutional Collapse," *Financial Times*, July 21, 2016. For a Turkish commentator, see Semih Idiz, "Will Erdoğan Rise to the Occasion with Wisdom?," *Hürriyet Daily News*, July 19, 2016.

62. The *New York Times* called the purges "unprecedented" in terms of their size and gravity: Josh Keller, Iaryna Mykhyalysyn, and Safak Timur, "The Scale of Turkey's Purge Is Nearly Unprecedented," *New York Times*, August 2, 2016. For a comprehensive record of the purges, see http://turkeypurge.com/.

63. Rod Nordland, "Turkey's Free Press Withers As Erdoğan Jails 120 Journalists," *New York Times*, November 17, 2016.

64. The problem of the innoncent being hurt was brought up by a conservative journalist at a relatively early stage: Taha Akyol, "The Just and the Unjust Alike," *Hürriyet Daily News*, September 6, 2016. Subsequently President Erdoğan also raised the issue on his way back from the G20 summit in China; Taha Akyol, "At izi, it izi," *Hürriyet*, September 9, 2016.

65. Commentators warned that other than Belarus, Turkey would be the only country with capital punishment in Europe and that it risked raising tensions in the country: "Reinstating the Death Penalty: The Mother of All Mistakes," *Hürriyet Daily News*, October 31, 2016.

66. On concerns about torture and mistreatment of detainies, see Human Rights Watch, "World Report 2017: Turkey: Events of 2016" (www.hrw.org /world-report/2017/country-chapters/turkey).

67. "We Are Living in a Semi-open Prison: Turkey's Main Opposition CHP Head," *Hürriyet Daily News*, October 3, 2016; and "Turkish Government Building 'a Baathist Regime,' Main Opposition Head Says," *Hürriyet Daily News*, October 31, 2016.

68. Zeynel Bilginsoy, "Turkish Opposition Leader Ends 25-Day March, Rallies Backers," *Washington Post*, July 9, 2017.

69. For a recent discussion of the Kurdish problem in Turkey, see Ayşegül Aydın and Cem Emrence, "Two Routes to an Impasse: Understanding Turkey's Kurdish Policy," Turkey Project Policy Papers, no. 10, Brookings, December 2016 (www.brookings.edu/wp-content/uploads/2016/12/aydin-and -emrence-two-routes-to-an-impasse.pdf).

70. Ishaan Toor, "Turkey's Election Is a Blow to Erdoğan and a Victory for Kurds," *Washington Post*, June 8, 2015.

71. For an assessment of the damage by the time the rebellion had been crushed, see Berkay Mandıracı, "Turkey's PKK Conflict: That Death Toll," International Crisis Group, blog, July 20, 2016 (http://blog.crisisgroup.org/europe -central-asia/2016/07/20/turkey-s-pkk-conflict-the-rising-toll/). For an interactive account of the breakdown of casualties, see International Crisis Group, "Turkey's PKK Conflict: The Rising Toll," International Crisis Group, blog, February 2016 (http://www.crisisgroup.be/interactives/turkey/).

72. Nora Fisher Onar, "The Populism/Realims Gap: Managing Uncertainty in Turkey's Policits and Foreign Policy," Turkey Project Policy Paper, no. 8, Brookings, February 2016, 8–10.

73. Amberin Zaman, "Fury Erupts after Mayors Detained in Turkey's Kurdish Southeast," Al-Monitor, October 26, 2016 (www.al-monitor.com/pulse/originals /2016/10/turkey-arrest-mayors-diyarbakir-kurdish.html); and "Turkish Courts Arrests Diyarbakır Co-Mayors," *Hürriyet Daily News*, October 31, 2016.

74. Amberin Zaman, "Turks Spooked by 90s-style Disappearances," Al-Monitor, August 7, 2017.

75. Nicholas Danforth, "Erdoğan's Dilemma: Preserving the Nationalist Alliance or Making Peace," *Turkey Analyst*, October 16, 2016 (https://turkey analyst.org/publications/turkey-analyst-articles/item/567-erdo%C4%9Fan %E2%80%99s-dilemma-preserving-the-nationalist-alliance-or-making-peace .html).

76. "Turkey Threatens to Expel 100,000 Armenians," *BBC News*, March 10, 2010.

77. Constanze Letsch, "Turkish PM Offers Condolences over 1915 Armenian Massacre," *The Guardian*, April 23, 2014. For the concept of "shared pain," see Altay Cengizer, *Adil Hafızanın Işığında* (İstanbul: Doğan Kitap, 2014).

78. For a list of such countries as of 2015, see Zeynep Gürcanlı, "Türkiye'nin yedi ülkede büyükelçisi yok," *Hürriyet*, April 24, 2015; and Selcan Hacaoğlu,

"Erdoğan Says He Will Ignore European Parliament Genocide Vote," Bloomberg, April 25, 2015.

79. Ayhan Aktar, "Yüzleşme yerine acıları yarıştırma hamlesi: Ankara 'biz de mağduruz' diyecek," *Taraf*, January 25, 2015 (www.taraf.com.tr/guncel /yuzlesme-yerine-acilari-yaristirma-hamlesi-ankara-biz-de-magduruz-diye -cek); and Robert Fisk, "The Gallipoli Centenary Is a Shameful Attempt to Hide the Armenian Holocaust," *The Independent*, January 19, 2015.

80. "Van ve Diyarbakır Ayinleri İptal Edildi," *Dünyadavan*, September 18, 2016 (www.dunyadavan.com/haber/van-ve-diyarbakir-ayinleri-iptal-edildi-h1517 .html).

81. "88 yıl aradan sonra Sümela Manastırı'nda ayin," *Hürriyet*, August 15, 2010.

82. "Sümela Manastırı'ndaki Ayin Restorasyona Takıldı," *Milliyet*, June 25, 2016.

83. Ayla Jean Yackley, "Turkey's Oldest Indigenous Culture Fears Extinction," Al-Monitor, July 9, 2017. For a denial of these reports by the government, see "Diyanet İşleri, Süryani Kiliseleri ile ilgili iddiaları yalandı," *Posta*, July 7, 2017 (www.posta.com.tr/diyanet-isleri-suryani-kiliseleri-ile -ilgili-iddialari-yalandi-haberi-1312624).

84. "Police Use Teargas against LGBT Activists in Istanbul," *The Guardian*, June 19, 2016; and "Police Detain 44 People at Istanbul's Banned LGBT Pride March," *Hürriyet Daily News*, June 25, 2017.

85. Elif Shafak, "Turkey's LGBT Community Is Fighting for Freedom: That's Why It's a Target for Extremists," *The Guardian*, June 23, 2016.

86. Onur Bülbül, "Türkiye Ekonomisinin 'Alternatif' Gerçekleri," *Yeni Arayış*, May 12, 2017 (http://yeniarayis.com/genel/2017/05/turkiye-ekonomisinin -alternatif-gercekleri/).

87. Mahreen Khan and Mehul Srivastava, "Turkish GDP Contracts 1.8 per cent in Q3, Worst Pace since 2009," *Financial Times*, December 12, 2016.

88. Cited in International Monetary Fund, "4. Report for Selected Country Groups and Subjects," World Economic Outlook Database, April 2017.

89. On July 16, 2016, right after the attempted military coup, it was 2.95 Turkish lira and at the end of 2016 the exchange rate had fallen to 3.52 Turkish lira to the U.S. dollar. In July 2017 the exchange rate remained unchanged. Türkiye Cumhuriyeti Merkez Bankası, "Gösterge Niteliğindeki Merkez Bankası Kurları" (http://tcmb.gov.tr/wps/wcm/connect/TCMB+TR/TCMB+TR /Main+Menu/Istatistikler/Doviz+Kurlari/Gosterge+Niteligindeki+Merkez+Ba nkasi+Kurlarii).

90. "Turkey's Economy Grows 5 Percent in First Quarter of 2017, Exceeds Forecasts," *Hürriyet Daily News*, June 12, 2017. OECD predicts a slower growth rate of 3.5 percent for 2017 and 2018, "Turkey—Economic Forecast Summary (June 2017)," OECD, June 2017 (http://www.oecd.org/economy /turkey-economic-forecast-summary.htm).

91. Mahfi Eğilmez, "Büyüdük Ama Sorunlar da Büyüdü," personal blog, June 12, 2017 (www.mahfiegilmez.com/2017/06/buyuduk-ama-sorunlar-da

-buyudu.html); Uğur Gürses, "Büyüme neden şaşırtıyor?," *Hürriyet*, June 14, 2017; and Mustafa Sonmez, "The Turkish Economy's Mysterious Rebound," Al-Monitor, June 23, 2017. Assessing this growth rate has also been complicated by the decision of the Turkish Statistical Institute (TUIK) to introduce a new method to calculate Turkish GDP and GDP growth rates. Mustafa Sonmez, "How Turkey Used Math to Drastically Boost Its Economy," Al-Monitor, December 20, 2016. As a result of this retroactive revision, Turkey became "the fastest growing country after China in the past six years, 'readjusting' GDP upward by 20 percent" (Sonmez, "The Turkish Economy's Mysterious Rebound").

92. Unemployment increased from 9.3 percent to 10.5 percent from April 2016 to April 2017, "İşgücü İstatistikleri, Nisan 2017," *Haber Bülteni*, TUIK, July 17, 2017 (http://www.tuik.gov.tr/PreHaberBultenleri.do?id=24629). During the same period youth unemployment (ages 15 to 24) increased by 3.8 percent to almost 20 percent. Inflation increased from 7.64 percent in June 2016 to 10.9 percent in June 2017, "Tüketici Fiyat Endeksi, Haziran 2016," *Haber Bülteni*, TUIK, July 17, 2017 (http://www.tuik.gov.tr/PreHaberBultenleri .do?id=21690).

93. Ali Bayramoglu, "Erdoğan's War on the Market Economy," Al-Monitor, December 12, 2016 (www.al-monitor.com/pulse/originals/2016/12/turkey -erdogans-war-on-market-economy.html); "Gül ve TÜSİAD'dan 'demokrasi- hukuk devleti' uyarısı: Türkiye yol ayrımında," *Cumhuriyet*, November 16, 2016; and Serkan Demirtaş, "Only an Upgraded Democracy Can Save the Turkish Economy," *Hürriyet Daily News*, December 17, 2016.

94. David Segal, "Turkey Sees Foes at Work in Gold Mines, Cafes and 'Smurf Village,'" *New York Times*, July 22, 2017. Segal reports that the "government has seized more than 950 companies, from a baklava chain to a major construction firm, over suspected ties to a coup attempt last year."

95. "FDI in Turkey," *Invest in Turkey*, accessed July 30, 2017 (http://www. invest.gov.tr/en-US/investmentguide/investorsguide/Pages/FDIinTurkey.aspx).

96. Stephen Walt, "10 Ways to Tell If Your President Is a Dictator," *Foreign Policy*, November 23, 2016; and Halil Karaveli, "Erdoğan's Journey: Conservatism and Authoritarianism in Turkey," *Foreign Affairs* 95, no. 6 (November/December 2016), 127.

97. For a succinct discussion, see Güven Sak, "Why the Growth Slowdown in Turkey Now?," *Tepav Günlük*, October 30, 2016 (www.tepav.org.tr/en/blog /s/5729).

98. World Bank vice president Cyril Muller observed that Turkey "has been very successful in moving from an agriculture-based economy into a modern manufacturing and services economy" but that "it needs to enhance its position in the areas around use of technology." Reported in Fatih Erkan Dogan and Muhammed Ali Gürtaş, "Turkey Needs Better Education, Innovation: World Bank," Anadolu Agency, October 31, 2016 (http://aa.com.tr/en/economy /turkey-needs-better-education-innovation-world-bank/675768). See also, Zülfikar Doğan, "Erdogan Pens Education Plan for Turkey's 'devout Generation,'"

Al-Monitor, June 29, 2016 (www.al-monitor.com/pulse/originals/2016/06 /turkey-education-Erdoğan-devout-generation-plan.html#ixzz4REw3WkEH).

99. *Turkey's Transitions: Integration, Inclusion, Institutions* (Washington: World Bank, December 2014), 18–21.

100. Luigi Narbone and Nathalie Tocci, "Running around in Circles? The Cyclical Relationship between Turkey and the European Union," *Journal of Southern Europe and the Balkans 9*, no. 3 (2009), 21.

101. Ibid., 27–28. There is a wide body of literature that discusses the EU's weakening interest in Turkish membership adversely affecting Turkey's reform zeal; see, for example, Philip Gordon and Ömer Taşpınar, "Turkey on the Brink," *Washington Quarterly 29*, no. 3 (2006), 57–70.

102. Hale and Özbudun, *Islamism, Democracy and Liberalism*, 157.

103. Quoted in Mark Beunderman, "Turkey Threatens to Turn Its Back on EU," *EU Observer*, September 5, 2005 (https://euobserver.com/political/19788).

104. Ziya Öniş and Şuhnaz Yılmaz, "Between Europeanization and Euro-Asianism: Foreign Policy Activism in Turkey during the AKP Era," *Turkish Studies 10*, no. 1 (March 2009), 7–24, 13.

105. Quoted in Senem Aydın-Düzgit and Fuat Keyman, "EU-Turkey Relations and the Stagnation of Turkish Democracy," *Global Turkey in Europe* (Rome: Edizioni Nuova Cultura, 2013), 112.

106. Gamze Avcı, "Turkey's EU Politics: Consolidating Democracy through Enlargement," in *Questioning EU Enlargement: Europe in Search of Identity*, ed. Helene Sjursen (London: Routledge, 2006), 62–63.

107. "Başbakan Erdoğan'ın AK Parti 4. Olağan Büyük Kongresi konuşmasının tam metni," September 30, 2012 (www.akparti.org.tr/site/haberler/basbakan -Erdoğanin-ak-parti-4.-olagan-buyuk-kongresi-konusmasinin-tam-metni /31771#1).

108. "İşte AK Parti'nin 63 maddelik 2023 hedefleri," *T24*, September 20, 2012, (http://t24.com.tr/haber/iste-ak-partinin-63-maddelik-2023-hedefleri,214191).

109. Düzgit and Keyman, "EU-Turkey Relations and the Stagnation of Turkish Democracy," 108.

110. Ali Resul Usul, "The Justice and Development Party and the European Union: From Euroscepticism to Euro-enthusiasm and Euro-fatigue," in *Secular and Islamic Politics in Turkey*, ed. Ümit Cizre (London: Routledge, 2008).

111. His speeches can be accessed at *Başbakanlarımız ve Genel Kurul Konuşmaları 9*, ed. İrfan Neziroğlu and Tuncer Yılmaz (www.tbmm.gov.tr /yayinlar/basbakanlarimiz_genelkurul_konusmalari/basbakanlarimiz_cilt9 .pdf).

112. For a detailed discussion of resistance by the CHP and "Kemalist" civil society, see Sinan Ciddi, "Kemalist Advocacy in a post-Kemalist Era?," in *Turkish AK Party and Its Leader: Criticism, Opposition and Dissent*, ed. Ümit Cizre (London: Routledge, 2016).

113. Interview with Aykan Erdemir, Washington, August 23, 2016.

114. Ersin Kalaycıoğlu, "Turkish Popular Presidential Elections: Deepening Legitimacy Issues and Looming Regime Change," *South European Society and*

Politics 20, no. 2 (2015), 157–79. See also İlter Turan, "War at Home, Peace Abroad," *PrivateView* (Autumn 2008), 8–15.

115. Hale and Özbudun, *Islamism, Democracy and Liberalism*, 74; and Ersel Aydınlı, "Ergenekon, New Pacts, and the Decline of the Turkish 'Inner State,'" *Turkish Studies* 12, no. 2 (2011), 227–39; for a discussion of the politics behind the e-memorandum, protests, and the court case, see Hale and Özbudun, *Islamism, Democracy and Liberalism*, 90–92.

116. E. Fuat Keyman and Şebnem Gümüşcü, *Democracy, Identity and Foreign Policy in Turkey: Hegemeny through Transformation* (Houndsmill: Palgrave Macmillan, 2014).

117. "The Worrying Tayyip Erdoğan," *The Economist*, November 27, 2008.

118. Susan Corke and others, eds., "Democracy in Crisis: Corruption, Media, and Power in Turkey," Freedom House Special Reports (Washington: Freedom House, 2014), 1–2. One such media group was Doğan Media, which saw a U.S. $3 billion fine imposed on it by the government: "Dogan v. Erdogan: The Travails of Turkey's Dogan Yayin," *The Economist*, September 10, 2009.

119. Nuray Mert, "Sivil istibdat," *Radikal*, November 17, 2009.

120. Ergun Özbudun, "AKP at the Crossroads: Erdoğan's Majoritarian Drift," *South European Society and Politics* 19, no. 2 (2014), 155–67.

121. Selim Koru, "Erdogan Goes for the Death Blow Against Turkey's Bureaucracy," *Foreign Policy*, April 14, 2017.

122. Senem Aydın-Düzgit and E. Fuat Keyman, "EU-Turkey Relations and the Stagnation of Turkish Democracy," *Global Turkey in Europe* (Rome: Edizioni Nuova Cultura, 2013), 104.

123. Timur Kuran, "Turkey's Electoral Dictatorship," Project Syndicate, April 20, 2014 (www.project-syndicate.org/commentary/timur-kuran-warns -that-recent-local-elections-will-reinforce-recep-tayyip-erdo-an-s-authoritarian -turn).

124. Kalaycıoğlu, "Turkish Popular Presidential Elections," 172.

125. Özbudun, "AKP at the Crossroads," 163. See also Özbudun, "Competitive Authoritarianism," *Turkish Review* 4, no. 6 (November–December 2014).

126. Mehul Srivastava, "Erdogan Sews Up Turkey's 'Second Revolution,'" *Financial Times*, February 27, 2017; and Zia Weise, "Erdoğan, the new Atatürk," *Politico*, December 26, 2016.

127. For a detailed discussion of the package, see Alan Makovsky, "Erdoğan's Proposal for an Empowered Presidency," Center for American Progress, March 2017 (www.americanprogress.org/issues/security/reports/2017/03/22 /428908/erdogans-proposal-empowered-presidency/).

128. "International Referendum Observation Mission, Republic of Turkey— Constitutional Referendum," April 16, 2017, and "Statement of Preliminary Findings and Conclusions" (www.osce.org/odihr/elections/turkey/311721 ?download=true). For the final report, see *Republic of Turkey Constitutional Referendum 16 April 2017: OSCE/ODIHR Limited Referendum Observation Mission—Final Report*, OSCE/ODIHR, June 22, 2017 (http://www.osce.org /odihr/elections/turkey/324816?download=true).

129. "Binali Yıldırım'dan son gün sitemi: 18 maddenin içeriğini konuşmaya fırsat olmadı," *Cumhuriyet*, April 15, 2017.

130. "The Functioning of Democratic Institutions in Turkey," Parlimentary Assembly of the Council of Europe, no. 14282, April 5, 2017.

131. Başak Kale, "Avrupa demokrasisinde kümeye düşerken," *BirGün*, April 30, 2017 (www.birgun.net/haber-detay/avrupa-demokrasisinde-kumeye -duserken-157514.html).

132. Suzan Fraser, "EU parliament advises freeze of Turkey's membership talks," *Washington Post*, July 6, 2017.

133. Howard Eissenstat, "Erdoğan as Autocrat: A Very Turkish Tragedy," POMED, Project on Middle East Democracy, April 2017, 11–12 (http://pomed .org/wp-content/uploads/2017/04/erdogan_as_autocrat.pdf).

134. "President Gül Urges Extended Democratic Rights," *Hürriyet Daily News*, October 1, 2009.

135. "President Gül Calls PM, Minister as Police Withdraw from Taksim," *Hürriyet Daily News*, June 1, 2013.

136. Sebnem Arsu, "Turkish Premier Blames Extremists for Protests as Two Are Killed," *New York Times*, June 3, 2013. For a discussion of the differences between Gül and Erdoğan and the latter's discomfort, see Semih Idiz, "Abdullah Gul Steps Up during Turkish Crisis," Al-Monitor, June 7, 2013 (www.al -monitor.com/pulse/originals/2013/06/abdullah-gul-turkey-protests-increased -role.html).

137. "Twitter ban: Turkey's President Gul Challenges PM's move," *BBC News*, March 21, 2014.

138. Tulin Daloglu, "Gul's Return to Turkish Politics May Not Be So Easy," Al-Monitor, August 18, 2014 (www.al-monitor.com/pulse/originals/2014/08 /daloglu-pro-islamists-akp-parliament-gul-prime-minister.html).

139. "Başbakan Ahmet Davutoğlu: Türkiye'de fikir özgürlüğü mutlak anlamda hayata geçirilecektir," *Radikal*, December 25, 2015; and "Did PM Davutoğlu Fall from President Erdoğan's Grace?," *Hürriyet Daily News*, April 6, 2016.

140. The Erdoğan-Davutoğlu rift became public with the publication of a blog post on Pelican Brief in May 2016. The post called Davutoğlu a traitor and characterized him as a disappointment. Mustafa Akyol, "How Mysterious New Turkish Blog Exposed Erdoğan-Davutoğlu rift," Al-Monitor, May 3, 2016 (www.al-monitor.com/pulse/originals/2016/05/turkey-rift-between-Erdoğan -Davutoğlu.html). See also interview with a former AKP deputy, November 23, 2016; and Cengiz Çandar, "The Davutoğlu Era Is Over," Al-Monitor, May 5, 2016 (www.al-monitor.com/pulse/originals/2016/05/turkey-Erdoğan-time-of -Davutoğlu-over.html#ixzz47tEdReJC).

141. For purges, the weakening of diversity within the AKP, and Erdoğan's growing dominance, see Özbudun, "AKP at the Crossroads," 158–60; and Toni Alaranta, *National and State Identity in Turkey: The Transformation of the Republic's Status in the International System* (Lanham, Md.: Routledge, 2015), 107. Yalçın Akdoğan, who had invented the term "conservative democrat" and

was made a deputy prime minister in Davutoğlu's cabinet, was purged when the new cabinet was formed by Binali Yıldırım for his "differences" with the "new" party line on the Kurdish issue. Semih Sakallı, "Erdoğan'ın gözden düşen yol arkadaşları," Medyascope.tv, September 1, 2016 (http://medyascope.tv/2016/09 /01/Erdoğanin-gozden-dusen-yol-arkadaslari/).

142. The current list of AKP's founders can be accessed at www.akparti.org .tr/site/yonetim/kurucu-uyeler. For a reporting of the names removed from the list, see "Gül ve Arınç AKP'nin kurucuları arasında neden yok, kimler listeden çıkarıldı," *T24*, February 23, 2016 (http://t24.com.tr/haber/gul-ve-arinc-akpnin -kuruculari-arasinda-neden-yok-kimler-listeden-cikarildi,329227).

143. Murat Yetkin, "Is AKP Revolution Devouring Its Own Children Too?," *Hürriyet Daily News*, February 3, 2016.

144. Interview with Aykan Erdemir, former deputy for CHP, August 23, 2016, and with Suat Kınıklıoğlu, former AKP deputy, November 23, 2016.

145. Ioannis N. Grigoriadis, "The People's Democratic Party (HDP) and the 2015 elections," *Turkish Studies* 17, no. 1 (2016), 39–46. Demirtaş became especially popular among liberals when he declared to Erdoğan, "We shall not make you president [Seni başkan yaptırmayacağız]" to quell suspicion among Turkish liberals that the HDP might have been tempted to strike a deal with Erdoğan on the Kurdish issue in return for supporting Erdoğan to achieve his executive presidential constitutional reform (ibid., 41–42).

146. Mehmet Bardakçı "2015 Parliamentary Elections in Turkey: Demise and Revival of AKP's Single-Party Rule," *Turkish Studies* 17, no. 1 (2016), 4–18, 7.

147. "Absurdity in Power: Turkey's Latest Trial of Journalists Is Surreal Even by Its Own Standards," *The Economist*, July 29, 2017.

148. "Prosecutor Seeks up to 142 Years in Prison for Jailed HDP Co-chair," *Hürriyet Daily News*, January 17, 2017.

149. Karaveli, "Erdoğan's Journey"; and Soner Cagaptay and Oya Rose Aktas, "How Erdoganism Is Killing Turkish Democracy," *Foreign Affairs*, July 7, 2017.

150. Burcu Taşkın, "Voter Turnout in Turkey's Parliamentary and Local Elections (1950–2014): Does Participation Increase when Competition Decreases?," *Turkish Studies* 16, no. 4 (December 2015), 465–86.

151. Birol A. Yeşilada and Peter Noordijk, "Changing Values in Turkey: Religiosity and Tolerance in Comparative Perspective," *Turkish Studies* 11, no. 1 (2011), 9–27. For a comparative study of Turkish attitudes with respect to civil liberties that fall considerably behind European and U.S. averages, see Richard Wike and Kathy Simmons, "Global Support for Principle of Free Expression, but Opposition to Some Forms of Speech," *Global Attitudes & Trends*, Pew Research Center, November 18, 2015 (www.pewglobal.org/2015/11/18/global -support-for-principle-of-free-expression-but-opposition-to-some-forms-of -speech/).

152. Birol Yeşilada and Peter Noordijk, "Religiosity and Political Values in Post-2000 Turkey," in *Democratic Consolidation in Turkey*.

153. Ibid., 34.

154. Turam, "Are Rights and Liberties Safe?," 116. For a similar in-depth assessment, see Sabri Sayarı, "Opposition Parties and Democratic Consolidation in Turkey," in *Democratic Consolidation in Turkey*.

155. F. Michael Wuthrich, *National Elections in Turkey: People, Politics, and the Party System* (Syracuse University Press, 2015), 90–91.

156. Etyen Mahçupyan, "'Reisçilik' denen bir tümör AKP içinde yoğunlaştı," *T24*, February 19, 2016 (http://t24.com.tr/haber/etyen-mahcupyan-reiscilik -denen-bir-tumor-akp-icinde-yogunlasti,328817).

157. Karaveli, "Erdoğan's Journey," 122.

158. Jenny B. White, "The Turkish Complex," *American Interest*, February 25, 2015.

159. "Chapter 2: Religion and Politics," *Religion & Public Life*, Pew Research Center, April 30, 2013 (www.pewforum.org/2013/04/30/the-worlds -muslims-religion-politics-society-religion-and-politics/).

160. Levent Gültekin, "Tek adam partisinden tek adam rejimine," *Cumhuriyet*, May 4, 2016; and Oral Çalışlar, "AK Parti, tek adam ve Erdoğan olgusu," *Radikal*, September 5, 2015.

161. "Davutoğlu'nun restine Saray cephesinden yanıt: İster sağdan, ister soldan oku," *Cumhuriyet*, May 3, 2016.

162. Ishaan Tharoor, "How Russia's Putin and Turkey's Erdoğan Were Made for Each Other," *Washington Post*, December 2, 2014; and Yaroslav Trofimov, "Turkey's Autocratic Turn," *Wall Street Journal*, December 10, 2016.

163. The full quotation is much more revealing: "In Kısakürek's formulation, a society is better off if its people participate merely in a moral way by electing leaders. The leaders have discretion to do what they think is best without much regard for what people want. The major point to be respected by the leaders is the moral standards of Islam, not the wishes of the people." Burhanettin Duran, "Transformation of Islamist Political Thought in Turkey from the Empire to the Early Republic (1908–1960): Fazıl Kısakürek's Political Idea" (Ph.D. diss., Bilkent University, 2011), 278.

164. See remarks by Ömer Taşpınar at the conference titled "Turkey's Political Dynamics after the Attempted Coup," Middle East Institute, September 30, 2016 (www.mei.edu/events/turkeys-political-dynamics-after-attempted-coup).

165. Christopher de Bellaigue, "Welcome to *Demokrasi*: How Erdoğan Got More Popular Than Ever," *The Guardian*, August 30, 2016.

166. Jose Casanova, "The Long, Difficult, and Torturous Journey of Turkey into Europe and the Dilemmas of European Civilization," *Constellations* 12, no. 2 (2006), 234–47; and Ziya Öniş, "Globalisation and Party Transformation: Turkey's Justice and Development Party in Perspective," in *Globalising Democracy: Party Politics in Emerging Democracies*, ed. Peter Burnell (London: Routledge, 2006).

167. Anne Applebaum, "Erdogan, Putin and the strongman ties that bind," *Washington Post*, August 11, 2016; and David Hearst, "The Putinisation of Erdogan," *Middle East Eye*, April 12, 2017.

168. *Freedom in the World 2017: Populists and Autocrats: The Dual Threat to Global Democracy* (Washington: Freedom House, 2017).

169. A full-page ad in the *Washington Post*, July 15, 2017, attests to it.

170. Yaşar Yakış, one of the original founders of AKP and its first minister of foreign affairs, remarked just ahead of the constitutional referendum that "I don't remember periods where Turkish public opinion was as divided." Quoted in Patrick Kingsley, "Turkey's Erdogan: Democracy's Savior or Saboteur?," *New York Times*, April 14, 2017.

171. Quoted in Shadi Hamid, "How Much Can One Strongman Change a Country?," *The Atlantic*, June 26, 2017.

172. Yusuf Kaplan, "Türkiye'nin önündeki iki takoz: Batılılar ve Batıcılar," *Yeni Şafak*, July 10, 2016 (www.yenisafak.com/yazarlar/yusufkaplan/turkiyeunin -onundeki-iki-takoz-bat%C4%B1l%C4%B1lar-ve-bat%C4%B1c%C4%B1lar -2030281).

173. Samuel P. Huntington, "The Clash of Civilizations?," *Foreign Affairs*, Summer 1993.

174. Daniel Heinrich, "Opinion: Turkey's History Is One of Division," Deutsche Welle, January 5, 2017 (www.dw.com/en/opinion-turkeys-history-is -one-of-division/a-37030046).

175. Kemal Göktaş, "60 yıllık politikacı Cindoruk, 'Yeni Türkiye'yi değerlendirdi: Çok partili hayat bitmiştir," *Cumhuriyet*, June 11, 2017.

176. Quoted in Luke Baker, "After Failed Coup, What Sort of Turkey Does Erdoğan Want?," Reuters, October 11, 2016.

177. Karaveli, "Erdoğan's Journey," 130; and Cagaptay and Aktas, "How Erdoganism Is Killing Turkish Democracy."

CHAPTER 7

1. Ahmet Davutoğlu, "Turkey's Foreign Policy Vision: An Assessment of 2007," *Insight Turkey* 10, no. 1 (2008), 77–96; and Ahmet Davutoğlu, "Turkey's Zero-Problems Foreign Policy," *Foreign Policy*, May 20, 2010.

2. Meliha Benli Altunışık, "The Possibilities and Limits of Turkey's Soft Power in the Middle East," *Insight Turkey* 10, no. 2 (2008), 41–54, 44–45.

3. Cengiz Çandar, " 'Sıfır Sorun'dan 'Herkesle Sorun'a Geçerken," *Radikal*, September 23, 2011.

4. Tarık Oğuzlu, "Soft Power in Turkish Foreign Policy," *Australian Journal of International Affairs* 61, no. 1 (March 2007), 95; and Altunışık, "The Possibilities and Limits of Turkey's Soft Power in the Middle East."

5. Kemal Kirişci, "Turkey's 'Demonstrative Effect' and Transformation of the Middle East," *Insight Turkey* 13, no. 2 (2011), 33–55, 47; and Ziya Öniş, "Turkey and the Arab Spring: Between Ethics and Self-Interest," *Insight Turkey* 14, no. 3 (2012), 45–63, 60.

6. Ömer Taşpınar, "The End of the Turkish Model," *Survival* 56, no. 2 (April–May 2014), 49–64.

7. Kaya Genç, "Turkey Is About to Change," *Huffington Post*, May 26, 2016.

8. "Turkey's Foreign Policy: An Eminence Grise," *The Economist*, November 15, 2007.

9. His readiness to work closely and constructively with the Ministry of Foreign Affairs was greatly appreciated, according to "one highly experienced career diplomat" cited in Gerald MacLean, *Abdullah Gül and the Making of the New Turkey* (London: OneWorld, 2014), 238–39.

10. For a detailed analysis of this legacy in a comparative framework, see Emirhan Yorulmazlar, "The Role of Ideas in Turkish Foreign Policy: The JDP-Davutoğlu Paradigm and Its Role after 2002" (Ph.D. diss., Boğaziçi University, 2015).

11. For a perspective on the negotiations, the deal, and its aftermath by the chief negotiator for Turkey, see Deniz Bölükbaşı, *1 Mart Vakası: Irak Tezkeresi ve Sonrası* (Istanbul: Doğan Kitap, 2008). Aylin Güney, "An Anatomy of the Transformation of the U.S.-Turkish Alliance: From the 'Cold War' to 'War on Iraq,'" *Turkish Studies* 6, no. 3 (2005), 341–59.

12. MacLean, *Abdullah Gül and the Making of the New Turkey*, 231.

13. For a detailed account of the diplomatic efforts and the complicated geopolitical scene facing the AKP in its first days in office, as well as a discussion of the domestic political scene in Turkey and in the ranks of the AKP, see Gürkan Zengin, *Hoca: Türk Dış Politikası'nda 'Davutoğlu Etkisi' 2002–2010* (İstanbul: İnkılap, 2014), 115–51. See also MacLean, *Abdullah Gül and the Making of the New Turkey*, 231–33.

14. The deal fell short by three votes in parliament. For an analysis of the results and the consequences, see Füsun Türkmen, *Kırılgan İttifaktan "Model Ortaklığa": Türkiye-ABD İlişkileri* (İstanbul: Timaş Yayınevi, 2012), 203–08.

15. In Turkey, polls revealed that 88 percent of the public was against the war, and almost two out of three respondents thought Turkey should stay out of it; reported in Güney, "An Anatomy of the Transformation of the U.S.-Turkish Alliance," 348.

16. Sabri Sayari, "New Directions in Turkey-USA Relations," *Journal of Balkan and Near Eastern Studies* 15, no. 2 (2013), 129–42, 131.

17. "Turkish FM Stresses Importance of Ties on Iraq Visit," *Hürriyet Daily News*, November 1, 2009.

18. "Erdoğan: Dev bir adım," *Milliyet*, October 4, 2005.

19. The neighborhood is composed of Turkey's immediate land and sea neighbors: Greece, Bulgaria, Romania, Ukraine, Russia, Georgia, Armenia, Azerbaijan, Iraq, Syria, Egypt, and Israel.

20. "Turkey, Syria's New Best Friend," *The Guardian*, October 1, 2009.

21. For a detailed coverage of the diplomacy leading to the protocols, and then the eventual failure to put them into effect, see Thomas de Waal, *Great Catastrophe: Armenians and Turks in the Shadow of Genocide* (Oxford University Press, 2015), 214–34.

22. Kemal Kirişci, "The Transformation of Turkish Foreign Policy: The Rise of the Trading State," *New Perspectives on Turkey* 40 (2009), 29–56.

23. "Democracy in the Middle East, Pluralism in Europe: The Turkish Perspective," address by H. E. Recep Tayyip Erdoğan, Prime Minister of Turkey, Harvard University, Kennedy School of Government, January 30, 2003.

24. "The Speech at the Meeting of the Foreign Ministers of the OIC," Tehran, May 28, 2003, in Abdullah Gül, *Horizons of Turkish Foreign Policy in the New Century* (Ankara: Dış İşleri Bakanlığı Yayınları, 2007).

25. Independent Commission on Turkey, "Turkey in Europe: Breaking the Vicious Cycle," Second Report of the Independent Commission on Turkey (September 2009), 26 (www.independentcommissiononturkey.org/pdfs/2009_english.pdf).

26. Nicholas Danforth, "Ideology and Pragmatism in Turkish Foreign Policy: From Atatürk to the AKP," *Turkish Policy Quarterly* 7, no. 3 (2008), 83–95; Tarık Oğuzlu, "Turkey and Europeanization of Foreign Policy," *Political Science Quarterly* 125, no. 4 (Winter 2010–2011), 657–83; and Burak Akçapar, *Turkey's New European Era: Foreign Policy on the Road to EU Membership* (Lanham, Md.: Rowman and Littlefield, 2007). See also Commission of the European Communities, "Turkey 2008 Progress Report," which praises Turkey's "constructive role in its neighborhood and the wider Middle East through diplomacy," 5.

27. Kemal Kirişci, "Comparing the Neighborhood Policies of Turkey and the EU in the Mediterranean," in *Turkey: Reluctant Mediterranean Power*, ed. Meliha Benli-Altunışık et al., Mediterranean Paper Series (Washington: German Marshall Fund of the Unted States, February 2011), 37.

28. Senem Aydın-Düzgit and Nathalie Tocci, "Transforming Turkish Foreign Policy: The Quest for Regional Leadership and Europeanisation," *CEPS Commentary* (November 12, 2009), 2.

29. Ziya Öniş and Şuhnaz Yılmaz, "Between Europeanization and Euro-Asianism: Foreign Policy Activism in Turkey during the AKP Era," *Turkish Studies* 10, no. 1 (2009), 7–24.

30. Pelin Turgut, "Behind the Turkish Prime Minister's Outburst at Davos," *Time*, January 30, 2009.

31. Banu Eligür, "Crisis in Turkish-Israeli Relations (December 2008–June 2011): From Partnership to Enmity," *Middle Eastern Studies* 48, no. 3 (April 2012), 437–38.

32. Zengin, *Hoca: Türk Dış Politikası'nda 'Davutoğlu Etkisi'*, 72.

33. The remarks were made during an address to an AKP party congress in Düzce. "Erdoğan İsrail Karşıtlarına Çattı," *Milliyet*, May 24, 2009.

34. "Sudanese President Bashir's Visit to Turkey in Limbo," *Hürriyet Daily News*, November 8, 2009.

35. Cihan Tuğal, *The Fall of the Turkish Model: How the Arab Uprisings Brought Down Islamic Liberalism* (London: Verso, 2016), 189.

36. Ahmet Davutoğlu, "Turkey's humanitarian diplomacy: objectives, challenges and prospects," *Nationalities Papers: The Journal of Nationalism and Ethnicity* 42, no. 6 (2013), 869.

37. Soli Özel and Gencer Özcan, "Turkey's Dilemmas," *Journal of Democracy* 22, no. 4 (October 2011), 124–38.

38. Ilgın Yorulmaz, "Turkey Criticizes World Leaders for Lack of Syrian Refugee Response," *Huffington Post*, September 25, 2016; and Semih Idiz, "What's behind Ankara's 'Deafening Silence' on Aleppo?," Al-Monitor, October 4, 2016 (www.al-monitor.com/pulse/originals/2016/10/turkey-syria-ankara-deafening-silence-over-aleppo.html).

39. Vijay Prashad, *The Defeat of the Nation and the Future of the Arab Revolution* (University of California Press, 2016), 194.

40. For a discussion of the impact of the Davos and MV *Mavi Marmara* incidents on the Arab public, especially in Egypt, and their contribution to the Arab Spring, see Nuh Yılmaz, "Change in Turkey Has Shown Another Way for Middle East," in *SETA 2011 Yıllığı* (Washington: SETA Foundation, 2011) (http://file.setav.org/Files/Pdf/20130117163007_seta_2011_yilligi_web_low-res.pdf); and Nuh Yılmaz, "Orta Doğu'da Davos Süreci," in *SETA 2011 Yıllığı.*

41. Quoted in Behlül Özkan, "Turkey, Davutoğlu and the Idea of Pan-Islamism," *Survival* 56, no. 4 (2014), 119–40, 128. In *Stratejik Derinlik*, he describes Israel as a creation of vaguely worded colonialism-related developments in Europe and "international political will" in the aftermath of World War II. Ahmet Davutoğlu, *Stratejik Derinlik: Türkiye'nin Uluslararası Konumu* (İstanbul: Küreyayınları, 2014), 329.

42. İhsan D. Dağı, *Kimlik, Söylem ve Siyaset: Doğu-Batı Ayrımında Refah Partisi Geleneği* (Ankara: Imge Kitapevi, 1996), 71–72.

43. Tarık Işık, "Bu da Türkiye-Suriye vize açılımı," *Radikal*, September 17, 2009.

44. "Turkey Has Strategic Cooperation Councils with 13 Countries," Anadolu Agency, December 24, 2012 (aa.com.tr/en/turkey/turkey-has-strategic-cooperation-councils-with-13-countries/292447).

45. "Yeni Bir Ortadoğu Doğuyor," *Milliyet*, June 10, 2010.

46. Republic of Turkey, Ministry of Foreign Affairs, "Joint Political Declaration on the Establishment of the High Level Cooperation Council Among Turkey, Syria, Jordan and Lebanon" (Ankara, n.d.) (www.mfa.gov.tr/joint-political-declaration-on-the-esthablishement-of-the-high-level-cooperation-council-among-turkey_-syria_-jordan-and-lebanon.en.mfa).

47. Ünal Ünsal, "T.C. Dışişleri Bakanlığı ve Yeni Teşkilat Kanunu," in *Türk Dış Politikası: Kurtuluş Savaşından Bugüne Olgular, Belgeler, ve Yorumlar*, vol. 3, ed. Baskın Oran (İstanbul: İletişim Yayınları, 2013), 236.

48. Figures were calculated from TUIK databases.

49. "Anatolian Tigers" is used to describe the entrepreneurs and industrialists rooted in the provincial heartland of Turkey, in towns such as Aksaray, Bursa, Çankırı, Çorum, Denizli, Düzce, Gaziantep, Kahramanmaraş, Kayseri, Konya, Malatya, and Yozgat. There is no common agreed-upon list of Anatolian Tigers. The list in the text has been compiled from a number of sources, including Ömer Demir, Mustafa Acar, and Metin Toprak, "Anatolian Tigers or Islamic Capital: Prospects and Challenges," *Middle Eastern Studies* 40, no. 6 (2004), 166–88; Şevket Pamuk, "Economic Change in Twentieth Century Turkey," *Cambridge History of Turkey* 4, ed. Reşat Kasaba (Cambridge University Press, 2008), 266–300.

50. Kemal Kirişci and Neslihan Kaptanoğlu, "The Politics of Trade and Turkish Foreign Policy," *Middle Eastern Studies* 47, no. 5 (2011), 705–24. For a broader analysis of the close political relationship between the AKP and the Anatolian business elites, see Ziya Öniş, "The Triumph of Conservative Globalism: The Political Economy of the AKP Era," *Turkish Studies* 13, no. 2 (2012), 135–52; and Ayşe Buğra and Osman Savaşkan, *New Capitalism in Turkey: The Relationship between Politics, Religion and Business* (Cheltenham: Edward Elgar, 2014).

51. Ahmet Davutoğlu, "The Three Major Earthquakes in the International System and Turkey," *International Spectator* 48, no. 2 (2013), 1–11.

52. Murat Yeşiltaş, "The Transformation of the Geopolitical Vision in Turkish Foreign Policy," *Turkish Studies* 14, no. 1 (2013), 661–87, 678. On the Arab Spring and its signaling the end of the Western order, see the interview with Taha Özhan, Murat Aksoy, " 'Camp David' Düzeni'nin sonu geldi," *Yeni Şafak*, March 28, 2011 (http://www.yenisafak.com/roportaj/camp-david-duzeninin -sonu-geldi-310652).

53. Cemil Haşimi, "Yeni Türkiye ve Arap devrimleri birbirini besliyor," *Sabah*, September 24, 2011; and Taha Özhan, "The New Middle East and Turkish Foreign Policy," SETA Policy Debate 2, October 2011, 6–9 (http:// setadc.org/wp-content/uploads/2015/05/SETA-The_New_Middle_East_and _Turkish_Foreign_Policy.pdf).

54. "Turkish PM Erdoğan Urges Mubarak to Heed Egyptian Outcry," *Hürriyet Daily News*, February 1, 2011.

55. "Erdogan Receives Gaddafi Human Rights Prize," *Tripoli Post*, December 6, 2012 (www.tripolipost.com/articledetail.asp?c=1&i=5195).

56. Zeynep Gürcanlı, "AK Parti Kongresi'nde ağır konuklar," *Gündem*, September 30, 2012.

57. Semih Idiz, "The Muslim Brotherhood Ascends," *Hürriyet Daily News*, September 4, 2012.

58. Davutoğlu, "The Three Major Earthquakes in the International System and Turkey," 7–8.

59. Behlül Özkan, "Dış politikada Davutoğlu parantezi kapatılacak," *BirGün*, June 11, 2016.

60. Ahmet Davutoğlu, "Dışişleri Bakanı Sayın Ahmet Davutoğlu'nun Diyarbakır Dicle Üniversitesi'nde Verdiği 'Büyük Restorasyon: Kadim'den Küreselleşmeye Yeni Siyaset Anlayışımız' Konulu Konferans," March 15, 2013 (www.mfa.gov.tr/disisleri-bakani-ahmet-davutoglu_nun-diyarbakir-dicle -universitesinde-verdigi-_buyuk-restorasyon_-kadim_den-kuresellesmeye-yeni .tr.mfa). Here the "order" that is mentioned is defined as resulting from a combination of the Sykes-Picot order, referring to the British and French agreement that drew the initial borders of the current Arab states of the region during World War I, supplemented by the Camp David order resulting from the agreement between Egypt and Israel reached in 1978. Taha Özhan, *Turkey and The Crisis of the Sykes-Picot Order: From Foreign Relations to Foreign Policy* (İstanbul: Okur Akademi, 2015); and Taha Özhan, "The Arab Spring and Turkey:

The Camp David Order versus the New Middle East," *Insight Turkey* 13, no. 4 (2011), 55–64.

61. Interview with Davutoğlu in İbrahim Karagül, "Yüzyıllık parantezi kapatacağız," *Yeni Şafak*, March 1, 2013 (www.yenisafak.com/yazidizileri /yuzyillik-parantezi-kapatacagiz-494795).

62. For Davutoğlu's remarks, see Taha Özhan, Ahmet Davutoğlu, and Rafik Abdessalem "Arab Spring, Tunisia and Turkey," SETA Policy Debate 7, January 2012, (http://file.setav.org/Files/Pdf/arab-spring-tunisia-and-turkey.pdf). Davutoğlu elaborated on his notion of the flow of history at an address at the Center for Strategic and International Studies, Washington: "Turkey's Foreign Policy Objectives in a Changing World," February 10, 2012 (www.csis.org /events/statesmens-forum-his-excellency-ahmet-davuto%C4%9Flu-minister -foreign-affairs).

63. Karagül, "Yüzyıllık parantezi kapatacağız."

64. Interview with a former deputy of the AKP, November 23, 2016, Washington, D.C. For the notion of a "Muslim Brotherhood belt," see İbrahim Karagül, "Müslüman Kardeşler Dünyası kuruluyor!," *Yeni Şafak*, June 19, 2012 (www .yenisafak.com/yazarlar/ibrahimkaragul/m%C3%BCsl%C3%BCman -karde%C5%9Fler--d%C3%BCnyas%C4%B1-kuruluyor!-32883).

65. "Kaybettiğimiz topraklarda buluşacağız," *HaberTurk*, January 21, 2012 (www.haberturk.com/gundem/haber/708252-kaybettigimiz-topraklarda -bulusacagiz).

66. Bipartisan Policy Center, "Turkey Transformed: The Origins and Evolution of Authoritarianism and Islamization under the AKP," BipartisanPolicy. org, October 2015, 71 (http://bipartisanpolicy.org/wp-content/uploads/2015 /11/BPC-Turkey-Transformed.pdf). See also Aaron Stein, "Turkey's New Foreign Policy: Davutoğlu, the AKP and the Pursuit of Regional Order," *Whitehall Papers* 83, no. 1 (2014) (http://www.tandfonline.com/doi/pdf/10.1080/02681307 .2014.989694).

67. Ahmet Davutoğlu, "Dışişleri Bakanı Sayın Ahmet Davutoğlu'nun TBMM Genel Kurulu'nda Suriye'deki Olaylar Hakkında Yaptığı Konuşma," April 26, 2012 (www.mfa.gov.tr/disisleri-bakani-sayin-ahmet-davutoglu_nun-tbmm-genel -kurulu_nda-suriye_deki-olaylar-hakkinda-yaptigi-konusma_-26-nisan-2012.tr .mfa).

68. Reported in Baris Ornarli, "Davutoğlu: Turkey Poised to Lead in Syria and New Middle East," Voice of America, *Middle East Voices*, April 27, 2012.

69. For a comprehensive study of the AKP's involvement in the Middle East, including Syria, and how it fell into a state of loneliness see Gökhan Telatar, "AK Parti'nin Düzen Kurucu Dış Politika Söylemi ve Orta Doğu," *Alternatif Politika* 7, no. 3 (October 2015).

70. For a brief account of these efforts by Davutoğlu himself, see Davutoğlu, "The Three Major Earthquakes in the International System and Turkey," 6.

71. Prashad, *The Defeat of the Nation and the Future of the Arab Revolution*, 2–3.

72. Quoted in Davutoğlu, "The Three Major Earthquakes in the International System and Turkey," 6–7.

73. Tim Arango and Eric Schmitt, "A Path to ISIS, through a Porous Turkish Border," *New York Times*, March 9, 2015; David Phillips, "Research Paper: ISIS-Turkey Links," *Huffington Post*, November 9, 2014; and Ben Hubbard and Karam Shoumali, "Fertilizer, Also Suited for Bombs, Flows to ISIS Territory from Turkey," *New York Times*, May 4, 2015.

74. Deborah Amos, "A Smuggler Explains How He Helped Fighters along 'Jihadi Highway,'" NPR, *All Things Considered*, October 7, 2014; and Prashad, *The Defeat of the Nation and the Future of the Arab Revolution*, 3. For the personal account of a foreign fighter using this "highway," see Robert F. Worth, *A Rage for Order: The Middle East in Turmoil, from Tahrir Square to ISIS* (New York: Farrar, Straus, Giroux, 2016), 180–94.

75. Cengiz Çandar, "Türkiye'nin Suriyelileşmesi," *Radikal*, July 23, 2015; and Michael M. Tanchum and Halil M. Karaveli, "Pakistan's Lessons for Turkey," *New York Times*, October 5, 2014.

76. Aykan Erdemir, "The Creeping Pakistanization of Turkey?," *The Globalist*, July 9, 2016.

77. Kemal Öztürk and Kemal Fırık, "Rabia Sign Becomes the Symbol of Massacre in Egypt," Anadolu Agency, August 16, 2013 (aa.com.tr/en/turkey /rabaa-sign-becomes-the-symbol-of-massacre-in-egypt/225250).

78. "Seven World Capitals Now without Turkish Ambassadors," *Hürriyet Daily News*, April 23, 2015.

79. Faruk Loğoğlu, "Türkiye'den Yayın Yapan Dört Yabancı Televizyon Kanalını Sordu," *Haberler*, February 3, 2015 (www.haberler.com/faruk-logoglu -turkiye-den-yayin-yapan-dort-yabanci-6930607-haberi/).

80. "Erdoğan Slams Maliki for Not Protecting Turkish Consulate," *Daily Sabah*, June 18, 2014. For a discussion of the impact of sectarianism on Turkey's diplomatic relations, see Mustafa Akyol, "Turkish Islamists' Trial with Sectarianism," Al-Monitor, December 22, 2016 (www.al-monitor.com/pulse /originals/2016/12/turkey-islamists-trial-with-sectarianism.html).

81. Semih Idiz, "The 'Sunnification' of Turkish Foreign Policy," Al-Monitor, March 1, 2013. For accusations of sectarianism, see also Halil Karaveli, "Turkey, the Unhelpful Ally," *New York Times*, February 27, 2013; and Mohammed Noureddine, "Turkey's Sectarian Foreign Policy May Backfire," *New York Times*, August 3, 2012.

82. Semih Idiz, "UN Vote Confirms Turkey's Waning Influence," Al-Monitor, October 17, 2014.

83. "Turkey Not 'Lonely' but Dares to Do So for Its Values and Principles, Says PM Adviser," *Hürriyet Daily News*, August 26, 2013.

84. Yaşar Yakış, "Turkey after the Arab Spring: Policy Dilemmas," *Middle East Policy* 21, no. 1 (Spring 2014), 98–106. Similar warnings also had come from a retired general, three retired ambassadors, and two academics. Yalım Eralp, Şadi Ergüvenç, Sönmez Köksal, Ümit Pamir, Mensur Akgün, and Sylvia Tiryaki, "Suriye'ye Dikkat," Global Political Trends Center (GPOT), Policy

Briefs (December 2013) (www.gpotcenter.org/dosyalar/PB37_2013_High AdvisoryBoardReport.pdf). For an early questioning of the government's Syria policy by a leading columnist on Turkish politics, see Sedat Ergin, "Suriye politikasında nerede hata yapıldı (1-4)," *Hürriyet*, August 29–September 1, 2012.

85. The decision to stay the course was unequivocally stated at the time by Yasin Aktay, deputy chairman of the AKP, who said there would be no change of course in foreign policy: reported in Ali Ünal, "Our Foreign Policy Is Based on Humanity, Not on Sectarianism," *Daily Sabah*, September 1, 2014.

86. Giorgio Cafiero and Daniel Wagner, "Turkey and Qatar: Close Allies, Sharing a Doomed Syria Policy," *Huffington Post*, November 10, 2016.

87. "Russia Joins War in Syria," *BBC News*, October 1, 2015.

88. Alexander Mercouris, "Did Russia Just Threaten Turkey With Nuclear Weapons?," *Russia Insider*, February 19, 2016.

89. Ünal Çevikoz, "Dimyat'a pirince giderken evdeki bulgurdan olmak," February 2, 2016; and Taha Akyol, "Yine Ortadoğu," *Hürriyet*, December 25, 2015.

90. The survey concluded that those deeming Turkish foreign policy toward the Middle East "unsuccessful" or "neither successful nor unsuccessful" were 73 percent in 2013; 70 percent in 2015 and 82 percent in 2016; in contrast, those who deemed it "successful" were 27 and 30 percent in 2013 and 2015 respectively and 18 percent in 2016. In the case of Turkey's Syria policy, the corresponding figures for those who deemed it "unsuccessful" or "neither successful nor unsuccessful" were 76 percent in 2013; 74 percent in 2015; and 83 percent in 2016. In contrast, those who deemed it "successful" were 24 and 26 percent in 2013 and 2015 respectively and 17 percent in 2016. See slides 36 and 37 in a PowerPoint slide deck available from Kadir Has Üniversitesi, "Türk Dış Politikası Kamuoyu Algıları Araştırması," May 18, 2016 (www.khas.edu.tr/news/1367).

91. Calculated from TUIK (Turkstat) database.

92. Mustafa Kutlay, "Whither the Turkish Trading State? A Question of State Capacity," On Turkey Brief (Washington: German Marshall Fund of the United States, February 2016).

93. Taha Özhan, Hatem Ete, and Selin M. Bölme, eds., "Turkey in 2011," SETA Policy Report 8, January 2012, 51 (http://setadc.org/wp-content/uploads /2015/05/SETA_Policy_Report_Turkey_In_2011.pdf).

94. "Middle East Report 2016: Current Conditions and the Road Ahead" (Zogby Research Services, 2016), 6.

95. Ali Tuygan, "About Pipe Dreams" (blog post), DiplomaticOpinion.com, January 4, 2017 (https://diplomaticopinion.com/2017/01/04/about-pipe-dreams /#more-812).

96. "The End of Turkey's 'Precious Loneliness,'" *Hürriyet Daily News*, January 18, 2016.

97. Raymond Aron's original observation—"Ce sont les hommes qui écrivent l'histoire mais ils ne savent pas ce qu'ils écrivent"—can be translated as "Man are those who write history but they don't know what history they are

writing." The idea was also used by Philippe Aghion in "Can We Make Growth More Inclusive? A Trans-Atlantic Perspective: The 13th Annual Raymond Aron Lecture," December 20, 2016 (www.brookings.edu/events/13th-annual -raymond-aron-lecture-can-we-make-growth-more-inclusive-a-trans-atlantic -perspective/), 8;44 min. Aghion's translation is "Man are those who write history but they don't know what history they are writing."

98. Author's interviews of a former AKP deputy, November 23, 2016, Washington, D.C. and Yusuf Müftüoğlu, a former foreign policy adviser to Abdullah Gül, June 29, 2016, Istanbul. See also Cengiz Çandar, "The Davutoğlu Era Is Over," Al-Monitor, May 5, 2016 (www.al-monitor.com/pulse/originals/2016/05 /turkey-erdogan-time-of-davutoglu-over.html#ixzz47tEdReJC).

99. Kadri Gürsel, "Revisiting Davutoglu on Syria," Al-Monitor, May 27, 2013 (www.al-monitor.com/pulse/originals/2013/05/davutoglu-syria-admit -mistake.html).

100. "Davutoğlu Esad'a ömür biçti," NTV, August 24, 2012 (www.ntv.com .tr/turkiye/davutoglu-esada-omur-bicti,Nsez_e7zmEO7uz5O9Pv6hw).

101. Semih İdiz, "AKP Finally Acknowledges Its Foreign Policy Failures," *Hürriyet Daily News*, June 2, 2016.

102. Semih Idiz, "Resetting Turkey's Syria Policy," Al-Monitor, August 23, 2016 (www.al-monitor.com/pulse/originals/2016/08/turkey-syria-resetting -foreign-policy.html).

103. Quoted in "Turkey Entered Syria to End al-Assad's Rule: President Erdoğan," *Hürriyet Daily News*, November 29, 2016.

104. Amberin Zaman, "Russian-Rebel Talks Resume as Erdogan Backs Down on Assad," Al-Monitor, December 1, 2016 (www.al-monitor.com/pulse /originals/2016/12/erdogan-clarifies-syria-position-russia-rebels.html).

105. Quoted in Erin Cunnigham, "Syria's War Creates Myriad Problems for Turkey," *Washington Post*, January 18, 2017.

106. Abdullah Ayasun, "Erdogan: US Strike against Syrian Regime Welcomed, But Not Enough," *Global Post*, April 7, 2017.

107. Quoted in "Turkey Calls for Assad's Ouster, Says Supports U.S. Missile Strike," Reuters, April 7, 2017.

108. Author's interview with Yusuf Müftüoğlu who observed that these circles felt that the "U-turn was just too sharp," June 29, 2016, Istanbul.

109. "İHH'den tarihi çark: İsrail'le örtünen çıplak kalır ama . . . ," *Cumhuriyet*, July 3, 2016.

110. Calculated from TUIK. Turkish exports in 2016 to Israel and Russia were almost U.S. $3 billion and $1.7 billion, respectively.

111. Gabriel Mitchell, "The Risks and Rewards of Israeli-Turkish Energy Cooperation," Mitvim Israel-Turkey Policy Dialogue Publication Series, January 2017 (http://mitvim.org.il/images/Gabriel_Mitchell_-_The_risks_and_rewards _of_Israeli-Turkish_energy_cooperation.pdf).

112. Ralph Ellis and Andrew Carey, "Erdogan Slams Treatment of Palestinians; Israel Issues Angry Response," CNN, May 9, 2017; and Dan Arbell, "Tensions over Jerusalem Expose Vulnerability of Turkey-Israel Relations, One Year

After Normalizing Ties," *Markaz* (blog), Brookings, July 31, 2017 (www.brookings.edu/blog/markaz/2017/07/31/tensions-over-jerusalem-expose-vulnerability-of-turkey-israel-relations-one-year-after-normalizing-ties/).

113. "Erdoğan'dan o slogana yanıt," *Milliyet*, December 12, 2016.

114. Republic of Turkey, Ministry of Foreign Affairs, "Cumhurbaşkanı Erdoğan BM 69. Genel Kurul'unda dünya liderlerine hitap etti," daily briefing (Ankara, September 24, 2014) (www.mfa.gov.tr/cumhurbaskani-erdogan_-bm-69_-genel-kurulu_nda-dunya-liderlerine-hitap-etti.tr.mfa).

115. Murat Yeşiltaş, "Turkey's Quest for a 'New International Order': The Discourse of Civilization and the Politics of Restoration," *Perceptions* 19, no. 4 (Winter 2014), 43–76, 65; and "Erdoğan: Müslümanların BM Güvenlik Konseyi'nde tek bir temsicisi yok, bu düzen elbet çökecek," *T24*, May 8, 2016 (t24.com.tr/haber/erdogan-muslumanlarin-bm-guvenlik-konseyinde-tek-bir-temsilcisi-yok-bu-duzen-elbet-cokecek,339541).

116. Interview with Zeinab Badawi from BBC's HARDtalk, "President Erdogan tells BBC: EU Wastes Turkey's Time," *BBC*, July 12, 2017.

117. Serdar Karagöz, "Tired of EU's Delaying Tactics, Erdoğan Points to Shanghai Pact," *Daily Sabah*, November 20, 2016.

118. Remarks made by a former deputy undersecretary of the Turkish Ministry of Foreign Affairs, Ünal Çeviköz, quoted in Semih Idiz, "Is Erdogan Giving Up on EU aspirations?," Al-Monitor, November 22, 2016 (www.al-monitor.com/pulse/originals/2016/11/turkey-erdogan-resurrects-desire-to-join-shanghai-group.html).

119. Joshua Kucera, "Erdogan, in Plea to NATO, Says Black Sea Has Become 'Russian Lake,'" *The Bug Pit* (blog), Eurasianet.org, May 11, 2016.

120. Andrea Weiss and Yana Zabanova, "Georgia and Abkhazia Caught between Turkey and Russia," *SWP Comments* 54 (December 2016).

121. Murat Yetkin, "A Scary Scenario in the Ankara Political Backstage," *Hürriyet Daily News*, December 8, 2016; and Mustafa Akyol, "What the 'Russian Lobby' in Ankara Wants," Al-Monitor, December 15, 2016 (www.al-monitor.com/pulse/originals/2016/12/turkey-russia-what-russian-lobby-wants.html).

122. Quoted in Idiz, "Is Erdogan Giving Up on EU Aspirations?"

123. Quoted in Karen DeYoung, "Trump Administration Not Sending a Delegation to Syria Peace Talks," *Washington Post*, January 22, 2017.

124. "EU a Key Anchor and Turkey Not to Lose It: Deputy PM," *Hürriyet Daily News*, December 27, 2016.

125. "Talks between Turkey, EU to Update Customs Union Deal to Start in 2017," *Daily Sabah*, August 30, 2016.

126. Sinan Ülgen, "Negotiating Brexit: The Prospects of a UK-Turkey Partnership," Turkey Project Policy Paper, no. 11, Brookings, March 2017 (www.brookings.edu/research/negotiating-brexit-the-prospect-of-a-u-k-turkey-partnership/). See also Sinan Ulgen, "How Turkey and Europe Lost That Loving Feeling," *Financial Times*, April 30, 2017.

127. A statement in support of these positions can be found in various places: President of IKV Ayhan Zeytinoğlu's remarks on the EU-Turkey summit in

Brussels in May 2017 are accessible at www.ikv.org.tr/ikv.asp?ust_id=8; TÜSİAD president Erol Bilecik's remarks on the EU at the High Advisory Council meeting in Istanbul, May 18, 2017, are accessible at www.tusiad.us /press-releases/tusiad-president-at-high-advisory-council-calls-for-reforms/; TÜRKONFED'den AP'ye Tavsiye Mektubu: "Türkiye AB Sürecinde Sorun Kaynağı Değil, Çözümün Aracıdır," TürkonFed.org, April 27, 2017 (http:// turkonfed.org/tr/detay/1349/turkonfedden-apye-tavsiye-mektubu-turkiye-ab -surecinde-sorun-kaynagi-degil-cozumun-aracidir).

128. The EU's share in Turkey's exports increased steadily from 39 percent in 2012 to 47.9 percent in 2016, while the share of exports to the Arab Middle East dropped from 23.5 percent in 2012 to 20.1 percent in 2016; and whereas exports to Russia (almost U.S. $7 billion) had made up 4.38 percent of Turkey's overall exports in 2012, they accounted for only 1.22 percent of Turkey's exports in 2016 (U.S. $2 billion). Figures were calculated from TUIK databases. The Arab Middle East is composed of Iraq, Syria, Lebanon, Jordan, the Gulf Cooperation Council countries (UAE, Bahrain, Saudi Arabia, Oman, Qatar, Kuwait), Yemen, and North Africa (Egypt, Libya, Algeria, Morocco, Tunisia).

129. Safak Timur and Rod Norland, "Erdogan Threatens to Let Migrant Flood into Europe Resume," *New York Times*, November 25, 2016.

130. International Organization for Migration, "Migrant Presence Monitoring," *Situation Report*, December 2016 (http://migration.iom.int/docs/Sitrep _Turkey_December_2016.pdf). The flows for 2016 and 2015 to Greece from Turkey were 176,654 and 857,363, respectively: International Organization for Migration, "Mixed Migration Flows in the Mediterranean and Beyond: Compilation of Available Data and Information," January 12, 2017 (http://migration .iom.int/docs/Monthly_Flows_Compilation_12_January_2017.pdf).

131. Murat Yetkin, "AB Erdoğan'a ne 'olmazsa olmaz' dedi?," *Hürriyet*, June 22, 2017.

132. Remarks reported in Turan Yılmaz, "Turkey's EU Process a Necessity of Politics, Not Romanticism," *Hürriyet Daily News*, June 1, 2017.

133. Semih Idiz, "Turkey-EU Set to Seek New Path Forward in Ties," Al-Monitor, May 24, 2017 (www.al-monitor.com/pulse/originals/2017/05/turkey -european-union-seek-new-modus-vivendi.html#ixzz4imo4vMcz).

134. Andrea Thomas, Anton Troianovski, and Ned Levin, "Tensions Escalate Between Germany and Turkey," *Wall Street Journal*, July 27, 2017.

135. "Turkey Backs Down from Germany," *Handelsblatt Global*, July 24, 2017 (global.handelsblatt.com/politics/turkey-backs-down-to-germany- 802380?utm_ source=feedblitz&utm_medium=FeedBlitzEmail&utm_campaign=0&utm_content=23327); and Connor Murphy, "Turkey Withdraws Blacklist of German Firms Accused of Financing Terrorism," *Politico*, July 24, 2017.

136. Florian Eder, "Jean-Claude Juncker, Upbeat and Ready for a Fight," *Politico*, August 3, 2017. Juncker delivered similar remarks in his interview with the German news channel, ARD. Kai Küstner, "Martin Schulz bleibt mein Freund," interview with ARD Studios in Brussels, August 3, 2017 (www.tagess-chau.de/ausland/eu-juncker-101.html).

137. Recep Tayyip Erdoğan, "TÜBİTAK 2016 Yılı Ödüllerinin Tevdi Töreninde Yaptıkları Konuşma," *Türkiye Cumhurıyeti Cumhurbaşkanlığı*, December 12, 2016.

138. Amberin Zaman, "Turkey in Uproar over McGurk," Al-Monitor, August 1, 2017, and Murat Yetkin, "Two NATO Allies Accusing Each Other of Helping Terrorists," *Hürriyet Daily News*, August 3, 2017.

139. Reported in "Turkey Asks U.S.-Led Coalition for Air Support at Syria's al-Bab," Reuters, December 26, 2016.

140. Karen DeYoung and Greg Miller, "First Sign of Enhanced U.S.-Russia Relations under Trump: An Invite to Syria Talks," *Washington Post*, January 13, 2017. Turkish foreign minister Mevlüt Çavuşoğlu is quoted in the article as having said, "The United States should definitely be invited, and that is what we agreed with Russia. Nobody can ignore the role of the United States."

141. Serkan Demirtaş, "Turkey Optimistic for Ties with US during Trump Era," *Hürriyet Daily News*, January 5, 2017.

142. "Erdoğan Urges US and Saudi Arabia to Join Astana Peace Talks," *Sabah Daily News*, June 16, 2017.

143. Simon Tisdall, "Erdogan Outgunned at Trump Meeting in Face of US-Russian United Front," *The Guardian*, May 17, 2017.

144. See slide 12 in a PowerPoint slide deck available from Kadir Has Üniversitesi, "Public Perceptions on Turkish Foreign Policy," July 20, 2017 (www.khas.edu.tr/news/1588). The significant fall in threat perceptions for Russia is clearly a function of improved relations since the summer of 2016. For the figures on NATO membership, see slide 35. According to a survey by Pew Research Center from August 2017, 72 percent of Turks considered the "U.S. power and influence" a "major threat to our country." Jacob Poushter and Dorothy Manevich, "Globally, People Point to ISIS and Climate Change as Leading Security Threats," *Pew Research Center's Global Attitudes and Trends*, August 1, 2017 (http://www.pewglobal.org/2017/08/01/globally-people-point-to-isis-and -climate-change-as-leading-security-threats/).

145. "NATO Is a Terror Organization, Says Turkey's Ruling AKP Deputy Tayyar," *Hürriyet Daily News*, January 23, 2017.

146. Ben Kamisar, "Turkish Violence in Washington Presents New Trump Headache," *The Hill*, May 17, 2017; and Philip Bump, "Was Erdogan Personally Involved in His Bodyguards' Attacks on Protestors in D.C.?," *Washington Post*, May 19, 2017.

147. Author's interview with Namık Tan, May 27, 2017, Istanbul.

148. Fiona Hill and Ömer Taşpınar, "Turkey and Russia: Axis of the Excluded?," *Survival* 48, no. 1 (Spring 2006), 81–92.

149. Ziya Öniş and Şuhnaz Yılmaz, "Turkey and Russia in a Shifting Global Order: Cooperation, Conflict and Asymmetric Interdependence in a Turbulent Region," *Third World Quarterly* 37, no. 1 (January 2016), 71–95.

150. Aaron Stein, "How Russia Beat Turkey in Syria," Atlantic Council (blog), March 27, 2017 (http://www.atlanticcouncil.org/blogs/syriasource/how

-russia-beat-turkey-in-syria); and Cengiz Çandar, "Operation Euphrates Shield: A Postmortem," Al-Monitor, April 5, 2017.

151. "General Staff: Russia-Turkey Balance of Force in Black Sea Has Changed over Years," TASS Russian News Agency, September 14, 2016 (http://tass.com/defense/899730).

152. "Brothers in Arms: Turkey and Russia Cozy Up over Missiles," *The Economist*, May 4, 2017.

153. Can Kasapoglu, "Turkey's S-400 Dilemma," EDAM Foreign Policy and Security Paper Series, no. 5 (Istanbul: Center for Economics and Foreign Policy Studies [EDAM], July 2017), (edam.org.tr/en/IcerikFiles?id=3101).

154. Semih Idiz, "Turkey Squeezed between Russia, US in Syria," Al-Monitor, February 1, 2017 (www.al-monitor.com/pulse/originals/2017/02/turkey-squeezed-between-russia-and-united-states-in-syria.html); and Rengin Arslan, "Astana Suriye görüşmeleri: Ne oldu; bundan sonra ne olacak?," *BBC Türkçe*, January 25, 2017 (http://www.bbc.com/turkce/haberler-turkiye-38741741).

155. Maxim A. Suchkov, "Russia Offers Outline for Syrian Constitution," Al-Monitor, January 27, 2017 (www.al-monitor.com/pulse/originals/2017/01/russia-meeting-syria-opposition-moscow-constitution.html?utm_source=Boomtrain&utm_medium=manual&utm_campaign=20170129&bt_ee=BXpdxRWTd0D9CjxuBEJk/LPuYLtTRCehcv6x/7SFCS4YfyX4YyiuQthmU9Jqhkwq&bt_ts=1485768732772).

156. Anna Borshchevskaya, "Is Erdogan A Russian Ally Or Putin's Puppet?," *Forbes*, January 27, 2017.

157. See the interview with the Ukrainian ambassador Andrii Sybiha in *Daily Sabah*, April 17, 2017. These developments were also confirmed in an interview with a Turkish diplomat in Ankara, June 6, 2017.

158. For a discussion of Gülen issues in U.S.-Turkish relations in the aftermath of the coup attempt, see Jim Zanotti, "Fethullah Gulen, Turkey and the United States: A Reference," Congressional Research Service, August 4, 2016.

159. Bulent Aras, "Turkish Foreign Policy after July 15," Istanbul Policy Center, February 2017, p. 4 (http://ipc.sabanciuniv.edu/wp-content/uploads/2017/02/Turkish-Foreign-Policy-After-July-15_Bulent-Aras.pdf).

CHAPTER 8

1. Joseph S. Nye Jr., "Will the Liberal Order Survive?," *Foreign Affairs*, January/February 2017.

2. For his remarks, see "Turkey and the Failed Coup: One Year Later," speech, Washington Institute, July 13, 2017. The video recording of the conference can be accessed at www.washingtoninstitute.org/policy-analysis/view/turkey-and-the-failed-coup-one-year-later.

3. Halil Karaveli, "Erdogan's Journey: Conservatism and Authoritarianism in Turkey," *Foreign Affairs*, November/December 2016.

4. Pinar Tremblay, "How Erdogan Is Redefining Who Is a Turk," Al-Monitor, January 13, 2017.

5. Human Rights Watch, "Turkey," in *World Report 2017* (Human Rights Watch, 2017), 600–08 (www.hrw.org/sites/default/files/world_report_download /wr2017-web.pdf).

6. Mustafa Akyol, "Erdoganism [Noun]: From 'National Will' to 'Man of the Nation': An Abridged Dictionary for the Post-secular Turkish State," *Foreign Policy*, June 21, 2016 and Mustafa Akyol, "Will Erdogan Be Turkey's Next Ataturk?," Al-Monitor, July 9, 2014.

7. Ghassan Salame, "Introduction: Where Are the Democrats?," in *Democracy without Democrats*, ed. Ghassan Salame (London: I. B. Tauris, 1994).

8. Quoted in Karaveli, "Erdogan's Journey," 127.

9. Soner Cagaptay, *The New Sultan: Erdogan and the Crisis of Modern Turkey* (London: I. B. Tauris, 2017), 127–42.

10. Hayrettin Kaplan, "İslam, demokrasi ve Medine Vesikası," *Yeni Şafak*, May 29, 2014 (www.yenisafak.com/yazarlar/hayrettinkaraman/islam-demokrasi -ve-medine-vesikas%C4%B1-53922). Meanwhile, political liberalism, a key component of *liberal* democracy, is frowned upon by an even bigger portion of religious conservatives. For an interesting debate on democracy and Islam, see Shadi Hamid, *Islamic Exceptionalism: How the Struggle Over Islam Is Reshaping the World* (New York: St. Martin's Press, 2016), and Mustafa Akyol, *Islam without Extremes: A Muslim Case for Liberty* (New York: W. W. Norton, 2011).

11. Binnaz Toprak, "Islam and Democracy in Turkey," *Turkish Studies* 6, no. 2 (2005), 167–86.

12. "Deep State of Crisis: Re-Assessing Risks to the Turkish State," Bi-Partisan Policy Center, March 2017 (https://bipartisanpolicy.org/library/re -assessing-risks-to-the-turkish-state/).

13. Garry Kasparov and Thor Halvorssen, "Why the Rise of Authoritarianism Is a Global Catastrophe," *Washington Post*, February 13, 2017; Philip Rucker, "Trump Keeps Praising International Strongmen, Alarming Human Rights Advocates," *Washington Post*, May 2, 2017; and Djene Bajalan and Michael Brooks, "The American AKP," *Jacobin* (blog), JacobinMag.com, July 8, 2017.

14. I thank Üstün Ergüder for pointing this out to me (May 27, 2017, Istanbul). For a similar argument, see Deniz Kavukçuoğlu, "İktidar sıkıntısı," *Cumhuriyet*, May 31, 2017.

15. For a discussion of the European Neighborhood Policy and the idea of having well-governed countries constituting a "ring of friends" around the EU, see Michael Leigh, "The EU's Neighborhood Policy" in *The Strategic Implications of European Union Enlargement*, ed. Esther Brimmer and Stefan Fröhlich (Johns Hopkins University: Center for Transatlantic Relations, 2005), 101–25.

16. There does not seem to be a written record of these intructions; nevertheless, the caution was part of the lore of traditional Turkish diplomacy. These instructions began to be received in the media as commentators have repeatedly referred to them as a piece of wisdom that the AKP and Davutoğlu should have heeded while formulating their Syria policy. This can be found in a TV debate

where Özdem Sanberk, a former ambassador and under-secretary of the Ministry of Foreign Affairs in the early 1990s, cited them. "Eğrisi Doğrusu," *CNNTurk*, December 25, 2015 (www.cnnturk.com/tv-cnn-turk/programlar /egrisi-dogrusu/dis-politikada-nereden-nereye). A brief listing of the instructions can be found in Nihat Dinç, *Gönüllü Diplomat: Bir diplomatın yaşamından notlar* (İstanbul: İthaki Yayınları, 1998), 40.

17. Gizem Karakış, "Numan Kurtulmuş izlenen politikayı eleştirdi: Suriye baştan yanlıştı," *Hürriyet*, January 5, 2017. He had made similar remarks as early as August 2016: Murat Yetkin, "Numan Kurtulmuş: Başımıza gelen birçok şey Suriye politikası sonucu," *Hürriyet*, August 18, 2016.

18. For the notion of "imperial fantasy," see Behlül Özkan, "Turkey's Imperial Fantasy," *New York Times*, August 28, 2014.

19. Rachid Ghannouchi, "Tunisia Shows There Is No Contradiction between Democracy and Islam," *Washington Post*, October 24, 2014.

20. Interview with Yaşar Yakış, former AKP deputy, May 18, 2016, Ankara.

21. See Michael O'Hanlon's reply to a question about Turkey's commitment to NATO membership at an event at the Brookings Institution: "I would simply say one of the basic concepts of an alliance like NATO is that you can get out if you want. And once you get out, you may or may not get back in, which is part of why I don't really think Turkey is going to invoke this option." "NATO At a Crossroads: Next Steps for the Trans-Atlantic Alliance," July 31, 2017 (https:// www.brookings.edu/events/nato-at-a-crossroads-next-steps-for-the-trans -atlantic-alliance/).

22. Ali Tuygan, "Turkey Needs a Serious Foreign Policy Review," *Diplomatic Opinion*, May 31, 2017 (https://diplomaticopinion.com/2017/05/31/turkey -needs-a-serious-foreign-policy-review/).

23. Theodore Piccone, *Five Rising Democracies and the Fate of the International Liberal Order* (Brookings Institution Press, 2016), 186–87.

24. Jan-Werner Müller points to Erdoğan's use of language that identifies himself with the people against those who are defined as standing against the will of the people as typical of populist leaders disregarding pluralism in a society. Jan-Werner Müller, *What Is Populism?* (University of Pennsylvania Press, 2016), 3.

25. Pinar Tremblay, "Even through All His Bluster, Erdogan's Fear Is Obvious," Al-Monitor, July 17, 2017.

26. David Goldman, "Turkey Is the Next Failed State in the Middle East: Spengler," *Asia Times*, October 20, 2015; and "Good Bye Modern and Secular Turkey," *International Policy Digest*, December 24, 2016.

27. Cagaptay, *The New Sultan*, 10. See also Soner Cagaptay, "Erdogan Is Dividing Turkey against Itself," *The Atlantic*, March 31, 2017.

28. Such an outcome was described by Levent Gültekin, a columnist and once avid supporter of the AKP, against the background of fear of a civil war. He foresaw the possibility of "the rich leaving Turkey in their yachts while the poor join the unfortunate masses trying to make it across the Mediterranean Sea." Interview held on June 29, 2016, Istanbul.

29. Zia Weise, "Turkey Loses Its Brains," *Politico*, January 17, 2017; and Cagan Koc, "Now Even Turkish Millionaires Are Fleeing Erdogan's Crackdown," *Bloomberg*, June 13, 2017.

30. According to Rıza Türmen, a former judge on the European Court of Human Rights and a current CHP deputy, the reintroduction of the death penalty would amount to Turkey "severing its ties with the West." Quoted in Semih Idiz, "Is Erdoğan Really Serious about Bringing Back Death Penalty?," Al-Monitor, November 1, 2016 (www.al-monitor.com/pulse/originals /2016/11/turkey-how-Erdoğan-serious-about-death-penalty.html#ixzz4QmEY 0ReZ).

31. Christopher de Bellaigue, "Welcome to Demokrasi: How Erdoğan Got More Popular Than Ever," *The Guardian*, August 30, 2016.

32. Shadi Hamid, "How Much Can One Strongman Change a Country?," *The Atlantic*, June 26, 2017.

33. For a discussion of three possible scenarios see Michael Leigh, "Scenarios for the Future of the EU-Turkey Relationship," Geopolitical Intelligence Services, September 4, 2017 (www.gisreportsonline.com/).

34. "Ahead of Key Vote, CHP Tells EU 'Turkey Is Bigger Than Erdoğan,'" *Hürriyet Daily News*, November 23, 2016; and Sinan Ülgen, "Turkey Is Much Bigger Than Erdoğan," *Carnegie Europe*, September 1, 2016 (http://carnegieeurope. eu/2016/09/01/turkey-is-much-bigger-than-erdogan/j53j).

35. For the divisions in the ranks of AKP on the referendum vote and anger expressed by a pro-Erdoğan media towards Gül and Davutoğlu for not lending their support, see Zia Weise, "5 Takeaways from Turkey's Divisive Referendum," *Politico*, April 18, 2017, and Mehtap Yılmaz, "Şimdi hesaplaşma zamanı," *Yeni Akit*, April 20, 2017 (www.yeniakit.com.tr/yazarlar/mehtap-yilmaz/simdi -hesaplasma-zamani-19134.html).

36. Recalled in interviews with academic Gün Kut, October 14, 2016, Istanbul, and a serving Turkish ambassador, interviewed on November 15, 2016.

37. Elif Ergu, "Cumhurbaşkanı Erdoğan'dan önemli mesajlar: Yapamıyorsak dükkanı kapatıp gidelim," *Hürriyet*, May 18, 2017.

38. "President Erdogan Tells BBC: EU Wastes Turkey's Time," *BBC News*, July 12, 2017 (interview with Zeinab Badawi of HARDtalk) (http://www.bbc .com/news/world-europe-40577216).

39. The term "de-Europeanization" encapsulates the concept that the normative appeal of the EU weakened and the Turkish public became increasingly lenient about abandoning the EU as a reference point with respect to the conduct of institutional, political, economic, social, and legal reforms. Senem Aydın-Düzgit and Alper Kaliber, "Encounters with Europe in an Era of Domestic and International Turmoil: Is Turkey a De-Europeanizing Candidate Country?," *South European Society and Politics* 21, no. 1 (2016), 1–14.

40. Michael O'Hanlon, *Beyond NATO: A New Security Architecture for Eastern Europe* (Brookings Institution Press, 2017), 58; Thomas J. Wright, *All Measures Short of War: The Contest for the Twenty-First Century and the Future of American Power* (Yale University Press, 2017), 216.

41. Author's interview with Ali Tuygan and Uğur Ziyal, May 26, 2017, Ankara.

42. Ömer Taşpınar, "The Rise of Turkish Gaullism: Getting Turkish-American Relations Right," *Insight Turkey* (January–March 2011), 11–17.

APPENDIX

1. Davutoğlu never appreciated the reference to Kissinger and argued that, unlike Kissinger, who only believed in "realist policy," he believed in "ideals and principles" in international relations. Eyüp Can, "Yeni Osmanlıcılık mı, Yeni Türkiye Vizyonu mu?," *Hürriyet*, May 5, 2010; Bülent Aras, "Oxford'da Davutoğlu Vizyonu," *Sabah*, May 5, 2010; and Gürkan Zengin, *Hoca: Türk Dış Politikası'nda 'Davutoğlu Etkisi,' 2002–2010* (İstanbul: İnkilap, 2014), 37–50.

2. For a discussion of the full range of these concepts and their meaning, see Murat Yeşiltaş and Ali Balcı, "A Dictionary of Turkish Foreign Policy in the AK Party Era: A Conceptual Map," SAM Papers 7 (Ankara: Republic of Turkey, Ministry of Foreign Affairs, May 2013) (https://sam.gov.tr/wp-content/uploads/2013/05/SAM_Papers7.pdf).

3. "Turkey's Foreign Policy: An Eminence Grise," *The Economist*, November 15, 2007, 6.

4. For an account of the phone call he received from Gül while in class, see Gürkan Zengin, *Hoca: Türk Dış Politikası'nda "Davutoğlu Etkisi"* (İstanbul: İnkilap Yayınevi, 2014), 107–10.

5. Remarks made in interview by Owen Matthews, "Davutoglu: Inside Turkey's New Foreign Policy," *Newsweek*, November 27, 2009.

6. Ahmet Davutoğlu, "Turkish Foreign Policy Vision: An Assessment of 2007," *Insight Turkey* 10, no. 1 (2008), 77–96, 83.

7. Ahmet Davutoğlu, "Turkey's Zero-Problems Foreign Policy," *Foreign Policy*, May 20, 2010.

8. Davutoğlu, "Turkey's Foreign Policy Vision."

9. Paraphrased from Zengin, *Hoca: Türk Dış Politikası'nda "Davutoğlu Etkisi,"* 467.

10. In Davutoğlu, *Stratejik Derinlik: Türkiye'nin Uluslararası Konumu* (İstanbul: Küre Yayınları, 2014), Davutoğlu compares history to a river and underlines the importance of having a strategic vision derived from one's own national culture in order to shape the "flow of history." Elsewhere, building on this metaphor, he argues the importance of "writing history" rather than just "reading it": Ahmet Davutoğlu, "Sabit ve Ufuk Coğrafyaları Açısından Türkiye," *Aksiyon* 89 (August 17, 1996).

11. Murat Yeşiltaş, "Turkey's Quest for a 'New International Order': The Discourse of Civilization and the Politics of Restoration," *Perceptions* 19, no. 4 (Winter 2014), 43–76, 46.

12. Ahmet Davutoğlu, "Dışişleri Bakanı Sayın Ahmet Davutoğlu'nun Diyarbakır Dicle Üniversitesi'nde Verdiği 'Büyük Restorasyon: Kadim'den Küreselleşmeye Yeni Siyaset Anlayışımız' Konulu Konferans," March 15, 2013

(http://www.mfa.gov.tr/disisleri-bakani-ahmet-davutoglu_nun-diyarbakir-dicle-universitesinde-verdigi-_buyuk-restorasyon_-kadim_den-kuresellesmeye-yeni.tr.mfa).

13. Alexander Murinson, "The Strategic Depth Doctrine of Turkish Foreign Policy," *Middle Eastern Studies* 42, no. 6 (2006), 945–64; and Ioannis N. Grigoriadis, "The Davutoglu Doctrine and Turkish Foreign Policy," ELIAMEP Hellenic Foundation for European & Foreign Policy Working Papers 8 (April 2010).

14. For a discussion of this literature, see Matthew S. Cohen, "Ahmet Davutoğlu's Academic and Professional Articles: Understanding the World View of Turkey's Former Prime Minister," *Turkish Studies* 17, no. 4 (2016), 527–43.

15. Emre Ersen, "The Evolution of 'Eurasia' as a Geopolitical Concept in Post–Cold War Turkey," *Geopolitics* 18, no. 1 (2013), 24–44; Şaban Kardaş, "Turkey: A Regional Power Facing a Changing International System," *Turkish Studies* 14, no. 4 (2014), 637–60; and Ziya Öniş, "Multiple Faces of the 'New' Turkish Foreign Policy: Underlying Dynamics and a Critique," *Insight Turkey* 13, no. 1 (2011), 47–65.

16. Toni Alaranta, *National and State Identity in Turkey: The Transformation of the Republic's Status in the International System* (Lanham, Md.: Rowman and Littlefield, 2015); Malik Mufti, "The AK Party's Islamic Realist Vision: Theory and Practice," *Politics and Governance* 2, no. 2 (2014), 28–42; Behlül Özkan, "Turkey, Davutoglu and the Idea of Pan-Islamism," *Survival* 56, no. 4 (2014), 119–40; Aaron Stein, *Turkey's New Foreign Policy: Davutoglu, the AKP and the Pursuit of Regional Order* (London: Routledge, 2015); and Murat Yeşiltaş, "Turkey's Quest for a 'New International Order': The Discourse of Civilization and the Politics of Restoration," *Perceptions* 19, no. 4 (Winter 2014), 43–76.

17. Bülent Aras and Rabia Polat, "From Conflict to Cooperation: Desecuritization of Turkey's Relations with Syria and Iran," *Security Dialogue* 39, no. 5 (2008), 495–515; Kemal Kirişci, "The Transformation of Turkish Foreign Policy: The Rise of the Trading State," *New Perspectives on Turkey* 40 (2009), 29–56; and Burak Bilgehan Özpek and Yelda Demirağ, "The Davutoglu Effect in Turkish Foreign Policy: What If the Bowstring Is Broken?," *Iran and the Caucasus* 16 (2012), 117–28.

18. Tarık Oğuzlu, "Turkey and Europeanization of Foreign Policy," *Political Science Quarterly* 125, no. 4 (Winter 2010–2011), 657–83; Burak Akçapar, *Turkey's New European Era: Foreign Policy on the Road to EU Membership* (New York: AltaMira, 2007); and Mesut Özcan, *Harmonizing Foreign Policy: Turkey, the EU and the Middle East* (Burlington, Vt.: Ashgate, 2008).

19. Burak Bilgehan Özpek and Yelda Demirağ, "Turkish Foreign Policy after the 'Arab Spring': From Agenda-Setter State to Agenda-Entrepreneur State," *Israel Affairs* 20, no. 3 (June 2014), 328–46; and Wayne McLean, "Understanding Divergence between Public Discourse and Turkish Foreign Policy Practice: A Neoclassical Realist Analysis," *Turkish Studies* 16, no. 4 (2015), 449–64.

20. See, for example, Murinson, "The Strategic Depth Doctrine of Turkish Foreign Policy," and Grigoriadis, "The Davutoglu Doctrine and Turkish Foreign Policy."

21. Baskın Oran, "2001–2012: Dönemin Bilançosu," in *Türk Dış Politikası: Kurtuluş Savaşından Bugüne Olgular, Belgeler, ve Yorumlar (2001–2012)*, vol. 3, ed. Baskın Oran (İstanbul: İletişim Yayınları, 2013), 136.

22. Ahmet Davutoğlu, *Stratejik Derinlik: Türkiye'nin Uluslararası Konumu* (İstanbul: Küre Yayınları, 2014). The book was originally published in 2001.

23. "Kaybettiğimiz topraklarda buluşacağız," *Haberturk*, January 22, 2012 (http://www.haberturk.com/gundem/haber/708252-kaybettigimiz-topraklarda -bulusacagiz).

24. Reported in "Erdoğan'dan önemli mesajlar," *Hürriyet*, September 5, 2012.

25. Alaranta, *National and State Identity in Turkey*, 101–02; and Stein, *Turkey's New Foreign Policy*, 89–90.

26. "Kaybettiğimiz topraklarda buluşacağız."

27. Davutoğlu, *Stratejik Derinlik*, 29.

28. Ibid., 556–62.

29. Ahmet Davutoğlu, "Türkiye Merkez Ülke Olmalı," *Radikal*, February 26, 2004. For a detailed discussion, see Murat Yeşiltaş, "The Transformation of the Geopolitical Vision in Turkish Foreign Policy," *Turkish Studies* 14, no. 1 (2013), 661–87.

30. Davutoğlu, *Stratejik Derinlik*, 103–04.

31. Noted in Şaban Kardaş, "Turkey: Redrawing The Middle East Map or Building Sandcastles?," *Middle East Policy* 7, no. 1 (Spring 2010), 115–36, 124.

32. Davutoğlu emphasized the importance of having a strategic vision based in one's own national culture in order to shape the flow of history as an active agent; he also emphasized the importance of "writing history" rather than just "reading it": Davutoğlu, "Sabit ve Ufuk Coğrafyaları Açısından Türkiye."

33. Davutoğlu, *Stratejik Derinlik*, 56–57.

34. Pınar Bilgin and Ali Bilgiç, "Turkey's 'New' Foreign Policy toward Eurasia," *Eurasian Geography and Economics* 52, no. 2 (2011), 173–95, 182.

35. On one particular occasion, he did raise the rhetorical question, "Why shouldn't Turkey rebuild its leadership in former Ottoman lands in the Balkans, Middle East and Central Asia?": quoted in Jackson Diehl, "The Turkish 9/11," *Washington Post*, December 6, 2010.

36. Ömer Taşpınar, "Turkey's Middle East Policies: Between Neo-Ottomanism and Kemalism," Carnegie Papers 10 (Washington: Carnegie Institution of International Peace, October 2008); Delphine Strauss, "Turkey's Ottoman Mission" *Financial Times*, November 23, 2009; Rasim Özgür Dönmez, *Türkiye'de Politik Değişim ve Türk Dış Politikası: Neo-Osmanlıcılığın Sosyo Politiği* (Bursa: Dora Yayınevi, 2014); İlhan Üzgel and Volkan Yaramış, "Özal'dan Davutoğlu'na Türkiye'de Yeni Osmanlıcı Arayışlar," *Doğudan*, no.16 (March–April 2010); Göktürk Tüysüzoğlu, "Strategic Depth: A Neo-Ottomanist Interpretation of Turkish Eurasianism," *Mediterranean Quarterly* 25, no. 2

(2014), 85–104; Hugh Pope, "Pax Ottomana?," *Foreign Affairs*, November–December 2010; and Murinson, "The Strategic Depth Doctrine of Turkish Foreign Policy."

37. Behlül Özkan, "Turkey, Davutoğlu and the Idea of Pan-Islamism," *Survival* 56, no. 4 (2014), 119–40. This analysis is derived from a survey of almost all the published works of Davutoğlu. The influence of this Islamic perspective is also highlighted by Yeşiltaş, "Turkey's Quest for a 'New International Order'"; and Yeşiltaş, "The Transformation of the Geopolitical Vision in Turkish Foreign Policy."

38. Bilgin and Bilgiç, "Turkey's 'New' Foreign Policy toward Eurasia"; Ahmet Davutoğlu, *Alternative Paradigms: The Impact of Islamic and Western Weltanschauungs on Political Theory* (Lanham, Md.: University Press of America, 1994), based on Davutoğlu's Ph.D. thesis. Davutoğlu aims to show the distinctiveness of two paradigms based on Western and Islamic worldviews.

39. Yeşiltaş, "Turkey's Quest for a 'New International Order,'" 43–44.

40. Ahmet Davutoğlu, "Global Governance," SAM Vision Papers 2 (Ankara: Republic of Turkey, Ministry of Foreign Affairs, March 2013) (http://sam.gov .tr/tr/wp-content/uploads/2012/04/vision_paper_ing_02.pdf).

41. Ibid., 13 and 8.

42. Highlighted by Yeşiltaş, "Turkey's Quest for a 'New International Order,'" 57; and Yeşiltaş, "The Transformation of the Geopolitical Vision in Turkish Foreign Policy," 678.

43. Yeşiltaş and Balcı, "A Dictionary of Turkish Foreign Policy in the AK Party Era," 15–16. See also "Dışişleri Bakanı Davutoğlu: Türkiye Düzen Kurucu Ülke Olmak Durumunda," May 2, 2009 (http://www.haberler.com /disisleri-bakani-davutoglu-turkiye-duzen-kurucu-haberi/).

44. Recep Tayyip Erdogan, "Turkey: The New Indispensable Nation," Project Syndicate, December 13, 2010 (www.project-syndicate.org/commentary /turkey--the-new-indispensable-nation?barrier=accessreg).

45. Quoted in Özkan, "Turkey, Davutoğlu and the Idea of Pan-Islamism," 126. For the focus on the Muslim Middle East and the desire to reclaim a leadership role, see also Soner Cagaptay, "The AKP's Foreign Policy: The Misnomer of 'Neo-Ottomanism,'" *Turkey Analyst* 2, no. 8 (April 2009); and Mufti, "The AK Party's Islamic Realist Vision."

46. Özkan, "Turkey, Davutoğlu and the Idea of Pan-Islamism," 128.

47. Emirhan Yorulmazlar, "The Role of Ideas in Turkish Foreign Policy: The JDP-Davutoğlu Paradigm and Its Role after 2002" (Ph.D. diss., Boğaziçi University, 2015), 323. He reiterated his view that nationalism divided the Islamic world and his "dream" to see it reunited in an interview published in Cansu Çamlıbel, "Biz bu rüyayı terk etmeyiz," *Hürriyet*, September 17, 2012.

48. Burhanettin Duran, "Cumhuriyet Dönemi Islamcılığı," in *Islamcılık*, ed. Murat Gültekingil and Tanıl Bora (İstanbul: Iletişim Yayınları, 2005), 138 and 144. Davutoğlu in his published works does not have any reference to these authors; however, he did acknowledge how the works of especially Sezai Karakoç influenced the thinking of his generation, including Kısakürek: Behlül Özkan,

"Yeni-Osmanlıcılık ve Pan-Islamcılık," in *Türkiye'de Yeni Siyasal Akımlar (1980 sonrası)*, ed. Evren Haspolat ve Deniz Yıldırım (Ankara: Siyasal, 2014), 126.

49. The quotation is from Filibeli Ahmet Hilmi and appears in Duran, "Cumhuriyet Dönemi Islamcılığı," 135; the remark placing Turks at the center of Islam is from Kısakürek, in Duran, "Cumhuriyet Dönemi Islamcılığı," in *Islamcılık*, 136.

50. Yeşiltaş, "Turkey's Quest for a 'New International Order,' " 44.

51. Davutoğlu, *Stratejik Derinlik*, 47–48 and 33–34.

52. Ibid., 83.

53. Baskın Oran, "Giriş: Türk Dış Politikasının (TDP) Teori ve Pratiği," in *Türk Dış Politikası: Kurtuluş Savaşından Bugüne Olgular, Belgeler, Yorumlar (1919–1980)*, vol. 1, ed. Baskın Oran (İstanbul: İletişim Yayınları, 2001), 46–53; Mustafa Aydın, "Determinants of Turkish Foreign Policy: Historical Framework and Traditional Inputs," *Middle Eastern Studies* 35, no. 4 (October 1999), 152–86.

54. Malik Mufti, *Daring and Caution in Turkish Strategic Culture: Republic at Sea* (New York: Palgrave Macmillan, 2009), 16.

55. Ali Aslan, "Problematizing Modernity in Turkish Foreign Policy: Identity, Sovereignty and Beyond," *Uluslararası Hukuk ve Politika* 9, no. 33 (2013), 41. For Davutoğlu's objections to the "Westphalian order" in general, see Davutoğlu, "Global Governance," 7–8. For the continuity between this republican elite and the officials of the Ottoman Empire, see Eric-Jan Zürcher, *Turkey: A Modern History*, 3rd ed. (London: I. B. Tauris, 2003); and Frederick Frey, *The Turkish Political Elite* (MIT Press, 1965).

56. Alaranta, *National and State Identity in Turkey*, 102.

57. For a perspective from inside the Ministry of Foreign Affairs on this Western focus, see İsmail Soysal, "The Influence of the Concept of Western Civilization on Turkish Foreign Policy," *Foreign Policy* 6, nos. 3–4 (1977), 3–5. See also Metin Tamkoç, *The Warrior Diplomats: Guardians of the National Security and Modernization of Turkey* (University of Utah Press, 1976).

58. For a succinct discussion of these two worldviews, see Meliha Benli Altunışık, "Worldviews and Turkish Foreign Policy in the Middle East," *New Perspectives on Turkey* 40 (Spring 2009), 169–92 and Yorulmazlar, "The Role of Ideas in Turkish Foreign Policy."

59. This is puzzling because the speeches Davutoğlu delivered at the ambassadorial conferences during his tenure frequently praised the personnel of the Ministry of Foreign Affairs and recognized the continuity between the diplomatic traditions of the Ottoman Empire and the Turkish Republic. This practice began to weaken and take a more critical line in his speeches in 2013 and 2014. See www.mfa.gov.tr/disisleri-bakani-sayin-ahmet-davutoglu_nun-besinci-buyukelciler-konferansi-kapsaminda-izmir-universiteler-platformu-tarafindan-d.tr.mfa and www.mfa.gov.tr/disisleri-bakani-sayin-ahmet-davutoglu_nun-vi_-buyukelciler-konferansinin-acilis-oturumunda-yaptiklari-konusma_-13-ocak-2014_-an.tr.mfa.

60. Davutoğlu, *Stratejik Derinlik*, 57.

61. Quoted in Özkan, "Turkey, Davutoğlu and the Idea of Pan-Islamism," 128–29.

62. Noted by Salih Bıçakçı, "Between Neo-Ottomanism and Kemalism: Turkish Foreign Policy Recovers its Memory?," paper presented at the World Conference on Middle Eastern Studies, Barcelona, July 19–24, 2010; also quoted in Bilgin and Bilgiç, "Turkey's 'New' Foreign Policy toward Eurasia," 182.

63. Nora Fisher Onar, "Neo Ottomanism, Historical Legacies and Turkish Foreign Policy," EDAM Discussion Paper Series (Istanbul: Center for Economics and Foreign Policy Studies [EDAM], October 2009), 3 (www.gmfus.org /publications/neo-ottomanism-historical-legacies-and-turkish-foreign-policy). EDAM publications on the website go only as far back as 2012.

64. Marc Pierini, "Turkey is Turning its Back on the EU: Hypothesis of Reality," Judy Dempsey's Strategic Europe, Carnegie Europe (blog), October 23, 2012 (http://carnegieeurope.eu/strategiceurope/?fa=49764).

65. For a discussion of the origins of the term going back to Ottoman times and its connection to Turkish diplomacy, see Aydoğan Vatandaş, *Monşer: Saklı Seçilmişler* (İstanbul: Timaş Yayınları, 2009).

66. "Başbakan Davos'ta Diplomatik Davranmış," *Radikal*, February 3, 2009.

67. Damla Aras, "Turkey's Ambassadors vs. Erdoğan," *Middle East Quarterly* 18, no. 1 (Winter 2011), 47–57.

68. Ibid.

69. For a detailed discussion of the politics surrounding the adoption of the law, including a speech delivered before the Turkish National Assembly by Davutoğlu and its provisions, see Ünal Ünsal, "T. C. Dışişleri Bakanlığı ve Yeni Teşkilat Kanunu" in *Türk Dış Politikası*.

70. In 2009 the ministry had fewer than 1,000 diplomats employed compared to more than 1,500 in the case of Germany and France; see table in ibid., p. 235. The number of diplomats by 2016 had increased to 1,202 and its diplomatic representation bodies (embassies, consulates, offices with international agencies such as WHO and the FAO) had increased to 210 from 178. For the statistics, see "FETÖ Dışişleri Bakanlığı'na nasıl sızdı," *Hürriyet*, January 14, 2017.

71. Barçın Yinanç, "What Has Happened in the Turkish Foreign Ministry?," *Hürriyet Daily News*, July 28, 2016.

72. Aras, "Turkey's Ambassadors vs. Erdoğan."

73. "FETÖ Dışişleri Bakanlığı'na nasıl sızdı."

74. Ibid.; and Yinanç, "What Has Happened in the Turkish Foreign Ministry?"

Acknowledgments

This book is the product of more than three decades of research and study devoted to Turkish politics and foreign policy. Most of my career has been spent at Boğaziçi University in Istanbul, where countless colleagues, students, and friends made invaluable contributions to my academic career. The name and standing of Boğaziçi opened many doors in Turkey and beyond, and I was able to conduct research on sensitive topics. This affiliation allowed me to engage in in-depth conversations with hard-working and dedicated diplomats, military officers, judges, prosecutors, and bureaucrats, as well as business people and civil society representatives. Over three decades I gained from these interactions a wealth of insight and wisdom. In addition, I have been able to participate in many international conferences and teach at universities in Canada, England, Switzerland, and the United States—all experiences that made me aware of the outside observer's perspective with regard to Turkey.

Space does not permit me to acknowledge all the names of those who have shaped my understanding and assessment of Turkish politics and foreign policy during this long journey. Two names shine through, however: my university professor and later chair and then rector at Boğaziçi University, Üstün Ergüder, and my thesis adviser at City University of London, Peter Willetts. I owe them both a huge debt of gratitude for giving me the chance to develop as a young academic who may have on occasion seemed more interested in sports than academia. Others who provided invaluable knowledge and guidance while I was a fledgling student in foreign policy were Ahmet Acet, Balkan Kızıldeli, and Zergün Korutürk, and their late colleagues, Cenk Duatepe and Gündüz Aktan— all part of the Turkish Ministry of Foreign Affairs.

There are, of course, those whom I must acknowledge for their more direct and substantive assistance in the writing process of this book. First, Martin Indyk, the then Foreign Policy vice president and later executive vice president, kept the expectation very much alive after I joined Brookings in 2013 that I should produce a comprehensive work studying the richness and depth of Turkey's relationship with the West. The invisible whip that he held was taken over by his successor, Bruce Jones, the current vice president of Foreign Policy, who deployed it just as effectively. At the Brookings Center for the United States and Europe, Fiona Hill, my immediate "amir," her successor, Thomas Wright, and their deputy, Andrew Moffatt, as well as Vassilis Coutifaris, provided the warm social and intellectual milieu that made it possible to pursue my book project. I am grateful to Ted Piccone, senior fellow, for the insightful debates we have had on Turkish democracy in particular and democracy in emerging countries in general. Comments of Michael O'Hanlon, director of research in Foreign Policy, on the first cut of the manuscript were very helpful and no less encouraging. Thanks also to Laura Mooney, research librarian of Brookings, for her patience with me and effectiveness in locating pretty much every single publication I needed.

The work could not have "matured" substantively without the feedback of the two external reviewers who gently nudged me toward a more analytical and clearer narrative. Sinan Ekim, senior research assistant at the Center for the United States and Europe, provided instrumental and vital research assistance; his dedicated support over the course of the writing process was greatly appreciated. I must also express my deepest gratitude to Yalçın Ege Ercan, Karim Foda, Ezgi Likya İrgil, Sema Karaca, Barış Ornarlı, Galip Kemal Özhan, Kaitlin Staudt, Melis Cengiz, Ranu Nath, and Sezan McDaniel for helping me at various stages with the literature survey and research for the book. In addition, I would like to recognize the patience and effectiveness of Rachel Slattery who always responded with solutions to my calls for help with my computer.

There is a long list of colleagues who read the manuscript in whole or in part and gave me valuable feedback. These include Mustafa Akyol, Senem Aydın-Düzgit, Onur Bülbül, Ali Çarkoğlu, Serhat Güvenç, Gün Kut, Baskın Oran, Gencer Özcan, Soli Özel, Behlül Özkan, Raj Salooja, Sean Singer, Ömer Taşpınar, Füsun Türkmen, Kadir Üstün, and Hakan

Yılmaz. Many Turkish and other serving officials gave their time to talk to me and respond to my questions, but, for understandable reasons, prefer to remain anonymous; I extend to them my deepest appreciation and thanks.

The book also benefited and was significantly enriched by the formal as well as informal interviews and conversations I had with former ambassadors, businessman, civil society activists, deputies, journalists, officers, ministers, and officials: Taha Akyol, Hikmet Çetin, Ünal Çeviköz, Eric Edelman, Aykan Erdemir, Sedat Ergin, Sadi Ergüvenç, Abdullah Gül, Levent Gültekin, Amy Hawthorne, Can Kasapoğlu, Simone Kaslowski, Suat Kınıklıoğlu, Michael Leigh, Yusuf Müftüoğlu, Richard Outzen, Namık Tan, Tolga Tanış, Haluk Tükel, Sinan Ülgen, Akın Ünver, Yaşar Yakış, Zafer Yavan, Murat Yetkin, Muharrem Yılmaz, and Barçın Yinanç. Special thanks go to two former undersecretaries of the Turkish Ministry of Foreign Affairs, Ali Tuygan and Uğur Ziyal, who not only read parts of my manuscript, but also convinced me to reconsider some of my analysis.

I would like to thank the Brookings Press staff for their attention to the book, specifically Bill Finan and Janet Walker, and especially Marjorie Pannell, working through the press, who provided excellent suggestions and copyediting.

Last, much gratitude is extended to my dedicated and persistent wife, Candan, who converted my long incomprehensible sentences into a flowing narrative. Candan was also deeply involved in the project by poring through troves of reading material, giving feedback as the book shaped up, and most important, by lending a sympathetic ear to my incessant complaints and requests. Without her time and support, this book would never have seen the light of day. She deserves my biggest hug and acknowledgment. Contributing also in their own characteristic way were my children, Eda and Sinan. Eda's calm and quiet company was great comfort whenever I needed it most. Sinan's constant questioning, always delivered in the most fiery and challenging manner, kept me cognizant of the value of doubt and reconsideration in all matters concerning human behavior. I do hope that when they graduate from college they find a Turkey that is once more as liberal and thriving as it briefly was less than ten years ago.

I must also acknowledge the warm friendships of Seda and Mehmet Marşan as well as Petek and Alkan Dönmez. And not to be missed were the Stiebel children, Sloane, Tate, and Blake, our sweet little neighbors, who occasionally dropped by for candies, or "Kemal's eggs" as they called them, and reminded me each time of the innocence of young children and filled me with joy and happiness.

Not least, this book would not have been possible without the support of the Turkish Industry and Business Association (TUSIAD) for the Senior Fellowship at Brookings. I have been privileged to be the TUSIAD Senior Fellow since January 2013. I am also indebted to Lou Anne Jensen of the Jenesis Group for her enthusiastic support of the work of the Turkey Project and for the fascinating conversations we have shared about Turkey.

The book's findings are in keeping with Brookings's mission: to conduct high-quality, independent research and, based on that research, to provide innovative, practical recommendations for policymakers and the public. The conclusions and recommendations of any Brookings research are solely those of its authors and do not reflect the views of the Institution, its management, or its other scholars.

Index

Surnames starting with "al" are alphabetized by the subsequent part of the name.